m 9322324
15.95
MGAA

European Monographs in Social Psychology
Arguing and thinking
A rhetorical approach to social psychology

European Monographs in Social Psychology

Executive Editors:
J. RICHARD EISER and KLAUS R. SCHERER
Sponsored by the European Association of Experimental Social Psychology

This series, first published by Academic Press (who will continue to distribute the numbered volumes), appeared under the joint imprint of Cambridge University Press and the Maison des Sciences de l'Homme in 1985 as an amalgamation of the Academic Press series and the European Studies in Social Psychology, published by Cambridge and the Maison in collaboration with the Laboratoire Européen de Psychologie Sociale of the Maison.

The original aims of the two series still very much apply today: to provide a forum for the best European research in different fields of social psychology and to foster the interchange of ideas between different developments and different traditions. The Executive Editors also expect that it will have an important role to play as a European forum for international work.

Other titles in this series:

Arguing and thinking

A rhetorical approach to social psychology

Michael Billig
Department of Social Sciences
University of Loughborough

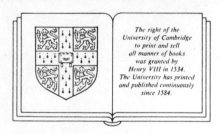

Cambridge University Press

Cambridge

New York   *Port Chester*

Melbourne   *Sydney*

Editions de la Maison des Sciences de l'Homme

Paris

Published by the Press Syndicate of the University of Cambridge
The Pitt Building, Trumpington Street, Cambridge CB2 1RP
40 West 20th Street, New York, NY 10011-4211, USA
10 Stamford Road, Oakleigh, Victoria 3166, Australia
and Editions de la Maison des Sciences de l'Homme
54 Boulevard Raspail, 75270 Paris Cedex 06

First published 1987
Reprinted 1989
First paperback edition 1989
Reprinted 1991

Printed in Great Britain at the
Athenaeum Press Ltd, Newcastle upon Tyne

British Library cataloguing in publication data

Billig, Michael
Arguing and thinking:
a rhetorical approach to social psychology. —
(European monographs in social psychology)
1. Social psychology
I. Title   II. Series
302   HM251

Library of Congress cataloguing in publication data

Billig, Michael.
Arguing and thinking.
(European monographs in social psychology)
Bibliography.
Includes index.
1. Social psychology.   2. Rhetoric.
3. Communication in the social sciences.
I. Title.   II. Series.
HM251.B47458 1987   302   87-14753

ISBN 0 521 32789 X hard covers

ISBN 2 7351 0159 2 (France only)

ISBN 0 521 33987 1 paperback
ISBN 2 7351 0301 3 (France only)

Contents

Acknowledgements

I am particularly grateful to Dick Eiser for his help and support. Whilst some other social psychologists might have adopted a professionally snooty attitude towards antiquarian endeavours, Dick has encouraged my eccentric wanderings. Rob Farr, too, has been constructively helpful, and made many useful criticisms. I am grateful to G. B. Kerferd for his specialist comments on the Sophists.

My colleagues in the Social Sciences Department at Loughborough University have provided an intellectually tolerant atmosphere, congenial to developing the themes of this book. It is a pleasure to work in such a genuinely interdisciplinary department. In particular, I am thankful to Alan Bryman, Susan Condor, Derek Edwards, Mike Gane and Alan Radley for their specific comments and general discussions.

My father, David Billig, would have recognized his influence on this work. He knew that I had begun another book, but there was something else that I should have mentioned to him during the last year of his life: this book, unlike the previous ones, would contain quotations from the Talmud and the Midrashim. That would have given him great pleasure.

Lastly there are my wife and children to thank. I cannot, in all honesty, thank them for providing the peace and quiet which an academic writer needs. But for much, much more I thank Sheila, Daniel, Rebecca, Rachel and Benjamin.

1　Introduction: antiquarian psychology

Psychologists are supposed to be modern. Take a look at any professional journal which reports the latest pieces of research, and you will see how up-to-the-moment most psychologists are. Each article will refer to a clutch of other articles, published not more than five years ago, mostly in the same journal, and some, tantalizingly, just about to be published. Perhaps, some older articles will creep into this showroom of intellectual modernity, often under the guise of being 'classics' or 'pathfinding researches'. It would not be good form to write an article in the 1980s which was filled with references to work done in the 1970s and 1960s. As for the 1950s, that would be stretching matters too far. We do not expect our refrigerators and our motor cars to be composed of thirty-year-old components, so our psychological theories should be constructed from the most modern elements possible.

In order to write such articles, the psychologists of today must keep up with the latest issues of their specialist journals. A sense of excitement should accompany the delivery of each new issue, which tells what colleagues in Iowa or Nebraska have been doing in their laboratories. Not for the modern psychologist the pleasure of wandering into the quiet parts of a library, selecting at random an old volume, blowing the dust off the edges and slowly opening the book to release the captured must. Nor should the psychologist experience a quickening of both heart-beat and mental quality, as the finger feels the rough surface of the old linen paper. Those feelings should be reserved for the latest professional journal, packed with its topical information on shiny, smooth wood-pulp. But should the psychologist who feels little but a painful sense of duty in front of smooth modernity give up either the wanderings amongst the old books or the claim to be a 'psychologist'? Surely there can be a place somewhere for the antiquarian psychologist?

A psychologist with unfashionably antiquarian interests should not be confused with a historian of the discipline. The historian of psychology will seek to make historical sense of the discipline's intellectual and social past, putting events into some sort of chronological organization. However, the antiquarian psychologist is someone who is interested in psychological, rather than historical, issues. Instead of approaching these issues in the sensibly modern manner of accumulating experimental data, the antiquarian suffers from uncontrollable urges to wander from the laboratory to the library. Passages from old and not-so-old books are haphazardly read, noted and thus collected, in a way which a modern psychologist might think pathological. If the resulting collection is to be arranged, the guiding principle will be psychological rather than historical. There will be no sort of chronology, which might be meaningful to the genuine historian, nor even respect for the integrity of different historical epochs. Instead, quotations from one era find themselves unhistorically placed next to those from a quite different age, as the antiquarian gathers material, with the enthusiasm of the amateur, to illustrate psychological issues. Above all, the antiquarian psychologist will seek out older psychologies, leaving the modern colleague to track down the latest references.

As far as social psychology is concerned, the archaeological sites offering the richest promise to the antiquarian souvenir hunter are to be found in the intellectual traditions of rhetoric. Stretching back to the Sophists of ancient Athens and forwards to the nineteenth century, the study of rhetoric has made a major contribution to the Western intellectual tradition. For centuries rhetoric formed a central part of education, as important as mathematics and certainly more important than psychology in today's curricula. Like psychologists of today, rhetoricians were frequently regarded with suspicion by members of the public. However, the odium against psychologists has not reached the strength of that shown against rhetoricians. Nor has it had legislative backing as it did in ancient Rome, when, according to Suetonius, "Latin rhetoricians" were forbidden from plying their trade because "young men spend whole days with them in idleness" (*On Grammarians*, 435). There is a strong similarity between the content of rhetoric and that of contemporary social psychology. As will be suggested, particularly in Chapter 4, many of the problems which are addressed by modern social psychologists were also issues studied by rhetoricians of old. Social psychologists might probe experimentally the foundations of 'attitude-change' or 'persuasive communication', in the hope of discovering important breakthroughs. In so doing, they are continuing to think about the same sorts of issues as those which filled the contents of Aristotle's *Rhetoric*, or Cicero's *Orator*, or Quintilian's *Institutes of Oratory*.

Typically, most social psychologists treat the ancient intellectual heritage of rhetoric as containing little of interest and promising even less of utility. The pressure to be up-to-date does not leave much space for antiquarianism. There is no need here to give examples of the way social psychologists dismiss the past, for some instances will be offered later. It is sufficient to say that social psychologists ignore their past, rather on the assumption that, just as one would not affix a chariot's wheel to a modern sports car, so one should not insert pre-scientific notions into a serious scientific discipline. It might be permissible to borrow the occasional idea from Aristotle or from Plato, but the borrowed idea would need to be re-sprayed with modern jargon and re-tooled with statistical precision, before the results of its test run could be allowed to take their place in the pages of the research journal.

The antiquarian shows no such disdain of the past, but deliberately raids it, digging up relics from old thinkers and delighting to find odd bits and pieces. These raids are conducted in a different spirit from the occasional borrowings of the up-to-date psychologist. Antiquarians will resist the urge to modernize everything that is encountered. Unconvinced that modernity is wholly satisfactory, antiquarians venture upon their raids in the hope of preserving relics of the past, and displaying them alongside modern possessions. The juxtaposition between the old and the new may reveal the limitations of the latter, in a way that would be impossible if one were totally and unselfconsciously immersed in the drive for modernity. Traditionalists may have been upset at the turn of the century by the shock of the new, but now in psychological theory, with tradition all but abolished by the scientific spirit of modernity, there may be space for the gentler shocks of the old.

Hannah Arendt described the German critic, Walter Benjamin, as a "pearl-diver", because, in the face of disappearing tradition, he searched the oceans of the past for quotations to disrupt the assumptions of the present. Benjamin even wished to publish an original work, composed entirely of quotations. His passion for collecting old books is beautifully described in the essay 'Unpacking my library'. Benjamin dived dangerously for his pearls, and it would be presumptuous to compare the limited ambitions of the present work with his scholarship and intellectual intensity. If Arendt's metaphor is to be continued, then it could be suggested that the present antiquarianism is content to wander safely at the edge of the sea, collecting pretty shells. No pearls are to be expected, but some of the shells are fine specimens. However, the tradition of rhetoric is as varied as the shells washed in by the tide. There is room in our collection for eccentrics like Lord Monboddo and charlatans like Stilpo. These and others will make their appearances alongside Aristotle, Cicero and Protagoras.

Rhetoric and social psychological theory

It would be misleading to present the present work as constituting a lone step into a neglected tradition of thinking. In fact, rhetoric has recently been creeping back into theoretical fashion, and there has been an awakening of interest in the old theories of communication. Much credit must go to Chaim Perelman, for the revival and development of the rhetorical tradition. His *New Rhetoric*, written in collaboration with Mme Olbrechts-Tyteca, and *The New Rhetoric and the Humanities* showed the wealth of insight, both psychological and philosophical, which can be gathered from the ancient texts. There are faint signs that this revival is being felt within the confines of the psychological world. The word 'rhetoric' has been making some recent appearances, as some psychologists have started labelling their inquiries into the symbolic and expressive elements of thought as being 'rhetorical inquiries' (e.g., Antaki, 1985; Weinreich-Haste, 1984). However, the word is more commonly used by the critics of the experimental methodology, and some of them have been recommending their colleagues to adopt a rhetorical approach to social psychology. The critics specifically contrast their own notions of a rhetorical social psychology with those of the experimentalists who supposedly neglect the expressive elements of social life (e.g. Harré, 1980 and 1981; Shotter, in press a, b). One leading critic of the experimentalists, Rom Harré, argues that psychologists should take as their basic theoretical model the image of "man as a rhetorician". He explains: "Such a model must begin as an analytical model, that is, we should look upon speech and action in a human being as persuasive, as expressive, as being used for the purposes of getting others to see events in the light that the orator, rhetorician, propagandist, etc, wishes them to be seen" (Harré, 1980, p. 205).

Harré's description seems to imply that the rhetorician is principally concerned with persuading others to see the world in a particular light. Certainly the traditional rhetoricians devoted much time to searching for hidden tricks of persuasion and to assessing the effectiveness of different styles of oratory. However, ancient rhetoric also contained a dimension which is missing in Harré's description: the argumentative dimension. The textbooks of the ancient theorists sought to equip the prospective debater with the wherewithal for conducting arguments. In addition, the best of such books are more than handy guides for those who lack the spontaneous skills of debate. Works like Aristotle's *Rhetoric* and Quintilian's *Institutes of Oratory* also analyse the nature of argumentation, and, in so doing, they reveal the importance of argumentation in human thought.

This theme of the importance of argument is introduced in Chapter 2 by way of a criticism of two metaphors commonly used in social theory. This chapter examines the notion that social life resembles either a game or a theatrical performance. Both metaphors will be found wanting, because they ignore the argumentative aspects of social life. In order to reinforce the long-standing link between oratory and argumentation, there follows a short historical chapter, looking at the origins of rhetoric. Chapter 3 traces the tradition of rhetoric back to the disputes of the Sophists in ancient Athens. The Sophists, in claiming to teach persuasive eloquence, were also claiming to offer instruction in the arts of disputation. Tribute will be paid to Protagoras of Abdera, the greatest Sophist of them all, and the founding spirit of the argumentative side to rhetoric. However, the antiquarian's prime purpose is not a historical one. The tradition of rhetoric is to be burgled, not organized *in situ*, and it will be the argumentative knick-knacks which will be carried from their ancient sites. Of all the relics, pride of place will be given to Protagoras's maxim that there are two sides to every question.

The collection of knick-knacks will have its tendentious side, for, starting in Chapter 2, a critical argument will be directed against current social psychological theorizing. After the brief historical interlude of Chapter 3, with its homage to Protagoras, will come the comparisons between ancient rhetoric and the modern psychology of persuasion. Here, in Chapter 4, are to be found the examples of social psychologists patronizing their past. The modern science of persuasion has not been as unambiguously successful as its protagonists might have wished. The suggestion will be made that today's experimentalists have had to come to terms with the inevitable limitations of social psychological knowledge, which Quintilian had predicted nearly two thousand years ago.

By Chapter 5, the main themes should be becoming clearer, as the old rhetorical ideas point to gaps in modern psychological theories. The biggest gap concerns the lack of attention paid to argumentation. Psychologists interested in thought processes have shown a tendency to venerate logical thinking to the neglect of the sort of rhetorical, or argumentative, thought to which Protagoras's maxim applies. In consequence, psychologists tend to give short shrift to those more fluid and imaginative styles of thinking, which form the basis of disputation. An example from the Talmud will be used to illustrate the depth, subtlety and general nature of argumentative thinking. There is, in addition, a psychological point to be made. It will be suggested that psychologists have overlooked the extent to which our inner deliberations are silent arguments conducted within a single self. If deliberation is a form of argument, then our thought processes, far from being inherently mysterious events, are modelled upon public debate. In consequence, the rhetorical handbooks, which provide guides to debate, can also be considered as guides to thought.

Just how easily Protagoras's maxim can be applied to social psychology itself will be seen in Chapter 6. There, a major contemporary theory will be considered: the idea that thought processes are based upon the categorization of information. Just as Protagoras had said that it was always possible to mount an opposing case, so the assumptions of this theoretical approach will be reversed. The intention is not to cause theoretical mischief for its own sake, but to pursue an old rhetorical notion about the forms of argumentation. If Protagoras's maxim is correct, then each form of thought can be contrasted by an opposing form of thought. Categorization, stressed in modern cognitive theory, can be contrasted by the opposing cognitive process of particularization. In fact, it will be suggested that we could not categorize information, if we were not possessed of the alternative skill of particularization. As far as rhetoric is concerned, these two forms of thought provide the basic outlines of argumentative forms. We can argue that a given particular should be placed in a category and we can oppose this by the counter-argument that the particular should be treated in its uniqueness. From this basic opposition between particularization and categorization, all manner of argumentative strategies can be constructed.

The remaining three chapters apply this perspective to a number of social psychological issues. Chapter 7 looks at the rhetorical nature of attitudes and why, as Protagoras's maxim would suggest, it is so hard to show that an opponent's attitudes are inconsistent. The chapter also suggests that attitudes should not be viewed merely as expressions of individual preference, but that they should be placed in their rhetorical context, as positions which are taken in wider controversies. Chapter 8 considers the topic of common-sense, for rhetoric, since Aristotle, has traditionally been concerned with common-sensical reasoning. Here we move from the forms of argument to the content of argumentation. Even so, the principle of rhetorical opposition is still important. Just as we possess opposing forms for expressing arguments, so also the content of our common-sense contains contrary themes. This point is exemplified by the ancient rhetorical notion of 'common-places'. Lastly, Chapter 9 considers the rhetorical flexibility with which we can express our attitudes. Not only are we like professional advocates, who can alter their tones to suit their audience, but also, on occasion, we seem capable of doing a complete about-turn in order to argue the opposing position. In these cases, we 'take the side of the other', in a way which would be incomprehensible if the rhetorical context were not taken into account, and if we did not possess contrary mental capabilities.

In outline, the social psychological themes of these chapters might appear stronger than the antiquarian ones. However, the tone in which the arguments are expressed differs from the tone of conventional social psychology. Most social psychological writing is firmly buttressed by references to experimental evidence, as writers feel obliged to cite all relevant laboratory studies, especially those conducted in the last five years. On the other hand, whatever are the odd compulsions driving the antiquarian, an obsession with a comprehensive bibliography of experimental findings is not among their number. Although general points of social psychological theory will be made, these will not inevitably be supported by examples of the strange, but precisely recorded, activities of experimenters and their subjects. Instead, the illustrative examples are gathered from the meanderings of the antiquarian: amongst other sources, classical oratory, Platonic debates, Dr Johnson's conversations, sporting sagas, the Talmud and Midrashim have all suffered from raids. It might have been possible to illustrate the same general points with examples from modern fiction. For example, Kafka and Heller provide rich testimony to the intricate argumentative capacities of humans. Perhaps a far subtler analysis of the argumentative aspects of twentieth century thinking could be gathered from these sources. However, for no good theoretical reason, except for antiquarian preference, fiction was generally avoided, although special exceptions are occasionally made for Borges's fictional antiquarianism. On the other hand, modern incidents, in particular those reported in newspapers, have been included. As a result, a modern argumentative incident, culled from an ephemeral source, can stand on a par with an ancient bit of oratory in a way that confirms the antiquarian's disrespect for chronology.

Some social psychologists might find the examples from such sources deeply unsatisfactory, because 'proper' evidence only comes in the form of the statistically analysed experiment. Such social psychologists seem to act as if the gods of knowledge are only appeased by offerings of experimental results: the journals record these dutiful sacrifices of time and money, and a touch of holiness can be gained at second hand by mentioning, with suitable reverence, the sacred sacrifices of others. To such psychologists, antiquarianism is, at worst, blasphemy, or at best, a foreign cult worthy of missionary attention. If the present approach might offend the sensibilities of the experimentalists, then so is it likely to upset some of the critics, who might find the present attitude insufficiently rigorous in its rejection of experimental rigour. The critics, following a very different religious preference from the experimentalists, tend to taboo all experimental findings, as offerings to false idols. The late Erich Fromm, a psychoanalytic social psychologist of great distinction, went through intellectual contortions in his book *The Anatomy of Human Destructiveness*, to avoid mentioning experimental results. Even when the experiments could hardly be ignored, so relevant were they to his themes, he added innuendoes and critical asides to show that he was no true worshipper. The antiquarian, however, shows no such inhibitions. Experiments are neither holy nor taboo, but, if interesting, they can take their place, along with the rest, in the promiscuous parade.

One obvious criticism can be levelled against the antiquarian – that of escapism. The antiquarian does not seem to seek an engagement with serious social issues, but runs away from reality to indulge in the pursuit of the quaint. However, as will be suggested in the course of the present work, attitudes must be placed in the context of controversy. Even the pursuit of the quaint can be seriously controversial. Walter Benjamin provides the obvious example. His antiquarianism was a despairing commentary on a world slipping into barbarity. Even the present low-keyed and playful antiquarian pursuit could, if required, be placed in the context of wider controversy. To do so might require a little act of imagination. For instance, one might imagine a totally hypothetical turn of events in Western civilization which leaves learning no longer being valued for its own sake. Instead, learning is to be quantitatively assessed in terms of its effect on such arcane matters as the Gross National Product or the Money Supply. Imagine that political leaders start to believe that the way to achieve the desired economic statistics is through training young people in scientific and computational expertise. Imagine, too, that those professionally enjoined to study human thoughts and wishes, hopes and dreams, can only imagine their fellow humans as computers, and that they are teaching a new generation of students to think in this way. Under such imaginary circumstances, to make antiquarian play in the traditions of the humanities is to show the old Protagorean 'spirit of contradiction'.

2 Rules, roles and arguments

To most psychologists rhetoric is an unfamiliar topic. Its history, its great works, and even its vocabulary are matters which will be strange to the average psychologist. That being so, the temptation is to treat rhetoric as an example of something which is much more familiar. For instance, we could view the occasions which produce great rhetorical set-pieces, not as oratorical events in themselves but as if they were theatrical or sporting events. It would not take great imagination to consider the rituals of a parliament or those of a law-court as being pieces of pure theatre. The orators, whether politicians or lawyers, deliver their speeches like actors, often combining the gestures of tragedy with those of pantomime. Defence and prosecution, government and opposition, judge and speaker, all have their allotted roles in the conventions of oratorical drama, just as Romeo and Juliet, Harlequin and Columbine have their parts to be played. With ease the point of comparison could be shifted from the stage to the playing-field, in order to view the grand rhetorical event as just a game. The parliament, then, would cease to be a theatre, full of actors hamming up their lines, but it would be transformed into a sporting arena. The teams would face each other, attackers would run for the winning goal, defenders would try to trip them up, and the final score would be assessed in the division lobbies. Then, both teams, metaphorical knees covered in mud and perhaps a smudge of greasepaint around the eyes, would troop off to the bar.

The images of rhetoric as either theatre or a game are important for two reasons: not only have rhetoricians frequently used these metaphors to describe their own skills, but also these two metaphors lie at the root of much current social psychological theorizing. In consequence, if we were to reduce rhetoric to being just a theatrical performance or to being merely a game, we would find ready concepts in social psychology to make the unfamiliar instantly familiar. For example, having categorized rhetoric as pure theatre we could then get on with the business of describing how orators act their roles and how they present themselves in public. It would be as if we had suddenly discovered a fast motorway, bypassing the blocked town centre, whose ancient, cobbled streets were never intended to carry motor vehicles. Rather than waiting in the inevitable traffic jam, we could speed cheerfully along a familiar route.

Superficially there would be much to recommend a translation of rhetorical matters into dramatic or ludic ones. After all, no less an authority than Aristotle stressed that benefits accrued to the oratorical politician who was a bit of an actor: "The honour of dramatic contests falls, as a rule, to the actors; and, just as, on the stage, the actors are at present of more importance than the poets, so it is, owing to the vices of society, in the contests of civil life" (*Rhetoric*, 1403b). Quintilian, like other teachers of rhetoric, recommended that actors should instruct the apprentice orator: "He will...insist that the speaker faces his audience, that the lips are not distorted nor the jaws parted to a grin, that the face is not thrown back, nor the eyes fixed on the ground, nor the neck slanted to left or right" (*Institutes of Oratory*, I, xi, 9). Or perhaps we could follow Seneca in using the gaming metaphor; introducing his published collection of famous controversies, Seneca commented that he felt just like a producer of gladiatorial contests (*Controversiae*, IV, preface). The same metaphor is contained in Quintilian's descriptions of the various strategies of debate as feints, parries and side-blows (*Institutes of Oratory*, IX, I, 20), and also appears in Kenneth Burke's account of argumentation's "holds and counter-holds, the blows and the ways of blocking them" (1962, p. 576). A gentler game appears in Adeimantus's complaint to Socrates that people "feel your arguments are like a game of drafts in which the unskilled player is always in the end hemmed in and left without a move by the expert" (Plato, *Republic*, 487b).

These same metaphors of the theatre and of the game appear in contemporary social psychological theorizing. This chapter will discuss perspectives which treat social life as if it were a staged drama or an organized sporting contest. There are social psychologists who view us as fulfilling roles and following scripts when we go about our daily business. Others see us as obeying the rules of some gigantic game. These approaches can provide much insight into the routines of everyday life and the properties of human cognitive processes. If criticisms are to be made, and they will be in this chapter, they should imply neither that it is erroneous, nor that it is utterly fatuous, to view social life in terms of games or theatrical performances. Instead, it will be suggested that these metaphors are one-sided, in that they omit another side to social life. As far as rhetoric is concerned, it is a crucial aspect which is omitted. In fact, it will be suggested that the role-playing or game-playing theories of psychology bypass the very essence of rhetoric. This resides not in dramatic display or the sense of organized competition, but in the notion of argumentation.

The intention is not to overthrow current social psychological approaches, but to draw attention to another side of the matter. There is a danger in psychology that theorists get so preoccupied with one sort of human activity that they produce one-sided theories, which overlook the contrary aspects of human endeavours. In order to remedy this, the following guideline could be adopted: if one psychological principle appears reasonable, then try reversing it, in order to see whether its contrary is just as reasonable. This very guideline represents a foretaste of the rhetorical approach of Protagoras, the great sophist, who will be discussed in the following chapter.

The reversal of the theatrical and ludic metaphors could take the form of turning the metaphors around on themselves. For example, instead of seeing rhetorical argument as being a game, we could see games as being rhetorical arguments. Such a reversal is contained in the joke of Polemo, who "on seeing a gladiator dripping with sweat out of sheer terror of the life-and-death struggle before him, remarked, 'You are in as great an agony as though you were going to declaim'" (Philostratus, *Lives of the Sophists*, pp. 129–131). Implicit reversals of metaphor are not unknown in psychological theorizing. Skinner's *Verbal Behavior* treated language as if it were bodily movement, whilst other analysts, including Julius Fast, the author of the best-selling *Body Language*, send the metaphor in the opposite direction to forage for those bodily movements which resemble speech. Closer to our central theme is Roland Barthes's double metaphorical reversals in his sparkling essay 'The world of wrestling'. Barthes sees the professional wrestling bout both as human comedy and as scholastic dispute.

Barthes's metaphors, which treat sport as something other than itself, imply that wrestling is something other than a sporting contest. Professional wrestling, so runs the implication, is not really sport, but it is theatre or rhetoric. In the same way, the gaming or theatrical metaphor, when applied to formal rhetorical occasions, suggests that the parliament or law-court is really nothing but a game or a play. It is not the present intention to dislocate reality in this, or the reverse, way. Any attempt to argue that wrestling, or any other physical activity, is really scholastic disputation, still represents a by-pass around the topic of rhetoric itself. To be sure, we might have changed direction in order to travel against the flow of the traffic, and we might catch different glimpses of scenery through the wind-screen. Nevertheless, we would still be circling around our destination, rather than approaching it directly. In place of reversing our direction on the bypass, the present intention is to suggest the irreducible importance of argumentation in itself. Even in the worlds of theatre and sport there is an argumentative dimension, which should be considered in its own right.

Life as theatre

The theatrical metaphor is contained within a set of theoretical terms, which are commonly used by social scientists and which imply that social life resembles a theatrical performance. Foremost among these terms is the concept of 'role'. Virtually every discussion of 'role' in the textbooks starts by noting the intended parallel between a 'social role' and a theatrical one. For example, Sarbin and Allen, in *The Handbook of Social Psychology*, write: "We begin by noting the fact of resemblance between the conduct of social man and the conduct of characters who pass before us on the stage" (1968, p. 489). Ordinary life is seen to be a staged drama, in which actors skilfully enact their roles. The actors must learn to present themselves, so that their audiences notice the requisite gestures. Like Quintilian's apprentice orator, we must all beware lest our lips become inappropriately distorted or our jaws part to a grin, which will undermine our everyday performances. Above all, we must practise our parts and learn the scripts appropriate to our roles. Some roles are major performances, demanding much rehearsal and line learning. To perform convincingly a role, such as that of doctor, lawyer or police officer, a vast amount of speeches, gestures, ways of entering and exiting scenes, and so on, have to be acquired. Other roles are more fleeting, but a walk-on part still involves the learning of appropriate cues and gestures. For example, a casual greeting in the street demands a skilled coordination of smile, half-inclined face, slowing down of pace, together with subtle gestures indicating that total stoppage and conversation are not to follow. The role must be skilfully performed, and it must be recognized by other actors sharing the scene. As Sarbin notes, a role describes "the behaviour expected of the occupant of a given position or status" (1968, p. 546). Unless we possess such expectancies and fulfil those of others, the theatre of everyday life would be unable to progress. In this sense, skilled role performance enables our mundane dramas to unfold undramatically.

'Role' may be the central concept (indeed the star theoretical performer) in the theatrical metaphor, or 'dramaturgical perspective', but other concepts play crucial supporting parts. Biddle lists some of them, when he suggests that "such terms as *role enactment, role playing, coaching, performance, actor, mask, persona, psychodrama, presentation of self*, and *as-if behaviour* imply the dramaturgical metaphor" (1979, p. 9). There is little doubt that the theatrical metaphor can be enormously illuminating, especially when used by as keen and witty a social observer as Erving Goffman. Looking in detail at everyday "performances", Goffman drew attention to the artifices of social life, particularly those involving a "pre-established pattern of action" (1959, p. 14). By applying the theatrical metaphor he was able to show how all of us are actors, as we strut our personal stages, attempting to impress our shifting audiences. To a greater or lesser degree, there are times when we all resemble the hotel staff, whom Goffman observed adjusting their public expressions, before entering through the kitchen door onto the stage of the dining-room.

The notion of a social role, and the other theatrical concepts used by social psychologists, draw attention to the expected regularities of social life. People must have shrewd ideas about what is expected of them in given contexts, or else life would be nothing more than a meaningless jumble of random activities. This applies as much to the big roles in life as well as the walk-on parts. The casual greeting in the street cannot be created afresh on every occasion someone wishes to wave to a passing acquaintance. There must be certain regular patterns of action which are recognized as constituting a greeting, otherwise the recipient of the greeting would be unable to distinguish the casual wave from the threatening fist.

If we are all actors, then we must be following some sort of script, which coordinates the various parts to be played. Rom Harré, in *Social Being*, underlines the importance of the script in the theatrical metaphor; he suggests that, just as "the action of the play is usually determined by a script, though actors and producers place their own interpretations on it", so the performance of everyday actions depends on learning and following the unwritten scripts of social life (1979, p. 192). In going about our everyday business, we need to possess the appropriate scripts for the scenes in which we find ourself at any given moment. Schank and Abelson, who have rewritten the dramaturgical metaphor in the language of computer simulation, have pointed to the cognitive implications of this. In their book *Scripts, Plans, Goals and Understanding*, they suggest that a script "is a predetermined, stereotyped sequence of actions that defines a well-known situation" (1977, p. 41). Schank and Abelson argue that we need to possess in our memories numerous different scripts, in order that we can act with appropriate coordination and direction in social situations. They illustrate their point with the detailed example of a person in a restaurant. Such a person needs to possess general restaurant-behaving scripts, with sub-scripts about self-service or waiter-service establishments, and special routines about tipping or complaining. The appropriate restaurant scripts must be summoned out of the memory-store and then be followed with permitted improvisations, if the meal is to be successfully ordered, consumed and paid for. Failure to act out the script is likely to lead to a hiatus in the action, which would be as embarrassing as the silent pause following a professional actor's lapse of memory on the public stage.

The theatrical metaphor emphasizes what is necessary for the smooth coordination of social life. Conflict has a rather minor billing in this production. To be sure, role theorists have often looked at the tensions which impede smooth role performance. A major concern has been 'role conflict', which occurs when an actor has to appear on stage in two roles at once. To quote a modern social psychology textbook, which puts the matter more formally and without reference to the metaphor, role conflict occurs when "a person holds several positions that have incompatible demands" (Deaux and Wrightsman, 1984, p. 12). As is customary with popular modern textbooks, there is a pictorial illustration of the abstract concept. A photograph shows a young woman sitting at an office desk, her right hand flicking through a pile of documents, whilst her left hand rests gently on the head of an infant seated on the office carpet. "An example of interrole conflict: A working mother brings her baby to the office", explains the caption. In this way, the abstract concept, having been removed from the physical context of the stage, is returned to a different physical context, which implicitly is then compared to the theatre. In this case, the serenity of the young woman's expression conveys that the skilled actor can manage two difficult parts at once. In fact, one might say that a third role, that of 'working mother', is emerging, with its own scripted demands and expectations. If the other actors recognize the intricacies involved in performing this new role, then there is little reason why the scene-shifts from office to family home cannot be made with a minimum of friction, to enable our heroine to play her part in both scenes.

The concept of 'role conflict' attempts to deal with the issue of tension without going outside the theatrical metaphor. Although life is still a stage, smooth performance is threatened, because unfair demands are being made on the actors. The company is a small one and actors are having to double up on their roles, without sufficient time being allotted for changing costume or shifting scenery. However, not all forms of conflict, or argument, can be quite so easily accommodated within the theatrical metaphor. It will be suggested that the metaphor is, in fact, poorly equipped to deal with the argumentative aspects of social life, principally because of its emphasis upon social regularities and the coordination of scripted performances.

Any metaphorical analysis of social life must necessarily be a partial one. If one aspect of social life is treated as a model for all social life, then other aspects will tend to be overlooked. Ordinary life might resemble a theatrical performance, but there must also be differences, otherwise we would not be able to distinguish a genuine theatrical performance from a metaphorical one. These differences between the real and the metaphorical are apt to be ignored if the analyst is driven by metaphor to search for similarities. In consequence, it might be necessary to rescue the differences, in order to demonstrate the limits of the metaphor. One strategy would be to take those parts of social life which seem as remote as possible from the world of theatre, and then to suggest that the dramaturgical metaphor can only be applied in a feeble or tasteless way. For example, critics of role theory have argued that the theatrical metaphor is unable to deal satisfactorily with phenomena like class-conflict (Popitz, 1972) or consumer choice (Boudon, 1981). The present approach adopts a different strategy. It aims not to select those portions of social life which seem far removed from the world of the theatre. Quite the contrary, it will concentrate upon the world of the theatre, in order to argue that the metaphor only partially covers this world, which is, of course, its own world. In particular, the dramaturgical metaphor only presents a view of the theatrical world from which the argumentative aspects have been removed.

What the dramaturgical metaphor does not do is to take the whole theatrical world as a model for social life. It narrows the world of the theatre down to the staged performance. If all the world is a stage, then what goes on backstage is being excluded. Thus, a complete sub-world, that of the theatre, is not being considered as the model for social life, but only one element of that sub-world: the public performance. The problem is that this is the one part of the theatrical world which demands the suppression of arguments. During a performance, all members of the cast must leave their disagreements in the wings, and must work together to produce the drama. On stage, a scene would be destroyed if an actor were to voice a backstage complaint, declaring suddenly that a fellow player suffered from bad breath or from a complete lack of talent. Instead, co-operation is the order of the moment. So it is for office-teams impressing a visitor, or sales-teams performing in front of an audience of potential customers. As Goffman observed, on such occasions a united front must be maintained by the repertory companies of everyday dramas, because "it seems to be generally felt that public disagreement among members of a team not only incapacitates them for united action but also embarrasses the reality sponsored by the team" (1959, p. 74).

However, the world of the theatre itself cannot be understood in its entirety in terms of following a script in public. Much backstage work has to be done to produce the script and the stage directions, so that the actors can play their parts on stage. At all times in the backstage work there is the possibility, if not the probability, of argument. From the moment the playwright starts conducting an internal argument, filling the waste-paper basket with rejected drafts, and right up to the moment when the curtain rises, there can be rows and disputes. It is these arguments, lasting months, years and sometimes lifetimes, which contribute to the activity which enables the performers to follow their scripts without argument for an hour or two in front of the footlights. Here is a successful playwright writing about the world of the theatre, in terms of anything but smooth and skilful coordination:

> Minor hazards stalk the play: actors quarrel with directors;
> directors quarrel with administrators; critics misunderstand;
> producers under-budget; sets are lost or burnt; stage-hands strike;
> newspapers strike. (Arnold Wesker, *The Observer*, November 18,
> 1984)

What marks out the actual public performances from all the backstage work is not so much the wearing of costumes or the presence of an audience: it is the deliberate suppression of argument. All the arguing must finish once the curtain is raised. It is for this reason that the theatrical metaphor, by taking for its central image one of the few social acts in which argument is taboo, underestimates the argumentative aspects of social life. And it is for this reason that the theatrical metaphor can give only such a partial understanding of the world of the theatre itself.[1]

One brief example can be offered of a theatrical event which is difficult to understand in terms of the performance itself, and which demands to be understood in terms of the wider world of argumentation. The Roman playwright Terence broke through accepted theatrical convention with his prologues. Terence's actors were not required to set the scene for the audience in the customary manner, by describing events occurring before the opening of the first scene. Instead Terence exploited the ambiguity of the prologue by having an actor appear, not in the character of another, but apparently 'out-of-role' as himself. The actor then seemed to speak his own words, not the playwright's, as Terence's critics were attacked and the playwright defended.

In his prologues, Terence argued with those who criticized him for adapting stories from Greek dramas. The ambiguity of these enacted attacks on real enemies is illustrated by the prologue to *The Self Tormentor*. The actor, who follows Terence's script, is forced to suffer the indignity of speaking lines such as "the author wanted me to represent him, instead of delivering the usual prologue" and "I only hope that my eloquence can match his skill in marshalling his thoughts when he wrote this speech for me to deliver" (p. 101). In this way, the prologue, instead of attracting attention to the world being created on the stage, draws attention to the wider world of controversy. The language of the law court is used: "In the guise of a prologue I stand before you to plead my case" is the start of the prologue to the third production of *The Mother-In-Law* (p. 293). The ensuing play, then, is presented as if it were a further argument in a continuing debate. *Phormio*, for example, is intended to be Terence's "answer" to his critics, and it is for the audience to judge how effective an answer it is: "Pay attention and give us a fair hearing in silence" (p. 227). Here we have the reversal of the metaphor of the oratorical debate as a piece of theatre. The piece of theatre is now presented on the stage as a piece of a wider argument. In this way, the stage, by exploiting its own ambiguities, draws attention to the world of controversy existing beyond its wings. No theoretical perspective which took literally the dictum that all the world was a stage could possibly understand the full force of this prologue enacted on the stage. Nor could it appreciate the dramatic contrast between the bitterness of the prologues and the lightness of the ensuing comedies. To grasp this tension, we must follow Terence's directions to think about the wider world of argumentation existing outside the theatre.

Life as a game

If we switch the metaphor for social life from the theatre to the game, then the emphasis changes slightly. No longer are presentation and display the uppermost characteristics. Instead, we would be concentrating upon those features of games which distinguish them from non-games. The most obvious characteristic would be that of fun. If something is called just a game, then perhaps it is being described as not being serious. It is as if real life is a serious matter, but games are a frolic. However, the game metaphor does not focus on the fun aspect, for it recognizes that organized games are played typically in full seriousness, and also that some, like ancient gladiatorial contests, are quite literally matters of life and death. Instead, the metaphor concentrates upon the importance of rules in games. The person playing a game follows certain rules and attempts to win the prize within the agreed framework of these rules. So it is with ordinary life: we follow the social rules. In the hands of social psychologists, the game metaphor tends to portray the social player as a rule-follower, rather than as the script-follower of the theatrical metaphor. What does not change, it will be suggested, is the overlooking of the argumentative aspects of social life.

The displacement of scripts by rules has certain advantages for the development of social psychological theory. Critics of role theory have argued that the notion of a 'script' is misleading, in that it implies that social actors have their words already decided for them. At best actors can decide how to interpret these words, but it is not their business to create new ones or alter the ones they have been allocated. The creation of scripts takes place off-stage in the author's study, and, being an activity removed from the public gaze, it does not feature largely in role theory. However, in ordinary life we do not need to wait for an author, or indeed The Author, to provide us with new speeches if our carefully memorized scripts fail us.

In fact, ordinary people are forever tinkering about with their sets of scripts. Schank has recently admitted that the idea of a 'restaurant-script' is a simplification, because "there is not one restaurant script but thousands"

(1981, p. 128). We do not simply enter a restaurant and plug into the correct script. All sorts of bits and pieces of previous restaurant-scripts have to be hastily cobbled together to deal with the particular restaurant which is being entered at that very moment. Therefore, our scripts are never fully worked out sets of directives. Role theory's critics have pointed out that there is a crucial distinction between social roles and theatrical ones: the social script, unlike the theatrical one, can only provide rough guidelines, not fully prepared speeches. Boudon, in *The Logic of Social Action*, stresses that, whilst words are put into the mouth of the actor, "roles are never in reality defined with such a degree of precision that no room is left for interpretation" (1981, p. 41).

These considerations have led some social psychologists to argue that it is not scripts as such which are of importance, but the underlying rules by which scripts can be generated. Thus, instead of possessing a fully determined script, we have rules or guidelines, which might provide us with the outlines of our performance, but which enable us to add our own flourishes to our roles. Social life, therefore, is more like a game, in which there are general rules which have to be obeyed; however, the rules provide the latitude for the players to develop their own individual strategies and styles of play. The players are not tightly constrained by the rules, in the way that an actor is a prisoner within the script. The rules may define the structural properties of the social occasion, but the players have autonomy to decide how they will react.

In a second respect, the game metaphor improves on the theatrical one. As has been suggested, the theatrical metaphor stresses the co-operative aspects of social life to the neglect of the competitive ones. The game metaphor, on the other hand, provides a perspective in which competition is central. For example, the comparison between an oratorical debate and a theatrical drama omits the competitive, or agonistic, element. The orators in a parliamentary debate, or the lawyers in a criminal case, are not merely showing off their powers of delivery in front of an audience. They are also attempting to do something else. Like Terence, but not like his actor, and like every player in a sporting contest, orators in parliaments and law-courts are attempting to defeat opponents. It is this element of winning and losing which is caught by the game-playing metaphor, but not by the theatrical one.

Despite the advantages of the game metaphor over the theatrical one, nevertheless both metaphors suffer from similar limitations. In arguing this, one point must be stressed. Just like the theatrical metaphor, the game-playing one can be enormously revealing. Again, Erving Goffman has pointed the way with his use of the gaming metaphor in *Strategic Interaction*. But, as always, there is another side to a metaphor. It would be possible to reveal the limitations of the metaphor by pointing to social events which hardly seem game-like at all. Such a task would probably be best achieved by feminist social scientists. There is a pronounced masculine dimension to the metaphor, as social life is presumed to resemble such predominantly male pursuits as soccer, cricket or boxing. Traditionally, it has been men, rather than women, who have had the time for games and who become obsessed by their rites. It is more than likely that the metaphor would sit bizarrely upon traditionally female activities, and that it could only be applied to feminist ones with insult. Although the whole business of seeing social life as a game might be a male, and thereby hopelessly partial, notion, it is not the present intention to demonstrate partiality in this way. Instead, we will follow the same path as for the theatrical metaphor. Rather than searching for untheatrical worlds, we looked at the limitations of the metaphor within the theatrical world. Similarly, it will be suggested that the game metaphor is limited even within the world of games. Its stress upon obedience to the rules of the game leads to a partial perspective, which, like the theatrical metaphor, fails to appreciate the argumentative element within its own chosen world.

One of the major exponents of what can be termed the rule-theory approach to social psychology is Rom Harré. In a series of books, Harré has criticized experimental psychologists for ignoring the rules which constitute the grammar of everyday life. He argues that coordinated social behaviour would be impossible, if there were not rules of conduct for the various situations in which people find themselves. One way to uncover these rules is to treat episodes of everyday life as if they were formal rituals or games, for we are accustomed to the idea that rituals and games have rules. The game metaphor is particularly appropriate for revealing the assumptions of rule-theory. Games require rules, if they are to be played. One cannot understand what happens on a football pitch without understanding the rules of football. However, a mere knowledge of the rules will not enable one to predict the outcome of a single match. Michael Argyle, in an analysis strongly influenced by the perspective of Harré, has stressed the importance of rules: "Continuing our analogy between social situations and games, I want to propose that all social situations are rule-governed" (1980, p. 81). According to Argyle, "even the most informal situations are governed by some rules" (p. 83). The idea is not a new one and is similar to George Mead's notion of society. Mead collapsed the theatrical and gaming metaphors when he pointed to the analogy between acting roles and playing games. According to Mead, the organization of society is like a ball game "in which the attitudes of a set of individuals are involved in a co-operative response in which the different roles involve each other" (1934, p. 256). In other words, when acting our roles in society, we adhere to the rules of the game, just as batsman, bowler and wicket-keeper have their parts in the drama of a game of cricket. All taking part in the drama must adhere to the rules, which in the case of cricket are actually called 'The Laws of the Game'.

Underlying the rule-theory perspective is an image of the social actor, not far removed from that of the theatrical metaphor. In both instances the actor is a follower. In the one case the actor follows a script, and in the other the player follows the general rules of the game. As such, both views are implicitly proposing a one-sided view of human activities. This one-sidedness can be illustrated by Harré's argument that social psychologists should adopt a "rule-following theory" (1974, p. 250). He goes on to assert that what is needed in social psychology is "a system of concepts appropriate to the analysis of an individual psychology of rule-following" (p. 255). Under-lying this is a one-sided, rule-following image of the social actor: "It can hardly be denied that we are rule-following, self-monitoring agents" (Harré and Secord, 1972, p. 142).[2]

The problem with one-sided images is not that they are untrue, but that they can be reversed without too much trouble or denial. If the bit about self-monitoring is left aside, the equally convincing statement can be made that 'it can hardly be denied that we are rule-breaking agents'. Or rule-bending agents. Or rule-disputing agents. Or rule-creating agents. The point is that a rule-following approach only tells a part of the story. It can pose and answer questions about the regularities of social events and about the ways people conform to expectations or social rules. What it does not probe is the controversial nature of rules, for there is more to rules than that they are, or even should be, obeyed. Rules can be objects of argument, just as much as Terence's plays could be the topic of heated debate. The game-playing metaphor, with its emphasis upon rule-following, tends to overlook the close connections between rules and argumentation.

The game metaphor contains similar limitations to those which restrict the theatrical metaphor. Both metaphors compare social life in general to a sub-world, either that of sport or of the theatre. Then, one aspect of this sub-world, and not the complete sub-world, is taken as the point of comparison. The part of the sporting world which is relevant to the game metaphor is the happenings on the field of play, once the referee has blown the whistle to start play. However, we should be cautious of seeking to understand sport purely in terms of sporting activity, for there is much more to the sporting world than takes place upon the pitch. The most perceptive book on cricket, and indeed probably on any sport, is aptly called *Beyond a Boundary*. C. L. R. James (1963) combines, in a unique work of art, the philosophy of Marx with the knowledge of cricketers, and he proves his own axiom that 'he who only knows of cricket, knows nothing of cricket'.

At one stage James deliberately uses both science and the history of the British Empire to settle a dispute about the techniques of batting.

The game metaphor, if strictly maintained, cannot do justice to James's axiom, which assumes that the world of sport is itself partly a non-sporting world. The metaphor does not preserve the necessary distinction between the game and the non-game, for it assumes that all social life is similar to a game. It provides no entry into the non-sporting world, which is very much part of the sporting world itself, just as the theatrical metaphor gives no access to its own non-theatrical dimensions. If the theatrical metaphor wishes to deal with backstage happenings, it must translate them into yet another drama. Similarly the game metaphor is forced to view the world of sport beyond the playing pitch as yet another game. The results in both cases are similar, in that the argumentative aspects are, if not lost, at least only glimpsed at, as we speed along the rhetorical by-pass.

It may seem odd to maintain that the argumentative aspects are overlooked when considering sporting occasions. In a straightforward sense this would seem to be absurd, because games settle arguments. In the late eighteenth century and early nineteenth, bizarre cricket matches were arranged to settle theoretical disputes, and to provide opportunities for betting. In Walworth, in 1796, a match was arranged between "eleven Greenwich Pensioners with one leg against eleven with one arm". So great was the interest that the game was halted by crowd disturbances, but in the event the argument was settled: the one-legged were shown to be the superior cricketers "by one hundred and three runnings" (original report in Phelps, 1977, p. 146). Sporting figures themselves can be aware of the argumentative nature of a contest. Gene Tunney, that most intellectual of heavyweight champions, saw his fights with Jack Dempsey as occasions for settling the argument about the merits of their respective approaches to boxing; the argument is clearly described in Tunney's own account *My Fights with Jack Dempsey*. In fact, any sporting occasion can be seen as an opportunity for settling the argument between the contestants. Moreover, sporting competitions give rise to arguments, despite the image of rule-following. The second Tunney–Dempsey fight produced what Tunney called the "real argument" about the referee's long count, an argument which he wished to settle by a third fight. Anyone standing near a football touchline will be aware of the constant appeals and counter-appeals to the referee, disputing what should or should not be classed as foul play.

All this hardly suggests that the game metaphor omits the argumentative dimension of social life. If anything, these examples suggest the close connection between games and arguments; so close is the connection that one might hesitate to consider that games constitute the basic term in any equation between the two. The reduction of arguments to games can easily be reversed by considering games as arguments, as Tunney did his fight with Dempsey. However, the parallel between games and arguments should not be pushed too far, because in one important respect the sporting occasion, like the theatrical performance, represents a cessation of argument. It is true that sporting occasions can be viewed as a means of settling controversy by using rules. Equally, it is true that the application of these rules can give rise to arguments at virtually any stage of the contest. However, the rules themselves are inviolate and thus beyond the realm of controversy. The participants agree to suspend argument over the rules during the contest, thereby accepting their legitimacy, if not their particular applications. In this sense, the rules are to be followed, and not disputed, during the sporting occasion. This ensures that the sporting occasion is a special event in the world of sport, just as the performance is in the world of theatre. At all other times there can be discussion and argument about the nature of the rules, but not when there are points to be scored and goals to be saved.

The problem with using the game metaphor to understand social rules is that the metaphor only deals with one aspect of rules: their acceptance. It does not deal with the creation of rules. Just as the writing of scripts occurs off-stage and out of range of the theatrical metaphor, so the creation of rules occurs in those committee-rooms situated away from the field of play. Here, the administrators of the game, often old players and enthusiastic philanthropists, can argue about the rules themselves. They may repeat the arguments which can be heard in changing rooms after contests, as players discuss the way their sport could be, or needs to be, improved. In these arguments, the rules are not a means for settling the disputes, but the rules themselves are the matter of dispute. Just as there is no formal sport whose rules are changed on the field of play, so there is no sport which off the field treats its rules as unchangeable writ.

C. L. R. James's axiom can be adapted to deal with this aspect of games: he that only knows the rules of play, knows nothing of those rules. The game and its rules are only comprehensible because there is more to social life than rule-following. Inevitably the metaphor of the game, by restricting itself to one aspect of social life and by treating this one aspect as a metaphor for the whole, produces a restricted image of the person. This is a person who essentially accepts the rules of life without question, although complaining about their application in particular situations. Again, a parallel between the theatrical and gaming metaphors can be made. The former assumes that social actors resemble the script-following actor rather than the script-creating playwright. Similarly the game-playing metaphor sees us all as rule-following players, rather than high level administrators, who make and change the rules, and who frequently are too old in body to engage in the sporting activity themselves. In short, it could be said that for rules to exist, there must be more than rule-following. There must also be rule-creation. Moreover, as will be suggested, rules are created in the context of argument.

Conversation as a game

At this point an objection might be raised. The critic might claim that the discussion about the weakness of the game metaphor has missed the point. The game metaphor, far from ignoring argumentation, is particularly apt for analysing arguments for a simple reason. Each game can be seen as an argument about a single issue: for example, whether the one-armed or the one-legged make the better cricketers. In order to conduct the argument, there must be agreement about rules. In this respect the game-argument is like an argumentative conversation. In order for two people to argue a point, they must agree upon far more than they disagree about. For instance, they must agree upon a common language, upon conventions for taking turns in speech, upon the meaning of gestures and so on. Therefore, an argument, like a game, depends on a wide area of agreement in order for the disagreement to be aired. In this important respect, the critic might conclude, an argument resembles a game.

This line of reasoning has been well put by Hans Gadamer. In *Philosophical Hermeneutics*, he has suggested that every dialogue can be seen as a form of a game (1976, p. 66ff). Like a game, a conversation has a momentum of its own, which carries it forward. Gadamer's point is caught in Thomas De Quincey's metaphor of the "vast tennis-courts of conversation, where the ball is flying backwards and forwards" ('Conversation', p. 422). For the ball to be hit back and forth there must be agreement between the players about the rules of play. This assumption of agreement occurs repeatedly in Gadamer's analysis, especially in his major work *Truth and Method*: "To conduct a conversation requires first of all that the partners to it do not talk at cross-purposes" (1975, p. 330). Just as the tennis-players must share common game-rules, so the conversationalists must share common rules of language: "Every conversation presupposes a common language, or it creates a common language" (p. 341) and "a conversation is a process of two people understanding each other" (p. 347).

There is a hint of one-sidedness in these quotations, for one can easily think of conversations which have proceeded from, and ended up in, mutual misunderstanding. To be fair to Gadamer, it must be stressed that his aim is to describe ideal processes of communication. As a result, he writes of the "true conversation", in which each participant "opens himself to the other person, truly accepts his point of view as worthy of consideration and gets inside the other to such an extent that he understands not a particular individual, but what he says" (p. 347). Gadamer's example of "true conversation" is the Socratic dialogue. Over and over again, Socrates stressed that the purpose of his conversations was not to score debating points, nor were they games. He expressed the pious hope that he and his fellow disputants would co-operate in their efforts to examine the issues under debate. Thus, according to Gadamer, the Platonic dialogues show how Socrates, by patient questioning, made sure that he and his debaters were at one, as they jointly approached the topic under debate.

Socrates's technique is often called the method of 'elenchus' (see, for instance, Robinson, 1971). By questioning, he gets the debaters to agree to certain propositions, and then by further questioning he examines the implications of this agreement. The method aims to give the debate a fixed starting point: there must be a proposition which is accepted, in order for the implications to be discovered. For the sake of the argument, the disputants must agree to the meaning of a particular proposition and then see where this agreement takes them. If the examination results in contradiction or absurdity, then the original proposition must be discarded and the process re-started with a different proposition. The process will continue until the participants find a proposition which withstands the test of cross-examination. The method of 'elenchus' seems to illustrate Gadamer's point about "true conversation" and to illustrate how argument proceeds from a measure of agreement.

However, in point of fact, the Socratic debates do not proceed in such an orderly fashion. They seldom, if ever, resolve anything, and the participants often end up expressing their frustration. The topics they want to discuss keep disappearing from view, as they find themselves bogged down in other issues. Moreover, the arguments have a habit of doubling back on themselves. What seemed to have been agreed upon earlier becomes, at a later point, a topic of dispute. An instance of this occurs in the Platonic dialogue *Protagoras*. Socrates gets Protagoras, under protest, to assent to the proposition that the various virtues are separate. Socrates, after some cross-examination leads Protagoras to agree that holiness is just, and Protagoras thereby seems to contradict the original proposition that the virtues are distinct. However, Protagoras, like many of Socrates's conversational disputants, reacts to the questioning by adding to his answer "if you like", in order to indicate that, since the questions are phrased in Socrates's terms, so too are the answers. What Protagoras wants to do is to shift the argument back to the starting-point, in order to claim that Socrates had treated the original proposition in far too simple a manner. It was not a question of saying yes or no, for, as Protagoras suggests, "I don't think it is quite so simple, Socrates" (*Protagoras*, 331c).

When Protagoras uses the innocent little phrase "if you like", he indicates, quite argumentatively, that he would prefer to use his own words, rather than accept the phrasing which Socrates is trying to pin on matters. The meaning of that first proposition, as well as its correct phrasing, then would become a matter of dispute. In this sense, Socrates's hope of giving the argument a firm starting-point is a failure, for disagreement breaks out in the very area in which he had hoped to establish agreement. By the end of the dispute, Socrates himself is expressing dissatisfaction with the course of their discussion. They had wanted to discuss the proposition whether 'virtue could be taught', but their discussions had been inconclusive and had kept wandering off the point. Another time, suggests Socrates, they should begin with "a determined attack on virtue itself and its essential nature" (361c). Only after they had clarified the concepts to be used, would they be able to return to their original topic for debate.

What we see here is something which occurs commonly in arguments: the point of disagreement shifts and points of agreement can quickly turn into points of disagreement. Therefore, it is too simple to say that it is a precondition that the participants must agree on the rules of language. Arguments frequently turn into disputes about language and the meaning of words. And it is this aspect of argumentation which so often leads to a feeling of dissatisfaction. Instead of talking about the 'real issues', participants find themselves trapped in semantic disagreements. It was to avoid this verbal entrapment that Socrates suggested clarifying the nature of 'virtue' before they started their next round of disputation. However, one would predict with a fair degree of confidence that a further debate between the two about 'virtue' would proceed as messily as the first one. It might even succeed in throwing into contention a whole new set of concepts. Once an argument starts, words which have been used non-controversially can suddenly find themselves in the forefront of controversy, as the momentum of the argument pushes the disagreement into hitherto unsuspected areas.

All this suggests that the game metaphor might oversimplify the extent to which disagreement can be contained in an argument. In the case of a game the rules can be set aside as beyond dispute. Elenchus may be all very well in sport, but it is hard to achieve in an actual argument. As Socrates kept discovering, what had seemed to be settled had an unsettling tendency of coming right back into the forefront of the dispute. If we wish to use a game metaphor to describe this process of shifting argumentation, then De Quincey's tennis metaphor would not seem to be the most apt. The same ball does not keep getting whanged across the same net, for at any moment the tennis-players might start arguing about the sort of ball they should be using and then they may drift into disputing whether they need a net at all, or whether the game should be played outdoors on grass or indoors on polished floors, and so on. If there is a resemblance between arguments and games, then also arguments can resemble games which never quite get played. It is as if two captains are picking sides in a playground before playing a game to settle an argument. However, they cannot agree how to pick the sides, and therefore they decide to play a second game, the winner of which can decide how to pick the sides for the first game. The second game requires that sides be picked, and that provokes a further row, which is to be settled by a third game. And, thus, there looms the prospect of infinite disagreement about the rules, all to be settled by further games, whose rules are disputable. Therefore, there is an infinity of disagreements which can be aired, before the teams can line up with agreed rules. Such disputatious captains might be thought to resemble Socrates and Protagoras, or any other disputants who cannot agree how to pick the words for their debates, and can only suggest further debate as a remedy.

Rules and arguments

If rules are treated as fixed and non-controversial entities, then it becomes difficult to explain their origins. The problem is a particularly acute one for theorists applying the game metaphor. The difficulty of discussing the origins of games by applying the game metaphor is well illustrated by Michael Argyle's article about the rules of social life. Argyle, having stated that "even the most fiercely competitive and aggressive games can only take place if both sides abide by the rules, of boxing or wrestling", adds the comment that "rules are developed gradually, as cultural products, as ways of handling certain situations; they can be changed, but changes are slow" (1980, p. 81). These comments suggest that the formulation of rules is something which somehow evolves with sluggish mystery, almost as imperceptibly as biological evolution. Just as the experimental social psychologist can safely assume that the course of biological evolution is not going to be changed in the middle of an experiment, so the rule-theorist can rest assured that the rules of social life will not be subject to sudden and troublesome alterations. However, this tacit dismissal of the issue of rule-formulation is based upon a misconception. The major sports of the modern world, such as football, cricket, tennis, and rugby, do not owe their rules to a slow process of accumulation, stretching over centuries of folk custom. On the contrary, the nineteenth century saw an energetic burst of rule-making. Elias and Dunning's important studies in the sociology of sport, not to mention C. L. R. James's analysis of Victorian cricket, have shown that this rule-making occurred at specific times of social change. Moreover, it was predominantly confined to a particular class. Needless to say, it was, like most else in the world of sport, the exclusive prerogative of the male sex.

The rules of rugby and soccer were formulated in order to transform informal agreements, which had permitted all manner of aggressive play, into defined codes to restrict violence. Above all, the rules were formulated against a background of argument. For example, the rules of football were intended to settle arguments, not just about the codes of game-playing, but also to end disputes in the public schools between ill-paid masters and their well-to-do charges. In introducing formal sports, and then having to legislate upon tricky decisions, the individual public schools found themselves elaborating different systems of rules. This led to further arguments between the schools and, in one famous instance, it ultimately provoked the split between the codes of rugby football and soccer.

Much of the early rule-formation arose directly out of argumentation, for it had been necessary "to develop more regular procedures for settling disputes" (Dunning, 1971, p. 143). For example, the 1846 rules of rugby were not exhaustive rules of procedure, covering all aspects of the sport, but, in point of fact, were little more than "decisions of certain disputed points" (Dunning and Sheard, 1977, p. 92). Things were not settled once-and-for-all when the various self-appointed rule-makers had codified their decisions into proper systems of rules. Disputes were still liable to arise, especially as tactics and styles developed. In fact, the administrators of all sports need to monitor the rules, in order to make certain that the delicate balances between attack and defence, between vigour and dullness, and so on, are maintained. If the authorities fail in this task, the new developments, which are so necessary if a game is to continue to be interesting, can so easily upset the balances on which all sports depend (Elias and Dunning, 1971a and 1971b). Within every sport there will be individuals or lobbies who will wish to change this or that rule, and there will be others who will deny that the change would lead to improvement. The continual monitoring of rules ensures that the process of rule-formulation is never ended.

If rule-following is a necessary prerequisite on the field of play, one might say that the existence of such rules implies an off-field structure to permit the alteration of rules amidst argument and debate. In fact, the more rules a sport may have, the more arguments and changes of rules can be expected. Cricket is probably the most ornate of all sports, demanding that the players obey both the formal rules and the informal spirit of the game. Not a season passes without the game's officials arguing amongst themselves about changing rules. In fact controversies on the pitch can end up in the committee rooms as controversies about the appropriateness of rules. This is certainly true of the most furious, and enduring, of cricket's on-the-field controversies. On the tour of Australia in 1932/3, the English bowlers adopted a tactic which the Australian team and public considered to be unfairly dangerous. The arguments stretched from the field of play right up to the highest levels of government. As with Socrates and Protagoras, the words used in the dispute would not keep agreeably still, but the choice of terms became a matter of controversy in itself, as well as being a signal of the speaker's sympathies. The British preferred to call their bowling tactic by the neutral, even academic, name of 'Leg Theory', as if nothing more than strategy were involved. The Australians insisted on 'Bodyline' to express their indignation with a ploy which they felt to be unsportingly intimidatory. What is significant is that the controversy led to a change in the rules of cricket, and that the merits of this change occasion arguments to this day amongst the legislators of the game.[3]

There is a general point which does not concern the details of that unhappy cricket tour, and which is not even restricted to the world of sport. The wider issue is the close connection between law-making and argumentation. Laws may exist to resolve disputes, but they are created out of dispute, frequently at the cost of provoking further argument. A simple syllogism might illustrate this: if there are laws, there will be lawyers (or experts in the law); if there are lawyers, there will be arguments (for it is by arguing that lawyers earn their living); therefore, if there are laws, there will be arguments. This same general point is better expressed in Plato's *Republic*, which looked forward to the creation of a well-ordered state. The citizenry of this ideal republic would obey the state's rationally founded laws without dispute. Such a perfect state, in the interests of maintaining its ordered harmony, would need to dispense with laws about trivia such as "contracts made in the market and contracts for manufacture, questions of slander and assault, the lodging of legal actions and empanelling of juries, exaction and payment of market or harbour dues and the general business of regulating business and police and harbour-charges and other similar affairs". If laws were formulated on such "minor matters", then the citizenry would waste their whole time "making and correcting detailed regulations" with the result that harmonious order would never be achieved (425c–e). Sextus Empiricus blamed the rhetoricians, rather than the existence of laws, for argumentation. He noted that amongst the barbarians there were no rhetoricians, and the laws remained unaltered and generally obeyed, "whereas amongst those who cultivate rhetoric they are altered daily, as is the case with the Athenians" (*Against the Rhetoricians*, 36). We could add that the "barbarians" Sextus Empiricus had in mind would not have codified their laws with the precision of the legislative bodies presiding over modern bat and ball games.

The close links between rules and arguments can be illustrated by considering a culture which has formalized its rules of everyday behaviour to an unequalled extent. The Talmud, containing the rules of orthodox Judaism, specifies in detail what are correct actions for every aspect of daily life. Even the most trivial action must be performed in a sanctified manner to prevent godlessness from entering into everyday routines. The novelist Jorge Luis Borges, in his story 'The Zahir', describes the Talmud as having "codified every conceivable human eventuality" (1971, p. 189). This is an exaggeration, for the continuation of Talmudic debates shows that complete codification is unattained but aimed for. The Talmud represents a self-produced anthropology, explaining to orthodox Jews the meaning of their rituals in a detail which the professional anthropologist, seeking the unwritten rules of social life, can only admire. Just as the behaviour of game-players is meaningless without knowledge of the rules of the game, so the customs of orthodox Jews are incomprehensible without the Talmud. However, this great code of behaviour, which seeks to leave nothing to chance but dictates detailed rule-following, is principally a record of arguments. From its opening page, through its sixty or so volumes of tractates, it describes the arguments of the ancient rabbis, as they disputed their interpretations of the Holy Law. Every pronouncement is a subject of argument, and, as Heilman has shown in his account of modern Talmudic study groups, even today the Orthodox learn the rules by reliving the ancient arguments. In fact, this style of argumentation may have deeply influenced the conversational forms of secular Jews (Schiffrin, 1984). All in all, the Talmud represents not merely one of the most detailed codes of behaviour ever produced, but is also one of the greatest collections of arguments in literature.

In addition to the rules and the arguments, the Talmud also contains stories. One famous story from the Tractate *Baba Metzia* (59b) shows that the sages knew full well the importance of earthly dispute for discovering the divinely correct rules of conduct. The sages were discussing whether or not a particular oven infringed the rules of ritual cleanliness. Surprisingly on this occasion the opinion of the great Rabbi Eliezer was rejected. Rabbi Eliezer, convinced of the correctness of his view, decided to enlist the help of the Almighty to prove his point. He declared: "Let this carob-tree prove that things are as I state." Whereupon the carobs were miraculously thrown a great distance off the tree. The other rabbis remained unimpressed and merely replied: "The carobs prove nothing." Rabbi Eliezer then said: "Let the walls of the college then prove I am right." The walls of the building, in which they were all gathered, began to shake and totter. The other rabbis shouted angrily to the walls: "If scholars are discussing the Law, what right have you to interfere!" The walls stopped their shaking. Finally, in desperation Rabbi Eliezer called out: "Let it be announced in the heavens that my statement was correct." And a heavenly voice was heard by all to say: "Why do you quarrel with Rabbi Eliezer, who is always right in his decisions?" That was not the end of the matter. Rabbi Joshua answered the heavenly voice back by quoting from the Bible: "The Law is not in the heavens." The Law, indeed all laws, lay now in earthly discussions. If heavenly voices wished to join in the debates, then they must do better than to shake walls or send carobs flying: they must present good arguments. Even a heavenly voice would have to conform to the dictum that "a legal decision depends not on the teacher's age, but on the force of his argument" (*Talmud, Baba Bathra*, 142b).[4]

In the Talmud there is a postscript to the story of Rabbi Eliezer and the ineffective heavenly voice. Apparently another sage managed to find out from the prophet Elijah how God reacted to having been put in His place: "He laughed and said 'My children have over-ruled Me, My children have over-ruled Me'" (*Baba Metzia*, 59b). There is a psychological moral to the story. Those who seriously seek the firmest and most absolute rules to follow cannot themselves only follow rules. Rules require more than that they be simply obeyed. At times even the highest authority must be over-ruled. And at all times there is the possibility of argument.

Because arguments are such a constant theme in the history of social rules, their psychological importance should be recognized. However, psychologists will be unable to give due attention to argumentation so long as they employ theoretical frameworks which subtract the argumentative aspects from human activities. If this point is accepted, then we now have our excuse to leave modern theory, and to enter the ramshackle old city centre of rhetoric: it is in ancient rhetoric, but not in recent social psychology, that argumentation is placed in the centre of human affairs. Consequently, the antiquarian psychologist is able to offer a justification for temporarily closing the modern psychology books, and for opening the texts of the ancient rhetorical tradition.

3   Protagoras and the origins of rhetoric

From the time of the ancient Greeks almost without interruption until the last century every well-educated person in the Western world was expected to have a grounding in rhetoric, or the art of speaking well. Rhetoric was no specialist study, confined to the ambitious few who hoped to make a career from public speaking. On the contrary, it was an established intellectual tradition, which offered practical skills of articulate expression and theoretical insights into the nature of communication. This heritage may now be strangely neglected, as rhetoric's classics of theory and instruction have long since passed from being compulsory schoolroom texts to items of antiquarian interest. The present work, by recommending that modern psychologists pay serious attention to the rhetoricians of old, can only paddle feebly, but obstinately, against a strong historical current.[1]

If rhetoric is to be so recommended, then it would not be difficult to act as sales representative, by promoting rhetoric as an ancient and well regarded art. The sales pitch might stress the lustre which could be acquired by psychologists, if they were to associate themselves with this classical tradition. Certainly, some impressive names could be dropped, as testimonials to the intellectual class of the old discipline. For instance, we could cite Aristotle, whose afternoon lectures for his most advanced pupils are preserved in *Rhetoric*. Or there is Cicero, whose great oratorical speeches have come down to us, alongside his theoretical works of instruction such as *Orator* and *De Inventione*. No mention of rhetorical study in Rome would be complete without reference to Quintilian's *Institutes of Oratory*, the most scholarly of ancient treatises on the subject. All the various aspects of rhetoric are discussed by Quintilian with copious examples from speeches by the famous and with references to other ancient academic theories. In the Middle Ages, Aristotle's *Rhetoric* might have been lost to the Christian world, although not to the Islamic culture, yet the Aristotelian heritage was preserved in *Rhetorica Ad Herennium*. This well organised, but rather simple, Latin textbook was learnt by generations of Mediaeval school children, for whom rhetoric took its place alongside grammar and mathematics to form the tri-partite core of the educational curriculum. Whilst famous names are being recruited to the gallery of rhetorical theorists, we can pause at the

Renaissance to collect Erasmus, Melanchthon and Francis Bacon. Next, we can travel forward to the seventeenth century to add Thomas Hobbes, who introduced Aristotle's *Rhetoric* to English readers, and then on again to gather up Adam Smith and Thomas de Quincey.

All this name-dropping would be a bit unseemly were it not for a paradoxical aspect to the rhetorical tradition. Whilst great stars can be summoned from the intellectual galaxy to give their encomia to the study of rhetoric, nevertheless there is something unsavoury about the topic. Despite a testimonial from Aristotle, it would not be too difficult to portray rhetoric as a discredited and far from venerated enterprise, to be avoided by all modern psychologists jealous of their reputations. The very word 'rhetoric' has an unfavourable connotation. It conveys speech which lacks substance, and the word seems to beg for the additional qualification of 'mere' or 'empty'. Mere rhetoric is often contrasted with the reality of deeds. The rhetorician is 'merely' a windbag, who trots out phrases full of sound and fury but lacking proper signification. Even worse, the rhetorician can be seen as a trickster, passing off empty words as the genuine article. Is it not absurd, the critic might ask, to recommend psychologists to associate themselves with a word of such dubious propriety? After all, psychology as a discipline has enough problems with its public image without calling upon itself the opprobrium attached to the word 'rhetoric'.

The critic could not be answered by the claim that the derogatory meanings of 'rhetoric' have been recently acquired. Even when rhetoric was well established doubts were common. In the nineteenth century Bishop Whately introduced his textbook *Elements of Rhetoric* with the comment that the title 'rhetoric' was "apt to suggest to many minds an associated idea of empty declamation, or of dishonest artifice" (1963, p. xxxiv). The very same accusation can be found one and a half thousand years before Whately. In the third century A.D., Philostratus complained that the public suspected rhetoric of "being rascally and mercenary". Whilst other professionals would rejoice to be called clever, the term "clever rhetorician" was a "far from flattering label" (*Lives of the Sophists*, p. 43). Sextus Empiricus thought that part of the trouble with rhetoricians was that they tended "to consort with knavish and double-dealing slanderers by going down to the same places as they" (*Against the Professors*, II, 30).

Such complaints about rhetoric, as well as the derogatory nuances contained within the word itself, all echo the famous criticisms made earlier by Plato; or, to be more precise, they echo the criticisms put into the mouth of Socrates by Plato. Again and again in Plato's dialogues, Socrates criticizes rhetoricians, impugning the motives of those who claimed to teach the art of public speaking. In *Gorgias* Socrates dismisses oratory as pandering to the feelings of the mob. Rhetoric was not a genuine art, but should be compared to cookery, "an occupation which masquerades as an art but in my opinion is no more than a knack acquired by routine" (463). Socrates went on to declare that oratory was a "counterfeit" activity, which stood in the same relation to genuine government as did cookery to medicine and beauty-culture to physical training: oratory, cookery and beauty-culture were all merely forms of pandering. Plato's distrust of the rhetorician was akin to the modern distrust of the advertiser, whose profession likewise lacks general respect. 'Clever advertiser' is not a term of unalloyed praise, but it indicates that a suspect cleverness has been rumbled. It is hard for the modern reader not to be struck by the parallel between rhetoric and advertising, when Socrates attacks the rhetorician Polus for "jingle-making, maxim-making, image-making" (*Phaedrus*, 267).

What Plato's criticisms and the modern misgivings about advertisers have in common is a distrust of those who put style above content. The rhetorician and the advertiser are accused of possessing the facility of presenting an alluring surface, which is likely to attract the unsuspecting for all the wrong reasons. Polus's jingle-making and maxim-making might win over an unsophisticated audience to a particular point of view, just as the advertiser, by creating images, hopes to charm us into buying a particular brand of chocolate or washing-powder. In both cases the suspicion is that our attention is being seduced by irrelevancies, and that there is something inherently counterfeit about these skills of promoting style over substance. As Boethius warned from his dungeon in Pavia, messages can "have a specious sweetness, honeyed as they are with rhetoric and music" (*The Consolations of Philosophy*, 185). Similarly, in the eighteenth century, Hugh Blair declared that the ordinary person distrusted eloquence as "the art of varnishing weak arguments plausibly; or of speaking so as to please and tickle the ear" (*Lectures on Rhetoric and Belles Lettres*, p. 309).

The charge against rhetoric is not entirely without foundation. Throughout rhetoric's history, style has been a major concern, as the ancient teachers stressed the importance of delivery and gesture. Large sections of the textbooks would be devoted to the ways speech could be adorned with stylish turns of phrase and with metaphorical allusions. Whole areas of rhetoric specialized in the creation of the purple passage, whose brilliant elegance would, it was hoped, impress the audience. In fact, from the seventeenth century onwards rhetoric came increasingly to be associated with little more than good literary style or impressive delivery. As a result, rhetorical study became, at worst, the empty jingle-making of its critics, or, at best, a guide to tasteful figures of language. In the next chapter, it will be suggested that modern social psychology has, in practice, taken up many of the themes associated with the old rhetoric of form. The modern social psychologists are not so interested in tasteful metaphors, but they are concerned with the packaging and presentation of messages, just like the jingle-makers of old. However, this is not the aspect of rhetoric which is to be recommended here. The present concern is with that element of rhetoric which raised the ancient discipline above the level of the advertising gimmick and which is strongly represented in Aristotle, Cicero and Quintilian. This is the element of argumentation.

When this dimension is removed from rhetoric, then the ancient art is liable to degenerate into the study of useless adornment. At times the study of rhetoric has appeared to be based upon a pedantic categorization of figures of speech. Stylistic conceits have been given grandiloquent labels, and schoolchildren must have spent hour after boring hour learning to distinguish one sort of trope from another apparently similar one. This tendency within rhetoric is well satirized in Samuel Butler's portrayal of the dry rhetorician:

> He could not ope
> His mouth, but out there flew a Trope:
> And when he happened to break off
> In the middle of his speech, or cough,
> He had hard words ready, to shew why,
> And tell what Rules he did it by. (*Hudibras*, Book i, Canto i)

Psychologists do not need to be told to follow this sort of practice, for they have plenty enough hard words of their own. Samuel Butler's pedant is concerned with little more than cataloguing, and the scope of his rhetoric narrowly excludes the topic of argumentation. When rhetoricians ignore argumentation in this way, their discipline is liable to slip into pompous triviality. Chaim Perelman has expressed the matter succinctly: "If their argumentative role is disregarded, the study of figures is a useless pastime, a search for strange names for rather far-fetched and affected turns of speech" (1979, p. 18).

The present intention is to promote an argumentative rhetoric, rather than a rhetoric of adornment, for it matters little whether tropes fly forth from the open mouths of psychologists, or whether old-fashioned labels can be put to the tricks of the modern advertiser. In this chapter, the origins of rhetoric will be discussed, and it will be suggested that the study of rhetoric, in its earliest forms, was not 'mere rhetoric', but it was rooted in the study of argumentation. This historical sketch will involve tracing rhetoric to its pre-Aristotelian and sophistical foundations. The Sophists, a much maligned group of ancient Greek philosophers, included the great figure of Protagoras, for whom radical innovation seems to have been a habit. Protagoras is to be heralded as the originator of a psychological principle, which will be used repeatedly in the present work, and which expresses the argumentative spirit of rhetoric.

Sophists and the origins of rhetoric

Public speaking may be as old as society itself, but the teaching and the study of oratory can be assigned a rough date. Custom has it that the Sicilians, Corax and Tisias, were the first professional rhetoricians. According to Quintilian, they were "the earliest writers of text-books" (*Institutes of Oratory*, III, i, 8). The connection between these early rhetoricians and the practice of the courtroom is well established. In 467 B.C. the people of Syracuse in Sicily had driven out their tyrannical ruler, in order to set up the sort of democracy which prevailed in Athens. This gave the citizenry an opportunity to pursue law suits, in order to recover property which had been confiscated by the erstwhile king. Inevitably there was an outbreak of legal actions. The problem was that ordinary members of the public were expected to present their own cases in court. However, the average person, having no experience of pleading a case in court, was liable to become tongue-tied or to blurt out irrelevancies. There was an obvious need for professional speech writers, who would know how to present the strong points of a case and to counter the arguments of opponents. Men like Tisias and Corax were quick to capitalize upon their skills. In addition to providing a practical service, these two were able to formalize their skills into a system which could be taught to others. According to Cicero, "while many had taken pains to speak with care and with orderly arrangement, no one had followed a definite art or method" (*Brutus*, 46).

Quintilian recounts that Tisias and Corax, as the forerunners of rhetoric, were quickly "followed by another from the same island, namely Gorgias of Leontini, whom tradition asserts to have been the pupil of Empedocles" (III, i, 8). Gorgias was one of the group of thinkers who were known as the Sophists. Greek society must have been undergoing profound changes in the fifth century, although it is not possible to specify what were the precise conditions which gave rise to an unprecedented outpouring of philosophy and rhetoric. What we can say with certainty is that in the second half of the fifth century, Athens offered excellent opportunities for employment to those equipped with quick wits, good speaking voices and a love of disputation. Provincials like Protagoras of Abdera, Hippias of Elis, Gorgias of Leontini and Prodicus of Iulis poured into Athens from all parts of Greece to seek their fame and fortune. The skills of argumentation were much in demand, and the Sophists offered a much needed educational service. They offered to train the young gentlemen of Athens for a career in public life, equipping them to be publicly articulate. In teaching about language and speech, the Sophists were offering, above all, practical skills. As has been written, "what they taught was the art of succeeding in a democratic State when you do not yourself belong to the ruling democracy, and, in particular, the art of getting off when you are attacked in the courts of law" (Burnet, 1962, pp. 109–110). Fathers, ambitious for their sons, and young men, ambitious for themselves, flocked to the Sophists, with the result that these successful, but provincial, experts of oratory made their fair share of enemies in Athens.[2]

Like the word 'rhetoric', the word 'sophist' has a derogatory implication. If the image of the rhetorician combines a mixture of an unscrupulous mob orator with the smooth public relations officer, then that of the sophist depicts someone too clever by half. Likewise, 'sophistry' invites the addition of 'mere', as the word has cut loose from its etymological root: originally derived, without irony, from *sophos*, or wise man, the word now indicates the sort of slickness held to be the very antithesis of genuine wisdom. This reversal of meaning has been long established. It was encouraged by Plato in his attacks upon the Sophists, but was not confined to him. Xenophon declared that "many others besides myself blame the sophists of our generation...because the wisdom they profess consists of words and not of thoughts" (*On Hunting*, 13.6). He added that the term 'Sophist' "is a term of reproach among sensible men" (13.9). The young Hippocrates, who intended to attach himself to Protagoras as a pupil, admitted, under pressure from Socrates, that he would be ashamed to present himself to his countrymen as a Sophist (*Protagoras*, 312A). In this there is more than a hint of Athenian prejudice against outsiders. Such prejudice surfaces unmistakably in the *Meno*. Plato puts into the mouth of Anytus bigotry against the Sophists: these foreigners were "the manifest ruin and corruption" of any genuine Athenian, who had the misfortune to come into contact with them, not that he personally "had anything to do with a single one of them" (91C-B).

It is clear that considerable fortunes could be made by the successful Sophist, and this very financial sucess would have produced its own envious reactions. Plato alludes to the fees charged by the Sophists, and later scholars have attempted to translate the sums into the currency of their day. Adam Smith, in his famous treatise on economics, *The Wealth of Nations*, calculated the orators' fortunes with precision: if Isocrates had a hundred pupils, and charged each ten minae, then for each lecture course he would have made, by eighteenth century standards, £3333 6s 8d (1911, p. 120). Of course, such translations can never be exact, but there are enough indications that the successful Sophist was indeed well rewarded. Cicero wrote that Gorgias "was held in such honour by Greece that to him alone of all men a statue was erected at Delphi that was not gilt but made of solid gold" (*De Oratore*, III, xxxiii, 127–130).

It must be admitted that some of the charges levelled against the Sophists, especially those made by Plato, do have some foundation. The Sophists were not just teachers, nor did they confine their practical rhetorical skills to the law-courts. They were also public figures, if not show business personalities. Their speeches provided entertainment for the crowds, who would flock to hear their set-pieces. The Sophists would earn their living with dazzling displays of logic, pseudo-logic, eloquence and philosophical disputation. Hippias and Gorgias would challenge their audiences to ask any question, and whatever they were asked, they were able to provide a clever answer. According to Philostratus, Gorgias would ask the audience to suggest a subject, and then he would extemporize a speech. In this way, added Philostratus, he would demonstrate that he apparently knew everything. The crowds loved this style, which combined the academic lecture-hall with the fairground boxing booth.

Under these circumstances, it is not difficult to find examples of disingenuous slickness or phrase-making for its own sake, especially from minor orators or Sophists. Even the very best seemed to court suspicion, especially with the controversial boast that they could make the worse argument triumph over the better. Nothing could be more guaranteed to upset sensibilities, whilst at the same time attracting customers. Philostratus claims that at one stage the Sophists were banned from the Athenian law courts, "on the ground that they could defeat a just argument by an unjust, and that they used their power to warp men's judgement" (*The Lives of the Sophists*, p. 11). Cicero, who was himself a practising orator enjoying triumphs with unpromising cases, was to take the Sophists' boast at its face value. In *Brutus*, he wrote that Protagoras, Gorgias, Hippias and "many others of the same time...all of whom enjoyed great honour in their day" used to claim "not without arrogance, to be sure, to teach how by the force of eloquence the worse (as they called it) could be made the better cause" (30). Aristotle, on the other hand, took a sterner line with this boast, declaring that it had no place in any art "except Rhetoric or Eristic" (*Rhetoric*, 1402a).

By 'eristic', Aristotle was referring to those competitive debating contests, which Protagoras was said to have started and in which no intellectual holds were barred. Socrates constantly maintained, and his sentiments were echoed by Aristotle, that genuine philosophy and wisdom could not flourish under such competitive conditions. The eristic games encouraged debaters to win at all costs, with the result that facile triumphs were the order of the moment. Socrates complained that the "professional debaters" played with words, basing their arguments on verbal quibbles, and "were satisfied to have got the better of the argument in such a way" (*Theaetetus*, 164c). By contrast, he continued, "lovers of wisdom" would not stoop to such low tricks because their aim was to discover, and then nurture, truthful arguments. The genuine philosopher must always disdain those virtuoso performances which seek nothing more than to dazzle the multitude with bad arguments.

Socrates's complaints may have been justified against certain Sophistical practices, but, as a sweeping condemnation of all the Sophists, they are unfair. In the first place, Socrates himself, at least as he appears in the Platonic dialogues, was not averse to mixing in the rough and tumble of debate. Secondly, the Sophists were not entirely trivial in their philosophizing, nor in their studies of discourse. As we shall suggest in the next section, there is profit in attending to the thoughts of Protagoras in particular. When Socrates debates with Protagoras in the famous Platonic dialogue, we do not see a clash between the philosopher, who uses pure logic, and the trickster, who employs underhand methods. Both argue their points with force, employing all the skills of argumentation. On occasion, both are liable to overstep the bounds of propriety by straying into slyness or ill temper. On this score, Socrates, the pure philosopher, is no moral superior to Protagoras, the professional rhetorician.

An example from *Protagoras* shows how the philosopher is willing to trade tricks in the debate with the successful Sophist. Socrates realizes that there is an advantage to be gained by cross-examining Protagoras and forcing him to give brief answers to a series of pithy, and often unfair, questions. If he allows Protagoras to expound at length, the audience is captivated by his "long and magnificent display of eloquence" (328D). Socrates therefore must take the initiative by insisting upon the cross-examination. He counters one of Protagoras's lengthy and well applauded contributions by claiming with mock modesty that "I'm a forgetful sort of man, Protagoras, and if anyone speaks at length I lose the thread of the argument...so now since you find me forgetful, cut down your answers and make them shorter" (334D). Protagoras now has to search for reasons why his answers should be lengthy: "What do you mean by 'make my answers short'? Am I to make them shorter than my subject demands?" (334D). Socrates dodges this challenge, sensing that it could lead to trouble. Instead he goads Protagoras directly: so it is not true that you are a master of the brief answer as you claim? With the great debate degenerating to the level of the playground squabble, Socrates prepares to leave, but he gives way to that most human of rhetorical impulses: the desire to have the last word. In this case, the attempted last word consists of a final put-down of Protagoras and a last justification of himself:

> Since...I have something to do and could not stay while you spin
> out your long speeches, I will leave you. I really ought to be
> going. Otherwise I should probably be glad to hear them.
>
> (*Protagoras*, 335C)

In the event Socrates is persuaded to stay, and the pressing engagement is not quite so pressing, as he finds himself asking his questions. Finally, Socrates remembers his lack of time, just after he has been able to deliver a speech of a length which he wished to deny Protagoras from making. This speech was also of a length which supposedly was too great for this own faulty memory. Having said his piece, Socrates really must depart.

Both Socrates and Protagoras might use quick tricks of debate and both might, when the occasion demands, produce the eloquent declaration. However, their dialogue is not fully described as an exhibition of professional skills. They are doing more than merely displaying themselves and their talents in public. Their conversation is more than a game, just as it is more than a staged performance. The two protagonists are also arguing, and, in their case, the argument concerns matters of importance. The debate is not between one who uses arguments and another who disdains them for noisy jingle-making or the striking of dramatic poses. Protagoras possesses arguments, not slogans, and he is an adversary whose message has content as well as witty and urbane packaging. Above all, Protagoras has a philosophy – one that is attuned to his practice of rhetoric – and it is this philosophy which Plato seeks to criticize, using, all the time, argumentation, and thereby rhetoric.

The genius of Protagoras

No other Sophist expresses the spirit of rhetoric better than does the remarkable Protagoras. It is clear that Protagoras was considered by his contemporaries as a major intellectual figure. This includes Plato, who may have criticized him, but never dismisses him as unworthy of serious debate. The *Protagoras* is a dialogue between two serious thinkers and, although tempers might become frayed, Socrates treats his older opponent with respect. In *Theaetetus*, a dialogue enacted after Protagoras's death, Socrates goes to great trouble to reconstruct the Sophist's arguments. Protagoras's views are not to be caricatured and Socrates allows himself no easy victory. At one stage he admits that he has refuted Protagoras's position too easily and that, if Protagoras were still alive, "he would have had a good deal to say in its defence". Therefore, Socrates supplies answers to his own criticisms, in order to assist the deceased Protagoras "in the name of justice" (164). It is clear that Plato does not consider Protagoras to be the sort of 'mere rhetorician', whose words are all adornment and whose thought is negligible. In *Phaedrus* sarcastic mention is made of Chalcedon, who was "a terrible man...for rousing the passions of a crowd, and lulling them again when roused, by the magic of his song". Socrates specifically distinguished this sort of base rhetoric and "piteous whinings" from the practice of Protagoras, who always showed "a correctness of diction" and "a great many other fine things besides" (267).

Protagoras seems to have been a prolific writer, for Diogenes Laertius lists fourteen books on issues as diverse as rhetoric, government, ambition and wrestling. Unfortunately none of the books has survived, and we have to rely on the fragmentary quotations given by later writers such as Diogenes Laertius, Philostratus and Sextus Empiricus. These quotations are too brief and too opaque for a proper reconstruction of Protagoras's wide ranging views. A vivid portrait of the man and his style is contained in *Protagoras* and, as has been mentioned, a detailed philosophical analysis appears in *Theaetetus*. Even so, there is always the problem whether the words which Plato put into the mouth of his Protagoras can be ascribed with fairness to the real Protagoras. Also, despite the care of Socrates in *Theaetetus*, it is possible to wonder whether Protagoras's views have been reconstructed and interpreted with total accuracy. In addition, those fragmentary quotations which have survived are too sparse to clear matters up. They must inevitably be ambiguous because their literary context has been lost, and we can only guess at the precise role of such quotations in Protagoras's books.

Although so much has been irrecoverably lost, there does seem little doubt that Protagoras was one of the most innovative figures of all time. There can be few figures in history who have been credited with such originality. According to Philostratus, he was the first person to charge for lectures, "not that he is to be despised for doing so" (*Lives of the Sophists*, p. 35). In *Protagoras*, he himself claims to be the first person to call himself openly a Sophist: others had tried to disguise what they did but "I...have always gone the opposite way of my predecessors. I admit to being a Sophist" (317). Protagoras has been hailed for inaugurating the study of syntax, because he was the first person to divide discourse grammatically into prayers, questions, answers and commands (see Barnes, 1982, p. 462). According to Diogenes Laertius, no one before Protagoras had distinguished between the tenses of verbs. In addition Diogenes ascribes to Protagoras the invention of what was to become known, unfairly it seems, as 'Socratic' questioning. Protagoras's rhetorical firsts were considerable. He was apparently the first person to institute "contests of argument" (Diogenes Laertius, IV). According to Cicero, Protagoras was the first of many rhetoricians who were to compile lists of common-places; these were general arguments, which could be inserted into particular speeches. If the Sophists provoked unpopularity, then Protagoras apparently did so in a spectacularly novel manner. One modern authority notes that Protagoras "gained the distinction of being the first man in history to have his writings burnt by public authority" (Hussey, 1972, p. 116). The tributes to the genius of Protagoras seem unending. In our century we find no less an authority than Karl Popper locating the origins of the social sciences in Protagoras's distinction between the natural and the social environment (1966, Vol. 1, p. 57). Nor were all Protagoras's inventions intellectual ones. Just for good measure, he also invented "the porter's pad for men to carry their burdens on" (Diogenes Laertius, IV).

From all Protagoras's innovatory ideas, it is those relating to the two-sidedness of human thinking which primarily concern us here. According to Diogenes Laertius, Protagoras was "the first person who asserted that in every question there were two sides to the argument exactly opposite to one another" (III). Here was the practice of rhetoric elaborated into an innovative philosophy. In the courtroom there will be things to be said both for the prosecution and the defence. Also, in legislative assemblies criticisms and justifications will be offered for the same proposals. Professional orators must believe that there is always something to be said to support their case. Protagoras can, therefore, be interpreted as drawing theoretical implications from what could be observed in rhetorical practice. He was suggesting that human affairs are of such a nature that pro and con arguments can always be found. Certainly, this assumption formed a central part of the oratorical training offered by Protagoras. Apparently he was the first person "who practised regular discussions on set subjects", in which pro and con arguments would be rehearsed in tandem with each other. It also appears that Protagoras himself used opposing arguments in his own speeches. Certainly in *Protagoras* we see him arguing two opposing points of view. If he did argue in this way, then, as Diogenes Laertius recounts and as would be expected, he was the first person to do so.

As befits a man who argued that there were two contrary sides to every question, contradictory stories circulated about Protagoras's own life. According to one story, favoured by Philostratus in his brief biography, Protagoras was the son of a wealthy family in Abdera. Philostratus suggests that Protagoras picked up his unorthodox turns of mind from associating with the Persian magi. On the other hand, Diogenes has none of this. He suggests that Protagoras's invention of the porter's pad was born out of necessity, for Protagoras was a humble gatherer of sticks before his talent was spotted by Democritus, another of Abdera's famous sons. Two contradictory stories have also come down to us about Protagoras's death. Plato, in the dialogue *Meno*, contains the account that Protagoras died as a well-respected figure at an advanced age in Athens (91E). Philostratus tells a more exciting story of Protagoras being chased from Athens in a sailing-ship, which was then wrecked at sea. Even if these issues cannot be fully resolved today, there is one thing of which we can be sure: the originator of the belief that there are two sides to every issue would have been delighted to know that such disputes can still continue, more than two thousand years after his well-bred/humble birth and his violent/peaceful death.

Although we cannot be certain of the exact implications Protagoras drew from his maxim that there are two sides to every issue, we can guess with confidence that he upset traditionalists. The maxim hardly encourages an unquestioning belief in absolute certainties, and Protagoras seems to have caused outrage by his provocative agnosticism. According to Diogenes Laertius, one of his books began with the words: "Concerning the Gods, I am not able to know to a certainty whether they exist or not. For there are many things which prevent one from knowing, especially the obscurity of the subject, and the shortness of the life of man" (III). Protagoras's own relativism is preserved in a famous statement, which appears to deny the validity of objective truth, whilst having a dig at traditional religious belief: "Of all things man is the measure, of things that are, that they are, and of things that are not, that they are not" (quoted by Plato in *Theaetetus*, 152A, and also by Diogenes Laertius and by Sextus Empiricus in *Against the Professors*, 60).

This none too lucid utterance seems to express the general rhetorical position that different cases can always be made on the same topic. It seems to imply some people may reasonably assess some things to be the case, and others may reasonably assess them not to be the case. Over and above this rhetorical interpretation, there has been a perceptual one. Plato in *Theaetetus* interprets Protagoras as talking about the relativity of perceptual impressions. To one person the wind may appear cold but to another person the same wind may not appear cold. Neither of the two perceptions, or judgements, is more correct than the other. In fact, both are correct, for people cannot be in error whether they feel the wind to be cold or not. There is, in addition, an existential interpretation which has been put to Protagoras's statement. Both Plato and Sextus Empiricus also take the statement to imply that, not only are there two sides to every issue, but that the opposing sides are both true. According to Sextus Empiricus, Protagoras suggested that "all sense-impressions and opinions are true and that truth is a relative thing being inasmuch as everything that has appeared to someone or been opined by someone is at once real in relation to him" (60).

In this way the Law of Contradiction was challenged, for both a statement and its negation could be equally true.

Controversially, Protagoras applied the same argument to judgements of 'goodness' and 'badness'. Since the same things are judged by some people to be good and by others to be bad, therefore things are not unequivocally good or bad. Anthropological arguments also appear to have been used: what is moral in one society is immoral in another, and so the same action is both moral and immoral. If this seems to lead inexorably to a complete relativism, then Protagoras, or at least Socrates in the name of Protagoras, was willing to put the other, and more conventional, side. All experiences or opinions might be equally true, but some were more useful than others: food may taste bitter to the sick individual and pleasant to the healthy person, but that was no reason to deny that health was preferable to sickness, just as one could say that the person who delights in bad thoughts suffers from "a bad condition of soul" (*Theaetetus*, 167). Despite this respectably moral side to Protagoras's arguments, there was much in his philosophy and tone to upset the non-reflective. In the *Protagoras* an example is given, which, by its nature, seems to add insult to the injury already suffered by believers in traditional rectitude. Protagoras argues that, since "goodness" is "multiform", all things have their good and bad points: even manure shares this complexity, being "good for all plants when applied to their roots, but utterly destructive if put on the shoots or young branches" (334B).[3]

This sort of argument inevitably brought Protagoras and other Sophists, like Gorgias, who denied the existence of single objective truths, into conflict with Plato. Professor Kerferd, in his book *The Sophistic Movement*, has shown that Plato was not offended by the assumption that there are contrary opinions or sense-perceptions. Plato accepted this as obvious and there are passages, particularly in *The Republic*, which make the very same point. Objects which appear beautiful to one person are likely to appear ugly to another, and similarly there are differences of opinion about which actions should be called just and which unjust (479b). Plato's quarrel was with the assumption that these differences of opinion had anything to do with knowledge. Whereas Protagoras seemed to be denying that anything truer than conflicting opinions existed, Plato argued that, behind the contradictions of shifting opinions, there lay "eternal, unchanging things". Knowledge, as opposed to opinion, derives from these hidden and constant forms. Because Protagoras and other relativist Sophists did not look for this reality behind differences of opinion, they were merely "lovers of opinion rather than lovers of wisdom" (480a).

The difference between Plato and Protagoras is a profound philosophical one. Plato recognizes, along with Protagoras, that the world of everyday experience is full of shifting opinions and impressions. It is a rhetorical world filled with contradictory arguments. Unlike Protagoras, Plato wishes to transcend this world of opinion, in order to discover the fixed essences of truth, which will put a stop to all the argumentation. His vision, therefore, is a vision of undisputable truths. In *Phaedrus*, Plato describes how the soul in the heavens might circle round the essences of truth, as it attempts to catch a glimpse of these unchanging verities. Unfortunately, the soul's wings become heavy before full knowledge has been acquired. All too soon, the soul must sink down from this rarefied atmosphere into the baser universe of life. Having been banished from "the spectacle of truth", the soul must "thenceforth live on the food of mere opinion" (248).[4] This vision is so different from Protagoras's. Man, not a divinely inspired spectacle, is the measure. On this earth we must conduct our measuring through argumentation, rather than hope to recapture the silent vision which will end all argument. Plato may have dreamt of an end to argument, but in Protagoras's philosophy there is no escape from rhetoric.

Logoi and anti-logoi

For present purposes, questions about the existence or non-existence of unchanging realities can be left to one side. Our concern with Protagoras does not rest with the existential aspects of his philosophy, but with its rhetorical and psychological implications, especially with respect to argumentation. Protagoras's maxim draws attention to the importance of contradiction in rhetoric. If there are always two possible sides to every issue, then there is always the possibility of contradiction. The importance of potential contradiction is expressed by the ambiguity of the word 'argument'. The word has both an 'individual' and a 'social' meaning. The individual meaning refers to any piece of reasoned discourse. As one articulates a point of view, one can be said to be developing an argument. Rhetoric, in this sense, aims to help the individual thinker to develop a chain of reasoning, in order to build up a convincing case. In addition, there is the social meaning of 'argument'. Here the word does not refer to an individual's chain of reasoning, but to a dispute between people. Opinions, or individual chains of reasoning, clash in the context of a social argument.

Protagoras's maxim suggests that these two meanings of argument, the individual and the social meaning, are inherently connected. If there are always two sides to an issue, then any single opinion, or 'individual argument', is actually, or potentially, controversial. Therefore, any individual argument is actually, or potentially, a part of a social argument. The use of the same word, 'argument', to express two apparently different phenomena is felicitous, in that it draws attention to the rhetorical connection between the two. In later chapters, some of the psychological implications of this connection will be discussed. For now, however, we can draw attention to the fact that 'argument' will here be used indiscriminately to cover both its senses. Because the link between individual reasoning and social controversy is to be stressed, there will be no attempt to unpick what common language has, with insight, bound together.[5]

There is a further linguistic connection, which emphasizes the Protagorean insight. The Greek words for debater and for contradiction are closely connected. In *Theaetetus*, Socrates at one point decries his own point-scoring and claims "we seem to be acting like professional debaters" (164). The Greek term is *antilogikos*. In *Phaedrus* the same term is used to describe the technique of Zeno, who argues in contradictions, so that his audience believes "the same things to be at once like and unlike, one and many, at rest and in motion" (261). Kerferd, in his analysis of the term 'antilogic', concludes that the word refers to the method of argumentation by which contrary positions are examined in relation to each other, and that Plato was not opposed to this technique as such, only to the philosophically superficial uses of it. If Protagoras employed antilogic in this sense, then this is to be expected. His philosophy implies that all debate, to a certain extent, involves placing opposing positions into conflict with each other.

If Protagoras is interpreted in this way, he can be seen as making a statement about the constant possibility that any speech can be opposed by a counter-speech. At this point it might be helpful to take liberties with classical Greek, at the risk of offending the purists. Rather than keep with the term *antilogikos*, the concept of 'anti-logos' (or 'anti-logoi' in the plural) can be introduced for the sake of convenience. Literally 'logos' is Greek for 'word', but, in both its singular and plural forms, it has a much wider significance, which makes the English 'word' or 'words' an impoverished translation. 'Logos' denotes word-making in general, and so can be used as a synonym for discourse, speech or talk. When the professional rhetoricians instructed their students how to present a persuasive case, how to deliver a mellifluous speech, or how to quibble about the double meanings of words, they were teaching about 'logos'. Rhetoricians like Gorgias saw themselves as masters of 'logos', and offered their services as such. Although there might be agreement that rhetoric could be defined in terms of being the art of 'logoi', or, at least, as its techniques, "the wide meaning of this word (from talking or speech-making, to argument, reason, thought) made possible very different conceptions of the art of which it was the subject" (Guthric, 1969, Volume III, p. 177).

Protagoras's assumption was that any 'logos' could be matched by a counter-statement, or what here will be called an 'anti-logos'. Of course, the 'anti-logos' is itself a form of discourse, and so it too is 'logos' in a wider sense. Therefore, 'anti-logos' does not represent any sort of non-verbal opposition to speech itself, such as physical force being used to silence arguments. Instead it refers to an individual argument opposing another view in a social argument. For Protagoras, the art of contradiction appears to have been a major rhetorical skill: his work *Antilogion* would appear to have consisted of arguments and counter-arguments on well-known debating issues. In the *Phaedrus*, Plato describes the method of Theodorus, who was a follower of Protagoras, as giving "rules...for refutation and counter-refutation, both in prosecution and defence" (267). Protagoras appears to have derived a typically striking conclusion from the ubiquity of contradiction, namely that it is impossible to contradict (e.g., Diogenes Laertius, III). This denial of the Law of Contradiction can be interpreted philosophically as a statement about the non-existence of Absolute Truth. However, it is Protagoras's psychology, rather than his philosophy of relativism, which is of prime interest here. Protagoras was certainly not suggesting that people are unable to offer contradictory arguments when hearing a 'logos'. Quite the contrary, he was suggesting that, because people habitually contradict one another, it is impossible to establish a contradiction as an unassailable truth. There is no absolute refutation, because every 'anti-logos' can become a 'logos' to be opposed by a further 'anti-logos'. In this way Protagoras's philosophical denial of contradiction rests upon the social psychological assumption that people possess, and frequently use, a capacity to contradict logoi.

Later chapters will examine in greater detail how 'logoi' are always haunted, if not by the actuality of 'anti-logoi', at least by their possibility. For the present, however, we can note how the Protagorean insight limits the claims of the rhetoricians themselves. In order to attract custom, the Sophists had to act as their own advertisers. They tended to make inflated claims for their teachings, as if they were offering guaranteed cures for stammering or unfailing guides to fame and fortune. Protagoras declares that his prospective pupil, Hippocrates, will learn nothing less than "the proper care of his personal affairs, so that he may best manage his own household, and also of the State's affairs, so as to become a real power in the city, both as a speaker and a man of action" (*Protagoras*, 318E). Gorgias speaks in a similarly enthusiastic way, when he claims that he will confer on his pupils "the greatest blessing man can enjoy". This greatest of all blessings was not the abstract truths, which the unworldly Socrates sought, but worldly success to be gained by the power of logos. Gorgias announced that his pupils would acquire "the ability to convince by means of speech a jury in a court of justice, members of the Council in the Chamber, voters at a meeting of the Assembly, and any other gathering of citizens whatever it might be" (*Gorgias*, 452).

In these self-advertisements, great claims are made for the power of logos. It is not a matter of displaying both sides of a single issue, but of being able to put one side so forcefully, that the other side slinks away vanquished. This one-sided image of the persuasive logos is expressed by a statement made by Gorgias, in his *Encomium on Helen*, one of the few writings of a Sophist to have survived. Gorgias is defending the behaviour of Helen, who in Homeric legend deserted Menelaus and ran away to Troy with Paris. She should not be blamed, according to Gorgias, for she could not help herself. She was seduced by the words of Paris and no opposition was possible because "logos is a powerful master". Here, Gorgias advanced the psychological theory that those "with frailest, feeblest frame" can be powerless to resist the force of logos which "can put an end to fear and make vexation vanish; it can inspire exultation and increase compassion" (pp. 56–57).

Gorgias may have imagined himself to be like Paris, playing with logoi upon the susceptibilities of the feeblest frames. However, the very practice and the philosophy of the Sophists was designed to ensure that, far from logos being a powerful master, it would always be opposed by a rebellious anti-logos. If, by chance, the anti-logos managed to usurp the logos, in order to become the new ruling master, it too would be likely to face the revolutionary uprising of an anti-logos, eager to tear down the authority of the powerful logos. In fact, the *Encomium on Helen* was itself a notable piece of anti-logos. Gorgias was deliberately challenging the established view, shared by all sensible Athenians, that Helen, a traitor to Menelaus, should be condemned. Gorgias, as a Sophist, was mounting a defence of what traditionally had appeared indefensible. In so doing, he was demonstrating that even the most self-evidently true cultural belief could be opposed by the creation of an anti-logos.

In constructing Helen's defence around the power of logos, Gorgias uses what might have seemed a good advertising line for his own rhetorical academy. Nevertheless, Gorgias's arguments about the power of logos are not to be taken at face value. They must be set in their argumentative context, and this itself is sufficient to limit the boastful, one-sided pretensions of logos. As Isocrates was to claim later, Gorgias was constructing "a defence of her (Helen's) conduct", as if rebutting the charges of a prosecuting counsel ('Helen', 15). In consequence, Gorgias's psychological theory must be understood as being a defensive argument, opposing a prosecution who talks the language of personal responsibility and who claims that Helen should have countered Paris's logoi by her own anti-logoi. Although Gorgias might have hoped that Helen's reputation could be restored, he would not have seriously believed that his argument about the power of logos would enjoy an unopposed triumph. However powerful his own force of delivery, he would not completely sweep away all contrary arguments, with the new one-sided psychology of persuasion utterly replacing the traditional language of responsibility. Nor would he wish to. Gorgias himself might one day be called upon to use this very language, should he find himself in the role of prosecuting counsel, and the defence were resorting to psychological pleas of mitigation. Then, despite any previous victories with those psychological arguments, Gorgias would need to sharpen the counter-arguments of responsibility for the battle with the psychological ones.

In the *Encomium on Helen* Gorgias one-sidedly exaggerates the power of logos, or, more exactly, he appears to exaggerate it. In fact, as a good debater he remembers to add a built-in qualification to the seemingly sweeping generalization: logos only works its unopposed will over the feeblest of frames. Those with more powerful constitutions can grasp the logos and hurl it mightily back. In fact, rhetorical training will build up the argumentative constitution, in order to strengthen the forces of anti-logoi. This, then, is the true power of logos. The power of speech is not the power to command obedience by replacing argument with silence. It is the power to challenge silent obedience by opening arguments. The former result can be attained by physical force as well as by logos, but the latter can only be achieved by logos, or rather by anti-logos.

The importance of dialogue

There are a number of social psychological implications, as opposed to philosophical ones, which can be drawn from Protagoras's maxim. In the first place, Protagoras can be interpreted as pointing to the importance of argumentation for thought. His world, as a rhetorician, is a world of argument and discussion, and his special skills are based on a familiarity with the ways and means of this world. This world of rhetoric is a less certain world than that to which Plato looks forward. In Protagoras's world of rhetoric, there are no transcendental forms to be gazed at in silence, safely beyond the reach of all anti-logoi. Instead, it is a world in which thoughts are to be tested in argument, and wits are to be sharpened through controversy. As all the Platonic dialogues illustrate, it is a world in which debates between rhetorically sophisticated adversaries are unlikely to produce an agreement, which then dispenses with the need for further words. Instead the dialogues are liable to end in disagreement, with the two sides begging to differ, either amicably or grumpily.

One obvious psychological implication of Protagoras's maxim is that human thought is characterized by variety. We do not possess just one way of looking at, and talking about, the world. Instead, our species is characterized by the existence of contrary views. The same point was expressed by Cicero, when he declared that there is nothing which can be said which is so absurd that it has not been said by some philosopher (*On Divination*, II, 58). These sentiments were to be echoed later by Descartes, who reported that he became aware, early in his college career, "that no opinion, however absurd and incredible, can be imagined, which has not been maintained by some one of the philosophers" (1962, pp. 13–14). It is not merely that the philosophers have entertained absurd notions, but also that they have argued for their views, promoting their own ideas by criticizing as even more absurd the notions of their rivals. All this should be borne in mind by the psychologist who theorizes about the nature of human thinking. The psychologist should be cautious about formulating general theories, which stipulate that humans must fill their minds with particular sorts of ideas. The history of philosophy, not to mention the annals of practical rhetoric, will doubtless be able to produce instances where people have held the reverse of those ideas, and where the same ideas have been a matter of controversial debate.

A rhetorical approach stresses the two-sidedness of human thinking and of our conceptual capacities. A rhetorician is brought face to face with the contrary aspects of thought, and the teachers of rhetoric specifically aimed to develop a mental two-sidedness in their pupils. As was mentioned, Protagoras trained his students to argue both sides of an issue, and in his treatises he compiled pro and con arguments which might be of use to both prosecutors and defenders. This practice was to be followed by the great rhetorical textbooks of antiquity. Modern scholars have stressed the sophistical heritage of Aristotle's *Rhetoric*. According to Hunt, "Aristotle's rhetorical theory bears more resemblance to that of Protagoras and Gorgias than to that of Plato" (1961, p. 70; see also Grimaldi, 1972). In later chapters it will be suggested that these rhetorical theories contain important psychological insights. Above all, they draw attention to the human power of contradiction, or the role of anti-logos in thought.

Any psychological theory of thought which omits the role of anti-logos will therefore be incomplete. For example, the rule-following and script-enacting approaches, discussed in the previous chapter, can be said to give undue weight to the role of logos at the expense of anti-logos. These approaches stress the power of logos to constrain our actions, as we conform to rules and scripts. To this extent, they fail to put the other side of the matter: we argue with our rules and our scripts, creating anti-logoi with which to oppose their logoi. In Chapter 6, it will be suggested that a number of other social psychological theories of thinking are similarly one-sided. Protagoras's maxim, therefore, can be applied to psychological theory itself. One-sided psychological theories seem to invite a Protagorean response, which points out a contrary, and neglected, aspect. Theories which stress our inherent aggressiveness call forth counter-theories which stress our capacity for co-operation; behaviourist theories, which suggest that we behave but do not think, will be followed by cognitive theories which are all thought and no action. Of concern to us here, however, are those theories which appear to omit, or at least underplay, the argumentative aspect of thought. In such theories anti-logos hardly gets a look in. When faced with such approaches, the psychologist needs to summon up the spirit of Protagoras, and, by means of anti-logoi, to put the case for anti-logos. In this endeavour, there can be no escape from argumentative rhetoric. The psychologist who wishes to study rhetoric must also employ it, as arguments are made to argue the case for argumentation.

4   The science of persuasion

In classical times, rhetoricians often seemed to make two opposing claims for their skills. On the one hand, rhetoricians saw themselves as teaching the principles of eloquent speech, with the pupil being instructed in the art of speaking well. According to Crassus in Cicero's dialogue *De Oratore*, the finished orator is "a very near kinsman" of the poet, "rather more heavily fettered as regards rhythm, but with ampler freedom in his choice of words" (I, xi, 69). On the other hand, there was the more pragmatic aim of persuasion. As Gorgias had advertised the new skill, rhetoric would bring success in public life by persuading audiences. The orator's business was not to prettify debates, but to win them. Antonius spoke for this aspect of rhetoric, when he said that the orator produced "arguments suited to convince, in law-court disputes and in debates of public business" although he added that the orator should be "endowed besides with intonation, delivery and charm" (I, xlix, 213). Most textbooks combined these two conceptions of rhetoric – the aesthetic and the pragmatic – and acted on the assumption that the study of rhetoric would enhance students' eloquence as well as their persuasiveness. In fact, it was sometimes claimed that aesthetic speech was inherently persuasive. For example, Longinus, a great supporter of the aesthetic approach, claimed that sublime genius produces "consummate excellence and distinction of language", which gives the speaker "an irresistible power over the audience" (*On the Sublime*, p. 125).

Unfortunately for the aesthetes, in practice the beautiful does not always triumph. The problem was that audiences might not always be most impressed by good taste. Cicero, a practising orator, who inclined to the pragmatic approach, claimed that "the supreme orator...moves the minds of his audience", whilst using "good Latin" and diction that is "faultless and pure" (*De Optimo Genere Oratorum*, II, 5). It is a sad fact that there have always been orators who have been able to move audiences with appeals which fall below the highest standards of linguistic purity, and which are not even distantly related to poetry. This was noted by the classical teachers of rhetoric. Quintilian, claiming that puns indicated a lack of refinement, conceded that they could be effective and that "devices of the pettiest kind, which seriously considered are merely ludicrous,...at the moment of their production flatter their authors by a superficial semblance of wit" (*Institutes of Oratory*, VIII, v, 22). Aesthetics might be all very well, but good taste and eloquence provided no guarantee of effectiveness in the hurly-burly of debate. Demosthenes may have been the most eloquent of orators, but, as Plutarch recorded, he was not considered to have been "the most influential speaker", an unthinkable paradox if persuasiveness and aesthetics were based upon similar principles (*Lives of Demosthenes and Cicero, Parallel Lives*, p. 25).

If the pragmatic themes in classical rhetoric can be distinguished from the aesthetic ones, then the present approach could be said to concentrate upon the former. The focus will be on the psychological aspects, and, as a result, the eloquent side of rhetoric will tend to be ignored, although historically it has occupied large parts of the subject. Most textbooks contain long lists of different figures of speech, minutely distinguishing between various types of metaphor. In fact, during the Renaissance there was a pronounced shift from a persuasive rhetoric to an ornamental one. In 1481 Caxton could define rhetoric in terms of persuasion, as "a science to cause another man by speech or by writing to believe or to do that thing which thou wouldst have him for to do" (in Cox, 1899, p. 26). By 1630, Comenius was unambiguously placing rhetoric in the aesthetic domain: "A rhetorician searcheth out the forms and manner of speaking, exercises the style for eloquence, and for pleasant speech, varieth the words with tropes, the sentences with figures, the action with gestures" (*Porta Linguarum Trilinguis Reserata*, 751).

Once the criteria for recommending the various figures become purely aesthetic, then rhetoric has little direct connection with psychological matters. On the other hand, the pragmatic side of rhetoric has always been closely connected with psychological issues. In order to be effective persuaders, orators must study their audiences and gauge the effectiveness of their words. More generally, they should be sensitive to the ways opinions are changed and emotions are roused. These concerns are also central to modern social psychology, and this chapter will discuss the relations between the ancient rhetoric of persuasion and the modern techniques of social psychology. It will be suggested that the modern techniques, for all their scientific claims, have not totally superseded the old rhetoric.

Rhetoric and psychology

The pragmatic side of rhetoric was inevitably based upon psychological assumptions, whether or not these were just shrewd intuitions held by practising orators, or were fashioned by the theorists into an academic system. The ancient teachers of rhetoric recognized that, to be successful as a persuader, the orator must possess psychological insight. The experts might have disagreed amongst themselves about the other skills required of an orator, but they all stressed the need to study the thoughts and feelings of audiences. Cicero, in his dialogue *De Oratore*, depicts a group of Roman orators arguing about the nature of their profession. Crassus takes a particularly high-minded view, suggesting that the orator should be the complete intellectual, possessed of wide-ranging knowledge and impeccable aesthetic taste. Antonius takes a shamelessly pragmatic approach to the education of the orator: "His philosophical books he should keep back for a restful holiday." One matter on which Crassus and Antonius can agree is the necessity for psychological insight. According to Antonius, philosophy might not win political debates, but psychology might help, because the practising orator needs to develop "a keen sharpness" about the "thoughts, feelings, beliefs and hopes of his fellow-citizens" (Cicero, *De Oratore*, I, li, 223). Crassus does not demur, for the orator needed to be "familiar with the characters of men and the whole range of human feeling" (*De Oratore*, I, xii, 53).

There is even evidence that ancient orators occasionally employed their persuasive skills and psychological insights for psychotherapeutic purposes. Antiphon, who was nicknamed 'Nestor' because of his "extraordinary power of persuasion", set himself up in business near the market-place in Corinth. He announced "a course of sorrow-assuaging lectures", with the boast that "no one could tell him of a grief so terrible that he could not expel it from the mind" (Philostratus, *Lives of the Sophists*, pp. 39f).[1] The psychological dimension was not confined to ancient rhetoric, but later rhetoricians, who recognized the pragmatic aspects of their disciplines, also recommended that orators should study psychological matters. Edward Manwaring, in his *Institutes of Learning* (1737), paid tribute to the way "the Ancients made the Affectations the Life of Eloquence", and asserted that "to make a proper Use of human Affectations and human Nature, we must be well acquainted with both" (1968, p. 57). Similarly, John Mason, in *An Essay on Elocution* (1748), urged the aspiring orator to "study the natural Dispositions and Affectations of others", for "an Orator should be acquainted with all the Avenues to the heart" (1968, p. 30).

Of all the rhetorical works which attempted to map the convoluted course of these avenues, the greatest was Aristotle's *Rhetoric*. This treatise, which was to have an enduring impact on future rhetorical studies, aimed to provide more than a handbook for the aspiring orator. *Rhetoric* was an academic analysis of the various skills demonstrated by the practising orators. At the start of his treatise, Aristotle distinguished between the practice of rhetoric and the analysis of the principles on which this practice was based. The practising orator might be preoccupied with trying to persuade an actual audience, but the rhetorical theorists seek to understand how that persuasion is possible. Aristotle defined the academic aims of rhetoric as being "not to persuade but to discover the available means of persuasion in each case" (1355b). In order to discover the available means of persuasion, the rhetorical theorist must possess the sort of knowledge which nowadays falls under the heading of 'social psychology'. The rhetorician must know about the principles by which attitudes are retained or changed, how audiences resist or accept suggestions, how individuals who wish to make an impact should present themselves in public, etc. In fact, it can be asserted with probably little exaggeration that all the major themes of modern social psychology can be found in classical rhetoric, and in particular in Aristotle's *Rhetoric*.

Despite Plato's expressed hostility to the professional rhetoricians of his day, he was not inimical to an academic study of persuasion. He supported the idea that rhetoric should be based upon the sort of knowledge which nowadays would be termed scientific psychology. The problem was, according to Plato, that the professional rhetoricians did not seek this sort of knowledge, but preferred to practise glib tricks. As was discussed in the previous chapter, Plato accused orators of placing victory in debate above the supreme goal of seeking knowledge. Persuasion was an ignoble aim in itself, and could only be justified if the orator were seeking to convince others of the truth. A much quoted passage towards the end of *Phaedrus* reveals that Plato's opposition was not to rhetoric as such, but to those rhetorics which were not properly rooted in a scientific knowledge of psychology. According to Plato, anyone who "endeavours to effect persuasion" should enquire scientifically into the nature of the soul, noting "in what part it is active, and upon what it acts; in what part passive, and by what it is acted upon". The scientific rhetorician will inquire into "the different kinds of speech and different kinds of soul, and their different conditions". Having done this, the scientific rhetorician will "enumerate all causes that act, and suiting kind by kind, will show what sort of soul is of necessity persuaded, or not persuaded, by what sort of speech, and for what reason, in either case" (271). The modern social psychologist, so long as the references to 'soul' are overlooked, or are treated as an etymological pun on the word 'psychology', could find no better defence of contemporary research programmes into persuasiveness. In fact, it could be suggested that modern social psychology has set itself the task of translating into actuality Plato's dream of a complete science of persuasion.

The divisions of rhetoric

The sort of rhetorical science which Plato envisaged would be based upon fixed truths. The eternal verities of human nature would be discovered, and these would enable the orator to derive definite rules for persuading audiences. Only if such rules were enumerated, linking different means of persuasion to different types of 'soul', would oratory be able to progress from pandering to genuine science. These rules might take the form of suggesting that a particular sort of soul will be likely to be swayed by a message of a given characteristic. The resulting psychological laws of this new science might well encompass the accusations which critics of rhetoric traditionally made. For example, Thomas Browne complained that illogical and emotional rhetoric was liable to appeal to those who were "so illiterate in the point of intellect and their sense so incorrected" that they cannot determine truth from falsity (*Pseudodoxia Epidemica*, p. 16). This complaint could be rewritten as a social psychological law about the relations between education, intelligence and perceptual acuity on the one hand and the susceptibility to non-logical, emotional communications on the other.

The practising orator might have hunches about the susceptibility of various audiences, but the scientifically minded rhetorician hoped that regular laws could be substituted for the hunches. It will be suggested that, unfortunately for Plato's dream, fixed rules for rhetoric have failed to materialize, despite the efforts of the old-style rhetoricians and their modern psychological descendants. However, before discussing rhetorical or psychological laws, it might be useful to say a few words about the sorts of issues which rhetoricians studied and for which they hoped to discover laws. In this way, it will be possible to see the similarity between some of the topics of pragmatic rhetoric and those of modern social psychology.

Just as modern psychology contains a number of different sub-specialities, so too did ancient rhetoric. In fact, rhetorical theorists often spent considerable efforts categorizing the parts, sub-parts and sub-sub-parts of their own discipline. The details of their different schemata need not detain us here except to say that, by the time of Cicero, rhetoric was conventionally divided into five branches. Cicero himself favoured the five-fold classification, citing the authority of Aristotle for dividing up the discipline in this way. Quintilian was also a supporter of this division, which he claimed to be the one accepted by the best authorities (*Institutes of Oratory*, III, iii, 1). According to these authorities the five main branches of rhetoric were: Invention, Arrangement, Expression, Memory and Delivery (e.g. Cicero, *De Inventione*, I, VII).

(a) Invention

This was the part of rhetoric which was concerned with inventing arguments for the orator to use: "Invention is the discovery of valid or seemingly valid arguments to render one's case plausible" (*De Inventione*, I, VII). This is one of the most important aspects of rhetorical study and much of Aristotle's analysis was concerned with problems of this branch of rhetoric. Broadly speaking, invention involves discerning what are the crucial arguments on a particular issue. Francis Bacon in *Of the Dignity and Advancement of Learning* wrote that the skill involved was not, strictly speaking, one of invention, "for to invent is to discover that we know not, not to recover or resummon that which we already know" (1858, p. 421). Nevertheless, Bacon may have underestimated what was required. Invention was not simply a matter of recovering well learnt arguments from memory, but it also included the analysis of new situations. Even after possible arguments had been invented, the orator must exercise judgement. Not all arguments which could be devised would be suitable for use. Antonius put the point well in *De Oratore*: "When I am collecting arguments for my cases I make it my practice not so much to count them as to weigh them" (II, lxxvi, 309). As a branch of rhetoric, invention has tended to suffer from comparative neglect, despite its undoubted importance. It will be suggested in the next chapter that this division could most usefully be incorporated into modern social psychology. However, as will be seen, a revival of invention might not be painlessly uncontroversial for social psychologists, for it may necessitate the revision of some basic assumptions.

(b) Arrangement

Rhetoricians recognized that it is no good inventing superlative arguments, if they come tumbling out, one after another, in a confused order. Arguments, however good they might be, need to be organized into flowing and convincing discourse. As Longinus wrote, sublime ideas should be "well-ordered and built into one coherent structure" (*On the Sublime*, p. 161). The textbooks of rhetoric, therefore, attempted to present ground-rules for the satisfactory arrangement of speeches, or, to quote Cicero, for "the distribution of arguments thus discovered in the proper order" (*De Inventione*, I, VII). Typically, arrangement involved classifying the various parts of a well-constructed speech with technical labels. On top of offering a classification, the theorists also sought to discover what were the most efficacious, and aesthetically pleasing, ways of organizing speeches.

(c) Expression or style

Many of the classic theories of rhetoric were preoccupied with issues of style. Ancient theorists disputed endlessly whether the plain Attic style, which built upon the rhythms of ordinary speech, was preferable to the florid styles of orators like Demosthenes. Should the orator try to copy poetic modes of speech, or should the language be kept as straightforward as possible? To what extent should a speech be adorned with metaphorical figures? Some theorists preferred to offer their answers in terms of pragmatic criteria, some in terms of aesthetic ones, and others naively hoped that the two sets of criteria happily coincided. Critics sometimes turned the issue of style against the rhetoricians, suggesting that the standard rhetorical styles were both ineffective and absurdly pompous. Sextus Empiricus claimed that the simple style of the ordinary person was often more persuasive than the airs and graces of the orator (*Against the Professors*, II, 76). This may have been a dig against the practising orator, but it was an observation which, if true, should have its own place in the rhetorical science of Plato.

(d) Memory

It would be useless for professional orators to have carefully arranged their speeches and to have adorned them with the most elegant of metaphors, only to find their minds a blank once they ascended the public rostrum. A training in memorization was, therefore, considered an essential part of rhetorical instruction. In fact, many of the public orators were famed for their amazing powers of memory. According to Philostratus, Hippias "after hearing fifty names only once...could repeat them from memory" (*Lives of the Sophists*, p. 35). This ability seems paltry when compared to the feats of which Seneca the Elder boasted: "When two thousand names had been reeled off, I would repeat them in the same order" (*Controversiae*, I, preface, 2). Seneca also described how Latro, a fellow orator, would sit all day at an auction, and when the business of the day had been concluded, he "listed without a mistake and in the right order all the articles, their prices and purchasers, with the bankers authenticating the details" (I, preface, 19). As Frances Yates in her definitive *The Art of Memory* shows, the old mnemonic tricks of classical rhetoric were to have a long lasting impact, as the later mnemonists of the Renaissance took their inspiration from early rhetorical works such as *Rhetorica ad Herennium*. Phenomenal memory may now be relegated to computers and to the occasional variety-show act, but in former times it was of vital importance to the public figure. It is difficult nowadays, in an era of plentiful supplies of pens, paper and print-outs, to appreciate the absolute importance of human memory, when orators spoke perforce without notes.

(e) Delivery

Cicero may have listed Delivery, or "the control of the voice and body" (I, VII) last in his divisions of rhetoric, but its importance was generally recognized. Oratory did not end once a speech had been composed, but the words had to be delivered in public. Not all oratorical experts were able to cut an impressive dash in public. For all the technical brilliance and inventiveness which Isocrates displayed in constructing his speeches, his public appearances fell flat, for want of a commanding physical presence. The career of Demosthenes provided ample testimony to the importance of good delivery. In his early public appearances, Demosthenes was mocked, all the more so because of the obvious care he had shown in the preparation of his speeches. The problem was his weak and breathless voice. An actor advised him that it was "of little or no use for a man to practise declaiming if he neglected delivery" (Plutarch, 'Demosthenes', VII). In consequence, Demosthenes retreated to a subterranean cave to teach himself the art of delivery by exercising his vocal chords in private and by rolling stones around his mouth. The success of these exercises became legendary, and Demosthenes never forgot what had caused his change of fortune. In later life, he was once asked which branch of oratory occupied first place in importance. He replied without hesitation: delivery first, delivery second and delivery third (Quintilian, XI, iii, 6).

If Invention, Arrangement, Expression, Memory and Delivery were the five basic divisions of rhetoric, then all of them have a clear psychological element. An understanding of invention seems to call for a knowledge of the more imaginative faculties of the mind. Memory has been historically a central part of psychological study. As for expression, arrangement and delivery, they can all be incorporated into a pragmatic rhetoric.[2] That being so, the same basic social psychological question can be raised in all three divisions: what forms of expression, delivery, or arrangement are liable to be persuasive and with which types of audience? In addition, these three divisions seem to possess a similarity, which distinguishes them from the other two. Firstly, memory seems to be very different from all the other four. Memory is a skill, which enables rhetoric to occur, rather than being a skill of rhetoric itself, as are the other four. In addition, a distinction can be made between invention and the divisions of arrangement, style and delivery. This is a distinction between the content and the form of rhetorical communications. Invention refers to the content of the messages to be transmitted, and in particular to their argumentative content. The other three divisions all refer to the presentation, or form, of this content.

This distinction between form and content is an important one, especially in relation to rhetorical and social psychological rules. The theorists sought to formulate rules to guide both the content and the form of messages. However, much of the emphasis has been upon trying to discover rules of form. It was just such rules which the opponents of rhetoric particularly feared, rather than the rules of content. If the rhetoricians had hit upon effective strategies for improving the content of arguments, then no-one could reasonably complain. In fact, the critics would have been disarmed, and they would have had to acknowledge that everyone should be packed off to rhetorical college in order to raise the general standard of argumentation. Rules of form were a different matter entirely. Possession of these rules would give the orator the power to make the unreasonable appear reasonable. Argumentative content would be devalued, as the adornment, or non-argumentative aspects, of messages became crucial. Arguments of poor content would be delivered in stunningly persuasive ways. Such a science of persuasive rhetorical forms would have dangerous implications, and Demosthenes's boast about the importance of delivery could only exacerbate fears that rhetorical form would triumph over argumentative content.

The rules of rhetoric

The critics of rhetoric often feared that the rhetoricians had indeed succeeded in discovering effective rules of rhetorical form. For example, Philo of Alexandria, whose philosophy combined neo-Platonism and Judaism, urged the virtuous, who were unskilled in argumentation, not to engage in discussion with the rhetorically sophisticated, "for who are there that unarmed could meet armed men and fight them on equal terms?" (*The Worse Attacks the Better*, p. 225). Interpreting history in terms of the story of Cain and Abel, Philo saw smooth-tongued orators as the descendants of the evil Cain, who should be avoided by all latterday Abels.[3] On one level, Philo was offering sound advice to earnestly simple believers, who had "never learned arts of speech". On another level, he was expressing a fear that the powers of rhetoric might be irresistible. Such a fear would be well grounded if rhetoric possessed its own secrets, which could guarantee to make practitioners unstoppably persuasive by virtue of the way they arranged, adorned or delivered an argument, regardless of its content.

If this was the fear of rhetoric's opponents, and indeed on occasion it was the boast of rhetoricians themselves, nevertheless the textbooks on rhetoric rarely offered the sort of rules which would have constituted the secrets of persuasion. In Cicero's dialogue, Crassus, as a respected teacher and successful practitioner of oratory, is urged by the others to divulge his secret rules of rhetoric. In answer, he stresses that there is no magic trick: "I shall tell you no mystery, nothing worthy of your waiting, nothing that you have not heard already or that is new to anyone" (I, XXXI, 137). Crassus was not holding back, unwilling to divulge trade secrets. On the contrary, he was aware that the 'rules' of rhetoric turn out, on inspection, to be somewhat less than the fixed verities which Plato believed to constitute a genuine science. Certainly they hardly constitute dramatic secrets.

One can search works like Quintilian's *Institutes of Oratory* or Aristotle's *Rhetoric* in vain for the magic formulae which will make audiences captive. Instead of hidden secrets, there is, as Crassus implied, abundant commonsense, but sense which is common is hardly novel. I. A. Richards in his *Philosophy of Rhetoric* complains that Bishop Whately, a rhetorical theorist of the nineteenth century, offered nothing more than "prudential Rules about the best sorts of things to say in various argumentative situations". According to Richards "we get the usual postcard's worth of crude commonsense:- be clear, yet don't be dry: be vivacious, use metaphors when they will be understood not otherwise..." (1936, p. 8). Admittedly, Whately's *Elements of Rhetoric* is a ponderous tome, but not too dull to catch the attention of Coleridge. To be fair to the Bishop, it is not difficult to find a similar postcard's worth in some of the very best rhetorical treatises. For example, Aristotle was scarcely saying anything provocatively original, when he asserted that a speaker should try to convince an audience that he possesses "intelligence, virtue and good-will" (1378a), nor when he asserted that "diction ought to be neither too low nor too dignified" (1404b).

In fact the rules of rhetoric are something less than rules, resembling guidelines which offer no guarantees and which contain their own disclaimers. For example, Quintilian, whose discussions of the limitations of rhetorical rules are particularly pertinent, starts his analysis of arrangement with a disclaimer. It is not possible "to lay down general rules which would suit all subjects", but, instead, the orator must always be prepared to be flexible. Similarly *Rhetorica Ad Herennium*, which derived its popularity from its concise and orderly arrangement of rules, emphasized that any rules of arrangement can only be provisional: there might always arise situations which the orator must judge as appropriate for departing from "the order imposed by the rules of the art" (III, ix, 17). Again and again, the rules of rhetoric are accompanied by statements of limitation. Nor were later rhetoricians to discover hidden certainties which evaded the classical theorists. Adam Smith in the eighteenth century was still arguing that it is difficult to have firm rules on arrangement (*Lectures on Rhetoric*, pp. 16f).

By this time rhetoric had encompassed the written word, as much as the spoken, and Smith noted that "the best authors frequently deviated" from grammatical and rhetorical rules, especially "in the most striking and beautiful passages" (p. 23). Even Bishop Whately realized that only very general rules were possible, and that precise ones could not be fixed for "each individual case" (*Elements of Rhetoric*, p. 72).

Most rhetorical theorists were aware that the only strict rules that could be offered would be inoperable or absurd. For example, Quintilian declared that the length of the introduction to a speech, or 'exordium', will vary depending on the situation: "As for those who have laid it down as a law applying to all 'exordia' that they should not be more than four sentences long, they are merely absurd" (IV, i, 62). Later rhetoricians have not always heeded the advice of Quintilian but have laid down rules of unrealistic rigidity. For instance, Abraham Fraunce, in *The Arcadian Rhetorike* (1588), recommended rigid gestures to accompany different rhetorical stances. The left hand joined with the right was fit for expressing "addubitations or doubts", but that was about all the left hand was fit for, because absolutely "there is no gesture of the left hand alone" (1969, p.K). John Mason, in his *Essay on Elocution* (1748) was even more precise in his rules of gesture: "In deliberate Proof of Argumentation, no Action is more proper or natural than gently to lay the first Finger of the Right-hand on the Palm of the Left" (1968, p. 38). Occasionally, absolute rules in rhetoric have a medical quality to them: "Always when you read or speak, learn to preserve an ERECT ATTITUDE...Keep your Throat and Nostrils always clear and open" (Herries, *The Elements of Speech*, pp. 96–97). The laws of Nature should be followed, so that the orator's speaking instruments should be preserved in top condition. If moisture is lodged in the wind-pipe, Nature "provides a remedy": "An unusual quantity of air is discharged from the top of the lungs, with a sudden explosion called COUGHING, which dislodges the obstruction" (Herries, p. 97).

The medical, or physiological, rules hardly constitute the rhetorical rules of persuasion. Moreover the absolute rules of gesture appear more like prescriptive rules of etiquette than descriptive scientific ones. Their very definiteness precludes them from being sensible laws of science. Any theorist who makes an absolute statement that the left hand alone is unfit for gesturing, or that a particular hand movement is the most proper gesture to accompany proof, exposes themself to easy contradiction. As Quintilian recognized, there may always be occasions when it is socially appropriate or pragmatically effective to lay aside any general rhetorical law, and for this reason the laws of rhetoric could only be provisional. So too, the psychological laws on which a pragmatic rhetoric was based must be provisional. For example, a rhetorical theorist might express the advice, or the social psychological conclusion, that an orator will obtain a clearer diction and more persuasive manner by speaking standing up. This might be true on most occasions and for most orators, but exceptions are always possible: Suetonius recounted that Albucius attained distinction by speaking from his seat, only rising when he had warmed to his subject (*On Grammarians*, p. 445). The success of Albucius's eccentric style of delivery raises other questions about the relations between delivery and persuasiveness, the answers to which must likewise be provisional.

Quintilian gave good reasons why the student should not expect rigid rules for persuasiveness: "Let no one...demand from me a rigid code of rules such as most authors of textbooks have laid down, or ask me to impose on students of rhetoric a system of laws immutable as fate" (II, xii, 1). Any system of fully determined rules would fail to make due allowance for the particularities of every rhetorical situation. Rhetoric can never be a simple matter of mechanically classifying the particular case as being an instance where this or that tactic will be persuasive. All classifications involve an element of risk, for each instance may be the one where the general guideline falls down. There can never be absolute certainty that a present case will be crucially similar to those where a particular strategy worked in the past, and we must constantly be aware that our successful strategies may not always work in the future: "Since cases in the courts have always presented an infinite variety, and will continue to do so, and since through all the centuries there has never been found one single case which was exactly like any other, the pleader must rely on his sagacity, keep his eyes open, exercise his powers of invention and judgment and look to himself for advice" (VII, preface, 4).

The rules of rhetoric do not lack the certainty required by Plato because of the insufficiencies of the rhetorical theorists themselves. Quintilian was arguing that the rules must necessarily be provisional. It is the novelty of each moment and each situation which produces uncertainty, and thereby the need for hunches or judgement. Past experience can never be an infallible guide for dealing with the particular novelties of every current situation. Each prediction that the current situation is just like those which have occurred in the past must be haunted, to a greater or lesser extent, by the doubt that some unique features of the present situation may prove crucial in the end. For these reasons, the sensible rhetorician must be prepared to lay aside any fixed plan of action in order to judge the particularities of the present situation. We can call these arguments against the possibility of definite rules Quintilian's Principle of Uncertainty. The principle asserts that we can never capture the infinite variety of human affairs in a finite system of psychological laws. At any moment the finite laws are likely to be embarrassed by unforeseen and unforeseeable events.

It is only because of the possibility of such embarrassment, that the rhetorician can learn from experience. Experience gained from each novel situation contributes to this learning, as the rhetorician builds up more sagacious hunches and guidelines. However, this process of learning can never be finished. There is an infinity of possible situations, and therefore an infinity of things to be learnt.

Social psychology and persuasion

Brewster Smith, in the foreword to *Cognitive Responses in Persuasion* (1981), describes the modern research into the psychology of persuasion as being 'the new rhetoric' (p. xii). So long as one ignores the aesthetic dimension of the old rhetoric the description is apt: the new rhetoric follows Aristotle in aiming to uncover systematically the means of persuasion. Much of its impetus came from the work of Carl Hovland, and especially from the research he conducted during the Second World War into the effectiveness of propaganda. After the Second World War, Hovland (1954) continued his work into the social psychology of persuasion in the famous Yale University Communication Programme. The often expressed motto behind the research of the team was "the formula of *who* says *what* to *whom* with *what effect*" (i.e., Hovland, Janis and Kelley, 1953, p. 12). This formula, which originally was contained in Smith, Lasswell and Casey's *Propaganda, Communication and Public Opinion*, can be seen as a modern, and theoretically soulless, version of Plato's formula for a science of rhetoric, as expressed in *Phaedrus*. Both the modern and the ancient formulae contain the idea that the various aspects of persuasion should be carefully documented and their contributions assessed. Only by doing this systematically can the uncertainties of the old rhetoric progress to the certainties of a new science.

Brewster Smith's comment that the social psychological research into persuasion is a 'new rhetoric' is not typical of modern research workers, for most social psychologists do not look at present preoccupations in the light of past ones. By and large, practising social psychologists are not particularly interested in connecting their 'scientific' concerns to an 'unscientific' past. If they do glance backwards, it is in a way which emphasizes the differences between the dark ages of the past and present enlightenment. Instead of defining the present in terms of the past, as the label 'the new rhetoric' implies, psychologists more commonly view the past in terms of the present. In this way past rhetoric is to be seen as the old, and thereby unsatisfactory, social psychology.

A number of comments by social psychologists can be cited to illustrate this attitude towards the past. Perlman and Cozby, introducing the aims and methods of social psychology in their textbook *Social Psychology*, include some unidentified quotations from Aristotle's *Rhetoric* on the topic of friendship. Having allowed the reader to enjoy the anonymous words of Aristotle, they then reveal all with the comment: "These passages were actually written by Aristotle, but contain insights that are still worthy of our consideration today" (1983, p. 7). The 'actually' indicates surprise that a book so old may nevertheless still have retained its wisdom. The conjunction 'but' cautions the reader not to approach the past with too much wide-eyed enthusiasm, for the past, at best, is only worthy of our modern 'consideration'. In this way, the past is being patronized in terms of a present which is confident that progress has been and is being made. Aristotle was surprisingly acute – he gets a beta plus for effort – but he did not know what we know now. Aronson implicitly emphasizes this view of the past by calling Aristotle "the world's first published social psychologist" (1976, p. 58), and by not calling Hovland a 'recently published rhetorician'. Aronson goes on to express present confidence through his historical comments: "Although Aristotle first asserted some of the basic principles of social influence and persuasion around 350 B.C., it wasn't until the middle of the twentieth century that those principles were put to the experimental test by Carl Hovland and his associates." Petty, Ostrom and Brock write similarly in the first chapter of the book in whose foreword Brewster Smith refers to the 'new rhetoric'. Like Aronson, these authors qualify their reference to Aristotle with a cautionary 'although'. They write: "Although the first set of principles governing the art of persuasion was recorded in the fourth century B.C., it was not until the present century that attitude change was investigated experimentally" (1981, p. 9).

These quotations illustrate a confidence which is not to be found in older rhetoricians. No modern experimental psychologist investigating persuasion would dream of starting a book, as Edward Manwaring did his *Institutes of Learning* (1737), with the comment that modern writers "have never been capable of equalling the Ancients in Knowledge and Learning" (1968, p. 1). Nor is the modern psychologist, except perhaps a wilfully antiquarian one, likely to recommend unequivocally Aristotle's *Rhetoric* or Quintilian's *Institutes of Oratory*, with Lord Monboddo's remark that one "cannot perfectly understand any art or science without the study of those unfashionable books to which I refer" (1967, p. 87). Modern rhetoricians might sometimes try to catch this tone, but an element of doubt tends to intrude. For example, Bryant asserts that "though modern psychology is very different from that of the Greeks, and doubtless more scientific, modern enlightenment has produced no new method of analyzing an audience which can replace Aristotle's" (1965, p. 36). Towards the end of Bryant's article, the confidence in the past has cracked: "Psychology, especially social psychology, and cultural anthropology have much to teach modern rhetoric and to correct or reinterpret in traditional rhetoric" (p. 50).

Psychologists assume that there is a qualitative difference between the older rhetoric and their modern scientific researches. Around 1940 a decisive rupture occurred, when the experimental methodology was adopted to solve rhetorical problems. As Petty, Ostrom and Brock, as well as Aronson, implied, it is the experimental method, above all, which separates the 'old social psychology' from the 'new rhetoric', and which thereby divides the era of pre-scientific guesswork from the streamlined age of established fact. The attitudes of modern theorists of persuasion towards the rhetoricians of the past parallel those of Plato towards the sophistical theorists of his day. The modern social psychologist considers Aristotle as Plato did Protagoras: cleverness can be expected and even on occasions fortuitous truths, but cleverness and happy accidents are no substitute for scientifically based knowledge. Unlike Plato, the modern psychologists believe that they possess practices and routines, which, if followed, will reveal the hidden truths.

An immense amount of effort and ingenuity has been devoted in the last forty or so years to the experimental validation of older rhetorical hypotheses. The words of a successful orator, or those of an advertising executive, are not to be taken on trust about the relative effectiveness of various rhetorical strategies. All has to be put to the test and to be seen to be tested. Originally much of the work of Hovland and his associates had specific, pragmatic purposes. During the Second World War, Hovland was part of the United States War Department's Information and Education Division, being involved in the construction and evaluation of training and propaganda films. In much of this work he was required to discover the most effective ways of presenting the information which the army wished to transmit. As Hovland was to write of this work, "in nearly all cases...the studies had an immediate practical purpose and did not constitute a systematic research programme" (Hovland, Lumsdaine and Sheffield, 1949, p. 3). For example, a series of films, entitled 'Why We Fight', was designed to improve the morale of the troops, and Hovland was allotted the task of discovering whether they succeeded in doing so.

Towards the end of the war, the Information and Education Division wished to produce radio programmes designed to counter the optimistic assumption that the war with Japan would soon be successfully concluded. Hovland used the opportunity to test the old rhetorical problem, whether it is better to mention only those arguments which support one's own case, or whether 'counter-arguments', going against one's own position, should also be mentioned. Quintilian may have advised against appearing too certain, because "doubt...may give an air of truth to our statements" (*Institutes of Oratory*, ix, ii, 19). However, Quintilian never put the matter to a strict test, by giving speeches, differing only in the amount of counter-arguments expressed, to large captive audiences of army recruits and then noting any changes of opinion. By doing just this, Hovland and his associates were able to produce evidence that the effects of presenting counter-arguments were not uniform. Much depended upon the prior attitudes of the audience. Those soldiers who tended to believe that the war would be protracted were liable to become even more convinced after hearing the one-sided broadcast of this opinion. On the other hand, those who believed that the war would be a short one tended to be more influenced by the two-sided broadcast, which mentioned both sides before coming firmly down in favour of one of them. Therefore, even if the receptiveness to such messages was not shown to be dependent upon the souls possessed by the soldiers, it was affected by their attitudes.

Throughout the army research, Hovland and his team never confined themselves just to the evaluation of specific films. At all times Hovland wanted to transcend the details of the particular question of whether this or that film achieved its effect. No science could be built upon an interest in particular evaluations alone, for general principles had to be discovered. Thus, Hovland was not merely concerned with the means of convincing American soldiers (erroneously, as it turned out) that the war in Japan would be prolonged but he took the opportunity to go beyond the specific issue. In that instance he looked at the relative effects of one-sided communications, as opposed to two-sided communications, hoping to discover general laws about the persuasiveness of such messages. Like Aristotle, Hovland appreciated the limitations of an investigation which remained rooted in the particular case. Rhetoric, Aristotle had written, "will consider, not what is probable to the individual, as to Socrates or Hippias, but what is probable to a given class" (*Rhetoric*, 1356b). A Socrates or a Hippias only become relevant if they can be classified as members of a particular class of speakers who have a different effect on audiences because all members of that class of speakers possess a relevant characteristic. It is that characteristic which the theorist seeks to identify, and so have more to say than that Socrates and Hippias were marvellously and mysteriously persuasive.

Similarly the films advocating a lengthy war against Japan only became relevant to scientific investigation if they could be classified with other sorts of film, or indeed speech, and their effects could be considered representative of all members of that class. Even when reporting the war work, Hovland argued that the evaluation of the specific film had "little scientific value in contributing to testable hypotheses which may lead to the development of principles" (Hovland *et al.*, 1949, p. 5). After the war, when freed from the pragmatic demands of the military research, Hovland was able to apply the scientific criteria more fully. When describing the strategy of the post-war Yale research programme, he wrote that "practical problems are investigated only to the extent that there is clear indication that they will contribute to the formulation of important theoretical issues" (Hovland, Janis and Kelley, 1953, p. 2). In this way, Hovland's research strategy was based upon attempts to eliminate particularity, in order to observe general features.

Hovland may have shared Aristotle's belief that it was necessary to transcend the particular, but their respective rhetorics differ, not only in methodology, but also in emphasis. In Hovland's case the desire to get away from particularity seems to have led to a psychological rhetoric concerned with the form, but not with the content, of messages. To use the ancient classification, Hovland's investigations, unlike Aristotle's *Rhetoric*, have ignored invention, being more concerned with arrangement and presentation. This avoidance of content can be clearly seen in *Communication and Persuasion*, in which Hovland, Janis and Kelley summarized the results of their Yale studies. They include sections which are specifically devoted to discussing the "content of communication". Nevertheless these sections turn out to be concerned almost entirely with either the forms or the effects of communications, rather than with their contents. For example, one of the major issues, which Hovland, Janis and Kelley discussed under the heading of 'content', was whether communications which aroused fear were persuasive. If this were a discussion of content, then content had been defined in terms of the effects of the message on the emotions of the audience. Other issues, discussed as issues of content, were ones which had been traditionally discussed by rhetoricians as problems of arrangement. The following topics comprised the greater part of the discussion of 'content': "implicit as compared with explicit statement of the conclusion, presentation of one side versus two sides of an issue, and primacy versus recency effects produced by different orderings of the arguments" (Hovland *et al.*, 1953, p. 14). To be sure, the experimentalists provided evidence on matters of great rhetorical interest, often supporting the hunches of the rhetoricians, for example, that one's weakest arguments should be hidden in the middle of a speech. As any ancient theorist would have recognized, all this refers to the arrangement of messages, regardless of what their content might be.[4]

For the scientific purposes of Hovland and his associates, the actual content of the arguments was irrelevant. It did not matter whether the message was advocating a lengthy war with Japan, or advertised a consumer product. If both shared similar formal properties – whether they were arranged in a two-sided way, or whether they hinted at, but did not spell out their conclusions, or whatever – they should produce psychologically similar effects. This concentration on form was connected with the elimination, or attempted elimination, of particularity in the search for scientific certainty. It was assumed that the general scientific laws would be laws of form, which would hold true for all messages, regardless of their particular contents. For example, this assumption is clearly expressed in the textbook of Freedman, Sears and Carlsmith, three social psychologists all of whom have made major contributions to work on attitude change. They write:

> Social psychologists tend to concentrate on factors that increase the effectiveness of a message rather than on the content of the message itself. This is because we are looking for general laws that determine the effectiveness of all messages.
>
> (Freedman, Sears, and Carlsmith, 1978, p. 321)

In the early work of Hovland and the Yale team, it is easy to detect a bold optimism. Experimentation would provide the answers to age-old questions, and each experiment was making a definite contribution to the discovery of the hidden laws. When sufficient experiments had been conducted, varying the features of audience, message, and source in systematic ways, the fixed laws would become manifest. This optimistic vision foresees a triumph of the general over the particular, whereas Quintilian, with world-weary resignation, had accepted that any general law is always liable to be subverted by a novel particular. In Hovland's vision, far from the particular subverting the power of the general, eventually the general laws would be firm enough to be able to tame the uncertainties of the particular. He concluded his description of the war research with the statement: "It is believed that research of this kind, closely related to theory, will have greater practical value until a point is reached at which general principles have been established in the field and there remains only the working out of details of how most effectively to apply these principles to specific content" (Hovland, Lumsdaine and Sheffield, 1949, p. 279).

When such knowledge is attained, all that would be necessary would be for the particular to be categorized under the appropriate general class, and the most suitable means of persuasion would be calculated scientifically for each instance. Klapper and Loewenthal, who also conducted radio research of a military nature, foresaw a time "in an ideal world" when "the factors of content, audience, medium and effect would be merely elements in a precise formula, which could be algebraically solved for any one element" (1951, p. 651). Not without concealed warning, Klapper and Loewenthal hinted further at this future world of orderly and scientific persuasion: "The psychological warrior would need only to stipulate to the researcher the effects he desired, and the researcher, now a mere technician, would need only to work out the mathematics to stipulate in turn the requisite content that should be disseminated over specific media to specific people in order to achieve the desired effect" (p. 653). In such a world, rhetoric would have finally attained the certainty asked of it in *Phaedrus*. It would be a world which is as tightly organized as the republic of Plato, and which has little place for the mischievous spirit of Protagoras. In this world, the dialogue between the 'logos' of the general and the 'anti-logos' of the particular would have finally given way to a monologue from the possessors of the powerful and unchanging truths of logos.

Particular limitations of social psychology

Social psychologists working in the area of persuasion would freely admit that the bold vision of Hovland remains unfulfilled. Certainly it has not been for lack of effort. Since the original Yale studies there have been literally thousands of experimental studies, devoted to discovering the principles of persuasion and attitude change. Future generations will admire the energy and seriousness with which the traditional problems of rhetoric have been tackled in the mid years of the twentieth century. Nor can this upsurge of interest in solving rhetorical problems be credited solely to the energy of one or two individuals – a modern Prodicus here or a scientific Gorgias there. Following Hovland's pioneering studies, there has been concerted effort by teams of researchers based in practically every North American and European university, all contributing to the vast output of research. Incalculable numbers of undergraduates have given of their time, in order to collaborate in these projects as experimental subjects. Despite the vast accumulation of evidence, which is far too great even to be conveniently summarized, let alone remembered, by a single individual, there is, nevertheless, a noticeable sense of disappointment. Social psychologists have conceded that the end product of this research has not been commensurate with the effort involved.

It is generally admitted that the clear principles whose discovery Hovland anticipated have not emerged. For example, Fishbein and Ajzen, in a critical review of the evidence, claim that the result of all the experimental endeavour "has been an accumulation of largely contradictory and inconsistent research findings with few (if any) generalizable principles of effective communication" (1981, p. 340). Even the textbooks of the discipline, which generally attempt to simplify matters in an optimistic style, express disappointment. Roger Brown, writing of the Yale programme, commented that "the work has been well done...but it lacks something of intellectual interest because the results do not fall into any compelling pattern" (1965, p. 549, also quoted by Perlman and Cozby in their recent textbook of the same name, 1983, p. 116). Jaspars wrote similarly in another popular textbook:

> The most disturbing aspects of those results is their inconsistency. It is apparently difficult to make general statements about the

influence of message variables. Other factors also seem to determine the effect of these variables on attitude change, but it is not always clear which other factors should be taken into account in each case. (Jaspars, 1978, p. 295)

If the general principles have not been discovered, then there is little hope that the psychological expert can solve all the practical problems of the orator. Just like Crassus in *De Oratore*, the textbooks of social psychology disclaim any secret and guaranteed knowledge which can be put at the disposal of the speechmaker. For example, Aronson, whose book *The Social Animal* outstrips most classical textbooks of rhetoric for wit and kindness to the less scholarly student, poses an old problem from the rhetoric of form. He asks his readers to imagine themselves faced with the choice of either opening a debate or of replying to the first speaker. There seem to be good intuitive reasons in favour of both alternatives. Why not consult a social psychologist: "surely he must know which order has an advantage"? Aronson, however, cautions: "I'm afraid that if you expect a one-word answer you are in for a disappointment" and adds ironically that "if you wait to hear all of the social psychologist's elaborations and qualifying remarks, you might miss the opportunity of ever delivering your speech at all" (1976, p. 69). Later in the same chapter, Aronson asks the readers to imagine that they have inherited a television station: "Here is a golden opportunity to change people's opinions on an important issue" (p. 79). All you need to do, you might suppose, is to follow the recommendations of the experts in persuasion, construct your programmes accordingly, "and then you sit back, relax and wait for those opinions to start changing". Again, Aronson, well aware of the complexity of the research findings, discounts such easy optimism: "it's not that simple", he says simply (p. 81).

Aronson implies that when advice is given it is, or should be, hedged with qualifications. The general principles are not so general that they have firm control over the particularities of individual situations. The Principle of Uncertainty undermines any attempt to be too certain. Like Quintilian, the modern rhetorician is aware that occasions might always arise when the general principles should be laid aside. As a result, seemingly clear advice is immediately complicated by qualifications such as 'but it all depends on the circumstances' or 'you must take into account all factors'. A few examples can be given here, but any good textbook, which with the honesty of Crassus does not seek to claim more for itself than it can deliver, will contain many more. Deaux and Wrightsman, discussing whether one-sided or two-sided communications are more effective, comment that "few answers are 'all or none'; instead, specific conditions must be considered in each case" (1984, p. 283). The ubiquitous challenge of particularities to general principles can be seen in Hollander's summary of the research investigating whether speakers are well advised to inspire fear in their audiences:

> There may be circumstances where high fear appeals are needed to get action. But there is the risk that they may be too overwhelming especially for someone already concerned. Moderate fear appeals seem generally to be more effective in producing recommended action. But this depends still on the particular individual and the arousal needed for action in a *given situation*. (Hollander, 1981, pp. 160–162, italics in original)

Here each sentence seems to qualify the preceding one, and internal qualifications such as 'generally' rob the general laws of their generality.

The result is not far removed from the postcard's worth of commonsense of which I. A. Richards complained: we should make our audiences fearful, but not too fearful, although on occasion we should be extra careful of even that. The technical language may have changed, but the spirit is similar to Aristotle's conclusion on the same topic – a conclusion, which, like that of Hollander, follows a general statement with an immediate qualification: "Fear makes men deliberative; but no one deliberates about hopeless things" (*Rhetoric*, 1383a). When the modern social psychologist offers advice on the traditional matter of public speaking, the results would give I. A. Richards little more to applaud. Knapper, after carefully examining the experimental evidence, gives the prospective public speaker thirty-four hints, together with the general warning that "there is no single effective way of making an oral presentation". Thirty-four statements may be too many to fit on a post-card, but there are few surprises: "Be prepared in presentation". Hint number thirty-two expresses, as clearly as Quintilian, the readiness to lay aside any general rule: "Be as flexible as possible in your presentation to take account of audience needs (expressed through questions or comments) and any special circumstances that may arise" (1981, p. 166).

The qualification 'it all depends on the situation' is not then followed by an exhaustive list of situations, which definitively distinguishes those occasions when one sort of message is effective from those when it is not. Certainly, much of the social psychological research is devoted to discovering such situations in the hope of then formulating the general rule by which situations can be classified. However, attempts at formulating general rules about situations are themselves subject to the same qualifications as are the simpler rules about 'message variables'. In discussing why this should be the case, one point must be stressed. The social psychologists who formulate open-ended, or qualified, principles of communication, or who seem to be offering a disappointing post-card's worth, are not doing so because they are poor social psychologists who have failed to take into account all the evidence. In fact, the reverse is the case. The more accurately psychologists summarize the evidence, the less likely they are to offer the sort of confidently clear guidance which the inheritor of the television station might wish for. Similarly, Quintilian's careful qualifications reveal a greater sensitivity than do the more confident pronouncements of Fraunce or Mason. The layperson, overestimating the rhetorician's powers, might choose to believe that Crassus was concealing some esoteric knowledge, which perhaps Aristotle taught in his exclusive afternoon seminars on rhetoric, or that there is, tucked away in the most abstruse of social psychological journals, some vital experiment which reconciles all other findings. Fortunately for all audiences who receive the words of the powerful, there is no evidence that such secret knowledge exists. Nor is it likely that such knowledge is about to be uncovered. However, in order to justify this last claim, it will be necessary to return to the implications of Quintilian's Principle of Uncertainty.

Uncertainty and social psychology

Hovland's project for uncovering the principles of persuasion rested on an assumption that social psychological knowledge would be cumulative. Each well-conducted experiment would settle a small problem, and, thereby, it would remove a small portion of uncertainty. As more and more experiments were conducted, the total amount of uncertainty would be reduced. Thus, there would be a steady advance to a state of certainty, by courtesy of experimentation. Each hypothesis has to be tested systematically under differing conditions: "Only in this way can one ultimately determine whether or not the hypothesis is a valid generalization and, if so, whether it requires specification of limiting conditions" (Hovland, Janis and Kelley, 1953, pp. 5–6). The view that each investigation, satisfactorily completed, reduces uncertainty can be contrasted to an opposing image. In this image, experimentation does not solve problems in any straightforward manner, but each investigation increases uncertainty by throwing up new problems. Instead of a confident advance to ultimate certainty by the systematic reduction of uncertainty, there is a growth of uncertain complexity. Karl Popper has expressed this view of social scientific progress clearly: "With each step forward, with each problem which we solve, we not only discover new and unsolved problems, but we also discover that where we believed that we were standing on firm and safe ground, all things are, in truth, insecure and in a state of flux" (1976, p. 87). It will be suggested that Popper's description more accurately fits the practice of social psychology than do the expressed hopes of the practising social psychologists.

Early in Hovland's research programme, it must have been apparent that it was not going to be easy to discover general rules linking the form of a message to its possible effects upon audiences. One particular problem, not fully appreciated by all social psychologists, was that the content of a message was likely to influence the effects of its form. Not all messages which were arranged in the same way would have similar effects upon audiences. Since all messages, including those used in experimental conditions, have to possess both form and content, the 'pure' effects of form, uncontaminated by content, could never be investigated with certainty. The implications of this can be illustrated by considering one of Hovland's early experiments. Hovland and Weiss (1951) were interested, amongst other matters, in the differential effects of messages coming from highly and lowly valued sources. Subjects were presented with a number of essays and were told that some of the essays came from highly-valued sources (i.e., from an American nuclear scientist), while others came from lowly-valued sources (i.e., from the pages of *Pravda*). The experimenters arranged matters so that the same essay appeared to some subjects as if it came from a low status source, while to other subjects it apparently was the work of a high status source. Since Hovland and Weiss were interested in the general effects of form, not the specific effects of a particular message said to come from *Pravda*, a variety of high and low status texts were used, as well as a variety of high and low status sources.

Hovland and Weiss, in analysing their results, added together the subjects' estimations of all the texts ostensibly coming from high status sources and compared them with the estimations of all the low status communications. They did this in order to assess the effects of high status *per se*, rather than the particular different high statuses used in the experiment. The results indicated, as might be expected, that in general the high status communications produced more overt attitude change than did the low status communications. However, by treating all the high status communications as a unitary group, Hovland and Weiss tended to overlook the fact that not every single high status communication produced attitude change, nor did all the low status ones provoke less attitude change. In the case of the essays on the future of the cinema, the low status communicator produced more attitude change than did the high status one. Instead of producing clear cut results about the effects of source, the experiment raised problems, or at least should have raised them, about the possible effects of content upon form. From its results, the psychologists could have gone on to enquire what it was that separated the cinema essays from the others: is there something peculiar about all messages on the topic of the cinema, or was there something special about the particular cinematic sources employed in the experiment, or perhaps it was the phrasing of the actual messages used? Of course, there are many other possibilities besides these. To put it bluntly, the experiment raised more questions than it answered.

Nor is this peculiar to the study of Hovland and Weiss, but subsequent studies are haunted by the possibility that content affects form in unpredictable ways, so that a particular message may produce unforeseen effects. For instance, Eagly, Wood and Chaiken were interested in the effects of speakers who advocate positions which their audiences did not expect them to advocate. A careful experiment was conducted, using a complicated design in order to isolate the relevant variables. In the essential experimental condition, audiences expected a speaker to take a pro-business and anti-environmentalist line, but in the event the speaker spoke in favour of environmentalism. In discussing their results, the authors very properly caution against generalizing their effects to all messages, speakers and situations, because their study "did not incorporate multiple renditions of messages, or positions or multiple versions of the communicator and audience variables" (1978, p. 434). Had they done so, and had they included even more experimental conditions, it is doubtful if matters would have become clearer, but further examples of particular content producing discrepant results would have been obtained. In fact, the authors report that, before they were able'to run the experimental sessions, they had found it necessary to conduct a great number of pretests and trial runs. When the content of the messages had been varied in these trial runs, from a pro-environmental stance to an pro-business one, different patterns of response had been produced. The authors comment that the "pretesting of even these communicators and audiences in relation to another position (i.e. pro-business) on the same issue yielded a pattern of pretest expectancies inappropriate for implementing the design" (pp. 434–435). One could expect that more drastic changes in the experimental set-up would have produced even more unevenness. Nor is this peculiar to that particular experimental design. Jaccard has suggested that there are so many variables affecting any study of communication that 'inconsistent' results between different experiments are to be expected: "A pessimistic viewpoint might even go so far as to suggest that in those areas in which consistent data do exist, it is simply a matter of time until new conditions are (implicitly and randomly) sampled that yield inconsistent data" (1981, p. 262).

It may be helpful to represent the issue schematically, rather than to go into details about particular experimental situations. It can be asserted that social psychologists hope to produce general laws of the sort that "Stimulus X (Sx) produces Response Y (Ry)", where Sx and Ry refer to classes of stimuli and responses, and not to particular ones occurring once in a specific context. However, as has been shown, social psychologists do not feel confident in proposing such laws about the effects of 'message variables' on responses relating to persuasion. The one constant factor to emerge from the research into persuasion is that there is little constancy and that laws like "Sx produces Ry" stand in need of qualification. Because of this, we can make the following assertion: any law of the form "Sx produces Ry" needs, at the minimum, a qualification of the type "but there may be occasions when Sx does not produce Ry". Having made the qualification, it then becomes the task of the social psychologist to specify those occasions when Sx does not produce Ry.

This task is not completed when the social psychologist manages to discover a recalcitrant situation, in which the hypothesized effect does not occur. Because social psychologists are interested in general classes of stimuli and responses, it is not sufficient to produce a unique exception. It will be necessary to class the particular recalcitrant situation in a wider group of recalcitrant ones, in all of which Sx does not produce Ry. Let us assume that a particular group of social psychologists, after a series of careful experiments, has shown that there appears to be a certain type of situation in which the original law does not hold true. As a result, the psychologists put forward a second law, to the effect that "in Situation B, Sx does not produce Ry, but Rz". If the situation is seen as part of the general stimulus-environment, as it is by most psychologists, then this second law can be contracted to the assertion: "Sbx produces Rz". It can be seen that this second law has the same formal structure as the first law: both assert, without qualification, that a class of stimuli produces a class of effects. However, it is precisely this type of statement which needs to be qualified. Therefore, following the original logic, we must assume that our second law needs the qualification "but there may be occasions when Sbx does not produce Rz". Then the business of finding the recalcitrant situations starts again, in what is potentially an infinite process.

The result of all this is not the production of statements which in themselves are any more certain and less in need of qualification. Instead we obtain statements about more and more restricted ranges of phenomena. The more often the process is repeated and the more often the situations which produce exceptions are found, then the greater the confidence there is for insisting that the qualification must always be added to all general laws. On the other hand, we cannot abandon this assumption with confidence. Even if the psychologist, after many attempts, fails to identify situations which are exceptions to a general law, we cannot assume that no such situations exist. As Quintilian realized, and as experimentalists like Jaccard appreciate, the list of possible situations is infinite. At best, experimentation will only investigate a tiny proportion of all possible situations. In fact, each experiment draws our attention to many more possible situations, and in this sense each experiment increases, rather than decreases, the possibility of further experiments. This being so, it will always be reasonable to retain the qualification that there may always be exceptions to the rule that "Sx produces Ry". In consequence, it will always be unreasonable to suppose that, with just one more burst of experimentation, we will be in a position to abandon the qualification.

It is now possible to identify the nature of the problem, or at least what is a problem for those who believe that experimental knowledge is cumulatively approaching general laws. The problem is one of scientific imagination, but not in an obvious sense. It is not the lack of imagination which is impeding the discovery of universal laws. It is true that many experiments in social psychology, and particularly those in the field of persuasive communication, have an air of dull routine about them. However, it is not the pedestrian nature of experimentation that is preventing the discovery of general principles. To call for more imaginative research is, in fact, to call for more of the sort of research which shatters the optimistic notions of cumulative progress. This paradox occurs for a simple reason: it is the imaginative research which succeeds in finding the exceptions to the general laws. For example, it does not take great imagination to devise an experimental situation in which highly-valued communicators will produce more attitude-change than do lowly-valued ones. On the other hand, it is the imaginative social psychologists who discover the recalcitrant situations, which have demonstrated that the obvious findings cannot be generalized into a universal law. In a classic experiment, involving subjects eating cooked grasshoppers, Zimbardo was able to set up a situation in which the lowly-valued communicators were the more persuasive (Zimbardo, Weisenberg, Firestone and Levy, 1965). As is always the case with imaginative experimentation, it is possible to offer different explanations for the results: an experiment like Zimbardo's, in shattering preconceptions, also opens up all manner of other possibilities (see Nuttin, 1975, for alternative explanations of 'dissonance experiments' like Zimbardo's).

These comments should not be seen as an attempt to 'debunk' experimentation in a destructive manner. Such an attitude, although common amongst many critics of social psychology, is not particularly helpful. Nor is an attitude which naively assumes that greater clarity will emerge from more experimentation. Instead, the experiments should be taken as demonstrations of the infinite complexity of the rhetorical phenomena involved in persuasion. Above all, the experimental results underline the necessity for qualification and the need for alertness at all times to the possibilities of exceptions. In this sense, experimentation has proved successful. It is hard to imagine a competent social psychologist proposing, with the certainty of Fraunce, a universal law about the non-persuasiveness of left-handed gestures. Were any foolish enough to do so, one would expect a burst of experimental energy from unconnected laboratories, all producing situations where left-handed gestures are statistically demonstrated to produce persuasion. Quintilian may have had to rely on his memory to think of occasions when there were exceptions to general laws. However, the modern social psychologist possesses the means to go one better: with imagination the exceptional situation can be artificially produced.

Social psychology as dialogue

The flow of social psychological research can be compared to dialogue, oscillating permanently between logos and anti-logos. A categorical law is proposed, and then someone, applying their skills of invention, points out a recalcitrant exception. Perhaps there is a discussion whether the original law has been contradicted, whether it can be modified, or whether researchers ought to start out in a new direction. Even if there is no polemic between rival theoretical schools, there is the momentum of a dialogue, as the recalcitrant experimental result acts as a criticism against the theoretical law, which then will be justified, or re-worked, in terms of the critical challenge. This re-worked law acts as a provocative challenge to all potential critics to come up with a recalcitrant example. In this momentum there is no identifiable resting place, and the potential infinity of the process matches what Hans Gadamer, in his *Philosophical Hermeneutics*, called the "inner infinity" of all dialogues.

It is as if the scientific enterprise, which reaches out for fixed truths beyond the fluidities of everyday conversation, is itself contained within the universe of rhetoric. Again an analogy can be drawn with the intellectual ambitions of Plato. Searching for fixity, and attempting to reject the infinite uncertainties of dialogue, Plato nevertheless expressed himself within the format of dialogue. Although he may have dreamt of an end to dialogue, Plato's own works end in disagreements between the discussants, thereby exemplifying the Protagorean world he hoped to transcend.[5] Similarly, social psychology, and especially the social psychology of persuasion, might seek an undeniably true knowledge of the soul, but itself resembles a continuing argument. This resemblance can be seen both in terms of form and content. The form of social psychological activity is the form of a dialogue, and the content of its theories also reveals a two-sidedness, as if two viewpoints are attempting to make themselves heard.

(1) *Content of social psychology of persuasion*

There are two contrasting images in much recent psychology. One image views the person as a response machine, whose reactions are determined in a most rigorous way by external stimuli. This view sees us as automatic responders to messages. It suggests that, if the sender only gets the arrangement correct, then audiences will succumb to the charms of the communication. On the other hand, cognitive approaches stress that messages have to be processed and that there is not one simple way which humans have for digesting incoming information. Neither image is completely incorrect, and both can produce experimental results which show more or less thoughtful responses to messages. Rather than attempt to choose between a thoughtless or a thoughtful image of the person, contemporary approaches to the issue of persuasion embrace two-sided notions. For example, Hass (1981a) points to a 'basic antinomy' in human thought. People frequently dismiss messages without seriously examining them, especially if such messages threaten cherished beliefs. However, it is too simple to say that people only dismiss novel messages, for people also will seek out new information and revise beliefs.

This 'basic antinomy' is well expressed in the work of Petty and Cacioppo, who in recent years have been continuing the traditions of the Yale research into persuasion. Petty and Cacioppo write that "a general framework for understanding attitude change must consider that in some situations people are avid seekers and manipulators of information, whereas at other times people are best described as 'cognitive misers' who eschew any difficult information-processing activity" (1984, p. 79). The proviso 'it all depends upon the situation' is built into their theoretical perspective, and, of course, they have conducted experiments to distinguish which sort of situation produces which sort of response.

Although it would be an infinite task to detail the sorts of situations affecting such responses, the social psychologist can give broad guidelines. According to Petty and Cacioppo, there are two routes to persuasion – the central and the peripheral. The central route involves the assessment of the content of arguments. When the peripheral route is used, one is more likely to be overwhelmed unthinkingly by the form of a message. This is likely to occur, according to Petty and Cacioppo, when people are not paying full attention to an issue. When people are interested in the issue at hand, then they are likely to pay attention to content. If the peripheral route is taken, then an attractively packaged, but intrinsically worse, argument might succeed over an unadorned, but better, argument. If the content is being attended to, then people will sometimes accept the message and at other times they will argue back, either out aloud or in their thoughts.[6] Fundamentally, there is little new in this synthesis of the contrary tendencies in previous research. The cynic might trot out I. A. Richards's post-card once more. The practical orator still has no firm rules, but must pay attention to the competing demands of two voices of experience: one whispers seductively that people can be fooled and the other warns that the audience can argue back. For any given situation, orators must use their judgement to decide between these two voices of theirs.

Platonic scientists might profess disappointment with this state of affairs, but on another level this position is reassuring. The academic search for a science of persuasion has, of course, coincided with a massive growth of the mass media, which has given great possibilities of power to the controllers of information. An old orator like Demosthenes needed a powerful voice, lest his words be lost in the wind, unheard by the assembled hundreds. The modern politician or advertiser can whisper slogans, confident that they will reach millions. Each half-smile, each prepared gesture, each movement of the eye will be seen. Demosthenes, as well as Cicero much later, learnt his voice control from professional actors and, thereby, the public statesman became, in part, an actor. Today a retired actor can become a statesman, demonstrating on television sets around the world how the part of President of the United States should be played.

Despite all this and despite the immense effort by academics and professional advertisers, the secrets of persuasion still remain secret. As the latest research indicates, the power to argue back, which is perhaps threatened as in no previous age by the mass of planned information rather than by brute force, still remains a human power. The possibility of dialogue has not been ended by those who plan continually for monologue to be followed by cheers of acceptance. Those who value the power of 'anti-logos' to question 'logos' should be reassured by what, only at first glance, appears to be a failure of science.

(2) *The form of social psychology of persuasion*

In its formal structure, social psychological theory resembles a dialogue, whether or not persuasibility is the topic of this dialogue. The analogy can be put quite briefly. The form of the discipline, as portrayed above in admittedly a schematic way, is one where general statements are constantly being opposed by particular exceptions, which are then formulated as general statements. This implies a movement from categories to particulars and then back to categories in a potentially infinite process to and fro. It will be argued in Chapter 6 that this is a basic form of dialogue. General statements are constructed out of the qualifications, and then these general statements are opposed by fresh qualifications. This basic form does not depend upon there being several participants in the debate, for, as will be suggested in the next chapter, the deliberations of the individual can be modelled upon dialogue. Therefore the dialogic form can be found in the writings of a single person, whose thoughts reproduce the forms of everyday argument. Thus, the quoted passages of single social psychological authors contain this form, when a general statement is quickly followed by a qualifying "but...". It is as if someone else had chipped in with an objection, but, of course, in this case it is the same person who provides the qualification, thereby preventing anyone else from doing so.

If this characterization is correct, then there is a contradiction between the practice and the often expressed philosophy of some social psychologists. The practice exemplifies the position of Protagoras, in which both sides of an issue constantly dance around each other. The position of Petty and Cacioppo, based on the 'antinomy' of thought processes, captures the two-sidedness of Protagoras's position. The philosophy, on the other hand, is Platonic: there is a search for higher certainties behind the changing appearances of everyday reality. Through the practices of experimentation, it is hoped, the hidden universal laws or the essences of 'logos' will ultimately become apparent. Hovland's vision, thus, is the vision of someone who wishes to advance towards a transcendental truth. In this respect, it is the same vision of rhetoric which Plato outlined in *Phaedrus*.

The belief in ultimate answers and transcendental laws adds a mystic quality to the prosaic rituals of experimentation. Like the experimentalists, Kabbalists embark on an infinite quest in search of the absolute. Each word, indeed each letter, of the Torah is said to possess seventy layers of meaning. The mathematical precision seems to hold out the possibility that there are a distinct number of steps to be taken before the inner secrets of the universal law are fully revealed. Just seventy possibilities have to be circumscribed. However, every step taken branches out to infinity. Each of the seventy levels of meaning itself possesses seventy further, and each of those likewise has its seventy layers (see, for example, Gershom Scholem, *On the Kabbalah and its Symbolism*, Chapter Two). Similarly, the statistical calculations of the experimentalist open up new possibilities for experimentation. The more calculations which are made, the greater the number of possibilities that are revealed. The more 'situations' which are studied, the more situations there will be to study. The experimentalist is like the central figure in many of Borges's allegories: this is the person who, in searching for the ultimate, becomes trapped in an infinitely expanding labyrinth. In the 'Garden of Forking Paths', Ts'ui Pen is said to have constructed a maze, in which all futures can be simultaneously chosen. In this way Ts'ui Pen created "diverse futures, diverse times which themselves proliferate and fork...In the work of Ts'ui Pen, all possible outcomes occur; each one is the point of departure for other forkings" (1971, p. 51). The experiment-alist, too, creates a future, rather than waiting for it to occur, and this future is not 'the' future, but it points the way to diverse others.

The mystic element in social psychology may seem surprising. One might not expect to find the transcendental impulse in an activity whose practitioners pride themselves on pragmatism and who dismiss ancient philosophy as just so much unsubstantiated speculation. However, there is little reason for overestimating the neatness of human thought, in order to believe that categories such as 'mysticism' and 'science' are always kept apart. Perhaps the surprise may spring from an assumption which is itself as much metaphysical as it is scientific, and which is frequently accepted without critical reflection. This is the assumption that equates the categories of 'science' and 'mysticism' respectively with those of good and evil. But this assumption, like so much else, is a matter of controversy.

5   The art of witcraft

As one passes from a rhetoric of form to a rhetoric of content, one is dealing with invention, "the most important and the most difficult" division of rhetoric (*Rhetorica Ad Herennium*, II, 1, I). This aspect of rhetoric is not concerned with the presentation, or adornment, of arguments, but with argumentation itself. The inventive rhetorician would be one who could create devastating arguments, as opposed to delivering or packaging them with style. Since invention referred to the production of reasonings, whose content would do battle with the reasonings of opponents, this division was concerned with the nature of thinking. Thus a study of invention should also be a study in the psychology of thought. As will be stressed in the present chapter, this is not a psychology of the contemplative thinker, the Rodin figure who sits alone with hand on brow. The thinker of rhetorical theory is much more active, selecting and adapting thoughts, mutating and creating them, in the continual struggle for argumentative victory against rival thinkers.

All too often rhetoric has been associated with the comparatively narrow art of adornment, and rhetoricians, especially since the Renaissance, have neglected the study of invention. When John Smith published his book in 1657 with the eye-catching title of *Mystery of Rhetoric Unveil'd*, he offered no secrets, either of the psychology of persuasion, or of the invention of high quality arguments. His 'secrets' amounted to a dry typology of metaphors and tropes. The author's only secret was one he did not care to reveal: much of the work was lifted, without acknowledgement, from Blount's *The Academy of Eloquence*. Modern psychological books, protected by copyright laws, might not suffer from the same problems of plagiarism, but their titles still can sometimes excite the casual reader into believing that hidden secrets are about to be revealed. As was suggested in the previous chapter, there seem to be few psychological secrets of persuasion, waiting to be plucked like ripe apples from the forbidden tree. Although modern research has abandoned the preoccupation with figures of speech, it has tended, in common with the old lists of tropes, to neglect argumentation itself. There has been a great emphasis upon examining the effects of different types of messages, especially those coming from an organ of the mass media. The result has been a static rhetoric, in which the messages are seen to flow in a single direction from the broadcaster, advertiser or experimenter towards the audience. What is missing is a sense of the message being part of a debate, in which arguments flow back and forth, and in which skills are needed to invent excuses and accusations. It is in the context of argumentation that we see not so much the propagandist seeking a science of presentation, but disputants exercising the arts of thinking.

This chapter will discuss the rhetorical arts of thinking or invention. The evocative term of Ralph Lever, the sixteenth century rhetorician, will be used to describe these inventive arts. Lever, in his attempt to prove that English could be as good a medium for rhetorical study as Latin or Greek, sought to replace all "strange and inkhorn terms" with homely Anglicisms. Instead of referring to 'invention', he coined the word 'witcraft', using it to describe "the art of reasoning". According to Lever, witcraft involved "a cunning to frame and answer a reason" (*The Arte of Reason*, p. 1). Wit and craft well express the sorts of skills needed by the inventive rhetorician. Paradoxically, Lever himself was a follower of Peter Ramus, who more than anyone else was responsible for hiving off invention from rhetoric and treating it as a sub-branch of logic, with the result that the rhetoricians were left with little more than the pretty tropes.[1] However, in this chapter, Lever's term 'witcraft' will be used to argue against the view, held by Lever himself and by some modern psychological heirs, that thinking is, or should be, reducible to logic. Instead, the irreducibly argumentative aspects of thinking will be stressed.

Talk and argument

It would be a mistake to assume that witcraft is involved in all forms of talk or conversation. Instead, the term 'witcraft' will be used in relation to the skills of argumentation, and some types of conversation do not call upon these skills. An incident from Boswell's *Life of Johnson* can illustrate the distinction between talk which involves witcraft and that which does not. Johnson once mentioned to Boswell that he had "dined the day before at a friend's house, with 'a very pretty company'". Boswell enquired whether there had been "good conversation", to which Johnson replied: "No, Sir; we had *talk* enough, but no *conversation*; there was nothing *discussed*" (1906, vol. 2, p. 446). We can imagine the 'pretty company', which passed around polite platitudes all evening in a ritual of respectability. Where everyone agrees with each other it is not possible for discussion to flourish, and Johnson, that master of witcraft, craved the lively conversation which is fired by differences of opinion. In such discussions it is necessary to use the type of inventive wit which would have upset the prettiness of the well-mannered, but deadly boring, company.

If some conversations do not draw upon the skills of witcraft, then nor do some forms of oratory. It might be thought that all political oratory involves witcraft, since debate and controversy are the very stuff of politics. However, some political rhetoric can be based upon fixed rituals, which leave no immediate room for witcraft. The anthropologist Maurice Bloch has described the political oratory used by the Merinans in their village councils in Madagascar. All speeches are rigidly formal, following a traditional pattern, which determines both form and content. Even the audience is constrained by custom to express agreement. No debate is possible, for, as Bloch recounts, "on these occasions if you have allowed somebody to speak in an oratorical manner you have practically accepted his proposal" (1975, p. 9). Clearly no witcraft is needed on these occasions, although the technical skills of presentation might be handy to achieve the correct intonation, gestures etc. However, witcraft is not absent from the political decision-making of the Merinans, for, as in all societies, controversy can, and does, attend political decisions. With the Merinans, all the argument about a particular proposal takes place beforehand, and the formal oratorical speech signifies agreement. Or rather it is meant to signify agreement. Elinor Keenan recounts that she left her tape-recorder on after a formal speech, celebrating a marriage agreement. The argument, which should have been previously settled by the men, flared up again, as the women took over matters. This was, according to Elinor Keenan, a "match of wits", and this "verbal jousting" represented "the most developed art form in the culture" (1975, p. 110). In other words, the formalities of presentation had given way to the arts of witcraft.

It should be emphasized that an 'argument' does not imply ill-will or loss of temper. This sense of 'argument' should be distinguished from 'argument' meaning debate, lest it be thought that all debates lead to, or are caused by, ill-temper. On occasion, such feelings give rise to sharp debates, or they may result from exchanges of opinion. However, moods of anger are not a necessary part of argumentation, and, in fact, they may inhibit argumentation as discussion. When two people are said to be having an argument – that is, they are ill-disposed to each other – they might, in point of fact, be refusing to communicate by argumentation. Sulks and slammed doors typically signify an end to debate, and thereby to argumentation. In the Platonic dialogues, loss of temper and the introduction of personal animus normally indicate a breakdown of argumentation. For example, at one point Protagoras becomes angrily impatient with Socrates and indicates his unwillingness to continue. He has to be coaxed back into the debate, and the argument, as debate, only resumes when the argument, as a conflict of tempers, abates. Boswell stresses that, for all Johnson's ferocious intellect, the Doctor was an essentially kindly man. His love of argument stemmed not from any choleric aggression, but from a "spirit of contradiction." Witcraft is better fired by this spirit, than by anger. Contradiction is central to witcraft, as it is to the invention of anti-logoi to oppose logoi. If Lever's opposition to classicisms is to be respected, then words like 'logoi' and 'anti-logoi' should be avoided. Therefore, to adopt the language of Lever, one might say that witcraft involves reasons being framed cunningly to answer, and thereby contradict, other reasons.

Although witcraft forms an immensely important part of everyday life, the rhetorical aspects of argumentation have often been overlooked by modern psychologists. Those psychologists interested in conversation have often concentrated upon its 'prettier' aspects, in which harmonious agreement, or the coordination of responses, is the aim. On the other hand, psychologists interested in studying cognitive processes have a tendency to view thinking in terms of logic, rather than as a form of rhetorical argumentation. An example of a psychological analysis of discourse can be given, in order to show both the importance of witcraft in everyday conversation, as well as its neglect by contemporary psychologists. The example is taken from a paper by two psychologists, Hobbs and Evans, published in *Cognitive Science* in 1980. This paper includes a detailed transcript of a conversation between a woman and a man. The authors analyse the conversation in terms of their theoretical framework, which concentrates upon 'the goals' of the conversationalists and the 'plans' used to achieve these goals. As is common in modern 'Cognitive Science', or the Psychology of Thought, there is an urge to describe things in the language of computers. Using strange terms, which might not bear the smell of the ink-horn, but which echo the rattle of the print-out, Hobbs and Evans state that "a participant in a conversation is viewed as a planning mechanism whose behaviour is occasionally altered because of input produced by other such mechanisms" (1980, p. 374).

In the conversation detailed by Hobbs and Evans, the woman is presented as having clear 'goals'. She wants to impress the man, and also to interest him in the dissertation which she has just written and which she is carrying under her arm. The various ploys of conversation can be analysed, as she displays what modern social psychologists often term 'social skills'. Essentially, these are the skills of pretty company: they comprise the platitudes, the gestures, the smiles and so on, which allow inconsequential conversation to bounce along, and through which the largely unequal conversational dramas between men and women are enacted.[2] To judge by the transcript of the conversation, the woman is none too adept in these matters, and the man is hardly bothered with her plans. What interests the psychologists is how the woman's 'outputs' relate to the achievements of her goals and how she adapts her 'outputs' to the rather discouraging 'inputs' coming from her fellow 'planning mechanism'.

However, the conversation also contains something else besides the rather jerky tittle-tattle and the failure of the female planning mechanism to present herself in an interesting light. At one stage, the conversation finds itself spilling into argumentation. The woman is chatting about a competition which her children have entered, and which necessitated sending entry-forms through the post. She attempts to explain her children's lack of success in the competition: the postman might have maliciously altered the address on the entry-forms, so that no correct answers were delivered. The man rouses himself from his general indifference to the woman's remarks and expresses his incredulity: Why on earth should the postman do such a bizarre thing? Hobbs and Evans recount that "she retorts with 'Maybe the postman has children', thereby denying the force of his argument, and then says 'You never can tell', indicating that it is beyond their means at present to settle the issue" (p. 364).

At this point the pretty conversation has crossed the border into the realms of debate. For some reason, the woman's plans have led her to argumentation about the trustworthiness of the postal system. Such an analysis of the social world was never a part of her ulterior goals, but, having been started, this part of the conversation possesses its own internal momentum. The momentum is that of an argument, as a reason is framed to explain away failure at competitions. Then an objection is made by the fellow conversationalist. The objection takes the form of a question, doubting the reasonableness of the reason. In reply a further reason is framed to counter the objection. For all this, witcraft is needed: the woman required a sudden inspiration to justify the suggestion that postmen change addresses on competition entry-forms. Moreover, the woman's comment that 'you never can tell' signifies that the momentum could be continued, should the man pursue his objections, which he does not. His goals and plans are never made explicit.

However, the momentum of the argument is not of interest to the psychologists studying this conversation. They are concerned to view the elements of the conversation in terms of the plans and goals, and the momentum of the argument does not seem to serve a direct purpose for the achievement of the woman's plans. If anything, this outbreak of irrelevant, and rather artless, witcraft seems to threaten the success of these plans. Yet one can note the structure of this element of the conversation and see how easily the interchange drifted into argumentation. Indeed most conversations possess a potential for argumentation. All that is necessary is for one conversationalist to criticize another's platitude about the world, and for that other to offer a justification. Then the momentum will have begun. In everyday conversations there are few constraints to prevent this occurring, although in specific instances, such as the oratory of the Merinans, there may be rigid taboos against debate. In fact, if part of 'pretty' conversation involves presenting oneself as being 'interesting', then one might predict that any such conversation is always teetering on the brink of argumentation. The 'interesting' opinions of the 'interesting' person will always be likely to spark off a discussion, especially if others are desperate to be thought equally, if not more, interesting conversationalists. One might also predict that the potential for argumentation is increased when a woman offers the 'interesting' opinion: men are ill-trained for the role of smiling prettily and nodding their heads, when members of the opposite sex offer easily criticized opinions.[3] Whether or not any resulting arguments are used to further an ulterior purpose, they nevertheless possess their own dynamics. The rhetorical nature of these dynamics cannot be understood if argumentative interludes are seen as means to other, principally non-rhetorical, ends, rather than being treated in their own right.

The context of argumentation

If witcraft operates in the context of argumentation, then it is necessary to state what are the basic features of this context. As suggested by the example of the brief argument about the honesty of postmen, the essential features concern justification and criticism. The man is critical of the woman's hypothesis about the untrustworthiness of postmen, and she then justifies her supposition. Chaim Perelman points to the centrality of criticism and justification in rhetoric and he suggests that the two are rhetorically related to each other: "Every justification presupposes the existence or eventuality of an unfavourable evaluation of what we justify" (1979, p. 138), and "a question of justification ordinarily arises only in a situation that has given rise to criticism" (p. 33). As such, all justifications must be seen in terms of an argumentative context. Moreover, Perelman stresses that this context is a social context. Criticism, he argues, is meaningless "unless some accepted norm, end or value has been infringed upon or violated" (p. 33). Decisions or actions are criticized in relation to accepted rules or values; and, therefore, criticism "always occurs within a social context; it is always 'situated'" (p. 33). By implication, the same is true of justification.

It is possible to distinguish two different ways in which the context of argumentation can be called a social context. Firstly, the topics of argumentation can be seen as social issues, whereby arguments possess a social context. This is what Perelman is referring to, when he relates the social context of argumentation to disputes about norms and values. Thus the argument about postmen is an argument about whether or not socially acceptable standards of conduct have been transgressed, or are likely to be transgressed. In this way the topics of arguments frequently relate to wider social dilemmas. This aspect of argumentation will be considered in Chapter 8. For the present, however, the more immediate social context of rhetoric can be considered.

The context of rhetoric, as an argumentative context, is not confined to the relations between the speaker and the audience. The context might include the opinions which the speaker is attempting to justify to the audience, but it also comprises the counter-opinions which are implicitly or explicitly being criticized. Sometimes these counter-opinions might be held by the audience, but this is not necessarily the case. In fact, in the three main branches of classical oratory, the counter-opinions, which the speaker was attempting to defeat, were not typically the opinions of the audience. These three main branches, as delineated by Aristotle, were forensic oratory, deliberative oratory and epideictic oratory.

Forensic oratory described the oratory of the courtroom. In the context of the courtroom, audiences and counter-opinions are formally separated. Pleaders will direct their words to judge or jury as their immediate audience, but they will be attempting to defeat the anti-logoi of the counter-pleader. Although the courtroom drama resembles the 'pretty' conversation in that speakers address their words to audiences, and hope that certain favourable effects will follow from their speeches and interventions, there are important differences. In the pretty conversation, there are no anti-logoi to be voiced, and the logoi seek to interlock pleasingly with other logoi, so that the whole discourse forms a harmonious and complete jigsaw. However, the effect which is sought in the courtroom is for one's logoi to emerge victorious from their antagonism with anti-logoi. One's logoi need not only be directed to the audience of judge and jury, but, at times, the dialogue in a courtroom can be rhetorically complex. For example, a cross-examination represents a peculiar discourse, in which the audience overhear a conversation between the advocate and another person, which is spoken in order to be overheard.

The clear separation of audience from opponent distinguishes courtroom, or forensic, oratory from the other two main branches, the deliberative and the epideictic. In both these other two branches the conflict between logoi and anti-logoi is also detectable. Deliberative oratory refers to political speech-making. Speeches are given persuading to or dissuading from a course of action. If advisers are addressing their remarks to a ruler, then the audience and opponents are separated, as each faction, fighting for the favours of the governor, oppose the logoi of the other with their own anti-logoi. In legislative assemblies, speakers often addressed their opponents directly, urging them to convert their logoi to anti-logoi or vice versa. In modern democracy, politicians sometimes preserve the fiction that their professional opponents can be persuaded. More often politicians will address their views to 'the public', or to 'the people', by which they sometimes mean only their own supporters. The ambiguity of political audiences is revealed by the ambiguity of the term 'we', when uttered by a politician (Seidel, 1975 and 1978; Billig, in press a). Although a deliberate vagueness might be created about the extent of the 'we', the argumentative context always implies a 'them' to oppose the 'us'. 'They' are always a source of dangerous anti-logoi which threaten 'our' logoi.

Of the three classical branches of rhetoric, epideictic oratory occurs in the least overtly argumentative context. In this sort of oratory, the speaker formally praises an individual, as in a funeral oration. A consistently attractive picture of the subject has to be painted, and the skills of presentation are called for. Aristotle commented that proof is rarely used in this sort of oratory. Amplification, or the adornment of a given theme, was the requirement, "since the actions are taken for granted, so that it remains only to invest them with grandeur and beauty" (*Rhetoric*, 1367a). This sort of rhetoric at first sight seems far from the sort of argumentation for which witcraft is required. At the funeral oration, no alternative views are expected, and the speaker will be allowed to heap uncontested glory upon the memory of the departed. The sixteenth-century English rhetorician Cox stated that "confirmation of our purpose and confuting or reproving of the contrary which are parts of contention are not requisite in this kind of oration for here are not treated any doubtful matters to whom contention pertaineth" (*The Arte or Crafte of Rhethoryke*, p. 58).

However, matters are not quite as simple as Cox implied, for there is a hidden argumentative context to the funeral oration. The existence of such a context warns us not to equate the argumentative context solely with the scene in which the oration is taking place. To be sure, at the moment of speaking epideictic orators are not likely to face opposition, and their words are not addressed to obvious anti-logoi. Yet, the one-sided praises of the graveside can be seen as an implicit argument against the normal ambivalent estimations of everyday life. There would be less need for such praises, and for modern obituaries, if the tones of the panegyric were the normal tones of everyday life. Instead, the praises of the obituary help to drive away all criticisms of the departed from the mourners' minds. The anti-logoi of criticisms might be expressible yesterday or tomorrow, but they are forbidden on the day of the panegyric. So forbidden are these anti-logoi, that they are presumed non-existent and it is poor taste even to refer to them. The panegyric ensures that, despite the criticisms of normal evaluations, whole-hearted praise will for once be heard. Therefore the wider context of the epideictic oration, not the narrow context of speaker and audience, is implicitly an argumentative one. Witcraft will be needed to argue a consistently one-sided case and, in this case, to circumvent, rather than answer, unspoken criticisms. Nevertheless, the exceptional features of the epideictic situation make it a poor example for argumentative oratory in general, and yet even here an element of argumentation can be detected.

The three great branches of oratory describe formal occasions, rather than the informal discussions of a Dr Johnson or a Socrates. In these informal discussions, the lines between audience and opponents will typically be less formally drawn than in court cases, and opponents will be more visible than in the epideictic situation. There will be no equivalent to judge, or jury, and the discussion will turn into pretty conversation if the skills of amplification are employed without counter. Of course, the noisier discussants might appeal to the quieter ones, as if appealing to a neutral audience. And sometimes there might be attempts to give such appeals a formal status. In *Protagoras*, Socrates refuses Callias's suggestion for there to be a referee to the debate, since it "would be unfitting to choose an arbitrator over our words" (338B). On the other hand, Thomas De Quincey suggested, in apparent seriousness, that there should be a "symposiarch" to preside over conversations at "every convivial gathering" (*Conversation*, p. 453). Most people in their ordinary discussions side with Socrates in believing a conversational umpire to be unnecessary. This illustrates that contesting, contradictory parties provide the necessary social context of argumentation, whereas a neutral audience is an optional extra.

Meaning and reasonableness

There are a number of theoretical implications which follow from an emphasis upon the argumentative context of discourse. Two in particular will be considered here. The first refers to a rhetorical approach to the problem of meaning, and the second to the reasonableness of contrary statements.

(a) Rhetorical concept of meaning

Philosophers and psychologists have traditionally been much concerned about determining what is the meaning of words, utterances and whole passages of speech. Some psychologists have concentrated upon the images which are supposed to exist in the mind when one utters something. Others draw attention to the dictionary definitions of the words involved. The rhetorical approach connects meaning to the argumentative context, at least for discourse involving witcraft. I. A. Richards in *Philosophy of Rhetoric* argues that words do not possess fixed meanings. That being so, one must understand words in relation to the contexts in which they are being used. Thus the same word, or even sentence, may possess different meanings when applied in different contexts.

Following from this, it could be suggested that the meaning of discourse used in an argumentative context must be examined in terms of the contest between criticism and justification. Therefore, to understand the meaning of a sentence or whole discourse in an argumentative context, one should not examine merely the words within that discourse or the images in the speaker's mind at the moment of utterance. One should also consider the positions which are being criticized, or against which a justification is being mounted. Without knowing these counter-positions, the argumentative meaning will be lost. Thus, the meaning of a defendant's speech will be dependent upon the accusations explicitly made by the prosecution. The same is true of the implicit argumentative context. Deeper meanings will be detected in epideictic speeches, if we can grasp their implicit argumentative contexts by knowing what was said about the departed during their lifetimes. In consequence, the meaning of logoi, used in an argumentative context, will be linked to the meaning of the anti-logoi, which are being criticized implicitly or explicitly.

An example will be given to illustrate the point that one cannot properly understand an argument, if one fails to grasp what it is arguing against. In the last chapter, Bishop Whately's rhetorical works were mentioned, as well as I. A. Richards's criticisms of the Bishop's rather dull approach. Whately's best-selling book was an altogether racier affair. In 1819 he published a thin volume entitled *Historic Doubts Relative to Napoleon Buonaparte*, and in this book Whately proceeded to argue that Napoleon, contrary to appearances, had never existed. All manner of inventive witcraft was employed to show that British newspaper proprietors had conspired together to construct a French menace, which would boost flagging newspaper sales. It was absurd to imagine that a single individual – a Corsican upstart at that – could achieve half of what the newspapers ascribed to Buonaparte. Besides, neither Whately, nor anyone he knew, had ever seen this alleged Napoleon. Whately's book went to several editions. In the preface to the second edition, Whately wrote that "some sensible readers have complained of the difficulty of determining WHAT to believe" (1881, p. 4). The meaning of the book escaped the more naive readers.

It was not that the words, sentences, paragraphs or chapters of Whately's best seller were obscurely composed. All the internal meanings were clear enough. It was the argumentative context which was unclear. Was Whately really concocting a conspiracy theory, which attacked common assumptions about reality? Or was he doing something else? In point of fact, Whately, so at home in his clerical and academic worlds, was not arguing, as Barruel had done a few years previously, that politics were a giant hoax engineered by the freemasons. The real target of Whately's work had precious little to do with Napoleon. Whately was countering the scepticism of David Hume, by suggesting that the logic of Hume's arguments against Biblical miracles would lead to doubting obvious facts such as the existence of Napoleon. Because this was not spelled out in a way which would have spoiled the joke, some readers were perplexed: the real argument seemed to be conducted just out of ear-shot, and all they could hear clearly were words whose meaning they doubted.

Whately's *Historic Doubts* presents a clear example of a more general point about the argumentative context of discourse: the meaning of a piece of discourse can become unclear, if its argumentative context is ignored. This general proposition can be applied, for example, to academic work and particularly to philosophy. To an outsider, philosophy can appear a bizarre activity. It would appear a meaningless preoccupation to argue that things exist. However, philosophy is part of an argument which seems to be without identifiable beginning and which shows no sign of ending. Thus, Wittgenstein recognized the argumentative context of philosophy when he answered his own question: "On what occasions do people assert 'There are no (objects)' or 'There are (physical objects)'? Only when they meet people of the contrary belief" (1967, 413). Similarly, in the twelfth century Moses Maimonides complained that he was forced to justify obvious truths only because strange views had been put forward by other philosophers. He compared himself to Aristotle, who had been forced to assert the existence of movement because sophists like Zeno of Elea had denied its existence (*Guide of the Perplexed*, I, LI). If the argumentative context is ignored, then the arguments of Aristotle and Maimonides must seem, to the naive reader, as eccentrically bizarre as did Whately's doubts about Napoleon.

One can summarize this by saying that to understand an individual philosopher's argument, one must understand the social argument, or debate, in which it is situated. Thus, if one is puzzling over an extremely difficult piece of intellectual work, whose meaning seems too abstruse to grasp, one should ask oneself, not 'What is this about?', but 'What is this attacking?' If one comes to the conclusion that nothing is being attacked and that there are no logoi opposed, then the work has scant rhetorical meaning and must stand on its aesthetic merits of prettiness. From this, one might make a suggestion about the quality of arguments. It might be asserted that the quality of an individual argument is generally constrained by the social argument in which it finds itself. If trivial arguments are being criticized, then the attacking philosophy has little chance of transcending the triviality, for there is little honour to be gained from defeating an unworthy opponent. In fact, one way of downgrading an individual's argument is to suggest that it is attacking 'strawmen', or unimportant targets. On the other hand, praise will be due to the thinker who can go the distance, without necessarily defeating the intellectual heavyweight. Of course, as with all rhetorical hypotheses, there are exceptions. Sir Robert Filmer has attained immortality through the honour of having his ideas attacked in the first of Locke's *Two Treatises of Government*. And who today would have ever heard of Karl Eugen Düring had not Engels seen fit to write his *Anti-Düring*? These examples show that just occasionally a vastly eminent anti-logos can drag a nondescript logos into the spotlight of history.

(b) Reasonableness of contrary statements

The context of argumentation is one to which the maxim of Protagoras directly applies. According to the great sophist, it is possible to argue both sides of a case. Thus, both pro and con can be given justifications and reasons. In a literal sense one might say that within an argumentative context contrary statements can each be reasonable and justified. Simultaneously, both can be open to criticism. Perelman has suggested that it is this aspect of rhetoric which traditionally has upset philosophers. Historically, Western philosophers have assumed the "unicity of truth" (1979, p. 12). Accordingly, it has been assumed of contrary statements that both cannot be true or reasonable. However, Perelman points out that in many legal, political and even ethical disagreements both sides have reasoned, even reasonable, points. He illustrates this with the Talmudic story of the argument between the School of Rabbi Hillel and that of Rabbi Shammai. The two great rabbis and their followers argued at length their respective interpretations of Judaic Law. Finally, a heavenly voice settled the controversy between Hillel and Shammai: "Both of them speak the words of the living God, but the decision in law is in accord with the School of Hillel" (*Talmud, Erubim*, 13b). Perelman comments that the story illustrates a wider truth about disagreements and reasonableness: "Between the two opposed interpretations, *both are seen as equally reasonable*; we will choose, but not on the falsity or irrationality of the one or the other" (p. 113, italics in original).

If both sides to an argument can produce justifications and both can counter the criticisms of each other, then arguments are potentially endless. As Protagoras's maxim would suggest, claim and counter-claim can be made indefinitely. A recognized arbiter might bring an argument to a halt by a decision in favour of one party or another. The arbiter could be a heavenly voice, a courtroom judge, or De Quincey's symposiarch. However, such a judgement frequently represents an intervention from outside, forcing a halt to the momentum of the argument, rather than a natural cessation of that momentum itself. In consequence, even an official decision may not close matters permanently. As soon as the official brake of the judge is removed, the argument might be resumed.

The official judgement from above might itself be disputed. For example, it may receive the brusque reception accorded to the heavenly voice in the Talmudic story outlined in Chapter 2. Nor did the heavenly voice, inter-vening between Hillel and Shammai, settle all the arguments. The story of the judgement between their schools appears in the Talmudic tractate dealing with the laws for the observance of the Sabbath, and especially those laws which permit 'legal fictions' to circumvent obvious inconveniences. For example, this tractate discusses the ways of legally extending the boundaries of one's house to cover common courtyards, so that one could still comply with the commandment not to carry objects outside one's property on a Sabbath, but nevertheless be less restricted. Hillel had taken a more lenient line than Shammai, and had been rewarded by the heavenly voice for this. Nevertheless, the same essential argument is continued by later sages, seeking to specify exactly where the general boundary between permitted and forbidden actions should be drawn, as well as the physical boundary between one's own property and that of others. All sorts of tricky cases and hypothetical instances are cited and argued about. Once again the spirit of Shammai's strict legalism can be heard in these disputes. In this way, the general guideline in favour of the leniency of Hillel did not prevent later argumentation over specific issues, as the argument ostensibly closed by the heavenly voice is opened up again and again.

The recognition of the potential endlessness of argumentation follows from Perelman's assumption about the reasonableness of contraries. If "two different decisions, on the same subject, can both be reasonable and be expressions of a coherent and philosophically justified point of view" (1979, p. 115), then one might expect there to be endless arguments. Sometimes these unresolvable arguments might surface as unimportant differences of opinion, expressed in the course of a conversation designed to pass the time. Sometimes the arguments themselves may be centre stage in major historical dramas, in which the highest skills of witcraft are demonstrated. In both cases, the arguments take place in a rhetorical context of justification and criticism. And this is a context which, it will be suggested, differs from that of strict logic.

The open and closed fist

One of the most famous distinctions between rhetoric and logic was offered by the stoic philosopher Zeno of Citium. His distinction proceeded from the side of oratory rather than from logic, and what it lacked in exactitude it made up for in elegance. According to Cicero, Zeno "clenching his fist...said logic was like that; relaxing and extending his hand, he said eloquence was like the open palm" (*Orator*, 113; the same story is also told by Quintilian, *Institutes of Oratory*, II, xx, 7, and by Sextus Empiricus, *Against the Rhetoricians*, II, 7). The logician might have preferred a more rigorous conceptual analysis, but in this case the metaphor expressed by Zeno's gesture conveys simply the essence of an important truth: rhetoric possesses an openness not to be found in the context of logic.

Because the voice of disputation is always likely to be raised, it is possible for different interpretations to be put upon Zeno's gestures. The logician, ill-disposed towards rhetoric, might take Zeno to be contrasting the rigorous thinking of logicians with the sloppiness of orators. Such an interpretation exalts the powers of logic, and condemns rhetoric as being illogical. It might also imply that all forms of reasoning which are not logical are illogical. On the other hand, a rhetorician might dispute this interpretation and its implications: the looseness of rhetoric is not an indication of inferiority, nor does it need to be pulled taut by a logical wrench. For the rhetorician, the looseness is an essential part of rhetoric and a necessary aspect of argumentation. Needless to say, it is the second interpretation which is taken here, and for which justifications need to be advanced.

The contexts of rhetoric and logic can be distinguished. As has been suggested, the context of rhetoric is marked by justification and criticism, logoi and anti-logoi. It is a social context in which different points of view clash, or threaten to clash, and there is a potential infinity to these clashes. The maxim of Protagoras suggests that an unarguable rightness and wrongness cannot be established, for critical challenges are always possible. Matters are different within the realm of logic. There is not the same context of justification and criticism, surrounding, for example, the logical deduction of a conclusion from the premises of a syllogism. Deducing that 'Socrates is mortal' from the premises 'All men are mortal' and 'Socrates is a man' does not involve entering into an endless argument between religious believers and sceptics about immortality. Such an argument is by-passed by the correct application of logical principles. Moreover, unarguably correct and incorrect deductions can be made.

The boundary line between logic and rhetoric might not be clearly demarcated, with border-guards patrolling on either side to prevent illicit immigration. However, once an argument has entered the territory of logic, it is in a stern, close-fisted state, which rigorously discourages disputes with the official laws. In ancient Greece, the sophist Stilpo enjoyed the open-palmed atmosphere of debate, in order to display his dazzling talents for argumentation to large audiences. Like a conjuror, he would defy the senses with magic tricks of logic. If someone held up a vegetable, he would declare: "That which is shown to me is not a vegetable; for a vegetable existed ten thousand years ago, therefore this is not a vegetable" (Diogenes Laertius, *Lives of Eminent Philosophers*, Stilpo, VII). However, once an audience can see the conjuror's sleight-of-hand, or when it knows how the rabbit is extracted from the top-hat, then the magic trick no longer has the power to fascinate. Thus Aristotle in his *Sophistici Elenchi* showed the logical errors in the displays of pseudo-logicians like Stilpo. When this was done, audiences could spot a false bottom in the logician's baggage. Then, Stilpo's act for all time lost its power to amaze. And the matter was closed.

However, rhetorical issues are never so comprehensively closed. Aristotle was well aware that the laws of logic could not settle the proper arguments of rhetoric. His rhetorical works, notably *Rhetoric* and *Topics*, showed how arguments could always be opposed by counter-arguments, justification by criticisms, etc., in the looser atmosphere of rhetoric. Moreover, there was no sense of this looseness having been based upon error, in the way that Stilpo's pseudo-logic had been. It was just that in legal, political and ethical matters, there were, and would be, differences of opinion, and no logical calculus could be guaranteed to still their argumentative momentum. As Aristotle emphasized in the very first sentence of *Rhetoric*, "Rhetoric is the counterpart of Dialectic" (1354a), not a rival, nor a poor half cousin.

Zeno's metaphor can be applied to the styles of thinking necessary for rhetoric and logic. Witcraft represents the open-palmed thinking, whereas logical or mathematical problem-solving is based upon tight-fisted thought. Traditionally, psychologists, investigating thinking, have shown much more interest in the tight-fisted forms than the looser-palmed varieties. Thus, psychologists have tended to equate thinking with 'problem-solving', and then have investigated the sorts of problems for which there are unarguably correct and incorrect solutions. The author of a recent psychology textbook has specifically stated that the terms 'thinking', 'problem-solving' and 'cognition' can be used interchangeably. He asserts that "thinking is directed and results in behaviour that 'solves' a problem or is directed towards solution" (Mayer, 1983, p. 7).

Just as the problems which Stilpo set his audiences possessed a correct solution, so too do the majority of problems which psychologists set their experimental subjects. By using such tasks, the psychologists can distinguish those who solve the problems successfully from the unsuccessful. The classic problem used in this sort of psychological research has been the

'Tumour Problem'. This is essentially a geometric problem. Experimental subjects have to devise ways in which dangerously powerful rays can be used to remove a cancerous tumour from a patient. There is a correct solution: many rays of low intensity have to be used so that they can all converge on the same spot, having harmlessly travelled along different routes. Other psychologists have used explicitly mathematical problems. The famous German psychologist Wolfgang Köhler asked his subjects to estimate the length of a line drawn between two radii within a circle. Luchins (1942), in a much quoted study, used the sort of problem which might appear on a school's mathematics examination: there are three jars of given sizes and the subjects have to obtain specified amounts of water by filling and emptying the jars in various combinations.

In modern cognitive psychology this trend has been continued. Many contemporary psychologists choose to view the problems of thinking as being similar to the sorts of problems which computers are programmed to solve. These, too, tend to be the close-fisted sort of problem. One critic of this tendency has argued that cognitive psychologists, interested in computer models, have almost without exception studied "logical generalizations", rather than "the pragmatic generalizations", which characterize everyday thought (Lebowitz, 1982). The earlier example from Hobbs and Evans shows the preoccupation with 'problem-solving'. The elements of a naturally occurring conversation were classified in terms of whether or not they accorded with the goals of the 'planning mechanisms'. The result was that the dynamics of argumentation did not easily fit into this theoretical network. As the psychologists hauled in their catch of goals-achieved and plans-executed, the argumentative aspects of the conversation trickled back into the deep seas of criticism and justification.

Cognitive psychologists have not only shown a methodological preference for studying logical or mathematical problems, but also from time to time they reveal a Platonic hostility to rhetoric. An example occurs in the book *Psychology of Reasoning*, in which Wason and Johnson-Laird, two major cognitive psychologists, describe their experimental research into logical reasoning. They show a tendency to equate reasoning with logical inference, and to assume that logic represents the highest form of thought. The book concludes with the statement that "at best, we can all think like logicians" (1972, p. 245). In the opening chapter, they state that they are not interested in the reasoning of everyday life, as opposed to the logical puzzles which they can set for their experimental subjects. Wason and Johnson-Laird justify this by claiming that most controversies in daily life "do not involve points of logic" (p. 2). This is then illustrated by extracts from an ill-tempered debate between a racist politician and a television interviewer, in which, it must be admitted, the level of witcraft is not of the highest order. However, Wason and Johnson-Laird suggest that the faults of the debate stem from its fundamentally "rhetorical" nature: instead of proceeding along sensibly logical lines, the debate involves "emotional decisions to accept or reject premises, the relevance of questions of fact, equivocation and differences in interpretation" (p. 2).

In this condemnation of rhetoric, there is an implication that reasoning which is not strictly logical is illogical, and thereby fallacious. This rigid distinction between logical and illogical reasoning leaves little space for the open-palmed reasoning of witcraft. However, there is a paradox in Wason and Johnson-Laird's condemnation of the sort of reasoning which allows differences of interpretation and arguments about relevant facts. Psychology as a discipline seems to be firmly situated within this deeply-fissured territory, rather than in the well-ordered land of logic. In the last chapter, it was argued that experimental psychology, at its best, relies on leaps of the imagination, rather than plodding through deductions from uncontested premises. In fact, the arguments used by Wason and Johnson-Laird against rhetoric possess a rhetorical, rather than logical, character. A single example of bad rhetoric is used as a criticism against all rhetoric. Rhetorical theorists have not been slow to point out the weakness of this tactic: "It is not enough to argue in a single case in order to show that an attribute belongs universally" (Aristotle, *Topics*, II, iii). The tactic invites counter-arguments: the relevance of Wason and Johnson-Laird's example could be contested, and an example of high quality witcraft could be produced. Of course, such a move would not settle the argument conclusively. Wason and Johnson-Laird might claim that their example epitomizes the inherent dangers of witcraft and that logic should always be accorded prime respect. At this stage, we are unmistakably well within the boundaries of rhetoric, trading in justifications and criticisms like all the other citizenry.

In his more recent work on reasoning, Johnson-Laird has stressed that people do not think like logical machines. He suggests that people create 'mental models', and then, if they are being rational, they try to test these models. Rationality is not equated with logical deduction, but logical deduction is seen as a wider form of rationality. In this wider rationality, the use of counter-examples is accorded prime importance. For example, if faced by the task of assessing the truth or falsity of the proposition 'All swans are white', the rational strategy is to search for counter-examples – i.e. to discover whether there are swans of any hue but white. According to Johnson-Laird, "counter-examples play a central role in rational thought" and "rationality depends on a search for counter-examples" (Oakhill and Johnson-Laird, 1985; also Johnson-Laird and Bara, 1984). Again there is no attempt to place reasoning within a social context, and especially within a context of justification and criticism. Reasoning is, for Johnson-Laird, primarily a matter of individual calculation, with counter-examples ensuring that the calculations do not go astray. In consequence, this picture of reasoning has no place for the reasoning of witcraft, The omission, however, is a potentially embarrassing one, because the reasoning of psychologists, including Johnson-Laird himself, is closer to witcraft than it is to the limited rationality of the counter-example.

Within rhetoric, the counter-example does not occupy a particularly privileged position. A telling counter-example might be used to criticize an opponent's argument, but an apposite example will be just as useful to justify one's own argument. Aristotle in his *Rhetoric* discusses the use of examples in argumentation. Historical parallels may be effective for emphasizing a point. For example, if a state is deciding whether to arm against, or to appease, a powerful foreign tyrant, the examples of Darius and Xerxes might be apposite (1393b). However, there is no suggestion that the supporter of armament is undermined by a counter-example that appeasement was once successful in the past. Nor is the case for appeasement undermined by the reverse counter-example of a successful incident of armament. In this situation, it is no more rational to seek counter-examples than it is to seek examples, but all historical parallels might be of interest. Moreover, these parallels will not settle the argument on their own, and, indeed, it is always possible to argue that all historical parallels are irrelevant to the particular case under question.

Within psychological writing, counter-examples do not find themselves in an especially privileged position. In common with most other experimentalists, Johnson-Laird supports his theories with experimental evidence. The experiments, then, become the examples, like the stories about Xerxes or Darius, and these are used to justify a point of view. This is true of the paper in which it is argued that rationality depends upon counter-examples. Instead of proving his own rationality by seeking a counter-example to this position (a self-defeating enterprise, if there was ever one), Johnson-Laird constructs an experimental example to back up his position.

From a rhetorical perspective there is nothing wrong with an experimentalist using examples to support a psychological argument. Within the context of psychological disputes, it is frequently unwise not to do this: the conventions of psychological discourse require disputants to cite relevant examples, just as traditionalists need to justify all present views in terms of historical examples. What this does imply is that there is a rhetorical, or argumentative, context to psychology itself. That being so, the justifications offered for theoretical perspectives, and the criticisms charged against them, need not be phrased in the tight-fisted language of logical calculation. There is still room for the open-palmed playfulness of witcraft, at least until the planning mechanisms of the computer programmers take complete control of things.

Witcraft in action

The nature of witcraft can better be understood by considering an example of the art. If the example is to illustrate the powers of invention, then one should be careful not to select too humdrum an instance. The brief exchange between the writer of the dissertation and her bored acquaintance hardly reveals witcraft to be a sublime art, although it might indicate the subtle constraints imposed in contemporary society upon women who wish to make the conversational running with men. However, no art can be fairly assessed by its shallower instances, nor by those moments which can be recreated routinely in the experimental laboratory. Therefore, our example is not intended to be a statistical representative of witcraft in daily use. Instead, it is an argument to be savoured for its aesthetic qualities.

The example comes from the Talmud, and from a rather surprising part of this great treasure store of arguments. There are two parts to the Talmud. There is the older Mishnah, which consists predominantly of the decisions of Rabbinical authorities on basic questions of Jewish Law. Typically, the Mishnah presents a compressed statement of the difference of opinion between two authorities, in particular the differences between Hillel and Shammai. Then there is a statement of the resulting decision, often without explanatory reason. The largest part of the Talmud is the Gemarah, which uses the decisions of the Mishnah as a starting-point for further discussions and story-telling. The reasons for the earlier decisions are debated as the sages ponder tricky cases and conflicting interpretations. The seemingly conclusive decisions of the Mishnah are thereby opened up into further debates. Although it is the Gemarah which by and large contains the detailed argumentation, our example is taken from the abbreviated prose of the Mishnah.

In the tractate *Avodah Zarah*, which summarizes the legal decisions regarding permitted contact with the worshippers of idols, there is to be found the outline of a debate, not between two rival Jewish sages, but between the Jewish Elders and unnamed, but presumably Roman, idolators (*Avodah Zarah*, 1, 4). The debate starts with the Romans challenging the Elders with the reasonable, but tricky, question: Why, if God so disapproves of idolatry, does He not destroy all the idols? The Elders reply that He would certainly do so, if the idolators only worshipped useless objects. The problem was that idolators worshipped necessary objects such as the sun, moon, stars and planets. Destruction of these would entail God destroying

His whole creation: "Shall He then make an end of His world because of fools?" The Romans are not satisfied by this answer, but they counter it with a further, and more difficult, challenge: If God does not want to destroy the world, then let Him destroy only the useless idols. Back comes the reply of the Elders. If God destroyed your useless idols, but kept the sun, moon, stars and planets, what would you say? You would, of course, say that these were the true deities, because they had been untouched by the destruction of idols.

The Mishnaic tractate ends at this point, leaving the idolators speechless on the written page. As near as is possible, this is an example of pure witcraft, for other aspects of rhetoric are absent or irrelevant. Niceties of presentation and technical expertise have been subtracted from the example, with the result that the bare art of witcraft is, so to speak, the remaining prime number. As will be suggested, the nature of this art can be more clearly seen by a contrast with matters of logic, technical expertise and presentation.

(a) Logic

The disagreement between the Elders and the Romans is not a disagreement over logic. Neither side is accusing the other of being illogical, and neither is attempting to argue as a logician might have argued against Stilpo's trick of the disappearing vegetable. Instead, each argues that the other's justifications are unjustifiable. Such an argument is clearly situated in the land of the open-palmed rhetorician. However, in this land, logic is not disparaged, nor is it flouted. Grice (1975) has shown that everyday conversations do not operate according to rules which transgress those of logic. Rather logic is assumed, just as grammar might be. In order to phrase one's arguments, one needs both grammar and logic, but the arguments are not necessarily about grammar or logic.

Aristotle, in *Rhetoric*, had suggested that the basic unit of a rhetorical argument resembled that of a logical one. In logic according to Aristotle, one argues in syllogisms, wherein one asserts two premises and deduces, tight-fistedly, a conclusion. In rhetoric one uses 'enthymemes', which were, according to Aristotle, shortened syllogisms. The second premise of an enthymeme was omitted for the sake of brevity, and, thus, the enthymeme was merely a conclusion supported by a single premise, or justification:

> To prove that Dorieus has been victor in a contest, for which the prize is a crown, it is enough to say that he has been victor in the Olympic games. It is needless to add that in the Olympic contests the prize is a crown; everyone is aware of that. (*Rhetoric*, 1357a)

Certainly the snap could be taken out of the Talmudic dialogue in order to extend the quick fire of enthymemes into syllogistic triads. For example, the first reply of the Elder could be constructed syllogistically: (1) If God wishes to destroy idols, he must destroy the sun, moon and planets; (2) The sun, moon and planets are necessary parts of his Creation; (3) Therefore, if God wishes to destroy idols, he must destroy necessary parts of His creation. The conclusion (3) follows inexorably from the acceptance of the two premises (1 and 2). However, recasting the Elder's argument into laboured syllogisms does nothing to resolve the debate. The participants are concerned with the invention of premises, rather than uninventive deductions. In this instance, an opposing premise is proposed in place of (1): If God wishes to destroy idols, he must *only* destroy idols other than the sun, moon and planets. The implication, which the Elders then draw from this premise, is not a logical deduction, but it is an imaginative construction of the consequences following the selective destruction of idols by the Deity. Of course, these enthymemes could then be recast into syllogisms, but nothing is gained by doing so, and much is lost.

In fact, Aristotle offered a second definition for enthymemes, in order to distinguish them from the logician's syllogisms. Whereas logical syllogisms produced deductions which were certainties, enthymemes dealt with probabilities. The internal mechanism of a syllogism might be non-controversial, but real arguments can always burst around its edges. The selection of premises can itself be a matter of dispute, and so the resulting argument is between competing, but equally valid, syllogisms. Such an argument would normally take on an enthymemic, rather than syllogistic, character. Basically, an enthymeme consists of a statement together with a justification. The justification might then be criticized, and it in turn will need an enthymemic support, which in its turn will be open to criticism, and so on *ad infinitum*. This open-endedness is quite different from the syllogism which comes to an uncontroversial full stop, once the premises have delivered up their unsurprising conclusion. If philosophy itself is an argument, then the debates of philosophy might have an enthymemic, rather than syllogistic, air to them. Rather than pursue this important, and highly complex, issue, we can be content with the comments of that eighteenth-century admirer of the Sophists, Lord Monboddo: "I have heard of a doctor in England, who had the curiosity to go through Aristotle's writings in order to find there complete syllogisms, and I was told he could find but three" (*Of the Origin and Progress of Language*, vol. VI, pp. 60–61).

(b) Technical expertise

Neither the Elders nor the Romans use any specialist knowledge to defeat the other. There is no attempt to confuse the opponent by citing arcane facts or by retreating into an impressively opaque jargon. Each side is equipped only with the tools of common-sense, to be used as wittily as possible. Anyone could have thought of the questions or answers, just as anyone, more or less two thousand years later, can appreciate the subtlety of the debate. In these circumstances, it takes a special genius to come up with something original, which could have been said by anybody, but which nevertheless can surprise everybody.

In its pure form, witcraft can be seen as a democratic art, because it does not depend upon technical expertise. Within an ideal context of pure witcraft, the powerful and the powerless meet upon equal terms. The Elders could celebrate their victory of wits over the might of Rome. Even the Emperor himself can be humbled by the weaponry of witcraft. The Talmud tells of the Emperor who demanded to see the Jewish God, knowing full well that no graven image would be produced. In reply, a rabbi tells the Emperor to look straight at the sun during the summer solstice. When the Emperor complains that the sun is too bright, the rabbi replies that if the Emperor cannot gaze at one of God's ministers, he could not hope "to look upon the divine presence!" (*Hullin*, 60a). Of course, it is not only Roman rulers who have found that political power does not guarantee victory in contests of witcraft. It is recounted that Alexander Jannaeus, king of the Jews, decided after a ruinous tyranny "to reach an understanding with his subjects by persuasion". He gathered his subjects to inquire in what way he could satisfy their wishes. Their answer, bitterly conclusive, was immediate: "By dying" (Josephus, *The Jewish War*, p. 34). A victory in the special circumstances created for debate is no protection in the bloody reprisals which can follow. However, for a courageous moment, when wits are the only weapons, subjects can triumph over their rulers.

In many sorts of debates witcraft does not appear in such a pure form but is allied to a necessary technical expertise. Lawyers must know the law, if they are to exploit fully the scope which law allows for witcraft. Similarly, academic debates often seem to the outsider to be weighted down by impenetrable matters. However, as we have seen in the case of experimental social psychology, there is still a context of argumentation, and thereby a need for witcraft. Sometimes an argument might find those who are slow moving, but equipped with the heavy weaponry of expertise, pitted against opponents lightly armed only with the nimble skills of witcraft. Each disputant might fear that the advantage will be with the other side: "Whenever Rabbi Hisda and Rabbi Shesheth met each other, the lips of the former trembled at the latter's extensive knowledge of Mishnahs, while the latter trembled all over his body at the former's keen dialectics" (*Erubim*, 67a). At one time, there was great debate whether "a well-read scholar", such as Rabbi Joseph, should take precedence over "a keen dialectician" (or, to use the metaphor of the Talmud, one "who uproots mountains"). The official answer was that the knowledgeable scholar was to take precedence, but Rabbi Joseph could not bring himself to accept the consequences: he always deferred to Rabbah, the most skilled uprooter of argumentative mountains (*Horayoth*, 14a).

(c) Skills of presentation

In the account of the debate between the Elders and the Romans, all details of presentation are absent. True to the economical style of the Mishnah, we are not told when and where the debate took place. We do not know the identity of the participants, nor, indeed, the language in which the argument was conducted. If these basic details are lacking, then certainly there is no information about the manner in which the participants delivered their arguments. Such details, however, do not matter, for the flow of the argument can be appreciated without them. Whether the idolators or the Elders had the more imposing gestures, and whose voice had the most resonant timbre are all irrelevant questions. Instead, the Mishnah presents a situation in which argument confronts argument, question with answer and answer with further question. In such a spare confrontation, attention is focussed on the arguments themselves, and not the manner in which they might be presented. It is the content of the arguments which provides the testimony to the participants' inventiveness.

Francis Bacon in *The Dignity and Advancement of Learning* stressed the importance of argumentative content over eloquence: "Eloquence is doubtless inferior to wisdom' (1858, p. 455). For an example, he cited the case of Moses, who, as a man of few words, needed Aaron to present his case to Pharaoh. Aaron may have possessed eloquent rhetoric, but, stressed Bacon, it was Moses's wisdom which should be accorded the greater respect. Bacon's distinction between eloquence and wisdom can be interpreted as a distinction between form and content. His example, then, suggests that the skills of witcraft are not to be dismissed as trivial skills, but they are a part of wisdom. Although Moses might not have had the confidence to present himself and his case in the court of an absolute potentate, he possessed, according to Jewish lore, the deeper art of argumentation.

The Midrash, the collection of rabbinical interpretations and legends, whose recension predates that of the Talmud, states that "all the righteous (in their pleas and prayers) come with skills before the Lord " (*Exodus Rabbah*,

XLVII, 9). The example given by the Midrash makes clear that these skills (or literally 'devices') are those of witcraft, rather than eloquent presentation. A story is told that Moses, after the affair of the Golden Calf, argued with God not to destroy the Children of Israel. Moses, with all the craft of a clever lawyer, disputed with God about the correct interpretation of His words. God is pinned down. Moses argues that technically the commandment, not to make graven images, had been given to him alone and not to all the Israelites. Had God wished it otherwise, He should not have used the singular form '*Thou* shalt not', but should have specifically employed the plural '*You* shall not'. Therefore, argued Moses "It was *I* whom Thou didst command", and "this being the case, then if I have made an idol, blot me, I pray Thee, out" (*Exodus Rabbah*, XLVII, 9). And besides, added Moses, what would God do with his Law, if He destroyed the Israelites, the only people who had opted to receive it? God is convinced by the arguments, but now it is His turn to use the skills of witcraft. Just as one argument is settled, so another one breaks out in heaven. And God now needs to reason with the angels, who start complaining about the special treatment Moses is receiving.

A further, and perhaps more remarkable, story in the Midrash shows the importance of witcraft. This story again finds Moses instructing God on the interpretation of His Laws. Extraordinarily, the expected roles of judge and pleader have been reversed. In this case Moses "wrapped himself in his cloak and seated himself in the posture of a Sage", and "God stood before him" as one pleading before a judge (*Exodus Rabbah*, XLIII, 4). It is hard to imagine how the human skills of argumentation could be elevated more highly than by the suggestion that even the Deity defers to them. These are the same sort of skills as used by the Elders in their argument with the Romans. Paradoxically, of course, the idolators too employ them. The Elders' final reply acknowledges this: if the useless idols were destroyed, then the idolators would be able to argue back strongly. From Deity down to disbelievers the arguments shuttle back and forth.

In search of the last word

The story of Moses approaching the Deity suggests that the purpose of argument is to persuade the other party. Yet, this is a simple view of argumentation, suggesting that arguments are countered and justifications are offered primarily in order to alter the opinions of the other. Certainly, as was discussed in earlier chapters, there has been, from Gorgias onwards, a long tradition in rhetoric of viewing argumentation in terms of persuasion. Richard Rainolde, a contemporary of Ralph Lever, wrote that "nothing can be more excellently given of Nature than Eloquence" by which "the most

stony and hard hearts can not but be incensed, inflamed and moved there-
to" (*The Foundacion of Rhetorike*, pp. i–ii). The skills of eloquence become
more excellent, when they are capable of moving not just the stony and
hard-hearted, but also the Deity as the symbol of perfect fair-mindedness.

Nevertheless, the link between argumentation and persuasion is not a
simple one. We cannot always assume that the audience, or the opponent,
possesses a fair-mindedness and is liable to be affected by good arguments.
Even when faced by an unbending opponent, we may still find ourselves
drawn into arguments, knowing full well that persuasion is not a realistic
possibility. In such cases, the arts of witcraft are not employed directly in
the service of a science of persuasion. The Jewish Elders would not have
entertained the hope, nor even the wish, that they might convert the
Romans from their idolatrous practices. For all that, the Elders could not
resist the argumentative challenge and leave their opponents' questions
unanswered. Therefore, the use of witcraft cannot be seen merely as a
mechanism for achieving persuasion. Instead, as will be suggested, its use
is linked to the search for the last word.

Another debate, which must have taken place around the same time as
the debate about idolatry, illustrates that the motive behind argumentation
is more complex than a simple desire to persuade the other. The Midrash
retells a debate between Rabbi Akiba (c. 50–130) and Tinneus Rufus, the
Roman governor of Judaea. Rufus is challenging Akiba to demonstrate
that the Sabbath is really different from other days, and, it must be admitted,
Akiba is struggling under the skilful questioning. Rufus declares that "if
it is as you say that the Holy One...honours the Sabbath, then He should
not stir up winds or cause the rain to fall on that day" (because such actions
would constitute forbidden work). Akiba's reply lacks the witcraft of the
Elder's final reply to the Romans in the Talmudic story. Instead, Akiba
withdraws from pure witcraft, and relies on a technical argument that the
world is God's personal property and that one is allowed to carry objects
short distances inside one's own home; therefore God's apparent work is not
really work (*Genesis Rabbah*, XI, 5). The answer may have been satisfactory
from a theological point of view, but in no sense could it be a serious attempt
to convince an opponent who is challenging basic principles and who would
be unimpressed by technical details. In such cases, the compulsion to argue,
or at least to continue with the momentum of an argument once started,
would seem to spring from something other than a simple desire to
persuade.

If opponents are caught up in the momentum of an argument, then they
find themselves in a situation whose dynamics suggest that criticisms
should be answered, and justifications need to be challenged. As charges
and counter-charges are made, each party is seeking for the last word, or

at least defensively attempting to prevent the other from claiming the last word. In this context, the last word would imply an unanswerable criticism or a failure to offer a justification. Through inventive witcraft, the debater may produce the sort of last word which catches the opponent off-balance. The decisive last word in the Talmudic story interrupts the momentum of question and answer, by taking the opponents' next answer and cleverly turning it around against the opponents. Against this turn of witcraft, opponents are left vulnerably speechless: their words have been taken out of their mouths and return to mock them. Philostratus recounts that Leon of Byzantium was particularly adept at this sort of witcraft, where the sallies resemble the punch-lines of jokes, which achieve their effect by surprise. According to Philostratus, Leon could achieve in a few words what took Demosthenes hours of speech-making, as a quick thrust upset the argumentative direction (*Lives of the Sophists*, p. 15).

However, the importance of the search for the last word goes beyond those occasions when witcraft has successfully upset an endless momentum. Other examples illustrate the defensive importance of attempting to have the last word. Akiba's retreat into technicalities signalled a refusal to be shifted: whatever criticism was thrown at him, he would produce an answer, whether or not his interlocutor wanted that type of answer. The woman in the conversation analysed by Hobbs and Evans also makes a play for the last word. The man has expressed incredulity at her idea that postmen may change the addresses of entries for children's competitions. The conversation is drifting away from this topic, and, indeed, she desperately wishes it to do so. However, before passing onto other matters, she cannot resist a parting aside: "you can never tell". This little remark, so common and so infuriating in conversations, lets the other person know that no persuasion has taken place, and that ideas which at present seem so bloodied by criticism live to argue another day.

The search for the last word should not be seen as the motive which leads to argumentation in the first place, but it is a motive which keeps the momentum going once the argument has started. Although it may be a powerful motive, it is not an overwhelming one. One can extract oneself from the momentum of argumentation, by signalling an end to the search for the last word. If the right to the last word is conceded, then the debate can be transformed into the pretty conversation. Perhaps an expression of agreement is the only way to silence a tiresome opponent, or perhaps the debate is not worth the effort. Whatever the reason, a conciliatory 'if you say so' or 'yes, very true' can stop the momentum. There will, of course, be occasions when, despite the conciliatory smile of the one who concedes the last word, a devastating riposte and a promise of revenge will pulsate silently around the brain.

One may not search for the last word to persuade the other, but to persuade oneself that one's own arguments have escaped unscathed by criticism. In this sense, the momentum of argumentation with its search for the last word can be a process of self-persuasion, or perhaps self-protection, rather than persuasion of the other. The danger of leaving the last word with the opponent does not arise because an occasion for conversion has been missed, but because there has been a failure to justify one's own arguments. Social psychologists have suggested that we have at our disposal many techniques for justifying ourselves to ourselves. Greenwald (1980) and Hastie (1981) have drawn attention to the ways in which people reconstruct their memories of past events in a way which accords favourably with their own images of themselves. In our memories we often over-emphasize our own contributions to a communal endeavour (Ross and Sicoly, 1979), and we might deny our own contradictory opinions (Bem and McConnell, 1970). If, in addition, we remember better the tasks in which we possess a vested interest, rather than those which concern us less, then we might expect persons on both sides of an argument to believe that they have had the last word. Each will remember their own answers to criticisms better than they will remember the answers of the other, since each will be more involved with their own tasks of providing answers than with the opponent's endeavours to answer. The result would be that both sides would feel that the same argument had produced very different last words, or unanswered criticisms.

Most contemporary psychologists, investigating memory, concentrate on how much an individual remembers from his own past experience. However, as Edwards and Middleton (in press) have argued, memory is also a social activity, in which groups construct their own images of past events. Myths, legends and newspaper reports are all social reconstructions of the past in this sense. So too are the stories of past arguments. In the Talmudic example, the last word is dramatically accorded to the Elder.[4] However, there is much reason for supposing that a Roman account of the same event might have ended with a different last word. Hyam Maccoby, in his discussion of the mediaeval disputes between Jews and Christians, has pointed to the extreme differences between Christian and Jewish accounts of the same debates. It was as if different debates were being described, as different last words are produced to protect opposing sets of justifications and criticisms.

The pursuit of the last word is in a real sense an illusory pursuit, for the final, uncriticizable word cannot exist. To be sure, social techniques may be devised in order to cut a debate short and to produce a socially usable final word. The political speeches of the Merinans constitute a last word of this type. Similarly, courts of final appeal ensure that arguments do not drag on interminably. It is probable that the competition which the children of the woman conversationalist sought to win contained some rule that the judge's decision was final and that no correspondence concerning that decision would be entered into. In such cases, social practices ensure that arguments are not permitted to develop their own endless momentum. However, the final words of Leon of Byzantium or of the Elder in the Talmudic story are not of this order. They are not the words which happen to be spoken when the time-bell is sounded. Rather their finality appears to arise from skilled witcraft, which disrupts the predictable argumentative momentum, leaving the opponent speechless for a crucial moment. If the Protagorean maxim is correct, and so, indeed, if the Elder's supposition about the inventiveness of Idolators is too, then such final words are unlikely to end all debate. If one uses the language of the 'problem-solving' psychologist, one might say that the 'final words' can solve the immediate problems facing the debater in the argumentative context. An opponent might be stumped for an answer, or might be reduced to a feeble and face-saving 'you never can tell'. However, these 'final words' seldom, if ever, succeed in creating a permanent stop to the debate, by solving the underlying problems of the argument, in the way that a mathematical problem may produce a final answer. In this sense their finality is at best temporary, and lasts until opponents can collect their wits or make their voices heard.

Philostratus recounts the story of Aeschines repeating for the benefit of his pupils the famous speech he made against his rival Demosthenes. The students are overcome by their teacher's masterpiece, but they are also puzzled as to how Aeschines could have lost his case with such an example of oratorical perfection. Aeschines reminds them of the rhetorical context: "You would not marvel thus, if you had heard Demosthenes in reply to these arguments" (*Lives of the Sophists*, p. 63). In the same way, the final word of the Elder's reply in the Talmudic example is not a necessarily final word. We do not possess a Roman account of the dialogue, which would certainly have ended with a different declaration. Nor do we know whether the Roman interlocutor woke up in the following night, clutching his head and crying out: 'Why did I not reply: if your God does not wish to destroy the useful or the useless idols, then why, oh why, does He not destroy us useless idolators?' Whilst we do not have a Roman account of the debate, we do have something just as interesting. In the Talmudic commentaries of the Gemarah, the debate is continued but there is an important difference: the debate is not between Elders and their enemies, but between different rabbinical sages. In this friendlier context, the question which the Roman should have posed in reply to Elder's final word is posed, and the sages argue the merits of various replies. The debate, which previously was sharply divided into the rival camps of insiders and hostile outsiders, is translated into an internal discussion of philosophical and theological dilemmas.

Since later generations of pious Jews studied to learn the Talmud, then we can see that they learnt arguments. This illustrates a point which will be discussed in more detail later: the cultural attitudes of a society comprise more than statements of belief, but they include the arguments, justifications and dilemmas associated with those beliefs. The unsophisticated members, whose Talmudic study might be based upon rote learning the Mishnah, might be satisfied by the Mishnaic argument with its clear presentation of a last word. The story suggests that criticism can be rebutted, and thereby doubts dispelled: a dilemma is neatly resolved and there is little need for further thought. On the other hand, the more sophisticated are encouraged to see the need for further thought, as the basic argument is opened up in more complex ways in the Gemarah. Here there is no clear last word, but different argumentative themes seek their last words in various directions. There is no easy dismissal of a cultural dilemma which is the same as that underlying the debate between Akiba and Rufus: this is the dilemma posed by the belief in God's omnipotence and the belief in the powers of natural objects to pursue their un-godlike courses. Moreover, as will be seen in Chapter 9, the idea of a last word can become psychologically questionable in such discussions. Participants may push their points as if pursuing the last word, but their own spirit of contradiction, and their awareness of the reality of the underlying dilemmas, can ensure that this is an unending pursuit. In these circumstances, witcraft is not merely a convenient weapon for warding off an outside challenge, but it provides the skills for discussing, puzzling over and thinking about fundamental questions. In this respect, witcraft represents a basic form of thinking, which at its best permits, not elegant deduction, but, as Bacon realized, wisdom itself.

Rhetoric and thinking

The connection between thinking and arguing was one which was frequently made by rhetorical theorists. Isocrates claimed that "the same arguments which we use in persuading others when we speak in public, we employ also when we deliberate in our thoughts" (*Antidosis*, 256). Similarly Francis Bacon suggested that we use the same processes "in argumentation, where we are disputing with another" as "in meditations, when we are considering and resolving anything with ourselves" (1858, p. 243). In this view, there is nothing specially distinct about thinking, as opposed to arguing. We might suppose that thinking is a silent and mysterious process, occurring in a private world inaccessible to others. This would seem to be quite different from the noisy bustle of argumentation, where public display is the order of the day. However, if the Eleatic Stranger in Plato's dialogue *Sophist* is correct, then the distinction between the two is only superficial: "thought and speech are the same; only the former, which is a silent inner conversation of the soul with itself, has been given the special name of thought" (263E).

If witcraft is a basic form of thought, then we can expect private thinking to be modelled upon public argument. In consequence, it should possess a dialogic, rather than monologic, character. Thought, then, would not be seen as a process which is inevitably locked within the recesses of the brain and which is only dimly reflected in our words. Instead, the structure of the way we argue reveals the structure of our thoughts. To put the matter in a paradox, which should not be interpreted too literally: humans do not converse because they have inner thoughts to express, but they have thoughts because they are able to converse.

From a developmental point of view, learning to argue may be a crucial phase in learning to think. In his early work, Piaget drew attention to the importance of argument in a child's development. In *The Language and Thought of the Child*, Piaget suggested that quarrels about actions precede genuine verbal arguments. From these very rudimentary disagreements, important cognitive processes might be formed. Piaget hypothesized that "it may well be through quarrelling that children first come to feel the need for making themselves understood" (1959, p. 65). In the genuine argument, children have to justify themselves, inventing reasons to fend off criticisms. Only when children have developed the conceptual forms for reasoning are they capable of arguing in this way, and they require these forms to pursue arguments with their fellows. Unfortunately, in discussing these issues, Piaget had a tendency to assume that argumentative forms of thought were identical to logical ones. For example, he referred to the verbal forms of such reasoning as being "verbal forms expressing logical relations" (p. 72). In Piaget's later work, the interest in the development of logic was much more apparent than his earlier interest in argumentation, and his followers still retain this bias towards logical and mathematical thought (e.g., Richards, 1985). Nevertheless what *The Language and Thought of the Child* drew attention to was the developmental connection between argumentation and reasoning – a connection which is delightfully illustrated by Gareth Matthews's accounts of his philosophical discussions with young children in *Dialogues with Children*. Matthews noted that, time and time again, the young children showed a philosophical sophistication far beyond that which would have been predicted by psychologists trained on testing, rather than debating with, children.

The present theoretical point is not a developmental one as such. It is the general point that our thinking, or at least our cogitations about loose-palmed matters, may be based upon dialogue. However, this point is strengthened if, as children, we learn to reason through dialogue, for our forms of reasoning will be forms of dialogue, especially argumentative dialogue. The comparison between rhetorical argument and internal thought, drawn by Bacon and Isocrates, refers to adult, rather than childish thinking. Their comparison suggests that we think to ourselves, as if addressing someone else. In this way we provide our own rhetorical context for our thoughts. Alternatively, and perhaps more interestingly, we may divide ourselves, in order to become our own critics and admirers. To use the words of George Mead, "all mental activity" involves the ability to take "the role of another" (1982, pp. 144–145), and, by taking the role of both proposer and critic, we are able to arrange our own internal debates. If our minds were like a radio set, whose volume could be increased by twiddling a knob, then outsiders might at times hear what seems to be a monologue: all the words are coming from the same person. However, if the outsiders listened closely, they would detect that the monologue possessed the content of a dialogue. It would be as if a single actor were playing all the parts in a drama, which has at times some quite stormy scenes.[5]

Some of the most dramatic occurrences of internal arguments involve the workings of conscience. Part of the self turns itself into a harsh critic against the rest of the self. To use Juvenal's courtroom metaphor, a guilty conscience is the "hostile witness in one's own breast" (*Satires*, XIII, 199). The phrase 'voice of conscience' is only metaphorical in the sense that nothing is spoken out aloud. Nevertheless, as psychologists have long recognized, the conscience noiselessly issues its criticisms as an insistent orator, and its rhetoric is a genuine rhetoric of argumentation. Freud, describing narcissistic patients, wrote:

> They are informed of the functioning of this agency (conscience) by voices which characteristically speak to them in the third person ('Now she's thinking of that again', 'now he's going out'). This complaint is justified; it describes the truth. A power of this kind, watching, discovering and criticizing all our intentions, does really exist. Indeed, it exists in every one of us in normal everyday life. (Freud, 1914, p. 95)

Perhaps the most compelling psychological descriptions of voices of conscience are contained in William James's *The Varieties of Religious Experience*, and in particular in the aptly named chapter 'The Divided Self'. There James quotes from the internal argumentative confrontations between the blasphemous and saintly voices of believers. According to James, the religious melancholic's "interior is a battle-ground for what he feels to be two deadly hostile selves" (1920, p. 171). The conscience, always seeking to have the last word against the workaday self, can work both ways: the voice of doubt can nag away in the believer's mind, just as the sinful can be beset by the voice of righteousness. James quotes from the testimony of a woman's growing scepticism:

> When I was sixteen I joined the church and was asked if I loved God. I replied 'Yes' as was customary and expected. But instantly with a flash something spoke within me, 'No, you do not'.
>
> (James, 1920, p. 177n)

William James's stories of believers and disbelievers being prompted by the insistent voice of conscience are all striking examples of a much more common process. In each case the individual was involved in a protracted and agonizing dilemma about which course of action should be taken: some were pondering whether to leave the religious life and some whether to adopt it. For each person a decision ultimately had to be reached. In this respect, the internal arguments between the different aspects of the self resemble the internal arguments which take place when someone is faced with a difficult decision. James in *Principles of Psychology* offers a beautiful description of the decision-maker's state of mind. There is an "inward unrest known as *indecision*" and "as long as it lasts, with the various objects before the attention, we are said to *deliberate*" (1890, p. 528). When we deliberate whether or not to take a particular course of action, we imagine different futures and contrast different reasons for avoiding or wishing for these futures. In our indecisive state we find ourselves favouring one alternative and then tending to another:

> Something tells us that all this is provisional; that the weakened reasons will wax strong again, and the stronger weaken; that equilibrium is unreached; that testing our reasons, not obeying them, is still the order of the day, and...we must wait awhile, patient or impatiently, until our mind is made up 'for good and all'. This inclining, first to one then to another future, both of which we represent as possible, resembles the oscillations to and fro of a material body within the limits of its elasticity.
>
> (James, 1890, vol. II, p. 529)

Deliberation is more than an uncomfortable state of uncertainty. It is an important thought process, which includes imagining future consequences and assessing the desirability of different outcomes. Since the vagaries of the future are being considered, there is little sense of one tight-fistedly correct solution existing amongst a pile of errors. To use Aristotle's terminology, there is not the certainty of the syllogism, but the possibilities of enthymemes. James's vivid descriptions of the decision-maker resemble the conclusions of Janis and Mann. In their excellent and carefully documented work *Decision Making*, Janis and Mann emphasize the tasks of a person faced with a major decision. Amongst other things, the decision-maker has to canvass a wide range of alternative courses of action, estimate the favourable and unfavourable consequences of such courses, and, when as much relevant information as possible has been gathered, carefully contrast the possible outcomes in order to choose between the two. These are no mean intellectual feats, and it is little wonder that Janis and Mann, like William James before them, emphasize that people tend to put off the moment when all oscillation must be ended and a decision made. According to Janis and Mann, "in the repertoire of every person is a proclivity to procrastination" (1977, p. 6).

Deliberation, as described by William James, is a thought process occurring within the individual's mind. However, it can be seen also in rhetorical terms. As the mind oscillates between alternatives, it successively champions the case for one decision or another, changing its set of justifications and criticisms. The considerations, calculations and reasons, which are entertained privately, would therefore resemble those which might be heard in public debate. One might ask how we ever learn to deliberate, unless there are publicly observable debates to copy. In fact, the psychological descriptions of individual deliberation resemble the rhetorical ones of deliberative oratory. According to Aristotle, deliberative oratory was concerned with matters of the future, as disputants discussed what course of action should be pursued. In its grand forms, the decisions would be major decisions of state, with, for example, those in favour of a declaration of war arguing against those in favour of peace. Such speeches required the same sort of estimations of the future and comparisons of outcomes as discussed by Janis and Mann. According to Quintilian, "all deliberative speeches are based simply on comparison, and we must consider what we shall gain and by what means, that it may be possible to form an estimate whether there is more advantage in the aims we pursue or greater disadvantage in the means we employ to that end" (*Institutes of Oratory*, III, viii, 34). Of course, in actual debates there is no need for the speaker to take the role of both sides, whereas the individual decision-maker, who considers all sides of the matter, must oscillate between the different arguments and has the responsibility for inventing both pro and con reasonings.

The similarity between modern psychological accounts of decision-making and ancient deliberative oratory does not end there. Janis and Mann outline the steps which should be followed by the 'vigilant' decision-maker. These steps do not guarantee that a successful decision will be made, but they lessen the chances of a dangerously thoughtless one. After observing the steps made by vigilant decision-makers, Janis and Mann propose a five-stage model. The details of this model are not of consequence here. What is of rhetorical interest is that Janis and Mann suggest that vigilant decision-makers ask themselves particular questions at each stage: e.g. 'Have I sufficiently surveyed the available alternatives?', 'Are the risks serious if I *don't* change?', 'Are the risks serious if I *do* change?' etc. (1977, p. 172).

The business of questioning oneself is one which would have been instantly recognizable to ancient rhetoricians. Theorists such as Cicero and Quintilian recommended orators to follow the practice of *stasis*. It was particularly important for forensic oratory, and for getting to the centre of an issue, in order to invent relevant arguments. Cicero, for example, suggested that the pleaders, in preparing their cases, should ask themselves "Why, with what intent and with what hope of success each thing was done" (*De Inventione*, II, xiv). If forensic oratory concerned past actions, then, according to Quintilian, the same method of self-questioning could be applied to the future actions of deliberative oratory. Unfortunately, Quintilian's discussion of the matter is none too clear. He suggested that the basic questions of *stasis* were suitable for all forms of oratory: "Everything that can form the subject of dispute or discussion is covered by the three questions, *whether it is, what it is,* and *of what kind it is.*" Decision-makers would be best advised to follow Janis and Mann's sensible list of self-questioning, rather than struggle to apply Quintilian's three basic questions to the practicalities of decision-making.

The self-questioning of *stasis* is the nearest that the oratorical textbooks came to offering rules for successful invention. The suggested lists of questions were intended to be guidelines, rather than sets of absolute procedures. In this, as in all other rhetorical matters, Quintilian realized that the self-questioner should be guided by the particularities of the case in hand, rather than adhering fixedly to pre-established procedures. Janis and Mann also stress that the decision-maker has no absolute rules to follow for every situation. They do not suggest for one moment that their five-stage model provides all the questions which need to be asked for every situation. Their list is a rudimentary guideline, which does not preclude the possibility that, as circumstances demand, imagination might be required to formulate the key perceptive question, or to provide the original answer. Not only is this a tacit admission of Quintilian's Principle of Uncertainty, but also we are quite firmly back in the land of witcraft.

The recommendation to question oneself, whether according to Janis and Mann's five-stage model or the various *stases* proposed by classical theorists, is, in effect, a recommendation to impose the structure of a dialogue upon deliberations. One is being advised to become one's own cross-examiner, by taking the roles of both questioner and respondent. In this way, a conventional form of discourse between people is to serve as a model for deliberation. Some theorists have gone further to suggest that cross-examination should provide the basis for thought in general, and not just for the deliberations specific to decision-making. For example, Hans Gadamer has proposed that every statement presupposes a question and that the art of dialectic consists of asking the right questions. In consequence "a person who thinks must ask himself questions" (1975, p. 338). The prescriptive consequences of this are that good thought depends upon rigorous mental cross-examination. John Stuart Mill, in his famous essay *On Liberty*, mentioned that Cicero's "forensic success" was based upon anticipating the adversary's case. Before stepping into court, Cicero had practised the arguments of both sides, so that he would be equipped with replies to likely challenges. Mill suggested that this was not just good oratorical practice, but was something to be "imitated by all who study any subject in order to arrive at the truth" (1962, p. 163) – if not *the* truth, at least a truth which can withstand the most obvious criticisms.

The example of Cicero suggests that, in terms of argumentative quality, the mental debates of the individual can be superior to actual public debates. Sometimes, of course, discussions between people are liable to throw up a wider range of opinions than each individual discussant would have proposed on their own. Experimental evidence (Vinokur and Burnstein, 1974) can be cited to support what De Quincey so graphically described: "In the electric kindling of life between two minds...there sometimes arise glimpses, and shy revelations of affinity, suggestion, relation, analogy, that could not have been approached through any avenue of methodical study" ('Conversation', p. 424). However, mere presence of numbers is not sufficient to ensure a satisfactory deliberation. One of the most useful aspects of Janis and Mann's analysis is their criticism of decision-making groups beset by 'groupthink'. For example, they discuss how Admiral Kimmel, the Commander-in-Chief of the U.S. Pacific Fleet, and his advisers ignored all the evidence that the Japanese might attack Pearl Harbour. An atmosphere had been created in which everyone shared the same opinion and all defensively avoided any counter-views. Anyone within the decision-making group who voiced criticisms of the prevailing view was strongly discouraged. In this way, full debate was avoided, and all 'spirit of contradiction' was suppressed. Under such conditions, according to the arguments of Janis and Mann, the quality of decision-making suffers.

In a group which is avoiding all discussion, no-one takes the role of the other. Just as an individual lacking Cicero's mental discipline might be unable, or psychologically unwilling, to entertain opposing contradictions, so in 'groupthink' no anti-logoi are proposed to test the prevailing logoi. The result of a one-sided deliberation will tend to confirm the existing beliefs, for there will be little electric life to kindle anything novel. It may be a situation in which a group readily accepts the words of its leader, and in which leaders consequently feel confident of their rhetorical powers. However, this confidence is misplaced. In reality, such a situation lacks one of the most important ingredients of the rhetorical context: the use of witcraft, or rhetorical thinking.

6   Categorization and particularization

The view of Isocrates and of the Eleatic Stranger, that thinking is like a quiet internal argument, has direct psychological implications. Most immediately, it suggests that psychological and rhetorical theories should be closely linked. However, this suggestion straightaway raises the problem of which sort of theory should be given primacy. If arguing and thinking are related, then it might be sensible either to base rhetoric upon the psychology of thinking, or to take the reverse strategy of constructing a psychology of thinking upon rhetoric. The first strategy is the one that would appeal to most modern-minded psychologists. After all, the psychology of thinking, or cognitive psychology, is very much in the mode. Academic theory, like so much in contemporary life, is affected by swings of fashion. Within psychology, the swing is frequently between the brightly coloured claims made for the emotions and the lighter pastels of cognitive theories, although some stylists still hope to recreate the craze for the harsh lines of behaviourism, with its denial that thoughts and emotions exist. At present, the fashion is quite definitely towards the calmer shades of thought. If nothing else, this current popularity of cognitive theory suggests that it might be an opportune moment to hitch the creaking old waggons of rhetoric to the computer-powered limousines of the cognitive psychologists.

However, despite all the expensive machinery at the disposal of the cognitive psychologists and despite the utmost modernity of their theoretical models and diagrams, it is the reverse, and certainly inopportune, strategy, which this chapter will recommend. The modern cognitive psychologist, it will be implied, can with profit cast an antiquarian eye over ancient rhetoric. The spirits of Protagoras and Cicero, Quintilian and Isocrates, can be allowed to run mischievously amongst the modern machinery. Their mischief is not that of the wreckers, who smash the power supply or who deliberately wipe clean a precious data-store. Instead, their spirits are invoked to suggest that there is something missing in the concrete and steel skyscrapers of modern cognitive theory.

Imposing though these structures might be, they often seem to leave little room for the messiness of argumentation. At times, cognitive psychology sees human thought as aspiring to little more than the utility of an efficient computer. For example, Isen and Hastorf suggest that cognitive social psychology assumes a particular model of the person. According to this model, people are viewed "as problem-solvers, who are evaluating situations, alternatives, and outcomes, planning actions, and trying to achieve goals" (1982, p. 8). Here we have the equation between thinking and problem-solving, which was critically discussed in the previous chapter. This model of the person, underlying much cognitive social psychology, tends to separate the individual from the argumentative or rhetorical context. Thinking is viewed in terms of the solutions it can provide for the individual's psychological functions. In consequence, thinking is not seen in terms of a wider conflict between logoi and anti-logoi, and the notion of conflict is not uppermost in this sort of psychology, as it is in the ancient rhetorical textbooks.

Cognitive social psychologists have devoted much effort to searching for the basic units of thought. Much of the present chapter will be taken up with discussing the assumptions underlying this search, and, in particular, how these assumptions have led to a non-rhetorical image of thinking. Although some of the issues may verge on the technical, the principal theme of the present chapter can be summarized fairly simply. If psychologists claim that a single psychological process constitutes the basic unit of thought, then they are in danger of constructing a one-sided theory of thinking. This one-sided theory is likely to stress a particular type of thinking and to ignore the contrasting type of thought. In short, the resulting psychology of thinking is liable to be a psychology of logos, which omits the psychology of anti-logos. Since this conflict is an important constituent of thought, the resulting psychology will be likely to produce only a diminished picture of thinking. To avoid the dangers of a one-sided psychology of thinking, psychologists should see the basic psychological units of thought as pairs of conflicting processes. If thinking is seen to be built upon conflicting tendencies, then there will be less danger of pushing the conflict between logos and anti-logos to a neglected siding. Instead, this conflict will be rooted in the psychological structure of thinking itself.

The particular process which cognitive social psychologists have concentrated upon is that of categorization. By basing theories of thinking upon the importance of categorization, psychologists have tended to construct one-sided theories of thinking. These theories seem to describe prejudiced and bureaucratic styles of thought, and opposing aspects of thought are correspondingly neglected. It is one-sided to suggest that as humans all we can do in our thoughts is to categorize information. It is at this point that the spirit of Protagoras will be invoked, in order to put the other side. The concept of categorization needs to be reversed in order to show that the conflicting process – that of particularization – is just as psychologically important. Instead of building a psychological portrait principally upon the single, and unopposed, process of categorization, the tensions between categorization and particularization will be seen as central. Thinking will be viewed in terms of the conflicts between these two processes. As the discussion moves from the perceptual level, at which much cognitive psychology is pitched, to matters of rhetoric, so categorization and particularization will be seen as strategies for thinking and argument, rather than as processes in the conventional way. This shift of emphasis will be quite deliberate. If the emphasis is upon strategies rather than processes, thinking is less likely to be viewed as being little more than an automatic process, from which all thoughtfulness has been subtracted.

Categorization and cognitive social psychology

Social psychologists who employ a cognitive perspective have set themselves the task of understanding how people make sense of their worlds. Although the area of cognitive social psychology covers a wide variety of interests, many of which will not be touched upon in the present discussion, a common set of assumptions is discernible. A basic assumption relates to the importance of cognition in human activity. This very assumption serves to distinguish the cognitive theorist from other theoretical persuasions. For instance, cognitive theorists will distance themselves from behaviourists, who tend to view the person as the unthinking respondent to outside stimuli. They will look askance at the more lurid stories produced by those motivational theorists who see the person as being powered by emotional forces.

The cognitive approach does not merely rest upon the assumption that thinking is important for understanding human action, but it also makes assumptions about the nature of thought. One of the leading textbooks in the area has discussed the assumptions at the root of the cognitive approach in the following way: "The individual is an active processor of information", and "the effect of a stimulus depends on how it is categorized and interpreted by the perceiver" (Eiser, 1980, p. 8). Eiser's characterization of the cognitive approach is revealing. He uses four typical phrases: 'the individual', 'processor of information', 'categorized' and 'perceiver'. These terms are of importance to cognitive social psychologists, who tend to see thinking, or cognition, in terms of isolated individuals, processing perceptual information by means of categories. It will be suggested that this view tends to produce a psychology which is one-sided and essentially non-rhetorical. Above all, it produces a psychology of thinking which removes some of the essential ingredients of thought from cognition.[1]

Much of the discussion will concentrate upon the notion that as thinkers we impart meaning by categorizing the information which our senses provide. Accordingly, cognitive theorists in social psychology have tended to assume that categorization is a basic unit of thinking. At its simplest level, categorization involves the placing of a particular object, or entity, within a general category. To say that 'this cup is red', or that 'stealing is wrong' or that 'Socrates was Greek' is to make a categorization. In each case, an entity – whether object, action or person – has been placed into a wider, or general, category. This cup has been categorized as belonging to the wider category of red objects, stealing to the category of wrongful actions and Socrates to the category of Greeks. In the last example, the use of the past tense indicates a more subtle categorization, as Socrates is inserted into the subcategory of deceased Greeks. All three statements involve locating a particular entity in a more general category. This is something which we do all the time, when we use language to make statements about entities. If we talk about anything, rather than make grunts or gestures, we can be sure that we will be using categories, and, thereby, making categorizations.

Psychologists have pointed to the link between categorizing objects and making judgements of similarity. To say that 'this cup is red' implies that this cup resembles, in some way, other cups also categorized as red, and differs from green, blue and yellow ones. Eleanor Rosch, who in recent years has probably done more than any other psychologist to awaken interest in categorization, has defined a category in terms of judgements of similarity: "A category exists whenever two or more distinguishable objects or events are treated equivalently" (Mervis and Rosch, 1981, p. 89). Thus, if we consider this red cup to be similar to that red carpet, we are categorizing both the cups and the carpet as belonging to the general category of 'red objects': to use Platonic language, one might say that both objects share the same essential quality of redness. Rosch and other cognitive psychologists make two crucial assumptions about such acts of categorization: (1) they assume that such acts represent fundamental psychological processes; (2) that this importance is based upon perceptual, and possibly biological, factors.

(1) *The importance of categorization*

Rosch, in studying categorization, has little doubt that she is studying a fundamental aspect of cognition. According to Rosch *et al.* "one of the most basic functions of all organisms is the cutting up of the environment into classifications by which nonidentical stimuli can be treated as equivalent" (1976, p. 382) and, in consequence, it is asserted that "categorization may be considered one of the most basic functions of living creatures" (Mervis and Rosch, 1981, p. 89). Other cognitive social psychologists also affirm the importance of categorization for thinking, and, indeed, for survival in general. Wilder describes categorization as "a pervasive cognitive process" (1981, p. 213), and Cantor *et al.* call categorization "a fundamental quality of cognition". Its psychological importance arises "because categorization schemes allow us to structure and give coherence to our general knowledge about people and the social world, providing expectations about typical patterns of behaviour and the range of likely variation between types of people and their characteristic actions and attributes" (Cantor *et al.*, 1982, p. 34). It can be noted that Cantor *et al.* refer to 'schemes'. Some cognitive social psychologists talk of 'schemas' or 'schemata', rather than categorizations, and schemata resemble categories but are generally held to be more complex and abstract. Like categories, schemata provide means for incorporating the particular instance into a more general framework. Fiske and Taylor state that "a schema contains abstract knowledge about types of people and events as a class, not a representative of every instance ever encountered" (1984, p. 179), and Anderson (1985) suggests that schemata are organizations of categories. (For an excellent discussion of schemata and categories, and their relations to the social sciences, see Casson, 1983.) Because schemata, in social psychological theory, are considered as forms of categories, many of the same psychological assumptions apply to the application of schemata as to categorization. In particular, there is the same implication that, if psychologists can uncover the principles of categorization or the application of schemata, they will have laid bare the basic units of thought.

(2) *The biological basis of categorization*

Psychologists like Rosch often add a biological air to their statements when talking of the importance of categorization. For instance, Rosch talks of "all organisms" or "living creatures", thereby giving the impression that categorization is not something peculiar to humans, but is a basic biological process. The argument for the biological importance of categorization is based upon the assumed need of organisms to reduce information. According to Rosch, "one purpose of categorization is to reduce the infinite differences among stimuli to behaviourally and cognitively usable proportions" (1978, p. 28). If every time we saw a red cup, we were preoccupied by its uniqueness, we would never be able to talk about or react to red cups in general. Animals, too, must group unique stimulus arrays under the general headings of 'food', 'foe' etc. If they did not simplify the infinite variety of the stimulus world, they would not be able to survive: "Without any categorization an organism could not interact profitably with the infinitely distinguishable objects and events it experiences" (Mervis and Rosch, 1981, p. 94).

Social psychologists who prefer to talk about schemata rather than categorizations tend to make a similar point, although their concern is with the social world of humans rather than with a wider biology. For example, Taylor and Crocker suggest that "because we cannot notice every detail in the environment", we need schemata to "tell the social perceiver what data to look for and how to interpret the data that is found" (1981, p. 90). In this quotation, the perceptual theme is quite clear, and for good reason. The link between human cognition and the tasks faced by all 'organisms' must be based upon conceiving human thought in terms of those psychological processes which we share with animals. Clearly there is much which we do not share with all other organisms, such as disputation, gossip and oratory, all of which are peculiar to humans. However, perception of external information is a process which unites the most arrogant human with the humble mollusc. Taylor and Crocker's assumption, about the impossibility of noticing every detail in the environment, would appear to be an eminently reasonable assumption about perception. Perceivers have available to them an enormous amount of redundant information. When we walk down a street, not all perceptual stimuli will be treated with equal interest, but we need to sort out the irrelevant stimuli from those which will prevent us from colliding with other pedestrians or motor vehicles. Presumably molluscs, too, have their marine equivalents of the busy street, full of information of scant immediate interest. Therefore, infinite variety must be reduced, so that an imminent danger can be categorized immediately. We need to recognize as 'dangerous' the car accelerating towards us, rather than be intrigued by the unique sequence of symbols upon its number plates. Similarly, molluscs do not need to pay attention to the unique features of every threatening predator. In both cases, complexity is to be reduced by categorizing incoming information. All in all, "in the cognitive approach the perceiver's groupings of objects into equivalence classes is viewed as a means of reducing the enormous complexity of the stimulus world with which he is confronted" (Hamilton, 1979, p. 56).

Both of these underlying assumptions – that categorization is a fundamental cognitive process and that it is of biological necessity – appear to be quite reasonable in themselves. However, as was mentioned in the previous chapter, arguments can be directed against quite reasonable positions, and, in fact, disputes frequently involve the conflict between two opposing, but equally reasonable, cases. Therefore the present strategy is not to argue that the assumptions of the cognitive approach are unreasonable as such, but that they only express one side of the many-sidedness of human nature. Another side of cognition will need to be put. As part of the argument for the necessity of this other side, it will be suggested that the very reasonable assumptions of the cognitive approach, if not qualified by equally reasonable counter-assumptions, tend to produce an unreasonably restricted view of human thought.

Prejudiced and bureaucratic thinking

From the assumptions of the cognitive approach, a rather narrow and unflattering image of the thinker can be drawn. This image is a very different one from the imaginative user of witcraft described in the last chapter. Unlike the crafty and witty arguer, dodging and weaving in the momentum of debate, the categorizing thinker appears as a rather dull person, destined to plod through the procedures of thought. The person as a categorizer of information can be compared either to a prejudiced individual, whose errors arise from a narrow thoughtlessness, or to a bureaucrat, who seeks little more than well-ordered routines. Both these metaphors – the thinker as a bigot, and the thinker as a bureaucrat – will be explored in this section, in order to illustrate the one-sidedness of categorization theory. The connections between categorization and prejudice are made by social psychologists themselves, but the unflattering image of the thinker as a bureaucrat is one that is being ascribed here to the cognitive approach.[2]

It might be objected that the cognitive approach is being unfairly caricatured for the sake of pursuing these two images. The defender of the cognitivists might claim that the present argument does not deal with every facet of the cognitive approach, and perhaps the defender might name several researchers whose work does not fit the caricature. Of course, it should be conceded that not all cognitive theorists, all of the time, stress the inflexible aspects of cognition. No doubt there are some who in their experiments and their theories paint a more dynamic picture of the thinker. However, the present argument is more concerned with the broad pattern, and the dominant emphasis in cognitive psychology is upon the inflexible aspects of thought. If it were not, then the remarks of the following two psychologists would be incomprehensible. Introducing a discussion of cognitive flexibility, Showers and Cantor comment: "To those familiar with this literature it may seem odd that we focus on flexibility and strategic cognition, since the preponderance of evidence in social cognition paints a very different picture" (1985, p. 277).

(1) *Categorization and prejudice*

Social psychologists adhering to a cognitive approach sometimes tend to see all thought as being inherently prejudiced, or, at least, they suggest that prejudice arises from the normal processes of categorization, which are assumed to lie at the basis of all thought. The very notion of categorization, as used by cognitive social psychologists, seems to invite this link with prejudiced thought. It is implied that reality is being distorted and simplified, when stimuli are categorized. The real world, existing objectively outside our perceptions, is assumed to be composed of infinitely different stimuli. Yet these infinite differences become simplified by categorization, and, therefore, the act of categorizing implies that objectively different stimuli are being perceived as if they were similar. This translation of objective differences into psychological similarities is necessary for perception, and it enables the overwhelming amount of information in the world to be reduced to manageable proportions. Fiske and Taylor refer to the model of the "cognitive miser": because "people are limited in their capacity to process information" they must take cognitive "shortcuts", and "consequently, errors and biases stem from inherent features of the cognitive system" (1984, p. 12).

Experimental evidence has been produced to show how categorization can simplify and distort the stimulus world. When stimuli are labelled, subjects will tend to underestimate the differences between stimuli falling under the same label and to overestimate the differences of stimuli from different categories (e.g., Tajfel and Wilkes, 1963 and 1964). In other words, the imposition of a category label leads subjects to overlook, and even to misperceive, the objective differences between stimuli which are grouped together. There is a serious implication from this sort of experimental evidence and from Rosch's definition of a category. This is the implication that all categories are distorting simplifications. Since language is a repository of categories, this implies that language functions to impoverish the richness of the outside world. Language does not create a complex, and infinitely rich, world of meaning, but shuts out complexity to protect the stability of the perceiver and to help in the task of processing information.

This image of thinking seems to be very similar to the image of prejudice, as traditionally discussed by social psychologists. The prejudiced person does not perceive social groups as they are, but is guided by prior conceptions and biases. These operate rather like the shortcuts of the "cognitive miser". The full richness of the social world is shut out by the imposition of stereotypes, or group schemata, and variety is reduced to simple categorical distortions. The prejudiced person exaggerates the extent to which members of the same group are similar to one another, and at the same time chooses to view people belonging to different groups as being very different. For instance the early work on stereotypes held by Americans suggested that Italians were seen to be excitable and violent (Katz and Braly, 1933). This stereotype glossed over the infinite differences between individual Italians, and imposed a composite picture on the whole group. In addition, the stereotype of the Italians was distinguished from that of the Germans ('ruthlessly efficient') or that of the Turks ('cruel') or whatever. The result was that the similarities between Italians, Germans, Turks, etc. were neglected.

If all thinking is assumed to be based upon distorting categorizations, then the implication is that stereotyping is merely an instance of normal cognitive processes. In fact, a number of cognitive social psychologists have accepted this implication. According to Taylor, "stereotyping is the outgrowth of normal cognitive processes" (1981, p. 83) and Wilder claims that "ingroup/outgroup bias may be a consequence of normal categorization processes" (1981, p. 232). Because the cognitive approach assumes that it is necessary to simplify the stimulus world, and because stereotypes are seen as examples of such simplifications, then it becomes a short step to conclude that stereotypes are necessary cognitive processes. The line of thinking is evident in the following quotation:

> As human beings, we exist in a world of many individuals performing many acts. As perceivers, however, we find it difficult to live in such a world and hence we seek out similarities and differences, reducing the degree of complexity around us by sorting people into groups and by sorting acts to behaviour patterns. When, as a consequence of this categorization process, the perceiver comes to associate certain patterns of behaviours or traits with certain categories of persons, then stereotyping has occurred. (Hamilton, 1976, p. 83)

In other words, when 'perceivers' start categorizing human actions, stereotyping is the inevitable result. Hamilton refers to this as the "depressing dilemma": categorizations, so necessary for reducing stimulus information, nevertheless produce the sorts of stereotypes which characterize prejudice. Therefore, prejudice is the inescapable outcome of thought. Gordon Allport, in his classic book *The Nature of Prejudice*, made the same point, when he suggested that "man has a propensity to prejudice". According to Allport, this propensity stems from man's "normal and natural tendency to form generalizations, concepts, categories, whose content represents an over-simplification of his world of experience" (1958, p. 21).

This image of cognition is not just depressing but it is also one-sided, for it does not consider that the reverse of prejudice is possible. The concept of tolerance, as the reverse of prejudice, has disappeared. In fact, worse than its disappearance is its assumed impossibility. If prejudice, or stereotyping, is the outgrowth of normal thought processes, then one can ask how, on this logic, is it possible to have tolerant thoughts, especially since we have a "propensity" for prejudice? In fact, according to the logic of categorization theory, tolerance is "strictly speaking" an impossibility, for all experience has to be mediated by distorting categories or schemata (*ibid*, p. 19). In fact, the very notion of tolerance is paradoxical if one follows the assumptions of categorization theory. To formulate tolerant thoughts one needs to use language, but, according to the logic of categorization theory, language contains categories and categories contain a built-in bias towards the simplifications of stereotyping. Therefore, the expression of tolerance involves further simplifications and distortions – in fact, further prejudice.

A similar view of cognition emerges from an analysis by Greenwald, who suggests that the human ego is inherently 'totalitarian'. Previous psychologists had assumed that it was bigots, especially racist ones, who showed totalitarian tendencies in their thought patterns (e.g., Adorno *et al.* 1950; Rokeach, 1960; and, more recently, Altemeyer, 1981). However, Greenwald suggests that the totalitarian nature of the ego is "pervasive in and characteristic of normal personalities" (1980, p. 603). Uncomfortable information is suppressed from consciousness, as we all bolster our own selves with as much care for the truth as a dictator's subservient functionaries at the Ministry of Propaganda: "With modest rewriting, Orwell's characterizations of thought control at the totalitarian-society level could stand as a summary of cognitive biases at the individual-person level" (p. 609).

However, there is a problem with this description of the totalitarian ego, as there is with Allport's equation of thinking with prejudice. We can ask how open-mindedness and tolerance are possible, if our thought processes are constitutionally inclined towards prejudice. How could Orwell direct his ego to a denunciation of totalitarianism, if his ego, like those of everyone else, was fundamentally totalitarian, and how could Allport, if prejudice were strictly impossible, have produced such a humanely tolerant book as *The Nature of Prejudice?* We could also apply the 'peritrope' criticism, which turns an argument against itself, as Socrates turned Protagoras's relativism back against the relativist (*Theaetetus*, 170E–171A): Is Greenwald's exposure of the totalitarian ego just another ego-driven self-serving distortion? If we wish to say, as we certainly ought to, that Greenwald's arguments, not to mention those of Orwell, represent more than the productions of a biased and distorting ego, then there must be more to the ego than psychological totalitarianism. Unfortunately, this other, extra, ingredient is missing from cognitive theories which are based too one-sidedly on the single process of categorization, at the expense of the two-sided argumentative aspects of thought.

(2) *Bureaucratic model of thought*

Generally speaking, the categorization approach leads to a rather limited view of thought. The typical thinker is seen as an individual who is faced with a complex and untamed stimulus world, which must be caught by the net of an appropriate categorization or schema. For example, if confronted by a stimulus, we ask ourselves "Is there an active schema for this event?". If the answer is 'yes', then all is safe, but if the answer is 'no', then we must search a bit harder in order to "find appropriate schema" (Hastie, 1981, p. 45). Once the schema has been found, the event can be categorized, and we will achieve the security of possessing instructions to tell us how to react. The untamed stimulus world will have been safely domesticated, as the complexities of the original stimulus fall away, leaving it to be remembered as just another instance of the schema.

A parallel can be drawn between the image of the thinker to emerge from this approach and a parodied image of the bureaucrat. Both need rules for dealing with the world. As Taylor and Crocker state, in a passage already cited, schemata "tell the social perceiver" what to look for. Low-level bureaucrats also have instructions telling them how to conduct themselves. In both cases the instructions forestall the panic which can occur, when it is discovered that there is no appropriate "active schema" to deal with the situation in hand. The parallel can be pursued by imagining that our bureaucrat deals with members of the public who wish to attract the attention of the bureaucracy. Both the perceiver and the bureaucrat are faced with the problem of processing the messiness of the outside world into orderly categories, and both tackle the problem in a similar way. The bureaucrat cannot treat each individual case as if it were unique, but each case must be placed into bureaucratically suitable pigeon-holes. Members of the public must fill out appropriate forms, which extract the information of interest to the bureaucracy. In this way the messy features of the general public's lives can become suitably regularized. Irrelevant information, for which there is no appropriate question on the official form, will be weeded out, and need never come to the attention of the bureaucratic system. Similarly, categories or schemata, like the official forms, serve to weed out the irrelevant stimuli and to organize the relevant features into ways which can be easily processed by the higher authorities of the system. Just as the bureaucrat will pass on the suitably completed forms to the higher cortical reaches of the bureaucratic system, so the processed information of the schema system will pass along the corridors of the nervous system: as Taylor and Crocker assert, "schemas determine what information will be encoded or retrieved from memory" (1981, p. 98). In this way, the individual case will lose its sense of uniqueness, to become just another instance of the official form, or schematic category, to be processed. This is inevitable, because both the bureaucrat and the ideal perceiver of the cognitive approach do not have the time to deal with each member of the public as a unique case. In both instances there is an image of inflexibility. All the bureaucrat or thinker can do is to impose pre-set categories which turn disorder into order. Our bureaucrat must follow the rules of the system, and the schemata equip the perceiver with rules to be followed, in order to escape the dangerous messiness of the outside world.

The bureaucratic image is particularly apt, because cognitive theorists tend to talk about the advantages of categorization in the way that a bureaucrat might defend office procedures. Thus, categorization and schemata theorists talk about the organization, order, management, and efficiency which are brought by schematic procedures to the stimulus world. For example, we are told that categorization "lends organization to our social world" (Hamilton, 1979, p. 56) and that it serves "to stabilize, make predictable and make manageable the individual's view of the world" (Snyder, 1981a, p. 183). Another cognitive theorist praises "the efficiency" of a cognitive system which provides such "stability" (Rothbart, 1981, p. 178). Those who describe thinking in terms of computer processes cannot help but strengthen the bureaucratic metaphor. Information is deposited into, and retrieved from, 'files' (e.g., Abelson, 1979; Schank, 1981). Quite literally these are the same sort of files which the modern bureaucrat uses in the name of mechanized efficiency.

This image of the thinker is not based upon any factual error, nor is there any reason to doubt the experiments which illustrate the ways in which memory or judgement are biased by categorization (e.g., Rothbart, 1981; Snyder, 1981a; Tajfel, 1981). It is just that this approach offers a very one-sided image, in which thinking has become reduced to the unthinking operations of the filing clerk. As was argued in Chapter 2, a rule-following model of psychological function is not incorrect – after all, people do follow rules – but it is incomplete. Not everyone thinks with the fixity of the timid bureaucrat, nor is everybody as intent as George and Weedon Grossmith's Mr Pooter to fulfil the commands of the administrative higher-ups. In fact, bureaucrats themselves frequently do not fit the image. Rather than being unimaginative rule-followers, they are often rule-benders and even rule-creators as well. As they fight their inter-departmental battles and as they enlist an unsuspecting public in these battles, bureaucrats need to show all the skills of witcraft.

It is precisely these skills which are missing in the categorization approach, with its implicit stress on rule-following and routine processes. Flair, wit and sagacity seem to have been edged out by the demands of organization and stability, with the resulting image bearing little relation to the open-palmed reasoning of witcraft. The potential of psychological theories to present a constricted view of mental capacities was noted over fifty years ago by Sir Frederick Bartlett. Although he is frequently credited with the introduction of the term 'schema' into cognitive psychology, Bartlett grew to reject his own word. He wrote that he strongly disliked the term 'schema', because it underestimated the dynamism of human thought. Our thoughts should not be viewed as being controlled by schemata, which tell us, as tyrannically as any totalitarian ruler, what to think. Instead, there is the constant possibility of "transcending" the schemata by using the "capacity to 'turn round one's schemata'" (1932, pp. 200–1).

The categorization approach gives the impression of telling only half the story, for, in stressing the constraints of schemata, it ignores the capacity for transcendence. Human thinking may express prejudice, but tolerance is not an impossibility; we can shut unpleasant truths from our mind, but we can also face up to them; we may behave like timid rule-following bureaucrats, but rule-creation, rule-breaking and rule-bending can also occur; we may process information, but that is not all we can do. In categorization theory, logos possesses a heavy-handed dullness, and the inventive force of anti-logos is hardly to be found. What is needed, therefore, is for anti-logos to establish its presence, by putting the other side to the categorization approach. In this way, the one-sided image can be opened out into a two-sided one.

Categorization and particularization

The problem with the categorization approach to cognition is that, from one-sided assumptions, a one-sided image of the person has been developed. Therefore in order to open out this one-sidedness, the strategy mentioned in Chapter 2 will be followed. There it was argued that, if a psychological theory concentrates upon a single principle, it often pays to reverse that principle. The notion of categorization as a fundamental unit of thought represents such a single principle. In consequence, the very principle of categorization itself will be reversed, and an opposing principle, that of particularization, will be proposed. Following from this, the assumptions of categorization theory can also be reversed. The intention is not to show that the original assumptions are erroneous or based upon badly constructed experiments. Instead, the broad aim is to show that Protagoras's maxim can be profitably applied to psychological theory itself, and the reverse case can be put to the categorization theory. The reversals of psychological assumptions, surprising as it may be, can turn out to be just as reasonable as the originals. What is more, these reversals can be attained within the broad domain of a cognitive approach and without wandering to the theoretically alien territory of behaviourism or motivational theory.

The obvious way to start reversing the assumptions of the categorization approach is to begin with the notion of categorization itself. The reversal does not take the form of denying that people categorize objects, for such a denial would clearly be absurd. In addition, it would be out of keeping with Protagoras's maxim, which states that the reversal does not replace the original but complements it. Therefore the aim of the reversal is to point to a process which seems to be the reverse of categorization and which might be just as fundamental to human cognition. The reverse of categorization will be described as 'particularization'. Categorization refers to the process by which a particular stimulus is placed in a general category: as a result of this process, the particular stimulus is robbed of its particularity, to become merely an instance of the general category. On the other hand, one might hypothesize that there is a reverse process: a stimulus need not be treated as being equivalent to other stimuli, but might be considered in its particularity. For instance such a stimulus might be extracted from a category into which it had previously been placed, or it might have been kept separate in the first place from that category and from all other stimuli. In either case, it can be said that the stimulus has been particularized.

The bureaucratic metaphor can be used to illustrate the differences between the two processes. We have already encountered the parody of the bureaucrat operating office procedures according to the strict demands of categorization. However, the bureaucrat, who routinely hands out standard forms to members of the public in order to process their cases in routine ways, might decide to do things differently when faced by a relative or a generous business contact. Instead of making them, or their documents, wait their turn, the bureaucrat may exploit the rules. A special case may be created and reasons may be found why the relative or business contact is different from the other members of the public. To create the special case, the bureaucrat must pay attention to the special features of the instance and must treat these special features as special. In consequence, the 'special case' is not robbed of its particularity. To achieve this, the bureaucrat will have needed to use wit and ingenuity to oppose routine categorization by particularization, and the same skills will be required should the special case be challenged by others.

The argument that categorization was the fundamental process of thought rested upon a number of assumptions, whose reasonableness was taken for granted. For example, cognitive social psychologists normally accept as intuitively obvious the notion that the stimulus environment demands simplification. However, the same sort of assumptions, which are used to justify the importance of categorization, can be turned around in order to justify the importance of the reverse process of particularization. For instance, Rosch, in arguing for the fundamental importance of categorization, states that "it is to the organism's advantage not to differentiate one stimulus from others when that differentiation is irrelevant to the purposes at hand" (1978, p. 29). The reversal of this assumption is equally plausible: it can be asserted that it is to the organism's advantage to be able to differentiate a special stimulus from the others when that differentiation is relevant to the purposes at hand.

Similarly it is not difficult to reverse Allport's statement about mankind having a natural propensity for prejudice because of the 'normal and natural' tendency to form categorizations and generalizations. Equally impressive would be a pronouncement to the effect that mankind has a natural propensity for tolerance because of a natural tendency to form particularizations and to make special cases. In neither case would anyone deny that humans have the abilities assumed by the respective statements, whether it is to form generalizations or to make special cases. Moreover, it would seem to be a political, or moral, decision to regard mankind as having more of a natural propensity for prejudice than for tolerance or vice versa. The evidence from cognitive psychology need not be taken as being conclusive in either direction.

A further two examples should be sufficient to show the ease with which the assumptions of the categorization approach can be reversed. In a typical statement, which seems to dismiss particularization as it stresses categorization, Rothbart asserts that "the amount of cognitive effort that would be required to treat every new stimulus as unique would lead us to be overwhelmed by events and would render us virtually immobile in a world that required action" (1981, p. 175). Just as plausibly it could be suggested that we would run the risk of being overwhelmed by a world which required action if no unique stimulus could be treated as being unique, but instead every unique stimulus had to be considered as similar to others. Lastly there is that statement by Mervis and Rosch, which directly links categorization with the need to cope with the infinite differences existing in the world: "Without any categorization an organism could not interact profitably with the infinitely distinguishable objects and events it experiences" (1981, p. 94). Again the statement seems eminently reasonable, and again an equally reasonable reversal can be made. For instance, it could be asserted that without particularization an organism could not interact profitably with the infinitely similar objects and events which it experiences. Nor is the concept of the infinite similarity of objects any more unreasonable than the assumption of their infinite differences. As Protagoras remarked to Socrates, "everything resembles everything else up to a point" (*Protagoras*, 331). If there are infinite ways of distinguishing between objects, then there must be infinite ways of finding them similar. At the very least, any two objects must resemble each other in infinite ways: there will be an infinite number of characteristics which neither possesses, and therefore the two objects are similarly non-possessors of these infinite characteristics.

However, there is no need to go into intricate arguments about infinite similarities and infinite differences. The basic point is a much simpler one. All the arguments which accord a special place to the process of categorization in cognition can be countered by similar arguments for the importance of the opposing process of particularization. Thus, if we need to put particulars into categories, in order to survive as perceiving and thinking beings, so then we need also to be able to pick out particulars. These reversals are not intended to suggest that we need to construct a cognitive approach on the basis of particularization, in order to rival the theories built upon categorization. The result of any such endeavour would be equally one-sided. What the ease of reversal does imply is that we should not necessarily accord a privileged status to the one process of categorization. Instead, we should examine cognition in terms of two opposing processes: categorization and particularization.[3]

It can be argued that the two processes are deeply interrelated, so much so that the ability to categorize presupposes the ability to particularize. Here, the notions of infinite similarities and infinite differences may be illustrative. If there are infinite ways of organizing the stimulus world in terms of similarities and differences, then we need to select appropriate patterns of similarities and differences, and reject a whole host of others. The notion of 'selection' is a crucial one in cognitive psychology. Any perceptual system which is attempting to categorize incoming information must engage in some form of selection. This point has been well made by Erdelyi in his review of theories about perceptual categorization. He writes that selection is "pervasive" in perception, and at all levels of the perceptual system information is selected (1974, p. 12). If we have a choice of ways of categorizing the stimulus arrays with which we are faced, then selection is involved in arriving at one appropriate categorization. This sort of selection is akin to what we have been calling particularization. Out of all possible categories, one is treated as uniquely appropriate, and it must be fished out of the general pool of categories. Thus, in order to categorize something by putting it into an appropriate category, we must have particularized that category. In this way, categorization depends upon the opposing process of particularization.

This general point can be illustrated by the work of Amos Tversky. In a series of elegant experiments Tversky has shown that judgements about similarities and differences depend upon prior categorization (Tversky, 1977; Tversky and Gati, 1978). Not always will the same two stimuli be categorized in the same way, but sometimes they might be seen as similar and on other occasions as different. Tversky asked his experimental subjects to make judgements of similarity and difference about various countries. Two countries, for example, might possess similar climates but be characterized by different levels of economic development. When economic issues are relevant they will be judged as dissimilar, but when geographical factors are uppermost they will be seen as similar. Tversky argues that the judgements of similarity and difference depend upon locating objects in the relevant 'feature space'. Therefore, the judgements of similarity depend upon the selection, or particularization, of one feature space from other possible feature spaces. Again, categorization on its own cannot be seen as the fundamental process of cognition, but there is a combination of particularization and categorization.

Categorization and particularization, inasmuch as they refer to human thought processes, are not to be considered as two distinct capabilities, as separate, for example, as the olfactory and visual senses. The two processes are interrelated, at least as far as linguistic categories and particularities are concerned. In order to use categories, we must be able to particularize and vice versa. The paradox is that these two processes seem to pull in opposite cognitive directions: the one pulls towards the aggregation of things and the other towards the uniqueness of things. The result is that the human mind is equipped with the two contrary skills of being able to put things into categories and to treat them as special. Thus, our thought processes are not held in the thrall of a single process, which inevitably leads to a distorting narrow-mindedness. Nor do our basic cognitive processes merely function to provide psychological stability and order. They also provide the seeds of argumentation and deliberation, as our logoi of categorization are always liable to be opposed by our anti-logoi of particularization. However, in order to see how this might operate, we need to move from the perceptual metaphor, used in much cognitive psychology, to consider directly logoi and their negations.

Locating the essence

Some cognitive social psychologists, taking their ideas about cognition from perceptual models, might talk about the processes common to 'all organisms'. However, if we are to examine the rhetorical implications of categorization, then we must concentrate on the one power which separates humans from all those other organisms: the power of language. Humans might resemble cats, rats and bats inasmuch as incoming perceptual information is selectively perceived and filtered into appropriate channels. Any resemblance ends when we consider the actual categories of language, rather than the inferred categories of perception. It is only the human organism which possesses these categories. This possession, and certainly not our rather moderate sensory capabilities, enables humans to be the only argumentative, and thereby the sole truly thoughtful, animal.

Selection may be, as Erdelyi claims, occurring throughout the perceptual system "from input to output", but the selection of categories is of much greater significance for humans than it is for other species. Much of the way in which other species select information is probably determined biologically, and their cognitive functions are strictly limited in the ways they can arrange the infinite varieties of stimulus material. If different species of animals segment the universe in different ways, then, from a rhetorical perspective, that is the end of the matter. The cat and the bat might possess their different 'categories', which serve their biological functions for the respective creatures. However, there is no known way for a cat to compare its categories with those of a bat, nor for each to argue with the other about the virtues of its own system. Nor can they gang up to criticize the thinking of the rat. For all these things one needs language. Moreover, with language it is hard to avoid arguments of this sort.

The possession of language ensures that the selection of categories is a serious problem, whose solutions are not provided by biology. A language provides us with whole varieties of ways of talking about the world. There is no language that is so impoverished that its users can only describe the world in one, rigidly determined, manner. Moreover, humans, through their use of language, possess that most important capability which makes rhetoric possible: the ability to negate. It is not just that we have different categories which we can apply to things; but we can argue the merits of categorizing one way rather than another. One category can be placed in opposition to other potential categories. This opposition of categories might then be a matter for justification and criticism. Even if the language does not provide us ready made with a suitable category for expressing our opposition, it will provide us with the raw materials for inventing such a category. For all these skills we need the power of negation. Holofernes, the pedantic schoolmaster in *Love's Labour's Lost*, chose to call the 'afternoon' the "posterior of the day", claiming that "the word is well culled, chose, sweet and apt" (V,i), thereby denying the merits of the more usually chosen term. No such deliberate culling and choosing, whether apt or not, is open to other organisms, and, just as importantly, no other organism would be able to justify the choice of an ugly pomposity. Nor would they be able to criticize it.

There is a tendency within cognitive social psychology to overlook the rhetorical context of categories, and thereby to underestimate the extent to which the selection of categories can be a matter of controversy. Some psychologists seem to dismiss the issue of selection by implying that selection is something which takes place automatically. They seem to say, to use a computing metaphor, that our systems of particularization are permanently set on default options, which readily come into play when the appropriate program is fed into the machine. In other words, the selection of categories is not much of a problem, for generally the appropriate selection is obvious. For example, Eleanor Rosch argues that we are equipped with hierarchies of categories, so that a single object can be categorized at different levels of generality. However, in such hierarchies there are Basic Categories, which tend to be selected in preference to other categories. The choice of what is to count as a Basic Category is determined by perceptual, rather than linguistic or aesthetic, factors: "In general, the basic level of abstraction in a taxonomy is the level at which categories carry the most information, possess the highest cue validity, and are, thus, the most differentiated from one another" (Rosch *et al.*, 1976, p. 383). To cite an example, Rosch argues that the category 'chair' exists at a more basic level than that of 'furniture' or 'armchair' and will tend to be used in preference to these less basic categories.

Rosch's notion of a Basic Category underplays the extent to which the selection of categories can be a controversial matter. She concentrates upon categories for natural objects, and she assumes that objective factors in the real world, which can be quantified in terms of information content and cue validity, will determine our level of categorization. The rhetorical context, as opposed to the informational, is well in the background. Rosch's point is illustrated because she has selected categories which, at least in normal use, appear relatively uncontroversial. With imagination one could envisage a situation where the choice between terms such as 'armchair' and 'chair' might be keenly contested; this could be a situation involving law-courts and allegations of broken contractual agreements between furniture manufacturers and wholesalers. Even so, a Holofernes, or a cunning advertising copy-writer, might always come up with a sweeter and better-chosen term than 'chair'. However, controversy is much nearer the surface when one considers the more abstract ethical, political and social categories which crowd argumentative discourse.[4]

Eleanor Rosch's assumptions about Basic Categories resemble some of the assumptions of Tversky. Although his experimental work seems to show the importance of selecting a 'feature space', Tversky steps back from developing the rhetorical implications of this. Rather than proceeding to examine the controversial aspects of categorization, Tversky seems to imply, in common with Rosch, that the selection of categories is no real issue. He suggests that 'feature spaces' are unambiguously linked to 'contexts'. Each situation will call forth the relevant dimension, and there will be little controversy, or confusion, about which feature space is being demanded: "With natural integral stimuli, such as countries, peoples, colours, sounds, there is relatively little ambiguity regarding the relevant feature space" (Tversky, 1977, p. 340). In other words, people will dutifully shuffle their patterns of similarities and differences to come up with the required, and non-controversial, responses. We are back with the thinker as obedient bureaucrat.

Nevertheless, Tversky's own results show that the issue of controversy about categories is not so easily pushed aside. In one of his experiments, Israeli students were asked to say whether Israel was more similar to England, Syria or Iran. There was no uniform response: a quarter opted for Syria, and the others were equally divided between England and Iran (see Tversky and Gati, 1978, pp. 92 f). Tversky, being primarily interested in technical problems concerning the psychology of judgements, did not explore the meaning of his subjects' choices. It can be assumed that this task, unlike many facing the volunteer subject in the psychological laboratory, was a highly meaningful one. Had Tversky then asked his subjects to justify their choices to each other, it is probable that sharp differences of opinion would have emerged. These disagreements would not have been confined to discovering which attributes the countries in question possessed. They would have revolved around the relative importance or unimportance of Israel's similarities and differences with these other countries. For instance, two subjects might have agreed that culturally Israel was a Middle Eastern country like Syria, but that economically and politically Israel resembled Britain. Despite this agreement about the existence of similarities and differences, two such subjects could have deeply disagreed about the relative importance of the patterns of similarities. To use Tversky's terminology, the dispute would have been about the selection of the appropriate 'feature space'. Such a dispute would as likely as not open all manner of controversial, or ambiguous, matters.

We might wonder what such an argument would be about. It would not primarily be a factual disagreement, although, like any argument, the focus of dispute can easily shift, especially into acrimony over who said what. Nor would the dispute necessarily concern matters of logic. Like the disputes discussed in the last chapter, both sides might be able to put forward reasons for their positions, and, to this extent, the dispute might be between two reasonable, and therefore unyielding, positions. If both sides agree on the existence of certain patterns of similarity and difference, but disagree about the selection of the relevant 'feature space', then they are disagreeing about where the heart of the matter lies. Particularization is here an issue of controversy, and, in all probability, a deeply felt controversy. What one side claims to be the essential set of differences, the other claims as less crucial. In this sense, they would be arguing about essences.

The idea of arguing about essences might sound a bit Platonic. The point, however, is not to advocate the philosophy of Plato, but to suggest that in our everyday thoughts and arguments we are all a bit Platonic. Suppose, however, that an objection is made to this last point. It might be suggested that arguments are not about essences. It is not necessary to elaborate such an objection, because the objection would be stating, in effect, that the 'essence' of argumentation lies elsewhere. Therefore, this objection would itself reinforce the original point about arguments and essences, since it relies on this very same form of argumentation.

Once we start bothering about what the essence of a matter is, we have transcended our immediate perceptions. It is not only professional philosophers and clever sophists who are concerned with essences. In all walks of life people ask themselves and each other questions about the significance of things, events and persons. This is a point stressed by Neville Cardus, the illustrious writer of music criticism and cricket commentary. Questions about essences were not confined to the high-brows whom he encountered at the classical concerts of Salzburg. The crowd at the popular end of Old Trafford were just as concerned with them:

> For human beings the essence of the object is the power
> consciously to perceive it – which is Bishop Berkeley for the
> masses. Maclaren was not just a cricketer any more than Wagner
> was just a composer; or any more than Phil May just drew comic
> pictures for *Punch*; or any more than Mr Squeers's blind eye was
> to Dickens only a blind eye and not very much like a fanlight.
> (Cardus, 1947, p. 33)

This does not represent a lurch towards the mysticism of Plato's higher world of forms. We are not talking about 'essences' as objects lying behind the objects of everyday experience, but of the fittest way of talking and thinking about these objects. In selecting one form of discourse, or one schema, over another, we state implicitly that this form captures the essence of the matter best. If we are challenged, and another set of categories is thrust at us, we might then make the implication explicit, and find ourselves arguing about the location of the heart of the issue. In consequence, it is not a matter of essences as such, but of arguments about the essence of the matter.

It is to Aristotle, rather than to Plato, that one should look for an examination of such arguments about essences. Aristotle in *Topics* attempted to give an exhaustive account of the different forms of reasoning which could be used in argumentation. These were, to use a term which will be discussed in greater detail in Chapter 8, the 'places of argumentation'. Much of Aristotle's *Topics* consists of detailed descriptions of the various forms of argumentative statements which can be made. For example, there can be an argument from size, claiming that something is bigger than another thing, or there is an argument from consequences, that one event is caused by another, or from inferences, that something is a sign for something else, etc. All these forms of argument are also forms of thoughts. In order to construct a case, or develop a sustained piece of reasoning, one must use the appropriate type of argument.

The selection of an appropriate argumentative form is by no means a simple matter, for it involves an element of choice. As Perelman and Olbrechts-Tyteca have stressed, the argumentative forms come in competing pairs, and, therefore, Aristotle's 'places of argumentation' represent '*loci* (or places) of preference'. Perelman and Olbrechts-Tyteca stress that, in using one of these argumentative places, one is expressing a preference for the appropriateness of that argumentative form, and is rejecting as inappropriate its contrary form. For example, two objects can be categorized as being similar, and reasons can be given for making such a judgement of similarity. In this case, a choice of categorization would imply a rejection of a particularization, which focussed upon the uniqueness of one or both of the objects in question. To use Aristotelian terms, a judgement of quantity would have been preferred to one of quality. As Perelman and Olbrechts-Tyteca point out, each place of argument has its opposing place: "It is amazing that even where very general *loci* are concerned, each *locus* can be confronted by one that is contrary to it: thus, to the classical *locus* of the superiority of the lasting, one may oppose the romantic *locus* of the superiority of what is precarious and fleeting" (1971, p. 85).

Since the *loci* of arguments represent basic forms of thought, negation is a basic, even essential, characteristic of thinking. The selection of a particular *locus* must be potentially or actually controversial, because it implies a rejection of the opposing *locus*. However, the rejection need not be a total rejection. The Romantic, to use the example of Perelman and Olbrechts-Tyteca, need not deny that some things, even desirable things, remain constant, nor need the Classicist reject all changes. They differ in their preferences for evaluating the relative significance of change and continuity: for the Romantic it is the movement of things which essentially, or in the last analysis, counts, and vice versa for the Classicist.

The strategies of categorization and particularization can likewise be seen as controversial and opposing forms of thinking. The argument for categorization stresses how much the object which is to be categorized resembles other objects, whereas particularization stresses the unique features of the object, and each is, at least implicitly, a critical rival of the other in the claim to be the essence of the matter. Xenophon describes an argument between Socrates and Anaxagoras, where a strategy of categorization comes into direct conflict with that of particularization. Socrates was edging towards Plato's position that each thing possesses its own unique essence, whilst Anaxagoras was propounding that all things were similar, because they were formed from the same basic substance. Anaxagoras drew parallels between the sun and other objects, such as stones and fire. Socrates countered all assertions of similarity with assertions of difference: "People can easily look upon fire, but they cannot turn their gaze on the sun" and "a stone placed in the fire does not shine, or last long" (*Memorabilia of Socrates*, IV, vii, 7). The argument reflects a choice between the most apt ways of talking about the sun, or indeed any other subject: should the similarities with stones and fires be culled from all available similarities, or would it be a sweeter choice to stress the sun's uniqueness? In such a debate, the similarities proposed by an Anaxagoras can always be countered with differences from a Socrates, until the participants grow weary of the debate. Each location of the essence lays claim to being the final word on the matter. However, in the end, there is no agreed procedure for settling whether the essence of the matter, indeed in this case the essence of all matter, is to be located in the similarities or in the differences.

In such a debate, the participants are not merely applying categories, but they are talking about their categories and the reasons for using or withholding such categories. Language, which equips us to express contrary forms of thought, enables us to do this. If we then wished to offer a location for the essence of thinking itself, we might propose the following to be considered. Categorization does not provide the basis of thinking in a simple sense. The automatic application of categories is the negation of thinking, in that it is essentially a thoughtless process. Thinking starts when we argue or deliberate about which categorization to particularize, or how to categorize a particularization. When we do this, we no longer obey unthinkingly the orders of our schemata, but we have, to use Bartlett's phrase, turned them around.

Arguing about particulars

If the emphasis in much cognitive social psychology is upon the way that categories and schemata give us commands, then the other side needs to be put, in order to show how we can unpick our schemata and question their categorical orders. This discussion of the ways in which our schemata can become objects of controversy will examine categorization and particularization at a linguistic level. It might be objected that, in so doing, we are stretching the concepts of 'categorization' and 'particularization' in far too loose a manner. Firstly, they were used in a discussion of non-verbal perceptual processes, and now these very same concepts will be employed in an examination of the linguistic strategies of argumentation. In defence, it can be pointed out that social psychologists typically use 'categorization' to cover a wide range of phenomena, and our term 'particularization' is only the counterpart of 'categorization', following it wherever it wanders. When psychologists conduct experiments on perceptual processes, in the hope of discovering the psychological basis of prejudiced stereotyping, they are using 'categorization' in a way that embraces non-verbal categories, as well as the verbal categories of prejudice. Similarly psychologists tend to use linguistic metaphors to describe the processes of non-linguistic categorization, which 'tell us what to do'. Even animals, with no powers of understanding or using speech, are presumably 'told' what to do by their schemata. However, if the critic persisted and claimed that it is no defence of muddled thinking to claim that others started the muddle, we could reply that, as far as we are concerned, the perceptual grouping of information could be cut adrift from the term 'categorization'. Our interest is primarily upon the rhetorical aspects of categorization, and it is little part of our case to draw analogies between these aspects and perceptual processes.

From the discussion of the previous section, it might be thought that a simple equation could be made: categorization is equivalent to logos and particularization represents the faculty of anti-logos. For instance, one might think that categorization is the heavy-handed process which gives us our orders, and that it is through particularization that we can rebel against conceptual authoritarianism. Such an equation is, however, misleading. Principally it ignores the inter-relatedness of categorization and particularization as forms of thought. The conservative is not stuck with using only categorization and the radical is not forbidden from visiting this place of argumentative form.[5] In order to see the inter-relatedness between categorization and particularization, we need to analyse how categorizations can be unpicked. Therefore, in this section and the subsequent one, there will be a discussion of the rhetorical strategies which turn around our schemata and unpick our categories. It will be seen that these strategies are not based upon a simple process of particularization. Rather, they are located within a continual argumentative momentum, oscillating between particularization and categorization.

If there is an argument about categorizing a particular, then the argument can centre around the nature of the thing to be categorized or about the nature of the category. One might dispute whether the particular resembles the sort of thing which is normally categorized in this way, or one might dispute the general meaning or legitimacy of the category itself. In short, the essence of the particular and the essence of the category can become matters of controversy. In both cases, conflicts between the opposing strategies of particularization and categorization can be involved. However, it will be suggested that the arguments involve more than a simple choice between particularization and categorization. In practice, an argument in favour of particularizing some object will involve categorizations and vice versa, as the momentum of argumentation swings back and forth between categories and particulars.

To begin with, we can treat the situation in which there is an argument, or dilemma, about what a particular should be called. The importance of applying a label to a troublesome particular should not be underestimated. As William James wrote:

> Concrete dilemmas do not come to us with labels gummed upon their backs. We name them by names. The wise man is he who succeeds in finding the name which suits the needs of the particular occasion best. (1890, Vol. 2, p. 1139)

In rhetorical situations each party will attempt to apply the label which suits their purposes best. The defence's 'unfortunate victim of circumstances' will be the prosecution's 'scheming criminal'. As was mentioned in Chapter 2, the famous cricketing dispute between England and Australia had its linguistic dimension, as disputants contested the labels of 'leg theory' and 'bodyline'. Such disputes often are not focussed upon individual words as such, but upon whole networks of meaning, or schemata, which an individual word brings to mind. Sometimes the debate might be between two terms which carry evocations of guilt and innocence. It was reported that the editor of *Meat Trades Journal* suggested a change of nomenclature in order to combat the growing menace of vegetarianism: in place of 'butcher' and 'slaughterhouse', pleasanter terms such as 'meat plant' and 'meat factory' should be employed (*Guardian*, November 30, 1984). Lance Bennett (1980) has argued that governing politicians have a tendency to define controversies in which they have become embroiled as being issues of motive rather than issues of fact. The politicians will suggest that what counts is their own intentions, and, of course, they always have the very noblest of intentions. They will avoid, if possible, publicly discussing the particular action in factual terms, lest their own incompetences or venality become matters of public debate.[6] Politicians are specially keen to contest the guilt-filled label which might be gummed upon their own actions. After American troops had been dispatched to Grenada to assist the overthrow of the government there, the President found himself insisting upon exact semantics:

> Mr Reagan objected to the description of the US operation as an invasion, saying it was a 'rescue mission'. He also grew visibly angry when a reporter asked how he felt about those who compared the action to the Soviet invasion of Afghanistan.
>
> (*Guardian*, November 4, 1983)

Since the rhetorical context is one of justification and criticism, the controversial label has to be justified and criticisms repelled. A reason must be found to separate a particular invasion from other invasions. Its essence must be seen to lie in factors which call for an alternative and sweeter description. Apparently, according to Mr Reagan, in Afghanistan "the Soviets used every vicious form of warfare...and in the process of changing forces there an American Ambassador was murdered". The 'rescue mission' was very different from the typical invasion: not every form of vicious warfare was employed against the tiny, and ill-defended, island, besides which the US forces were not involved in the murder of an American Ambassador. *Ipso facto* the invasion was no invasion. Such is the rhetorical force of language that the very choice of terms implies a position. In consequence, it becomes impossible to talk about such an invasion without implicitly or explicitly signalling a stance. Even a choice of ostentatiously neutral terms would indicate a position, for neutrality in the midst of conflict is every bit as much a position – and a controversial one at that – as is partisanship.

Reagan's argument depended upon claiming to discover 'special features' of a particular in order to argue against a damaging, but *prima facie* reasonable, categorization. Since all particulars contain their own particularities, there is always, in theory, the possibility of using the strategy of the Special Case. The British Chancellor of the Exchequer was recently arguing in Parliament that the introduction of low wages would reduce unemployment. He was challenged on the grounds that those areas with the highest unemployment rates were those with the lowest wages. He replied: "That is because of the special factors that affect industries in those areas" (*Guardian*, November 2, 1984). The strategy of the Special Case had been cited: the exceptions to the general rule have to be explained away in terms of their essential exceptionality.

The strategy is particularly common in legal disputes. As the textbooks of forensic oratory make clear, one can argue that the special features of a particular case are special enough to make it a legitimate exception to the law. In such a case, one is arguing that the essence of the particular resides in its special particularities, rather than in its *prima facie* similarities to those other cases, which have had the usual label gummed to their backs without argument. Although in theory any particularity can form the basis of an argument for a special case, the argument is likely to be facilitated if the particularities can be slid into familiar categories, backed up by values shared by pleader and audience. For example, under normal circumstances the deliberate shooting and killing of another is categorized as murder. Pleas of special circumstances can sometimes be successful to produce an alternative definition of the act: "A white who killed a black outside his house as he apparently stole 6 cents (49 US cents) of milk money has been cleared of criminal charges and praised by a South African judge for performing a civic deed" (*Guardian*, May 25, 1984). Because of "a rash of thefts of milk money in the white suburban neighbourhood", the judge announced that the killer "deserved a medal for what he did". Thus, the judgement located the essence of the case: the white gunman's act of shooting a suspected petty thief with dark skin was *essentially* a public service and quite the negation of murderous crime. In the courtroom the judge might have the power to impose a final word, but such powers are unable to still the momentum of controversy, which such a judgement inevitably sets rocking.

A classic case, which exercised ancient rhetoricians and lawyers, illustrates how a particular can be caught between two contrasting categories. The case of Epaminondas, the Theban general, was one where prosecution and defence fought over the essence of the matter. According to the letter of the law the case appeared as straightforward as the murder of the black petty thief. Theban law clearly stated that no individual should maintain supreme control over the army for more than a month. The facts of the case were not in doubt: Epaminondas did not relinquish control to his legally appointed successor at the month's end in accordance with the law. However, a few days later, Epaminondas won a famously heroic, but technically illegal, victory over the Lacedaemonians. He was prosecuted, and the defence, adopting the strategy of particularization, argued that this case differed substantively from cases of military disobedience. Epaminondas's actions were essentially those of a hero, not the misdeeds of a criminal. True he broke the law, but the essence of the matter lay in his famous victory and in the benefits it brought the state. Here was a dilemma with two opposing labels – hero and criminal – waiting to be gummed upon the back, or rather the neck, of Epaminondas (see Cicero *De Inventione*, I, xxxiii, 56, for details). The court decided against the general, but then changed its mind in the light of public feeling, which preferred to locate the essence of the case in the general's bravery. Nor did that end the matter, because the case was to become a classic matter of debate. Generations of aspiring orators would practise their skills by rehearsing the arguments.

The cases of Epaminondas and the rewarded South African murderer possess similarities. In both instances, there is a dilemma about the location of the essence. Particularities are invoked in order to shift the essence away from one set of social values to another set. These two sets of social values pull in opposing directions. Thus, in the case of Epaminondas, values for obedience to the letter of the law conflict with the values for brave service to the state. In the South African case, the value of respect for human life vainly battled with the stronger value of protecting small amounts of money belonging to white people.

In each instance, the strategy of particularization does not end with a statement of particularities but leads to further categorizations. The prosecutors of Epaminondas argued that, if an exception were made in this case, a dangerous precedent would be set. The defence countered by suggesting that the features of the case were so remarkable that a precedent would only be set for those few remarkable instances which would anyway stretch the existing law. Such discussions involve arguments about re-drawing the law in the light of a successful strategy of particularization. In other words, the particularization feeds back onto the original categorization, from which it is attempting to escape. In fact, the arguments about precedent can provide the fence, which prevents the escape, or, in the South African example, they can be heralded as the great example, which should be followed.

The basic structure of such an argument can be presented. Firstly there is a general rule or procedure stipulating something to the effect that 'all x's are Y'; for example that all acts containing a particular characteristic are illegal and anti-social. The difficult case arises. It clearly has the characteristic 'x', but it also possesses the characteristic of 'w', which is generally associated with socially approved actions. An argument ensues about which location is to be preferred for the essence of the particular matter. Such arguments typically will not confine themselves to the particular instance, but will examine the general consequences and the wider social values involved. The particular features of the specific case become conceived as generalities, and the particularization is translated into a categorization. One general consequence is that the original rule will not be left untouched, whichever way the decision goes. If the particularization is unsuccessful, then the rule 'all x's are Y' is strengthened by the additional rider 'including those x's with w's'. If the particularization is successful, then an exception clause must be built into the rule. In this way, simple rules, when tested in practice, become encumbered with all sorts of complicating sub-clauses resulting from instances which are controversially categorized.

The re-drawing of a rule in the face of a testing case can involve skills resembling those of tight-fisted problem solving. In psychological studies of concept-attainment, subjects often have to produce a rule, or criterion, for grouping a number of given particulars under a single category (e.g.,

Archer, 1966; Bourne, 1966). Similarly, law-makers may be required to draft emendations to the rule, so that particular cases find themselves categorized in the desired way. As in the concept-attainment experiments, this task can be done correctly or incorrectly. An incorrectly drawn rule will fail to have expressed the essence of the particular cases in a way which results in their being located on the desired side of legality. However, re-drawing rules often involves more than tight-fisted problem solving. Not only must the particulars of known cases be taken into account, but imagination must be used to envisage, and categorize, future problem cases. Nevertheless, because of Quintilian's Principle of Uncertainty, it is impossible to envisage all future possibilities. Each rule has its own areas of uncertainty, whether the rule be a legal statute, a psychological law or mental guideline for applying even the most basic of categories. However carefully re-drafted the categorization, it will always be vulnerable at some later date to the strategy of particularization, when an unusual and unforeseen event arises.[7] In this way the oscillation between categorization and particularization can be expected to continue without the resting place of a last word.

Arguing about categories

Arguments about difficult cases, such as that of Epaminondas, concern the drawing of the outer boundary of a concept. The dilemma is whether to include or exclude the problem case within the category and how to justify the decision. If all laws are vulnerable to the problem case, then it is never possible to draw their outer boundaries with any degree of finality. This is a point which Rosch stresses, when, following the analyses of Wittgenstein, she argues that the categories of ordinary language are fuzzy-edged. In consequence, disputes about the location of boundaries are to be expected. A crucial factor in these arguments is whether the particular problem case is essentially similar to those instances which are usually, or noncontroversially, placed inside the category in question. This seems to suggest that the centre of the category is not the locus of disagreement. However, arguments are not confined to the outer edges of categories. In addition to arguments about the essences of things placed on the fuzzier edges of categories, it is also possible to argue about the essences of the categories themselves. Just as the arguments about particulars can lead to arguments about categories, so, it will be suggested, the arguments about the essence of categories can lead to arguments about particulars.

Arguments about the essence of categories can be much more fundamental than those about problem cases. Disagreements about words need not be dismissed as trivial verbal quibbles, because "a dispute over words is not usually simply a dispute about words, even when both sides believe that the matter at issue merely concerns the choice of means by which a thought is to be formulated" (Ossowski, 1963, p. 171). A debate about the essence of a category can indicate a substantial difference of opinion or ideology. For example, drafters of legislation may debate about the outer edges of 'theft': whether, for example, unauthorized removal of property is theft or whether, in addition, there has to be an intention to keep the said articles permanently. Whatever legal decision is taken, the courts will then have the task of settling the boundaries, as and when the ambiguous problem cases arise.[8] The arguments involved in this will differ from an argument about the very essence of 'theft'. The careful drawing and re-drawing of boundaries will suddenly all look rather cosy, when an angry outsider bursts in to declare "Property is theft." No longer is there an essential agreement about the social undesirability of theft, but suddenly a whole system of values, not to mention the legitimacy of the courts which decide upon the problem cases, has become a matter for controversy.

Although Eleanor Rosch has investigated the fuzzy edges of concepts, her research has tended to assume that the centre of categories is non-controversial. She has argued, on the basis of her experimental studies, that not all particulars which are categorized together are considered to be equivalent. Some particulars are seen to be much more central to the concept than others. At the heart of categories are "prototypes", which are "representative exemplars" of categories. For example, a professional thief might be more prototypical of the category 'criminal' than was Epaminondas. According to Rosch, when we deliberate about the outer edges, we refer to the degrees of similarity to the prototypical examples at the centre. This process assumes that the centre of the concept is not the locus of dispute.

Rosch has provided impressive evidence about this aspect of categorization, yet there is the additional matter that the prototypes themselves may be a matter of controversy. Much of Rosch's research has focussed upon categories of natural objects, such as 'chair' or 'bird', which normally are not what Gallie (1962) would have termed "essentially contested concepts". However, the categories which frequently form the basis of rhetorical dispute are liable to have their prototypes questioned, as disputants seek to locate the essence in very different places. Political concepts are notoriously contestable. The Marxist-Leninist is unlikely to see the British parliamentary constitution as the prototypical democracy. By contrast, the British liberal will find great difficulty in understanding how a Soviet society can be portrayed as the epitome of democracy. Similarly, everyone champions the value of freedom, but the democrat's freedom is the fascist's 'anarchic degeneracy', whilst the fascist's idea of 'freedom', for anti-fascists, constitutes the essence of freedom's negation (see Billig, 1977).

The social sciences are particularly prone to arguments of this type. Theoretical writers are expected to define their terms in the first few pages of their books, as a token of their objectively scientific spirit. If a social scientist writes about 'democracy' or 'fascism', definitions will be expected, otherwise critics will pounce upon the lacuna. Such definitions have a rhetorical, or argumentative, meaning, for the academic definition of a commonly used term is not merely an elaboration of internal meanings, but is an argument against other definitions. The function of such a definition is to locate the essence of the matter in a direction which accords with the theoretical leanings of the writer, and to move it away from those of rival theoreticians. Sometimes the definition is an implicit criticism against the ordinary non-academic usage, in which essences anarchically sprout in a happy disorder. In this way, the academic selection of a definition and representative exemplars will be part of wider theoretical argument. What the academic does is not so different from the general argumentative strategy recommended by *Rhetorica Ad Herennium*: "The meaning of the term is first explained briefly, and adapted to the advantage of our cause" (II, xii, 17).

Examples of the argumentative definition are frequent in social psychology. Practically every writer on the subject of 'attitudes' has felt obliged to offer their own definition of the concept. As Jaspars and Fraser have shown, such definitions typically pick out one aspect as being the central one. Some theorists have stressed the emotional side of attitudes, whilst others play up behavioural or cognitive aspects. Their differing definitions are not random locations of preference, but each selection of an essence contains at least an implicit criticism of other preferences. Controversies over the definitions then will form part of wider theoretical debates, for the definitions themselves are part of these wider intellectual differences. As Eiser has noted, "the various definitions of attitude offered by social psychologists, while they appear uncontentious at a superficial level, frequently involve assumptions not only about the nature of attitudes, but also about the nature of learning, socialization, information processing, decision-making, memory, and so on" (1980, p. 18). In other words, the innocuous-looking definition, ostensibly clearing up matters to prevent misunderstanding, is like a jack-in-the-box, inside which arguments are tensely coiled, waiting to spring against the face of the curious critic.[9]

Perhaps the structure of arguments about categories can best be discussed in the light of examples. To begin with, there is a famous illustration of the fact that we are not cognitively powerless in the use of representative exemplars. Rosch's tables and chairs have no power to argue back against their selection of representativeness, but this should not imply that prototypicality cannot be unpicked. Karl Marx, the prototypical Marxist, was said by Engels to have reacted against his prototypicality. According to his friend and collaborator, Marx declared in exasperation that "what is certain is that I am no Marxist" (McLellan, 1973, p. 443). As is so often the case, the controversial statement is capable of provoking arguments along a number of directions, and therefore does not contain a simple unambiguous argumentative meaning. Marx's statement is simultaneously a statement about himself, about those admirers who misunderstood his position and about the category of 'Marxist'. Above all, he was arguing that there was a mis-match between the essence of himself and the essence of the category, of which he supposedly was the representative exemplar. As such, the argument about the essence of the category also involves arguments about the essence of the particular, and in this case, of course, the particularity of the debater.

It is probable that Marx did not object to the category of 'Marxist' as such, for who would seriously decline such a linguistic honour? What he wanted was to control the precise location of its essence, and as the acknowledged representative exemplar he felt uniquely, or prototypically, qualified to do so. On other occasions, an argument against the location of the essence of a category can also be an argument against the category itself. Here is an example of a challenge to the very existence of a category:

> I mentioned that Lord Monboddo told me, he awakened every morning at four, and then for his health got up and walked in his room naked, with the window open, which he called taking an *air bath*; after which he went to bed again, and slept two hours more. Johnson, who was always ready to beat down any thing that seemed to be exhibited with disproportionate importance, thus observed: 'I suppose, Sir, there is no more in it than this, he wakes at four, and cannot sleep till he chills himself, and makes the warmth of the bed a grateful sensation.'
>
> (Boswell, 1906, Vol. 2, pp. 123–124)

Lord Monboddo's early morning activities would be the representative exemplar of the category *air bath*, and the exercises of others would only qualify for the label to the extent that they resembled the noble lord's regimen. Johnson was disputing the particularity of this regimen: it contained no extraordinary essence, deserving of a special label. Johnson, in his description, was happily sliding the eccentric exercises into familiar words. The criticism of the category in this case depends upon disputing the essence of the particular instance. If the category of *air bath* is under dispute, then so is precisely what Lord Monboddo was doing, unclothed, in his Highland bedroom early on cold mornings.

The arguments about *Marxist* and about *air bath* were arguments about newly formed categories, whose eventual linguistic successes would be vastly different. These two examples might give the impression that only newly minted concepts can be controversial. However, well established concepts can find themselves under attack from new philosophies, whether metaphysical, political, ethical or religious. And it has been part of the long history of some concepts, such as 'good' and 'evil', that their essences have always been matters of controversy. In such controversies much more is at stake than in the debates about *air baths* or *posteriors of the day*, but even these debates could be opened up into controversies about wider issues, if the disputants so wished. What all these debates share in common is that disputants have turned round on their schemata, in order to locate the controversy right at the centre of categories.

In much of academic psychology, such disputes are quite common. Many scientifically-minded psychologists, especially behaviourists, urge us to dispense with our ordinary ways of talking about people, and to give new, and 'operationalized', meanings to old familiar words. However, the psychologists cannot expect others, or even their off-duty selves, to abandon comfortable words, or to relocate essences without an argument. In controversially advocating the wholesale revision of language, principally under the guise of preventing arguments about the ill-defined words of everyday life, the behaviourists are following Jeremy Bentham, who sought a psychological language which would dispense with the conceptual messiness of moral judgements. He recognized that he would need to create long-windedly new terms, or he would have to insist upon new, and restricted, meanings for old words – both strategies being familiar to modern psychologists. Bentham recognized that the endeavour would be controversial, and thereby would be in need of justification. Anyone using these new words would need "to confess, that for the sake of promoting the purposes, he has violated the established laws of language, and to throw himself upon the mercy of his readers" (*Introduction to the Principles of Morals and Legislation*, p. 102). Some of Bentham's neologisms, such as 'maximize' and 'minimize', have passed uncontroversially into the language, where they now do much messier jobs than he had wished for his linguistic offspring.

Bentham's readers were being asked to countenance with mercy the shifting of the prototypes of familiar categories. Instead of accepting common usage, with its imprecisions and implied essences, Bentham was urging his readers to seek a clear language which would transcend the strife of argument. However, this new language itself was, as Bentham recognized, controversial, in that it struggled against the old language, often using the old terms, in its dispute: Bentham, the unsentimental utilitarian, cannot prevent himself from asking for 'mercy' from his conventional readers in a most old-fashioned and non-utilitarian manner. Bentham, arguing for science over rhetoric, finds himself inevitably using rhetoric in order to justify his new words. His argument is not an empirical one to be settled by experimental evidence, just as the modern psychologist's strange terms are not threatened by the absence of statistically significant differences. Bentham's argument depends upon the rhetorical, and contestable, strategy of declaring the essence of an opponent's concept to be falsely located and of offering a truer location.

The ordinary usage, it is argued, finds its representative exemplars in false, or inappropriate, locations, and a 'true' version of the concept is proposed to replace the 'false' one. This basic strategy, which Perelman and Olbrechts-Tyteca have called 'dissociation', involves distinguishing between opponents' false use of a term and one's own true usage. It is to be found in many disputes about categories, especially when well established usages are challenged. The radical must argue against the false 'democracy' of the capitalists, often quarantining the word in inverted commas, so that its false and reactionary meaning does not infect the rest of the revolutionary discourse. The same strategy of distinguishing the false from the true essence is pursued by the anarchic challenge to 'theft'. Thus 'true' theft is not the unauthorized removal of property, but it is the authorized possession of property.

Similarly Plato's philosophy implied a wholesale shifting of essences from false to true locations. Plato argued that knowledge was obtained by remembering the divine truths implanted in humans before birth. This was the essence of 'true' remembering, and was to be distinguished from what we normally, in our philosophical ignorance, call 'memory'. Everyday remembering, such as remembering to buy something from the shops, or recognizing someone in the street, should not properly be called 'remembering', let alone be held to be prototypical examples. These sorts of things were merely 'recollection' (e.g. *Phaedrus*, 274). The prototypical example of remembering was then to be shifted to something which, hitherto, might have been thought to represent the opposite of memory. The famous example of Platonic memory is contained in the *Meno*. Socrates drew some geometric figures in the dusty earth, and by gentle prompting led an uneducated slave to solve some complex geometric problems. For Plato this was not, as it would be for many, a prototypical example of the way in which effective teaching could impart new information. According to Plato, the example illustrated quite the reverse: the slave, far from being taught something new, was 'remembering' information divinely given. Prototypes and essences were being shifted as learning becomes remembering ('true remembering'), and remembering ('false remembering') becomes recollecting. Such arguments about categories do not remain merely arguments about words. In addition, the argument will swing back from categories to particulars, as disputants prefer to locate in different places the essence of the incident between the famous philosopher and the anonymous slave.

A basic structure for arguments about categories can be suggested. It resembles the structure proposed for arguments about particulars in that there is a momentum between categorizations and particularizations. However, the starting-point is different. The structure of the argument about particulars started with a categorization and then proceeded to a particularization. The argument against a category can, but does not have to, start with a particularization: 'X is the epitome/perfect example/true instance of Y'. This is a particularization in that X has been picked out from all other instances of Y, and in this respect the statement differs from the categorization 'X is a Y'. The particularization might be countered by a categorization: 'X is essentially/really/truly Z' (where Z stands for 'recollect-ing', 'getting chilly in the morning' or whatever old concept is being defended against attack). Then the debate can focus on the nature of X, and thereby become an argument about the essence of a particular. Alternatively the original particularization could be countered by 'W is the epitome of Y', and again the matter would swing between the rival essences of particulars and that of the category, as opposing locations are preferred for the essence of the category. As was the case with arguments about particulars, the momentum between particularization and categorization suggests a contin-ual shuffle, rather than a progress to a natural resting place. And again, such arguments, and the thoughts they express, are impossible if we do not have the faculty for turning around the schemata which supposedly govern our cognitions.

Arguing about arguments

The foregoing two sections may imply that sometimes we argue about drawing the boundary of a category and on other, quite distinct, occasions we argue about the category itself. However, matters are not quite so straightforward, for sometimes we argue about arguments. Whether we are re-drawing a boundary along the fuzzy edges of a category or whether we are relocating its essence might itself be a contested issue. Let us put it this way: 'arguments about drawing boundaries' and 'arguments about changing essences' are themselves categories and there may well be controversy about which label to apply to a particular argument. The same strategies which enable us to unpick our categories and to dispute the nature of particulars will allow us to argue about the nature of our arguments.

It is possible to argue that an argument which ostensibly relocates an essence is really an argument about re-drawing a boundary. The argument could proceed in the reverse direction: the accusation then would be that an apparent re-drawing of boundaries is, in fact, relocating the essence of the concept. Typically, these arguments about arguments will hinge upon issues of whether the norms and values underlying the categories in question are being upheld or transgressed. A distinction between re-drawing a boundary and relocating an essence can be made: the re-drawing of the boundary usually does not challenge the basic values and norms, whilst a relocation does. Thus if we are arguing about arguments, it is likely that we are contesting whether values and norms are being upheld or being challenged.

The argument that essences, contrary to appearances, are really not being shifted might be made by a radical, complaining that a fellow radical is only a moderate posing in the battle fatigues of a revolutionary. After the revolution 'workers' justice' might be introduced as a complete negation of the reactionary 'bourgeois justice', which had hitherto prevailed. True justice would have been distinguished from the false justice of the old regime. However, the same courtrooms might still be employed and, apart from a few notorious judges, who had been shot without trial, there might be no dramatic change of personnel wearing the judicial wigs. Radicals within the party might dispute the official claims that these courts represented the new, and true, justice. Such radicals would complain that this was, in essence, 'bourgeois justice' and that the much trumpeted new workers' rights were merely an extension of the old bourgeois rights. The numbers of people benefiting from these rights had changed, but in essence the nature of the courts had not changed. To use Aristotelian terms, there would erupt a controversy pitting arguments of quality against those of quantity. The former arguments would assert that the essence of the matter had been changed, whilst the latter would deny this, claiming that only non-essential peripheral alterations had been made.

A strategy of re-drawing a boundary implies that the centre of the category, and the values it might express, are being left intact. The strategy itself becomes controversial when it is argued that the boundary is being re-drawn in such a radical way that the centre has been shifted. In fact, arguments to this effect will often accompany discussion of new legislation, especially that which deliberately seeks to open loopholes. Murray Edelman in his *Symbolic Uses of Politics* has provided a fascinating account of the way in which legislators deliberately present laws which in effect aim to permit that which is ostensibly being forbidden. Defenders of the legislation will deny that this is occurring, whilst critics claim that the laws are not essentially what they appear to be. Although Edelman claims that such laws are common in modern politics, our example is taken from an older dispute.

The 1571 Act Against Usury was not, in effect, an act against usury. It repealed the earlier act of 1552, which had forbidden all acts of lending money at interest, much to the inconvenience of the growing commercial classes, but greatly to the relief of the traditionalists. The 1571 Act presented itself as being fundamentally opposed to usury, stating with deceptive firmness that "all usury being forbidden by the law of God is sin and detestable" (Tawney, 1925, p. 169). However, its aim, far from upholding tradition, was to draw in the boundary of the concept of usury, so that what was formerly usurious could now be legally sanctioned. The supporters of the new act claimed that no traditional values were being infringed, but that it was essentially a matter of sensibly clearing up borderline matters. The traditional value was unambiguously asserted, yet the boundary was to be established by using a strategy of distinguishing true from false usury. The Act declared that usury was as different from "true interest" as "falsehood is to truth" (p. 155). Legally-sanctioned true interest would infringe neither respectable sensibilities, commercial interests, nor the laws of God.

Such a legislative move, with its introduction of the new category of 'true interest', did not fool the traditionalists. A *Discourse Upon Usury*, written by the rhetorical theorist Thomas Wilson, is a dialogue in which various fictional figures argue pro and con the new act. There is the doctor, who, unlike Wilson, is firmly on the side of the modern reformers, and asserts what no-one ostensibly denies, namely that usury is by definition evil: "The name usury is odious, ungodly and wicked" (1925, p. 319). However, fair commercial agreements are not truly usurious, but are based upon the charging of "true interest". Similarly, the lawyer suggests that only "they that are biters and oppressors" deserve the name usurer, and men of sound commercial sense and responsibility should escape the hateful epithet (p. 208). The opponents saw in all these sorts of argument a shifting of essence, rather than a slight adjustment of boundaries. The same prototype of the usurer – that of the Shylock and the hateful exploiter – might be employed by both sides, but the essence of the matter is not to be equated with the dominant image of the prototype. The essence of this image can be a matter of dispute. According to the traditionalists, the boundary of usury was being drawn so tightly around this figure that the nature of usury had altered qualitatively. Formerly, usury's essence lay simply in the charging of interest. As the preacher put it, "the very hope of gain upon money lent maketh a man to be a usurer" (p. 218). In the new economic age, this hope was insufficient to make one a hated usurer, but could lay the basis for a respectably successful career. Although the same prototype might be preserved, different aspects of the Shylock figure were being particularized as the basis for competing essences for the category. The modernists focussed upon the Shylock figure's excessive, and old-fashioned, styles, not to mention the figure's non-Christian tendencies. The traditionalists maintained that these undesirable characteristics stemmed from an essential fact: the essence of the hated figure of the money lender was that he lent money.

The traditionalists would be disputing that the arguments of the reformers were not 'really' arguments about setting the boundary, but that something much more basic was at stake. Similarly, it is not difficult to argue that one of the previous examples, which was presented as an example of categorizing a particular, is really an example of shifting the essence of the category. It would not be hard to claim that the white judge who praised the killing of the black petty thief had altered the whole concept of murder. So tightly was the boundary of 'murder' being drawn around the peculiar values of white South Africa, that murder was no longer murder, and 'public service' should be truly called murder; and that 'justice' deserved the name of injustice. Thus the arguments about the particular case can be challenged as being arguments about the fundamental nature of basic values.

In such disputes we have arguments about arguments. Nor are these arguments about arguments necessarily that uncommon. Our opponents in debate might frequently object to the way that we classify their arguments, and what we think we are doing may be disputed by our opponents. In consequence we may find ourselves arguing about the arguments, and the same argumentative strategies will be employed. Only in this case their subject matter will be other arguments. Of course, as these arguments develop, we might expect arguments about arguments about arguments. And so on. It might be possible to construct an analytic framework for these, but intellectual vertigo must strike at some point.

7   Advocacy and attitudes

Different psychological approaches suggest different images of the person. In cognitive psychology the person seems to be a rather unimaginative bureaucrat, whereas in the field of artificial intelligence, the human mind has become a complexly programmed computer. Old fashioned behaviourists continue to see us all as poor laboratory rats, chasing after the rewards of life. Game theorists view our activities as just so many games, whilst role theorists note the theatrical side of our endeavours. By contrast, a rhetorical approach argues for the oratorical image of the person. At first sight this seems straightforward, in that one set of metaphorical terms is recommended in place of others. In contrast to the other psychological metaphors, the rhetorical approach likens our conversations to scaled down versions of the great debates of history. In countless small living rooms we should hear the echoes of the Roman Curia, as we become domestic Ciceros and Catos.

However, the rhetorical image is not a straightforward one, but, as if to pay tribute to Protagoras, it contains two sides. One side of this rhetorical image has already been encountered in Chapter 5. There, it was suggested that, when people deliberate, their thinking resembles an argument. In consequence, the deliberator is not so much an orator, but is two or more contesting orators rolled into one person. If people can deliberate, first by advocating one side and then by advocating the other, then they are possessed of the skills of advocacy. The second part of the image does not show the individual person engaged in internal deliberation, but the person advocating a single position, or becoming the domestic version of the public advocate. In this second image, the argument is not unfolding within the self, but actually takes place with another orator, who is advocating a contrary position. In this way, the rhetorical image draws attention to two sides of the person. We see the person as the deliberator, uncertainly shuttling between contrary opinions. And then, we see a determined advocate, who has decided upon a single stance and is orating upon the virtues of the chosen position. Thus, the rhetorical image embraces both the uncertain and the certain, or the perplexed and the forthright, sides of human thinking.

This chapter will consider the advocate, rather than the deliberator, although a sharp distinction should not be made between the two. Certainly, the emotional states accompanying deliberation and advocacy might be very different, yet the same sort of cognitive process may underwrite the two sides of the rhetorical person. As we move from deliberation to advocacy, or in the reverse direction, we do not change from a mode of thinking which employs one set of cognitive and rhetorical strategies to a mode which uses a totally different set. Nor would this be expected: if deliberation is the internal oscillation between rival advocacies, then it is necessarily composed of the strategies of advocacy. As was suggested in the previous chapter, particularization and categorization represent basic rhetorical strategies, and these are to be found in advocacy as much as in deliberation. In fact, the inherently controversial nature of these strategies enables advocacy to take place. Because particulars do not slide uncontentiously into tight-fitting categories, there is the possibility for advocating alternative positions, and for exploiting the gap between the particular and the category. Therefore, the strategies of particularization and categorization, which were discussed in the previous chapter with respect to argumentation in general, are also crucial for advocacy.

Advocacy involves the use of strategies for justifying a particular case and for rebutting the critics of the case. One does not advocate, properly speaking, when one merely declares that one is in favour of this or that. Advocacy starts when the statement of belief is supported by reasons, whether they be direct justifications for one's own belief, or criticisms of competing positions. Therefore, advocacy involves the invention of reasons for possessing attitudes, as well as the formulation of escaping excuses, when the criticisms come hurtling in. Above all, as will be suggested, advocacy includes arguments about consistency, as we accuse our opponents of inconsistency and claim that our own stances are impeccably consistent.

What this discussion of advocacy will entail is the placing of familiar social psychological matters in a rhetorical context, which emphasizes the psychological importance of justification and criticism. For example, the topics of psychological consistency and attitudes have formed a major part of contemporary social psychological theorizing. It will be suggested that social psychologists have not always discussed the rhetorical, and controversial, aspects of these issues. By focussing upon the rhetorical dimensions, especially those which relate to the tensions between the processes of categorization and particularization, it is hoped that light will be thrown upon traditional social psychological issues, such as the limitations of motivational theories of consistency and the apparent gap between attitudes and actions.

As previously, the discussion will gather its examples of witcraft from antiquarian pathways. Often these examples are taken from philosophical disputes, and, in particular, from Socratic debates. However, no intellectual elitism is intended, for the choice of such examples, as opposed to the more common use of experimental studies, is in no measure meant to imply that only superior philosophical intellects can aspire to the cognitive complexities of advocacy. In fact, the reverse is the case. It is assumed that justification and criticism are fundamental components of thought. There is no reason to doubt Richard Rainolde, the sixteenth century English rhetorician, when he wrote: "Nature has indued every man with a certain eloquence, and also a subtlety to reason and discuss of any question or proposition propounded" (*The Foundacion of Rhetorike*, p. 1). Similarly Thomas Hobbes declared that "all men naturally are able in some sort to accuse and excuse: some by chance; but some by method" ('Brief of the Art of Rhetorick', p. 276).

Those equipped with a method of criticism and justification might be able to set themselves up as specialists offering advice to the less methodical. However, witcraft offers no hidden secrets to distinguish the professional expert from the layperson, and the public is well advised to look sceptically at those who offer, at a price, professional skills of inventing excuses. It was recently reported that a young French computer expert "is offering to provide excuses at about £5 a time to companies trying to wriggle out of embarrassing situations". The young professional Protagorean apparently "has already carried out some tricky paid diplomacy but believes the Rent-A-Liar company could take on several employees if the Government Aid to Business Fund will advance him money" (*Guardian*, October 18, 1984). It is unlikely that many companies will require such expertise, for most do quite well without the claims of method. It is worth recalling the gist, if not the innuendo, of Juvenal's comments on the wife caught in the act of adultery. She calls Quintilian:

> 'Find me a pat excuse.' 'I'm stuck', says the Maestro, 'you can get yourself out of this one.' And she does. (*Satires*, VI, p. 137)

When Cicero said that everyone can claim some part of the professional orator's qualities, he might have made an exception for the quality of eloquence, but he certainly included the invention of escaping excuses and of entrapping accusations (*Orator*, XVIII 60). That being so, the image of the orator is slightly different from some of those other images to be found in psychological theory. Psychologists can suggest that we may resemble laboratory rats and that it might be interesting to think of our minds as computers. However, these images are metaphorical, for even the most dedicated psychologist knows that we really are not rats and that neurophysiologists, probing the inner recesses of our cortexes, are not going to come across silicon chips from Japan. The rhetorical theorist need make no such concession. In our everyday lives, we do not merely resemble orators, but, quite literally, we are orators, as we offer up our daily excuses and send forth our accusations. Like Juvenal's surprised wife, we advocate for ourselves, possibly with even greater energy and imagination than any rented liar could summon.

The image of consistency

A wonderfully vivid description of the orator can be found in Thomas De Quincey's essay on 'Rhetoric', which ostensibly is a review of Bishop Whately's *Elements of Rhetoric*, but whose stream of arguments flows way beyond the Bishop's static pond. According to De Quincey, "the rhetorician exhibits his art by giving an impulse to one side, and by withdrawing the mind so steadily from all thoughts or images which support the other, as to leave it practically under the possession of a one-sided estimate" (p. 347). De Quincey's orator is clearly a single-minded advocate, who uses the traditional devices for 'colouring' all information to support the case in hand. Even when prosecution and defence have the same information to work upon, such as the testimonies of witnesses, they will offer very different 'coloured' interpretations. As Cicero wrote, "each will twist them to the advantage of his own case, making them tell in opposite directions though he follows a similar course of rules" (*De Inventione*, ii, xiv, 46). To use modern terms, the advocate will encode the information through a biased set of schemata, so that the output, whether on the rostrum, the courtroom floor, or the television screen, will give public support to the schematic assumptions.

It is easy to translate De Quincey's description of the orator into the language of modern psychology, because he is offering a psychological description of the one-sided mental state of the advocate. The mind has been withdrawn from contrary information, and all impulses are devoted to building up a particular case. In psychological theory, the image is a familiar one. It is the image of the bigot, whose mind is only attentive to what confirms the *idée fixe* lying at the root of the bigotry. In addition, the image is to be found in the cognitive theories of normal thought processes, discussed in the last chapter. Such theories of social cognition assume that the normal person experiences the world in a distorted, even bigoted, manner. The normal person is a 'cognitive miser', whose mind takes one-sided short-cuts, and possesses a 'totalitarian ego': all our thoughts are forced to support the party-line of the dominant schema, and signs of internal opposition are promptly repressed. In effect, these theories assume that the content of our thoughts is similar to the speeches delivered by De Quincey's orator. All incoming information has been coloured by mental schemata, which act as our *idées fixes*. Information which does not match these preconceptions is conveniently forgotten. As a result, we possess a bias towards confirming our assumptions, and our minds are habitually withdrawn from other estimates. Fiske and Taylor in their book *Social Cognition* write of the image of the 'social perceiver' which emerges from current social psychological theorizing and experimentation: "We find the rather unflattering picture of a charlatan trying to make the data come out in a manner most advantageous to his or her own already held theories" (1984, p. 88). Of course, there has always been a suspicion of charlatanry attached to the figure of the orator, burying the inelegant complexity of the world beneath a heap of elegantly one-sided phrases.

De Quincey's orator is seeking to tell a consistent story, all of whose sub-plots and sub-themes lead in the same direction. Such a story allows no room for doubt and dilemma. If De Quincey envisages his orator narrating this consistently one-sided tale to an audience, the one-sided charlatans of Fiske and Taylor tell their stories to their own selves. Both images view consistency as the outcome of psychological, or rhetorical, processes. In fact, the theme of consistency has been a pervasive one in modern social psychological theorizing. In the late 1950s and early 1960s a number of influential theories were proposed, all suggesting that we have a desire to order our thoughts and our actions in a consistent way. Probably the most famous of these theories was Leon Festinger's *Theory of Cognitive Dissonance*, which discussed the ways in which we avoid the unpleasantness of possessing inconsistent thoughts, or cognitions. Festinger argued that so unpleasant were the consequences of cognitive dissonance that we jerk our attitudes into line with our actions and we shuffle about our beliefs, until they all point in the same consistent direction.

The theories of cognitive consistency, like those of social cognition discussed in the previous chapter, seek to root the processes of cognition in 'basic' biological factors. Festinger, for example, argued that our thinking is governed by a biologically rooted motive to avoid inconsistency and that this motive is as strong as the motives for food and sex. He stated at the start of *Theory of Cognitive Dissonance* that if "someone cared to write a certain book about the hunger drive in human beings, it would turn out to be similar in nature to the present volume" (1957, pp. 3–4). Just as hunger, thirst and presumably sexual abstinence lead to physiologically uncomfortable states, so there is an analogously unpleasant state of dissonance produced by inconsistent thoughts. However, all such talk about basic, and thereby biological, motives removes cognition from a rhetorical context. In so doing it makes a strong assumption about one-sided thinking. The assumption is not that sometimes, when arguing a case, we behave like De Quincey's orator or like the charlatan of modern social psychological theory. Instead, there is the stronger assumption that we are continually driven by our own biological constitution to behave like the oratorical charlatan or the one-sided advocate.

The result is that these theoretical perspectives themselves have a tendency to one-sidedness. The remedy is not to deny the reality of the one-sided thinker. For example, cognitive dissonance theorists have provided convincing evidence about the mentality of consumers. When consumers, after much deliberation, come to a decision to purchase a particular brand of article, they are likely to become advocates of that brand, seeking out one-sided information in favour of the article of their choice and driving away all doubts that an erroneous decision might have been made (Ehrlich *et al.*, 1957). It would be silly to deny that this sort of thing occurs. However, the consistency theorists go further by seeing such episodes as representative of our thinking in general. They are not suggesting that we are occasional one-sided orators, but, that we are always, for biological reasons, driven to one-sidedness. It is this assumption which itself is one-sided.

It is necessary to set the topic of consistency in a rhetorical context, in which our motives are rhetorical ones rather than hypothesized biological drives. If one can speak of a basic rhetorical motive, as opposed to a biologically rooted one, then it is the motive to justify a position and to ward off criticisms. It is not that we are always motivated to justify and criticize, for sometimes we can let things ride, but if we stop being so motivated, we then remove ourselves from the rhetorical context of argumentation. This is the motivation which makes the actions of De Quincey's orator appear reasonable: the orator's mind is not necessarily one-sided in its constitution, but it has withdrawn itself from other estimations in order to get on with the job of advocacy. Inconsistency is uncomfortable to the extent that it represents an unanswered criticism, which threatens one's public advocacy or the preferred direction of one's private deliberations. The criticism of inconsistency is not the only criticism which can lead to discomfort. For example, it is not comfortable to be criticized on the grounds that our arguments are irrelevant or that they are ridiculously pompous. However, there is no reason for supposing that there are biologically rooted motivations to avoid irrelevancy and ridiculous pomposity. Similarly, within a rhetorical context there is no reason to suppose that we are possessed of a biologically rooted motivation to avoid inconsistency.

However, within the context of argumentation the accusation of inconsistency is a serious one. If we are arguing a case and we contradict ourselves, then our critics need only to draw attention to our own words, for we have done the bulk of their work for them: we have refuted and discredited our own case. As Aristotle noted, discrepancies between "dates, acts or statements" are "useful for Refutation" (*Rhetoric*, 1400a). This is why the *Rhetorica Ad Herennium* made the basic point: "It is a fault to be inconsistent with oneself in one's own discourse and to contradict what one has said before" (xxvi, 42). The fault is not to be avoided because inconsistent orators automatically experience a bodily discomfort, as if they had swallowed some sort of poison. It is that they lay themselves open to criticism that might be hard to rebut. The case at hand might be lost and their own skills of witcraft will be undermined. And that is seldom pleasant. But there again, neither is it pleasant to be exposed as a pompous buffoon or an irrelevant windbag.

This location of dissonance in a rhetorical context implies that inconsistencies in discourse can rest undisturbed, and undisturbing, should the argument rage around a different point. It is not inconsistency *per se* which is disruptive, but the criticisms of inconsistency, and it is the criticisms that raise the need for defensive justification. It does not matter whether such criticisms are made by others or whether they originate from our own internal voices of criticism. They still possess the capability to disturb and to provoke the invention of justification. Thus, the workings of our minds are not governed by the threat of inconsistency in any absolute sense, but only by those inconsistencies which form the basis of criticisms. This can be illustrated by an incident in Xenophon's *Banquet*, which describes the relaxed conversation between Socrates and his male friends. There is a homosexual undertone to the conversation, as flirtatious remarks are made to the prettier members of the company. For the group's entertainment, "a handsome girl" and "a beautiful boy" put on a display of dancing and gymnastics. The sight of the young girl throwing her cymbals in the air and catching them with perfect timing leads Socrates to declare that "the female sex are nothing inferior to ours, excepting only in strength of body, or perhaps steadiness of judgment". From this general statement, or attitude, Socrates then derives the specific recommendation that the wives of all the married men present "are capable of learning anything you are willing they should know to make them more useful to you" (pp. 166–167).

At this point the company senses a contradiction in the great Socrates, but it is not the same contradiction which might strike a modern reader. Antisthenes cries out that Socrates's own actions are inconsistent with his attitude, because he does not instruct his own wife, Xanthippe, who is surely "the most insupportable woman that is, has been or ever will be" (p. 167). The gathering hoots with laughter. Get out of that one, Socrates, they cry. Amidst even greater merriment, Socrates makes his argumentative escape. The strategy of the special case is used, as Socrates suggests that Xanthippe is uniquely insupportable and thereby an exception to the rule. No one present seems to have been troubled by the inconsistency between the statement of female almost-equality and the specific recommendation that wives should only be taught what is useful to their husbands. Nor does the company object when Socrates goes on to compare the instruction of women with the taming of horses. The only woman present was, of course, engaged in dance routines, and she was not expected to raise criticisms of the great men. It would take many years before such inconsistencies would be noted, at least by men.

This story illustrates the general point that potential inconsistencies can pass unnoticed, and unfelt. They might represent the potential for criticism, but only when criticisms are made is the rhetorical motive to deny contradiction set in motion. In addition, there is another theme in the anecdote. The charge of inconsistency is not accompanied by any mental *angst*, or bodily discomfort on a par with hunger or thirst. Instead, the charge of inconsistency is made in an atmosphere of hilarity, in the presence of food and wine, and the criticism is brushed aside in the same mood. A quick particularization rescues Socrates from being categorized as inconsistent. However, rhetorical contexts can change. Perhaps, in a context not dominated by male guffaws, the tone of the charges would be altered, and their force not so easily deflected. This suggests that the topic of consistency, at least as it relates to attitudes and not to logical calculus, should be firmly located within the context of argumentation.

Resolving inconsistency

Festinger's theory of cognitive dissonance presents a simple and intuitively appealing account of the way we think and, in particular, of the way we might change our thoughts. The theory is based upon a psychological idea that seems so reasonable: when two thoughts are inconsistent with each other, we will change one of them. Despite the widespread fame of the theory, its success within the world of the psychological laboratory has been limited. At the height of the research activity to produce 'dissonance effects' in the laboratory, one leading theorist wrote "in so many of the research areas inspired by dissonance theory, we seem to be dealing with slight effects that are very sensitive to subtle conditions of the experiment" (McGuire, 1969, p. 240). Even some of the early and most striking experimental displays of 'dissonance effects' have been questioned, or at least reinterpreted (e.g., Nuttin, 1975; Tedeschi *et al.*, 1971). Other psychologists have criticized the theoretical basis of dissonance and other consistency theories (e.g., Billig, 1982, chapter seven; Eiser, 1985). However, the theory still retains its adherents (Wicklund and Brehm, 1976) and still continues to inspire laboratory experimentation (e.g., Wicklund and Frey, 1981; Devine and Ostrom, 1985).

Much of the disappointment with dissonance theory has stemmed from its failure to provide a satisfactory theory of the way in which people might change their attitudes. Inconsistency has not provided the key to attitude change, and, thereby, the hidden secret of persuasion, for which orators have always yearned. This suggests that the key question might not be to discover how the hypothesized motivation for consistency operates, but how people cope with inconsistency. If dissonance between beliefs does not seem to produce the predicted change of a belief, then we should look at the ways people resolve or dismiss inconsistency without any fundamental changes of belief. The present intention is not to pick over the remnants of old, unsuccessful experiments, nor to announce new results. In fact, the famous dissonance experiments will be ignored here. Instead of inconsistency being assumed to be a guaranteed catalyst for mental change, it will be argued that inconsistency itself can be controversial and a matter for dispute. Because of this, there are a number of strategies for coping with inconsistency which do not entail a change of belief, and which might, in fact, serve to strengthen existing beliefs.

In talking of psychological or rhetorical inconsistency, one is not talking of logical inconsistency as such, although some models of thinking have concentrated upon deduction (e.g., Abelson and Rosenberg, 1958; Kruglanski, 1980). Within the confines of logic, inconsistency is a relatively straightforward matter. If 'p' and 'not p' are both asserted, then there is an inconsistency, and it is assumed both cannot be simultaneously true. Thus, one or other of 'p' and 'not p' should be dismissed as false. However, as has been argued principally in Chapter 5, the realm of rhetoric is different from the realm of logic. Within a rhetorical context, both a statement and its negation can be reasonable, and therefore inconsistencies between our 'p's' and 'not p's' are not so easily identified and dispatched as untenable error. In the course of a debate an advocate may appear to assert both 'p' and 'not p', as did Protagoras when he claimed that virtue could and could not be taught. The critic will eagerly pounce upon such an opportunity, in order to declare that the advocate has been illogical. In so arguing, the critic is seeking to move the locus of the argument from rhetoric, where unambiguous refutation is so elusive, to logic, which offers the possibility of the knockout blow. However eagerly the critic may pounce upon the inconsistency, and however certain the laws of logic are, no certain rhetorical victory is guaranteed. Rhetoric need not cravenly submit to the invasion of logic. In fact, even if the content of logic is not for dispute, the strategy used by the critic, of arguing from logic, is itself a rhetorical strategy, whose application can be contested.

Therefore, the advocate who has offered an apparent contradiction to a grateful critic need not passively await retribution. In reply, an attempt can be made to turn back the argument from logic into what Perelman and Olbrechts-Tyteca call a 'quasi-logical' argument. The form of such a defence is simple. The claim can be made that 'p' essentially possesses two different meanings, and therefore different 'p's' are involved in the assertion of 'p' and 'not p'. Within the abstractions of logic, no such defence is possible, because the 'p's' have no meaning except as counters in a logical calculation. On the other hand, within rhetorical discourse the meanings of words, phrases, sentences and indeed whole speeches can alter from context to context. In consequence, there is ample scope to escape from the precision of logical criticism by insisting upon the rhetorical, rather than logical, context of the debate.

An example of such a defence to a criticism of inconsistency is to be found in the section of the *Protagoras* in which, for the sake of argumentation, Socrates and Protagoras appear to swap roles (339–47). Protagoras becomes the Socratic questioner, searching out the contradictions in the assumptions of his fellow interlocutor. Socrates, on the other hand, becomes the Protagorean, justifying inconsistencies and wriggling rhetorically out of every logical trap. They are discussing a poem by Simonides, in which the poet had written that "Hard it is on the one hand to become/ A good man truly". Protagoras gets Socrates to assent that the poem is both "beautiful and well written" (339c). And would Socrates consider a poem to be beautiful and well written if it were contradictory? Of course not, replies Socrates. Then Protagoras proceeds to argue that there is a hidden contradiction in the poem. He quotes from a passage in which Simonides criticizes the sage, Pitticus, for saying that it is hard "to be noble". First Simonides is saying one thing and then the reverse: "How can a man be thought consistent when he says both these things?" asks Protagoras (339D). In fact, it was really Socrates's consistency that Protagoras was challenging.

Socrates's first reaction is to defend himself by defending Simonides. He denies that the two passages are inconsistent, although it is clear that he inwardly fears that Protagoras may have been correct. Having committed himself to the denial, Socrates has then to search for reasons to reconcile the two passages. He turns to Prodicus for advice, and Plato admitted that "this was a move to gain time to consider what the poet meant" (339E). Prodicus is famed for his ability to distinguish between the meanings of words which everyone else holds to be synonymous. By skilful particularization, Prodicus was always able to come up with distinctions, just as Abbé Girard in the eighteenth century claimed that all synonyms are in actuality "distinguishable from one another by some relative idea or quality which is peculiar to each of them" (*A New Guide to Eloquence*, p. vi). With Prodicus's help Socrates manages to distinguish between the two passages. The crucial difference, he argues, lies in the words 'to be' and 'to become'. In the one passage it is suggested that it is hard to *become* a virtuous man, whilst in the other it is not hard to *be* virtuous. Socrates explains away the inconsistency by asserting that when someone has succeeded in the hard task of becoming virtuous, it is not so difficult to remain virtuous. In other words, the 'p' and 'not p' are using different p's, which slide gracefully past each other without the crash of contradiction.

Protagoras remains unconvinced by Socrates's shift from logic to rhetoric: "Your justification, Socrates, involves a greater error than the one it sets out to defend" (340D). However, Protagoras finds himself displaced from logical to rhetorical territory, as he and Socrates wrangle on inconsequentially about the meanings of various words. Socrates playfully shifts the essence of a few categories, suggesting that the Spartans are the true, but hidden, Sophists of the world. Then Socrates attempts to put an end to this whole line of argument by dismissing the matter as trivial: "Conversation about poetry reminds me too much of the wine-parties of second-rate and commonplace people." Logic has little defence against that sort of remark.

Socrates's case was helped by the fact that the two passages to be reconciled contained different wording: one used 'to be' and the other 'to become'. The task of reconciliation does not depend upon such happy accidents, but it can always be argued that the same word means different things in the two passages. The basis of this rhetorical task is, then, to find differences between two apparently similar instances. To use the language of the previous chapter, one might say that some feature or features must be particularized, in order to locate the two instances in different 'feature spaces'. Then it can be argued that the two particulars are essentially different and should be slotted into different categories. That being so, there is no essential contradiction between upholding one instance and rejecting the other. As Prodicus and Girard showed, and as linguistic philosophers have done in our century, if one searches hard enough for linguistic distinctions, it is possible to discover them.

The rhetorical task for Socrates, therefore, depended upon finding reasons for shifting an apparent similarity to an essential dissimilarity. Sometimes this task is aided by making a contrast between levels of reality. Two things may appear similar, but at another, more important, level they differ. The exact spatial location of this new level does not matter: it may be basically, at bottom, below and deeper than the ordinary level, or it may belong to a higher conceptual order, above run-of-the-mill appearances. Whether up or down, the new level is the preferred location of the essence of the matter. The advocate, faced by the charge of inconsistency, then can argue for the choice of this essential level.

The same strategy can form the basis of intellectual study, rather than disputatious banter. Moreover, the task of reconciling contradictions may not emerge, as it did for Socrates, from the momentum of an argument. Instead it might be culturally determined, as the advocates of a particular perspective set themselves the task of such reconciliation. Examples of this will, it is hoped, show that under these circumstances, contradiction *per se* does not threaten belief, but that the rhetorical tasks posed by inconsistency may serve to strengthen belief by making it more reasonable.

Socrates and Protagoras are arguing about the correct exegesis of the poem. Although Socrates might affect to believe that such matters are best confined to second-rate wine parties, matters of exegesis form an important part of theological interpretation, and, as Northrop Frye has shown, of Western scholarship in general. The believer may be set the task of reconciling apparent contradictions in holy texts. Just as Socrates found himself assuming a higher, or deeper, unity in the poem of Simonides, so the believer will assume the essential harmony of the sacred work. As Maimonides said of contradictions between biblical passages, "a contradiction appears to have been said, whereas there is no contradiction" (*Guide of the Perplexed*, p. 17). The task for the exegete, then, is to show the underlying, or overlying, unity.

The Talmud is full of instances which quote seemingly contradictory texts from the Bible and then explain away the inconsistency. The format is roughly the same, and corresponds to the structure of Socrates's defence of Simonides. A few examples should be sufficient to show the pattern. For instance, a contradiction is mentioned between the verse about "visiting the iniquity of the fathers upon the children" (Exodus, xxxiii, 13) and that from Deuteronomy "neither shall the children be put to death for the fathers" (xxiv, 16). A statement of difference then settles the apparent contradiction:

> And a contradiction was pointed out between these two verses, and the answer was given that there is no contradiction. The one verse deals with children who continue in the same course as their fathers, and the other verse with children who do not continue in the course of their fathers. (*Berakoth*, 7a)

> R. Papa mentioned the following contradiction: It is written, 'God is angry every day' (Psalms, vii, 12), while it is also written 'Who could stand before His anger?' (Nehemiah, i, 6). But there is really no contradiction; the latter refers to an individual, the former to men collectively. (*Avodah Zarah*, 4a)

> R. Hama b. Hanina pointed to another contradiction: Scripture says 'Fury is not in me' (Isaiah, xxvii, 4), yet it also says 'The Lord revengeth and is furious!' (Nehemiah, i, 2). But there really is no contradiction: the former refers to Israel, the latter to idolators. (*Avodah Zarah*, 4a)

All these resolutions of inconsistency occur in a social context of limited rhetoric. Cultural norms have imposed a one-sided task: inconsistencies are to be uncovered and then resolved without an advocate of the counter-position that resolutions are impossible. True enough, there are debates between rabbinical scholars about the merits of various reconciliations, and even jealousies between rival scholars. However, within this cultural tradition, no one adopts the counter-position, to argue against the assumption that there is an underlying unity to the seemingly contradictory texts. Thus, no one is motivated, as Protagoras was in the debate about Simonides, to argue that the inconsistencies are really inconsistencies, regardless of the attempts at resolution.

The Talmudic examples illustrate that, once the rhetorical task has been set, a requisite pattern of differences can, with knowledge and witcraft, be found and justified. These differences then function to confirm the original belief, because they represent reasons for holding that belief. A cognitive theorist might describe the process in terms of adapting schemata, in order to provide the believer with self-confirming evidence (Snyder, 1981a and 1981b). Certainly social psychologists have often described cognitive processes which search for distinctions in order to remove inconsistencies. Rosenberg and Abelson (1960), in an early essay on inconsistency theory, perceptively discussed the 'micro-processes' for reducing dissonance. They suggested that, in order to take the psychological sting out of inconsistency, distinctions sometimes have to be made, with the result that two potentially inconsistent thoughts are cognitively insulated from each other. Similarly Taylor and Crocker (1981) speak of the "differentiation" of schemata, which creates new and neutralizing slots for inconsistent information. The Talmudic examples, and Socrates's defence of Simonides, involve a search for a distinction, which enables the two halves of the alleged inconsistency to be placed in non-antagonistic schemata, or sub-schemata. In addition, there is experimental evidence to suggest that the successful search for distinctions should reinforce, rather than undermine, the original beliefs. Role-playing experiments have shown that if one invents one's own arguments when required to defend a position, then one is likely to be persuaded by the truth of one's own argumentative creations (King and Janis, 1956; Greenwald, 1970). It is as if one feels particularly attached to one's own cognitive discoveries. Even Socrates, who initially seems sceptical of the position which he needs to defend, finds reasons for defending Simonides. To the extent that he finds reasons for his original position, it becomes that bit more reasonable. Similarly, each time Prodicus and Girard were able to produce distinctions between words commonly thought to be interchangeable, they must have become more convinced of the correctness of their linguistic theories about the essential uniqueness of words. In this way, the advocate may be set rhetorical tasks which lead to the production of new insights. Consequently, the advocate becomes more convinced, as the mind is withdrawn even further from other possibilities, and is directed towards new, and confirming, discoveries.

There is one difference between the Talmudic examples and the picture of the one-sided advocate of cognitive social psychology. The cognitive information processor supposedly avoids the problems of inconsistency wherever possible, although experimental evidence reveals that this is an exaggeration (e.g., Wicklund and Frey, 1981). In the Talmudic examples, we see the deliberate search for inconsistencies, just as Girard's *A New Guide to Eloquence* challenges his own linguistic theory by taking on the most similar of synonyms. The art of witcraft is not confined to the resolution of such puzzles, but immense scholarship is used to discover new inconsistencies. In this context, inconsistency is neither avoided, nor is it feared. Instead, it provides a medium through which cultural knowledge is advanced and new insights are gained.

The thinker to emerge from these examples is not the cognitive miser or the totalitarian, who desperately wards off all the psychological threats posed by the outside world to a fragile sense of self. Rather, the thinker is the student and scholar, working within a cultural tradition which is enriched by every new insight. The semantic investigations of Prodicus and Girard lead to greater awareness of the complexity of language, and the Talmudic scholars elaborate upon the infinite meanings within their texts. The distinctions made by these scholars are not psychological divisions made in the structure of the mind itself, but are distinctions in the sort of knowledge which can constitute the content of the mind. The exegetical distinctions resemble those made by social psychological theorists when their experimental evidence demonstrates that the supposedly general laws of psychological functioning are not so general. Situations in which a given psychological effect occurs must be distinguished from those in which the same effect does not materialize. In this way, the uncovering of unnoticed distinctions can represent a genuine, but nonetheless rhetorically contestable, discovery. Moreover, the process of discovering and explaining such inconsistencies is potentially infinite, for each discovered difference can provide the basis for further puzzles and more complex analyses. There is an infinity of situations, which can be distinguished by the experimentalist, and there is no end to the study of the holy texts.

In the debate between Socrates and Protagoras, there is no agreement about the hidden unity of the apparent discrepancies. In fact, it is the existence of such a unity which is at stake. Protagoras's comment, quoted in the previous chapter, that everything resembles everything else to a degree can be taken as a criticism of Prodicus's extreme theory of differences. Socrates's exegetical discoveries are rejected by Protagoras, who resists all Socratic attempts to shift the 'feature space' of the quoted extracts from Simonides. The relocated essence is returned to its original place, and Socrates's inner consistency is still, according to Protagoras's arguments, an outer inconsistency. The arguments about essences soon become arguments about arguments. Moreover, these arguments turn into arguments about consistency and inconsistency. The disputants find themselves disagreeing about what should be counted as being consistent and what is inconsistent, in a way which would be completely untenable in the tight-fisted context of logic. In the face of such basic disagreements about the nature of consistency, no easy resolution is to be expected to the argument about arguments.

Dismissing contradiction

The examples in the previous section show how inconsistencies can be creatively resolved, if not to persuade the critic, then at least to the satisfaction of the advocate. If the advocate is criticized for being self-contradictory, as Socrates was by Protagoras, then with imagination the criticism can be countered by a justification which tries to explain away the contradiction. Under these circumstances, dissonance theorists would not predict any change of belief, although they may have underestimated the ease with which a skilled advocate can smooth over the bumps of contradiction. On the other hand, dissonance theory would suggest that change should occur if the advocate searches without success for a way to distinguish safely between two dangerously inconsistent thoughts. Dissonance, therefore, might be thought to occur when there has been a failure of witcraft. For example, the dissonance theorist would predict that, if Talmudic scholars constantly produced Biblical passages containing contrary messages, and if, just as regularly, they failed to provide justifications for an essential unity, then discomfort would follow, and the certainties of faith would start to become eroded. Theoretically, then, the link between changing beliefs and a failure to resolve inconsistency would still be maintained. Nevertheless, this view of dissonance may be too simple, and may neglect the complexities of the rhetorical context. In particular, it ignores the possibility that unresolved contradictions can be dismissed, rather than left muttering dangerously inside the advocate's psyche.

The simplest strategy for the dismissal of a contradiction, as opposed to its resolution, is to claim that an undiscovered resolution exists. While Socrates was turning to Prodicus, he knew at that moment of no resolution, but was sure that one was possible. In this case, there was an expectation that a resolution would be immediately procured. The expectation that the solution is on the way is not necessary to allay the alleged feelings of dissonance. If the resolution depends upon locating a deeper, and harmonizing, essence behind apparently inconsistent particulars, then a declaration of humility and an assertion of the reality of the deeper level can provide the basis for a dismissal. Theological scholars can preserve their faith by admitting the limitations of human, as opposed to divine, knowledge, and theological justifications can be given for such a position. Judaic lore recounts Moses asking God why the virtuous of this world sometimes suffered misfortune and the evil enjoyed happiness. God did not provide a full answer to this apparent instance of divine inconsistency. He admitted that, in addition to rewarding the pious, "I am gracious to those also who may have no claim to My graciousness." When Moses pushes for an explanation, he is told "Thou canst not grasp all the principles which I apply to the government of the world" (Ginzberg, 1947, vol. III, pp. 135–136). If even Moses is not permitted to understand the hidden truths which unite the inconsistencies of the world, then how can the ordinary, humble believer be expected to resolve all inconsistencies?

This line of argumentation can be observed in a modern rabbinical writer, faced with an apparent contradiction in the writings of the great sages of old. On the one hand, the sages had prohibited prophesying the date of the Messianic age, yet they themselves made forecasts, and erroneous ones at that. Does not such an inconsistency conflict with a belief in their greatness? Such a conclusion is not inevitable: "We dare not say that they were mistaken in the conventional sense of the word", for "we cannot even begin to fathom their greatness". The deeper harmony may be obscure to us, but "the luminaries from whose mouths we live must have had a basis for saying what they did" (Rabbi Nosson Scherman, 1979, p. 1). In other words, the resolution of the mystery is beyond our comprehension, but resolution there is.

Such a defence would appear, at first sight, to be particularly suited to theological or metaphysical disputes. The very subject matter suggests a division between levels of reality: the world of appearances is separated from a hidden and essentially truer level. Inconsistencies in the world of appearances then can be justified in terms of the ineffable nature of the underlying harmony. However, this type of argument is not confined to theology, but its structure can be seen in mundane disputes. As was mentioned in the last chapter, particularization can be used to distinguish levels of essentialness in ordinary categories. Some matters can be seen as more essential than others, and the 'true' instances of an issue can be distinguished from the 'bogus'. When criticized for being inconsistent, the advocate can make a division between levels of discourse, which firmly places the criticism of inconsistency on a low level. If the levels of discourse are levels of importance, then the criticism can be categorized as trivial and dismissed accordingly.

This point bears directly on Festinger's theory of cognitive dissonance. According to Festinger, sometimes it is not possible to alter either of two inconsistent cognitive elements. In such cases, it is possible to reduce "the total dissonance...by reducing the *importance* of existing dissonance" (1957, p. 22). This strategy involves "reducing the importance of the whole area of cognitive content in which dissonance exists" (p. 271). Festinger admitted that he had little evidence to show how this might occur, although it is an important addition to the theory of dissonance. Nor does Festinger offer examples, although Socrates's high-minded dismissal of discussions about poetry as appropriate to second-rate drinking parties would count, had the philosopher not already extracted himself from the contradiction. On the other hand, it is not difficult to conceive examples where Festinger's process will not occur. The rabbinical scholar, puzzled by inconsistencies in the writings of great sages, is unlikely to dismiss suddenly the whole business of the Messianic Age as being of little import. What Festinger does not take into account is the rhetorical context of inconsistency. If what counts is the criticism of inconsistency, rather than any notion of absolute inconsistency, then dissonance can be avoided without reducing the importance of the whole "area of cognitive content". In fact, it might be wiser to stress the importance of the whole topic, for what needs to be downgraded is the criticism, at least in relation to the general topic. The criticism alleging contradiction must be seen as existing on an inappropriately trivial level, not befitting a topic of such importance. If this strategic move is made, an inconsistency, or more precisely, a criticism of inconsistency, can be dismissed unanswered.

Two examples of classical debates will be given, and in each a disputant, accused of inconsistency, distinguishes between levels of discourse. The escape from inconsistency is then effected by condemning the criticism to the trivial level. The first example, that between Socrates and Euthyphro, concerns religious issues, but its argumentative structure is not dependent upon the subject matter. The second example, a dispute between Alcibiades and Pericles, is very much a secular matter. Despite the differences in subject matter, and, indeed, in the atmosphere of the two disputes, there is an underlying similarity in the way Euthyphro and Pericles avoid changing opinions in the face of unanswered criticisms of inconsistency.

In the Platonic dialogue *Euthyphro*, we find Socrates tying in dialectical knots an earnest, but unimaginative, religious believer. Euthyphro prides himself on his piety, believing it pious to prosecute his own father for the manslaughter of a slave. Socrates demands a definition of piety. Euthyphro, who has long believed in his own undefined piety, is forced, by the demand, to particularize one aspect of a massively complex concept. He offers the sentiment that "piety is what all the gods love" (10). This is just what Socrates needed to show off his dazzling skills of philosophical cross-examination. Why do the gods love piety? Do they love piety because piety is pious? Or do they love it because it is loved by the gods? Euthyphro wilts under the dialectical onslaught, and soon stands contradicting his own definition. Nevertheless, the demonstration of the contradiction does not end matters, but off goes Euthyphro again trying to justify his basic belief in the divine nature of piety. And off goes Socrates in relentless pursuit. Whichever path Euthyphro takes, he comes back to his assertion that 'piety is what the gods love'. All Socrates's arguments that this belief is contradictory are not sufficient to shake Euthyphro. No matter what strange routes Socrates leads Euthyphro down, back like a homing pigeon comes the pious believer to his simple assertion. In the end Socrates declares that "we shall have to start our inquiry at the beginning again" (15).

Throughout the discussion, Euthyphro holds firmly to the belief that there is a way out of the verbal maze which Socrates has constructed. When Socrates asks Euthyphro to spell out what it is that the gods derive from human piety, Euthyphro struggles, until he dismisses his questioner's objections: "It would be too heavy a task for you to learn in detail how all these matters stand" (13). At the beginning of the dialogue Socrates had challenged Euthyphro to prove that the gods approved his decision to prosecute his father. Euthyphro had replied that "it would probably be no light undertaking" but "of course I *could* demonstrate it quite plainly" (9, emphasis in quoted translation). Perhaps by the end of the dialogue, the undertaking had seemed far heavier. Perhaps too Euthyphro was doubting his own strength to carry such a burdensome undertaking. What remained unchanged from start to end was the belief that the contradictions exposed by Socrates did not really matter: they could be answered, if only by the gods themselves.

Socrates and Euthyphro part on good terms, although each is a little puzzled by the other. The debate between Alcibiades and Pericles, as recounted by Xenophon, is much more waspish. The two are discussing the nature of law, and Pericles is arguing that all laws should be obeyed. The twenty-year-old Alcibiades shows himself to be far nimbler in witcraft than his venerable opponent. Soon Pericles is contradicting himself. Like Euthyphro he does not abandon his advocacy when the contradictions are exposed; he does make some concessions, such as admitting that the laws of a tyrant are not really laws, and therefore need not be obeyed. Pericles does not downgrade the importance of the issue being discussed. Instead, he downgrades the criticism of contradiction. Patronizingly, he replies to

Alcibiades: "I, when I was your age was very acute at such disquisitions; for we used to meditate and argue about such subjects as you now appear to meditate" (*Memorabilia of Socrates*, I, ii, 46). Alcibiades's disquisition, and thus his criticisms, were all rather immature, and Pericles claims that had he been younger he would have been more than a match for Alcibiades. The young man, however, is determined to have the last word. Instead of sliding the whole discussion into the category of immaturity, he prefers to particularize the mental agility of the young: "Would therefore that I had conversed with you, Pericles, at the time when you were most acute in discussing such topics!" (I, ii, 46).

Pericles's assumption, fiercely resisted by Alcibiades, is that under better conditions all the inconsistencies would be resolved. In this way, the present level of discourse is contrasted unfavourably with an idealized level, which Pericles, had he been younger and more energetic, would have surely attained. Similarly Euthyphro would have been able to explain everything clearly, had there been time and had Socrates not kept interrupting. Perhaps the ideal debate would have to await another world, when earthly contradictions would be divinely resolved. Whether the refutation would come in the next world, or would have been possible in the world that has passed, the assumption is the same: under ideal conditions of discourse, the criticisms will be exposed, and a higher, and harmonious, level of discourse will prevail.

The appeal to a higher level of discourse is not restricted to those answering the charge of contradiction. The appeal can also be made by those making the charge of contradiction. Clever resolutions can be dismissed as 'mere rhetoric', or what Philo of Alexandria called the "jugglery with words" (*The Worse Attacks the Better*, p. 225). Aristophanes parodied Socrates in *The Clouds* for his clever talk. Socrates, "the high priest of subtle bilge", is seen to be defending a physical theory of the weather, whilst Strepsiades attributes the natural elements to the bodily functions of Zeus. Every contradiction which Strepsiades raises in the physical interpretation of weather, Socrates brushes aside with an impressive answer about hydroelectric matters and such like. Strepsiades remains unimpressed and he turns Gorgias's proud boast into a criticism of Socrates: "You've an answer for everything" (I, i, 2). The implication is clear: the answer for everything is no real answer. Socrates's replies are to be placed upon a lower level of discourse than the question, to which they are essentially not proper answers. Strepsiades can continue to know that rainfall is Zeus urinating through a sieve, and that thunder is the sound of the great god's flatulence.

Such disputes turn into disputes about levels of discourse. One party's location of the essence of the matter is to be disputed by the other. How to classify the replies and questions is a matter for contention, as the disputants argue about arguments. Again, there is no agreement about what should count as a contradiction, nor what represents a satisfactory resolution. So long as advocates hold firm to their respective images of discourse and to their respective locations of contradictions, there can be no way of resolving the contradictions between them. Each, then, can dismiss the charges of inconsistency made by the other.

Rhetorical nature of attitudes

The strategies for arguing about consistency are of direct relevance to one of the central concepts within social psychology: the concept of attitudes. Festinger's theory of cognitive dissonance is a theory about attitudes and why they might be changed. The theory stresses that attitudes are altered in order that the individual may have a consistent outlook on the world. In particular, the theory predicts that if there is a discrepancy between our actions and our attitudes, it is the attitudes which will be changed, so as to be brought into line with the actions. Just as it was suggested that the notion of consistency possesses a rhetorical dimension, so too does the notion of an attitude. Certainly within the history of social psychology, the notion of an 'attitude' has been a troublesome one. Different psychologists have offered different definitions. Some have argued that our attitudes reflect our emotions, whilst others stress that our attitudes are habits of thinking. For other psychologists our attitudes are neurological states of readiness. All these psychologists will dispute with those others who see our attitudes as abstractions dreamt up by 'attitude theorists' (for a discussion of the concept of 'attitude' in the history of social psychology, see Jaspars and Fraser, 1984). It is not the present intention to enter into these intricate debates, except by way of pointing to the rhetorical context of attitudes.

Although social psychologists have been much concerned to provide exact, and official-sounding, definitions of 'attitude', the concept seems to be one of those which gives little trouble in everyday discourse. In everyday life, we take it for granted that we all have 'attitudes'. We would hardly be perplexed, if we were stopped on the street by a well-dressed stranger who wished to enquire about our 'attitudes'. We might not have time to reply to the questions, but it would be a strange response to say "I'm sorry, but I don't possess any attitudes at all." We would have a rough idea of the sorts of questions which might be asked. The stranger might ask about our views on political issues, or on moral or religious matters, or about our preferred ways of spending money. The vast compendia published by Gallup International and by other opinion samplers testify to the willingness of modern pedestrians to reveal their attitudes on wide ranges of topics to strangers (i.e. Gallup, 1976 and 1980).

The very familiarity of the word 'attitude', and our own plentiful possession of attitudes, makes it hard to appreciate just how modern a concept 'attitude' is. The present sense of the word has only arisen in the past hundred and fifty years. This is the period which has seen the emergence of mass media, mass politics and dictators, who like to believe that they represent the attitudes of their subjects. In the seventeenth century, when there were no opinion samplers with clipboards to bother pedestrians, the word 'attitude' was a technical term referring to the bodily poses of figures in paintings. By one of those odd quirks of etymology which fill the history of language, the meaning has been inverted, with the emphasis shifting from the posture of our bodies to the cast of our mind. And nowadays the term presents a controversial problem for psychologists, rather than for the teachers of different schools of portraiture.

Although social psychologists might disagree amongst themselves about the psychological processes behind our attitudes, they tend to agree about one aspect, which has important rhetorical implications. Attitudes refer to evaluations which are for or against things, issues, people or whatever. If a person dislikes the government, then psychologists are liable to say that such a person possesses a negative attitude towards the government. A number of social psychologists have suggested that the evaluative aspect of an attitude is its most important, or essential, component. Martin Fishbein argues that it is "only the evaluation or 'affective' component", which is "measured and treated by researchers as the essence of attitudes" (1967, p. 480). According to Melvin Manis, "attitudes are predominantly a matter of affective evaluation" (1985, p. 51).

Much of the psychological theorizing about attitudes has been concerned with the functions which the attitude might serve for the individual. For example, the affective aspects of an attitude might be linked to the individual's emotional and motivational needs. Alternatively, the attitude can be seen as a simplifying schema, which by its very simplifications gives the individual psychological security. This emphasis on what an attitude 'does' for the individual, however, ignores the social context of attitudes. As Palermino, Langer and McGillis have commented, "present day definitions of attitude effectively ignore the role of context" (1984, p. 181), and it is for this reason that a number of contemporary social psychologists hope to replace the concept of attitude by that of 'social representation' (Farr, 1977; 1984a and 1984b; Moscovici, 1981, 1982 and 1984).

One aspect of the wider context, which is largely ignored by psychologists who concentrate upon the individual's motives, is the rhetorical or argumentative context of attitudes. It can be asserted that all attitudes are situated within a wider argumentative context. This becomes apparent if we ask what it is that individuals have attitudes about. Having asked this question, we can see that people hold attitudes about controversial issues and that there are certain issues on which people are expected, or are liable, to take pro or con stances. Whether the topic is political, moral, religious, commercial, or whatever, an attitude refers to a stance on a matter of public debate and disagreement. In other words, an attitude represents an evaluation of a controversial issue or sometimes a controversial individual, such as a president or a queen. Therefore, the social context of attitudes is the context of controversy.

The controversial aspect of attitudes implies that not all beliefs are attitudes. Within a given society, there will be certain matters which are controversial, and others which are so obvious that no-one seriously questions them. About the latter sort of issue, one does not hold attitudes. In this way the uncontroversial beliefs of common-sense differ from those which are attitudes, for the common-sense belief is not an explicitly pro or con stance, which exists in controversial opposition to the contrary stance. Our opinion-sampler is not likely to ask modern pedestrians to locate their belief on a carefully graded scale about the issue of whether rainfall is the sieved urine of Zeus. In fact, someone troubling passers-by with such a question is liable to find themself removed officially and forcibly from the public highways. Instead of asking questions about issues on which no member of the public bothers to take a stance, the opinion sampler will be enquiring about matters of controversy. Of course, what is common-sensical and what is a matter of controversy can change within a community. For example, it was once common-sense knowledge that humans and apes had different origins. In the mid nineteenth century, in the wake of the Darwinian brouhaha, the whole matter suddenly became a loud controversy in which one would be expected to have attitudes. Slowly the controversy receded and evolution became as common-sensical as the roundness of the earth. Recently, however, there has been detectable movement in the reverse direction, as 'creationists' try to convince us that Darwinian theory is just an attitude. The creationists will happily mark their disagreement on the furthest point on any scale of evolutionary attitudes, whilst the scientifically minded will argue that, as this is a scientifically proven matter, it is not one on which persons properly should have attitudes (Handberg, 1984).

The implication is that attitudes are more than visceral responses for or against a stimulus. They are stances on matters of public debate. That being so, the possession of an attitude indicates a statement of disagreement as much as of agreement, and it signifies an implicit willingness to enter into controversy. In consequence, we can expect the possessors of attitudes to justify their stances, to criticize competing views, and generally to argue about the issues. All such criticisms and justifications are not, from a rhetorical perspective, extraneous matters tacked upon some basic movement of the gut, which constitutes the core of the attitude. On the contrary, the criticisms and justifications form an integral part of the attitude, for, without the argumentative context, there would be no attitudes. McGuire's (1964) experiments on persuasion are a good illustration of this point. McGuire wished to test subjects' resistance to arguments criticizing matters which they had never heard disputed previously. He found that subjects possessed few, if any, argumentative defences for 'cultural truisms' which had always been taken for granted, such as the desirability of cleaning one's teeth. Since such matters had not been issues of contention, the subjects did not possess the rhetorical wherewithal to repel the unexpected argumentative attack. One might say that, lacking such justifications, they did not possess attitudes about these unconsidered truisms. However, McGuire was able to demonstrate that, under the pressure of attack, defences, and thereby attitudes, can be easily formed, at least with a little help from the experimenter. Thus, in the experimental situation, the issue developed from being one of common-sense to one of controversy, on which attitudinal stances could be taken (see also the experiment of Szybillo and Heslin, 1973).

In psychological theory, the possession of an attitude implies more than that a stance has been taken in response to a particular stimulus. The notion of attitude suggests some sort of organization of beliefs, reactions, justifications and criticisms. There is, in short, a degree of generality to the concept of attitude. To say that we have a strong favourable attitude towards X implies that we will react favourably as, and when, we encounter instances of X. For example, Aristophanes's Socrates in *Clouds* possesses a general attitude favouring scientific views over theological ones. Not only does Socrates prefer an electrical explanation of rainfall to the common-sense view that it is Zeus's urine, but he also denies that lightning and thunder represent other eruptions of Zeus's bodily functions. Strepsiades, of course, has the contrary attitude upon this matter of controversy, and takes contrary stances on the specific questions. In this way, the general attitudes which Socrates and Strepsiades possess are linked to more specific beliefs and arguments.

If attitudes possess generality, then it can be said that the social psychological concept of an attitude rests upon notions of consistency. The general attitude implies some sort of consistency to the more specific beliefs and reactions. De Fleur and Westie, in their classic discussion of the concept, bring out this assumed link between attitudes and consistency. They distinguished between two concepts of attitude: the notion of an attitude as a "latent process" and the "probabilistic concept" of an attitude. When an attitude is considered as a "latent process", it is assumed to be a hidden force ("an unknown something") which generates our responses to specific stimuli. For example, Zimbardo and his colleagues assert that attitudes are "the core of our likes or dislikes for certain people, groups, situations, objects and intangible ideas". As such, attitudes, like Platonic essences, are beyond the reach of direct experience and "are thus internal private events whose existence we infer from our own introspection or from some behavioural evidence" (1977, p. 20). This notion of an attitude implies a degree of consistency: the hidden 'events' generate the more public psychological manifestations, and do so according to a meaningful and consistent pattern.

The "probabilistic concept" of an attitude also implies consistency, although in a much more direct way. Instead of implying that the attitude is the underlying cause of consistency, the probabilistic concept labels any observed consistency as constituting the attitude. Thus, according to this concept, Socrates's consistent rejection of the various aspects of The Zeus Theories of Weather constitutes his attitude. Had Socrates wavered on the issue, for example giving credence to rain as Olympian urine, but not to thunder as divine farting, we would feel less justified in ascribing a general attitude to him. Although the probabilistic concept denies that there is a hidden psychological entity called an attitude, it does resemble the 'latent process' concept in two respects: it assumes that an attitude possesses generality, and it also assumes that specifics, whether beliefs, reactions or whatever, are related in a consistent manner to this generality.

Despite these assumptions, attitude theorists have often been faced with evidence that there is frequently an inconsistency between general attitudes and specific beliefs. Often people claim to hold a general attitude, but some of their specific sentiments and actions are hard to square with that attitude. For example, racial bigots, who hold fast to general views about racial inferiority, can develop friendships with individual members of the groups against which they are bigoted. Rae Sherwood in *The Psychodynamics of Race* has detailed the instance of 'Mrs Chattoway', whose appalling prejudices against Asians did not prevent isolated acts of kindness, and even friendship, with individual Asians. On the other hand, those who are theoretically liberal can show some decidedly illiberal reactions: for example, Adorno *et al.* reported the "Genuine Liberal", who would not countenance marriage to a black person because she did not like dark skin (e.g., 1950, pp. 781ff; see Billig, 1982, chapter five, for a discussion of this case).

Above all, social psychologists have been discomforted to find that general attitudes are poor predictors of people's actions (Deutscher, 1973; Schuman and Johnson, 1976). People will often report to opinion samplers that they have strong general views on a particular issue, but in specific circumstances they seem to act in the opposite manner. Socrates may have announced to his friends at the boozy banquet that he believed in female almost-equality, but his actions towards the long suffering Xanthippe hardly squared with this general attitude. Even in the last moments of life, Xanthippe was nowhere near the equal of Socrates's philosophical friends. Plato recounts what happened when Socrates's friends arrived for their final visit to the philosopher's condemned cell:

> As soon as Xanthippe saw us she broke out into the sort of remark you would expect from a woman: 'Oh, Socrates, this is the last time that you and your friends will be able to talk together!' Socrates looked at Crito. 'Crito', he said, 'someone had better take her home.' Some of Crito's servants led her away crying hysterically. (*Phaedo*, 59E)

Let us assume that Socrates had been stopped in the street by an Athenian opinion sampler, who had asked him whether he agreed strongly, tended to agree, etc. with the statement that 'women are in no way inferior to men, except in bodily strength and perhaps steadiness of judgement'. Let us also assume that Socrates had 'tended to agree'. In reality, he would have probably been the dread of all opinion samplers – the awkward customer who objects at length to the phrasing of the question. The problem for the hypothetical ancient Athenian social psychologist would have been that the tendency to believe in female almost-equality did not seem to produce, or even be consistent with, Socrates's specific actions.

Faced with discrepancies between expressed attitudes and actions, some social psychologists have recommended that attitude researchers should avoid asking general questions. Ajzen and Fishbein (1980), for example, have suggested that researchers should turn their attention from 'attitudes in general', and that they should look at attitudes towards specific actions, and the perceived social desirability of such actions. As Ajzen has written, "attitude towards a behaviour – together with perceived normative pressures or subjective norms – determines a person's intention and thus his actual performance of the behaviour" (1982, p. 10). Therefore, if the Athenian social psychologists were interested in predicting Socrates's behaviour towards women, they should not ask general questions about female almost-equality. Instead a more accurate picture would have been obtained if their attitudinal surveys had contained items concerning the removal of wailing wives from prison cells, in order that important philosophical discussions could proceed uninterrupted. Socrates's answer to that question should have provided an accurate predictor of his final actions.

Ajzen and Fishbein's recommendations are designed to improve the predictive power of attitude surveys. In effect, their strategy for research is to narrow the gap between general attitudes and specific actions, by making the attitudinal statement as specific as possible. However, from a rhetorical perspective, there may be more to be gained by forgetting prediction and by concentrating upon that gap between the general attitude and the specific action. Instead of seeing the gap as a methodological weakness, to be eradicated by superior, and more precise, scales of measurement, it should be treated as something interesting in its own right. The person who professes support for democracy or for female equality, but who acts or speaks in undemocratic or discriminatory ways when it comes to specific situations, is no artifact.

It can be assumed that we all, from Socrates down to unthinking bigots, are prepared to defend some such general statements, or, in other words, to admit to the possession of attitudes. However there is no reason for supposing that we can conveniently slot all the messy particularities of the world into our general attitudinal categories. We might assume that no one is perfectly consistent, or, to be more precise, above possible criticisms, on this score. Moses even suggests that God was inconsistent with Himself, when He sought to administer particular punishment to Israel in the face of His own general recommendation to "turn into sweetness that which is bitter" (*Exodus Rabbah*, XLIII, 3). The results from the studies linking attitudes to actions reveal that most people can be criticized on the grounds that their general statements often appear to be inconsistent with their actions, and also with other beliefs which they might espouse. The evidence from cognitive consistency theory suggests that we need not crumple in the face of such criticism, beating our breasts and asking absolution from our attitudes. Instead we can argue back and attempt to justify ourselves, by widening the inevitable gap between particulars and general categories. As such, the problem of the inconsistency between attitudes and behaviour is not a methodological artifact. It is a problem with a rhetorical dimension, which can be examined in the context of arguments, and, in particular, in the context of arguments about consistency itself.

Attitudes and arguments

One might expect that general attitudes would not be good predictors of specific actions, if it is not difficult to justify seeming inconsistencies. Should criticisms, whether from outside sources or from the voice of conscience, be met with justifications, then there should not be the pressure to change the attitudes or recant the controversial action. Instead, those facing the criticism of inconsistency can become like De Quincey's advocate, presenting one-sidedly the arguments for their own essential consistency, in order to give a good account of themselves. As Scott and Lyman have so clearly argued, accounts are forms of justification, which aim to protect the identity of the person offering the account. Scott and Lyman, however, go further than the present analysis, by suggesting that accounts are successful in their aims. According to them, accounts "are a crucial element in the social order since they prevent conflicts from arising by verbally bridging the gap between action and expectation" (1968, p. 46). The present analysis, in contrast, suggests that the accounts can be controversial, rather than being devices which prevent controversy. In fact, accounts may stand more chance of convincing the accounters themselves than they do of persuading external critics, who are likely to counter with alternative accounts of the accounts.

If attitudes are seen as general statements and actions are specific instances, then the controversial relations between attitudes and actions will be instances of the relations between categories and particulars. Therefore, the strategies which might be used to avoid categorizing a particular in a rhetorically disadvantageous way will be used to justify apparent inconsistencies between attitudes and actions. In the previous chapter, the controversial aspects of categorization were discussed in terms of arguments about particulars, arguments about categories, and arguments about arguments. These same types of arguments can be observed in justifications, or accounts, which seek to separate a general attitude from a specific action, so that the action and attitude are not seen to collide with each other. Therefore, it is possible, at least theoretically, to distinguish *arguments about particular actions*, *arguments about general attitudes*, and *arguments about arguments about attitudes*.

Arguments about particular actions

One strategy to avoid the charge of inconsistency is to argue that the specific action should not *really*, or essentially, be classified as an instance of the sort of actions which the attitude covers. This strategy does not place the attitude initially in the centre of controversy, but it focusses on the nature, or essence, of the action. However, arguments about particulars so easily develop into arguments about general categories and their boundaries. For example, a strategy of particularization can be invoked, in order to argue that there are special features surrounding the action which separate it from the general attitudinal category. As Scott and Lyman argue, an excuse can be made which concedes that the action should be categorized as wrongful, but special mitigating circumstances are offered as the wrongdoer pleads for mercy or understanding". In classical rhetoric, this is the strategy of *concessio*, and Cicero's classification of three types of *concessio* – ignorance, necessity and accident – resembles Scott and Lyman's forms of excuse (*De Inventione*, II, xxxi). An excuse suggests that the offending action is not really similar to the genuinely offensive, inconsistent action, from which the special mitigating circumstances are always missing.

Scott and Lyman distinguish an excuse from a justification. Both these types of account can use the strategy of the special case, although the justification does not concede the wrongfulness of the action: "Justifications recognize a general sense in which the act in question is impermissible; but claim that the particular occasion permits or requires the very act" (1968, p. 51). We can admit that a particular sort of action runs counter to our attitudes, but, for reasons which must be given, we argue that the present act is very different: its essence suggests that it should not be categorized under the forbidding attitude, but that it should be classed very differently. If we pay attention to the special features of a case, then witcraft can prevent the automatic dominance of the general attitudinal category: "Mindful functioning... is more likely to result in attitude-behaviour inconsistency because the unique features of the context are actively considered and cause attitude variability" (Palermino, Langer and McGillis, 1984, p. 186).

A possible example of this strategy might be contained in the classic study showing that attitudes do not necessarily lead directly to action. When the social psychologist, LaPiere, travelled across the United States in the early 1930s with a young Chinese couple, he was met with unfailing courtesy by hoteliers and restaurant proprietors. However, when he wrote to the same hoteliers and restaurateurs about their willingness to accept Chinese guests, he received firm refusals. Even though the gap between the attitude and the action itself had been narrowed, almost to the point recommended by Fishbein and Ajzen, there was an apparent inconsistency between the hoteliers' actual actions and what they said, in theory, would be their actions. There was intolerance in theory and tolerance in the particular action.

The hoteliers, if accused of inconsistency, might have been able to mount a defence, which denied inconsistency by seeking to shift the essence of the action away from the expressed attitude. They might have claimed that they were, in principle, firmly opposed to serving Chinese guests, but LaPiere's friends were not just Chinese: they were, by all accounts, polite, respectable, educated, middle-class etc. In addition, when encountering the hoteliers, the Chinese couple also possessed more transient attributes. They were customers, or at least potential customers, who gave every indication of possessing that most important attribute of all – that of prompt bill-payers. In this situation, but not in the hypothetical letter LaPiere sent them, the Chinese dimension was not the essential one which cried out for special particularization: LaPiere's friends in person were primarily guests, who happened by chance to be Chinese, whereas by letter they were essentially Chinese, who wanted to be guests.

In order to justify their actions further, the hoteliers might use a further particularization. The general policy of refusing service to Chinese was not prejudice (it never is, according to the prejudiced!), but in their experience most Chinese are not polite, respectable, bill-paying customers ('well, not our personal experience exactly, but we did hear… '). In this way, the action and the general attitude might be given a justification, and the critic would find the argument drifting onto other matters. As has been observed by Schuman and Johnson, we have no real evidence about the state of mind of LaPiere's hoteliers: in particular, we would like to know "each proprietor's personal definition of the situation" (1976, p. 202), or which of the many features was particularized. It is possible that some of the hoteliers, if challenged about their inconsistency, might have attempted to argue that the respectable Chinese person was hardly Chinese at all: 'real' Chinese conform to a general stereotype, and it was 'that sort of Chinese', whom they wished to keep from their establishments. Such a strategy involves protecting the general attitude by particularizing the exception, and then recategorizing these exceptional particulars as polite people of foreign appearance, rather than as essentially Chinese (see Wilder, 1984, for an experiment which involved this sort of cognitive manoeuvre).

If the particular can be safely squeezed into a different attitudinal category by a redefinition of the situation, then the inconsistent attitude can be preserved, by being adjudged irrelevant to the special situation in hand. LaPiere approached the hoteliers directly without using any guileful witcraft. However, skilful manipulation can result in persuading others to shift the essence of their particular action. A variant of LaPiere's situation can be found in Boswell's *Life of Johnson*. Boswell had become captivated by the charm of John Wilkes, whose radicalism and moral dissolution were equally despised by Doctor Johnson. Under normal circumstances Johnson would never choose to share the company of such a fellow. Boswell, anxious to pit his two heroes together, knew he had to create propitious circumstances. He was aware that if he asked Johnson directly to dine with Wilkes at his publisher's house, Johnson "would have flown into a passion". Instead the particularities of dining with Wilkes must be shifted to a generalization, which Johnson would be unable to refuse. Boswell employed a tactic which modern sales representatives and social psychological theorists have called 'the foot-in-the-door technique', by which reasonable commitments are obtained as a prelude to a persuasive *coup de grâce* (e.g., Freedman and Fraser, 1966; Dejong, 1979).[1] Boswell asked Johnson whether he would accept an invitation to dine at Dr Dilly's house. Of course, he would. With his foot through the front door of Johnson's defences, Boswell sprung his trap: "Provided Sir, I suppose, that the company which he is to have is agreeable to you." The young Scotsman knew his prey well and Johnson replied with a huffy statement of principle: "Do you think I am so ignorant of the world as to imagine that I am to prescribe to a gentleman what company he wishes to keep at his table?" Even if that company were to include Mr Wilkes? Johnson's anger was rising nicely: "My dear friend, let us have no more of this. I am sorry to be angry with you; but really it is treating me strangely to talk to me as I could not meet any company occasionally" (1906, vol. II, p. 46). LaPiere's hoteliers would also not have been so ignorant of the world as to refuse hospitality to a couple who were essentially guests, but who happened to be Chinese. Similarly, Johnson was willing to meet someone who was essentially a guest, but who happened to be John Wilkes. Neither the hoteliers nor Johnson had any objections, so long as these exceptional occurrences did not occur too often.

It would appear that shifting the essence of the particular is an economical strategy when faced by the criticism of inconsistency. Westie (1965), in his study of The American Dilemma, found this to be a more popular strategy than shifting the essence of the general statement (to be discussed below). He found that whites almost uniformly agreed with general attitudes expressing fairness – 'Everyone in America should have equal opportunities to get ahead' – but many disagreed with applications of the principle, being, for example, unwilling 'to have a Negro as my supervisor in my place of work'. When confronted by this inconsistency, it was more common to qualify the particular than the general statement. Some respondents sought to find exceptions to the exception: "I guess it might be all right for a Negro to be a supervisor if he were unusually qualified." Such a line of argument might lead to a defence of the general principle, on the grounds that the typical (possibly proto-typical) black did not possess exceptional enough qualifications to satisfy the prejudiced white. Vilfredo Pareto, who well understood the rhetorical features of justification, wrote that "human beings have a conspicuous tendency to paint a varnish of logic over their conduct" (1935, para. 154). It is not, strictly speaking, logic which is applied, and, in the case of the justifications for prejudice, the varnish seems to peel off of its own accord.

Arguments about general attitudes

An alternative strategy for dealing with the charge of inconsistency between attitudes and actions is to focus upon the essence of the attitude, rather than upon the action. In so doing, it is the essence of the attitude which becomes the matter of controversy. This does not mean exchanging a pro position for a con or vice versa. De Quincey's orator is not expected to swap sides in the course of self-justification. Of interest here are those debates in which disputants all assume the rightness of a particular general attitude, even to the extent of treating it as common-sense, but for which different interpretations are offered. Participants in such controversies may claim that their interpretation fits the essence of the attitude. In the course of such an argument, it may be possible to arrange the essence of the attitude in such a way that it seems to marry happily, but controversially, with the disputed actions.

This strategy is particularly useful if one wishes to suggest that one's personal interests and actions conform to general principles or attitudes. Hypocrisy may be involved, but it need not be, for we may genuinely come to believe that the essence of our attitude lies where our desires wish it to lie. Having been motivated to search for an essence, which previously might have remained uncontroversially vague, we may find it in a convenient location. In fact, under the impact of hostile criticism, we are likely, with witcraft, to produce a friendly and harmonizing essence. Here a parallel might be drawn with the exegetical task, which can lead to genuine discoveries as well as the confirmation of belief.

The strategy here involves arguing about the meaning of the general attitude, by applying the rhetorical strategy of discovering a definition which best suits our cause. This assumes that most attitudinal statements possess an inherent vagueness, and that different prescriptions for behaviour can be derived from them. Salancik, in a perceptive critique, has suggested that most social psychological theories of attitudes do not take into account the "malleable and fluid character of a person's reactions to the objects in the world" (1982, p. 72). He notes that there can be disagreements over the sorts of behaviour which a general attitude might imply. Thus different interpretations of the attitude might lead to very different actions. He illustrates this by outlining a situation in which two lovers are lying on a couch. His sketch, which, in common with many jokes, draws upon common stereotypes, has the female complaining: 'If you loved me, you would leave me alone.' As is customary in such jokes, the male has the last word, replying, 'But I do love you and that is why I am bothering you.' In this sketch, two contrary actions – seduction and restraint – are derived from the same attitudinal form. Both parties claim to find the essence of 'true love' in different places, and each, should we eavesdrop upon their disagreement, would claim their love to be the truer sort than the other's.[2] It is possible that neither had defined their true love beforehand – whether in terms of respect or eroticism – but each can find a definition to be applied *post hoc* to their arguments, and their respective types of preferred action. Quick wits enable the male to come up with a justification for his conduct and, in this respect, he resembles Juvenal's wife caught in adultery. If our eavesdropping becomes clairvoyance, we may see that in the far future, when age and domesticity have taken their toll, the male has need of another definition. Should the reproach of inconsistency then be made, particularization may provide a justification, as the male, like Pericles, distinguishes between the present and past self: in those full-blooded days of youth, love had a different, more passionate, meaning to its present essence. Do our predictive powers enable us to foresee a female snort of derision or a smirking 'told-you-so'?

Arguing about the essence of the general attitude is a strategy which is well suited for political arguments. The general terms of political discourse can be suitably vague, especially those indicating general values. Much controversy will centre around the means to achieve the ends, as disputants claim that their opponents' means conflict with their stated ends. In the face of criticism, the essence of the end must be located to justify the means. A dictatorship (of the proletariat) will aid the cause of freedom (true freedom), and democrats will abolish electoral systems in the name of democracy (true democracy). Similarly, if two actions appear inconsistent with one another, witcraft can find a hidden harmony by referring to the essence of the general belief or ideology.

Lenin in 1905 strongly argued the Bolshevik position for boycotting the Duma, or parliament, set up by the Tsar. Two years later found Lenin arguing the opposite position, and no longer was the Duma to be boycotted. Surely, in the face of such a reversal, one or other action must conflict with the principles of Marxism. Lenin, in his essay 'Against Boycott', nevertheless argued that both strategies, boycotting and not boycotting, were derived from Marxist ideology, and all those who disagreed misunderstood the nature of Marx's thought. The two occasions needed to be distinguished: 1905 was a period of revolutionary "upswing", whilst 1907 marked a "lull" in the passage towards the inevitable revolution. Drawing a general principle from the distinction, Lenin asserted that boycotts were appropriate to moments of upswing, but not to those of lull. And all this was consistent with, or rather demanded by, the essence of Marx's teaching.

Neither a general ideology nor a general political attitude can stipulate exactly what action should be taken in every situation. New situations continually arise, and, as Quintilian's Principle of Uncertainty suggests, there will always be latitude, and thereby the potential for controversy, in the way that the novel event is defined or categorized. The practising politician will be faced with all sorts of decisions, in which competing alternatives can be arguably reconciled with the overall ideology. Yet a choice between theoretically justifiable courses of action must be made. Decision-making implies an end to deliberation, and the chosen alternative must be defined against criticism. The deliberator must then become the advocate. In the course of advocacy, whether in response to criticism or cleverly to forestall potential criticism, new essences of the ideology can be discovered. Lenin, in justifying the chosen action, discovers yet another principle of the Marxist theory of revolution. This new discovery of "upswings" and "downswings" is further proof of Marxism's "complete scientific sobriety in the analysis of the objective state of affairs" ('Against Boycott', p. 36). Thus, in order to argue that the ends justify a particular set of means, one may find that the means start creating the essence of the ends. As always, the location of essences is a matter of actual, or potential, controversy. The more the advocate claims, as Lenin did, that the essences of the ideology are so obvious that only blockheads fail to see them, the greater the indications of controversy.

Arguing about arguments about attitudes

Advocates may resolve inconsistencies between attitudes and actions to their own satisfaction, but critics can demur. Mensheviks responded that, notwithstanding Lenin's arguments, there was a contradiction between the 1905 and the 1907 positions, and, in consequence, the Bolshevik consistency was the Menshevik inconsistency (see Dan, 1964, pp. 383f). LaPiere's hoteliers might justify their actions to themselves, as Johnson did to Boswell, but others, refusing to shift the essence of the matter, can claim that the inconsistencies remain unresolved. Because the essence of the action and the essence of the attitude can be matters of controversy, so too can the essence of contradiction between attitude and action. As Salancik noted, "whether two things are consistent with one another is a matter of opinion" (1982, p. 56).

We cannot call in the psychologist to resolve expertly such arguments about consistency. The psychologist is unlikely to lift off the top of disputants' skulls, to show the psyche of one side as a mass of tangled knots, and the mental cords of the other as neatly arranged as the wires of a piano. Instead, psychologists themselves are often caught up in debates about inconsistency, arguing amongst themselves about arguments. For example, Donald Campbell (1964) and Irwin Deutscher (1973) have taken very different positions in their discussions of the LaPiere study. Campbell has denied that the hoteliers showed any real inconsistency. Using the rhetorical strategy of distinguishing the true instances of the general concept from the false, he suggests that the hoteliers showed only 'pseudo-inconsistency'. They possessed comparatively mild racial prejudices, and their actions were in conformity with this mild prejudice. Only the most virulent prejudices would have overridden all the other factors of the situation. Similarly, it might be argued that Johnson's opposition to Wilkes could not have been total, otherwise no social meeting between the two would have been possible. The form of Campbell's argument follows the accounts which those involved might have given to deny that their actions were inconsistent.

However, that is not the end of the matter, for one psychological account provokes a critical counter-account. Deutscher suggests that, for all Campbell's reasoning, there was a fundamental inconsistency in the actions of LaPiere's hoteliers: "Although the 'inconsistency' has been removed in the mind of the scientist (as a result of his understanding it), that same observable 'inconsistency' remains in the empirical world" (1973, p. 212). In other words, tolerance in practice and prejudice in theory are *essentially* contradictory. Similarly, it can be argued that there is a contradiction between damning John Wilkes one moment and sitting down to dine with him the next. The disagreement between Campbell and Deutscher is not a logical one. Nor is it an empirical one, for it is hard to see what facts the one could produce to convince the other. Their disagreement, like so much of psychological argumentation, is one that falls firmly within the territory of rhetoric, for it concerns the location of an essence. What is pseudo-inconsistency to the one theorist is genuine inconsistency to the other. Ultimately, their argument is an instance of the most basic, and irreconcilable, of disagreements: they are disagreeing about the nature of disagreement.

8 Dilemmas of common-sense

Thomas De Quincey's image of the one-sided advocate shows a determined battler, who blocks criticisms and hurls forth accusations in the defence of a precarious position. Some of the strategies for this type of argumentative warfare have been discussed in relation to the tensions between categorization and particularization. If the opponent challenges with a categorization, then the advocate can parry with a particularization. With block and counter-block, particularization and categorization, the arguments can flow back and forth between the two equally one-sided and unyielding advocates. Both advocates will be armed with the same strategic devices. We do not expect to see a contest between a champion of particularization facing a rival equipped only with the weaponry of categorization. The ancient gladiatorial contests might have pitted the light sword against the trident and net, but the oratorical gladiators will both possess the same forms of thought. Both will be able to push particulars into general categories and to slide them out again, although they may differ in the quick-witted application of these skills. The forms which they use to cast their arguments may be similar, but the content will be different, as they advocate opposing cases. In this chapter, attention will turn from the forms, or strategies, of argumentation to its content.

It might be suggested that De Quincey's image of the orator provides a good model of cognitive functioning. Certainly it would not be difficult to link De Quincey's images to modern notions of the thinker's 'totalitarian' or 'miserly' ego. Any such model would be based upon a metaphor, comparing the thinker with the advocate. However, the arguments of Chapter 2 should act as a warning about the limitations of such metaphors. The theatrical metaphor, so common in the social sciences, reduces the world of the theatre to the boards of the stage, and the game-playing metaphor ignores the sporting world beyond the field of play. Similarly a rhetorical model of thinking based solely on the image of the advocate would limit the world of the orator to the public performance upon the rostrum. Yet, there is more to the world of oratory than this, just as there is more than the formal oration within the mind of the orator.

In order to catch these other aspects of the orator's world, we must turn our attention away from those heated moments when we might catch De Quincey's advocate in full flow of speech, displaying gloriously closed-minded resolution. But let us follow the advocate at the conclusion of the case. The papers and notes have been stuffed back into the briefcase. The morning's work has been done, and rival advocates have been bid goodbye. Then it is back to the office to await the next call to action. There at the desk sits the orator, hoping for other clients and opportunities to display professional skills. It is the same orator whom we saw in action this morning. We know it is the same person, because we followed the footsteps back to the office. But in another sense, it is a different person, hardly recognizable from the one-sided advocate of the morning's endeavours.

This desk-bound orator is a much quieter person. Sipping a cup of coffee, or filling out a claim for expenses incurred, the orator now has no need of the morning's publicly florid gestures. There is, in addition, a deeper difference. The mind is no longer withdrawn from all estimates bar one. The tensions of the morning have been relaxed, and the orator, awaiting a professional engagement, is no one-sided advocate, whose mind has been folded around a single obsession. Quite the contrary, here is a professional who can offer the prospective client a whole array of different sorts of speeches. Should the client require a speech of stern accusation, the orator can expertly oblige. On the other hand, the client in need of an oration filled with appeals for pity need not pass by: the expert accuser can be transformed suddenly into the professional defender. The orator sitting at the desk knows full well how to praise as well as blame, to criticize and to justify, to defend and accuse. In short, the mind of the orator awaiting hire is stocked with potential arguments which can, two-sidedly, pull in opposite directions. Our orator at the desk now seems to resemble the deliberator, rather than the single-minded advocate of De Quincey's description. However, as discussed in Chapter 5, the mind of the deliberator seems to oscillate uncomfortably between contrary poles. By contrast, our orator at the desk appears a picture of well-adjusted calm, confident in the possession of two-sided skills. The advocate in action may feel the necessity to present a consistently one-sided picture. Away from the public platform, the germs of contrary speeches seem to be in comfortable repose, as the hours of the afternoon slip by.

This chapter will consider the possibility that the professional orator is not unusual in possessing the germs of contrary arguments. The ordinary person might also resemble the desk-bound orator, in that contrary thoughts may find their homes within the same mental spaces. In discussing these issues, the emphasis will be upon the content of arguments, rather than upon argumentative form. The strategies of categorization and particularization, for example, represent forms of arguments, as do the strategies for alleging contradictions and dismissing the charges of inconsistency. These strategies can be applied to all arguments and thoughts, regardless of content, and, as such, they can be distinguished from the contrary themes, which existed as content within the mind of the afternoon orator. The classic textbooks of rhetoric often referred to the content, or topics, of arguments as the 'common-places' of rhetoric, and the nature of these common-places will be discussed in the present chapter. Previously, in Chapter 5, it was argued that the arts of witcraft are arts of common-sense, as opposed to being the technical skills of specialists. This argument will be taken a step further in the present chapter with the suggestion that the argumentative 'common-places' are important aspects of common-sense.

The rhetorical aspects of common-sense suggest that, just as the mind of the orator might be filled with contrary possibilities, so too might common-sense be marked by a contrary nature. It is easy to think of common-sense as consisting of the communal wisdom which stamps the thinking of all members of a particular community. However, common-sense may not be a unitary store of folk wisdom, but instead it may provide us with our dilemmas for deliberation and our controversies for argument. The dilemmatic aspects of common-sense, in short, might fill our minds with the controversial things which make much thought and argument possible. If this is so, then there are social psychological implications. The contrary structures of our minds are not confined to the possession of those contrary forms which are used for shaping arguments, and which enable us to unpick categories by particularization and to bundle particulars into categories. In addition, the contents of common-sense thinking may also be marked by contrary aspects.

Orator and audience

In the social sciences, a comparison between two phenomena can provide a wide highway, in which the traffic of analysis can proceed in two contrary directions. For example, we can use the dramaturgical metaphor, which points to the similarities between the stage performance and ordinary social life. Using such a comparison as our vehicle, we then could travel from the theatre to the outside world, in order to show how the latter world is full of theatrical events. We could, however, proceed in the reverse direction to show how the realities of the outside world give force and meaning to theatrical productions. Similarly, two opposite analytical journeys are possible along that other metaphorical highway discussed in Chapter 2: ordinary life can be seen as a game, or games can be seen as extensions of the non-ludic parts of ordinary life. Many social scientists, equipped with conceptual road-maps such as 'roles' and 'rules', prefer to travel from the theatrical or sporting worlds to 'ordinary life'. Others, such as C. L. R. James in his profound works of literary, social and cricketing analysis, make the reverse journey, in which the comparisons are not so metaphorical. In the same way, we can walk along the conceptual road connecting the orator and the ordinary person in two directions. Like the role and rule theorists in social psychology, we could make the trek from a specialized world to the home territory of ordinary life. At the end of the journey, our souvenirs from the departed world of ancient rhetoric will add a touch of the exotic to our homes.

The analogy between oratory and ordinary life might be used to make the humdrum aspects of ordinary life take on a Ciceronian grandeur. We could suggest that our transactions in the supermarket, office and bedroom bear the eloquent echoes of past oratorical glories. The charm of any such analysis would depend upon not relinquishing knowledge of the basic differences between Ciceronian sublimity and our everyday rhetorical fumblings. The present purpose, on the other hand, is not to pursue the comparison in this essentially metaphorical way. In fact, far from suggesting that the ordinary person resembles the extraordinarily eloquent performer, the present argument will proceed in the reverse direction to highlight the ordinariness of the orator. We will not be travelling the whole way down this particular road, but, instead, there will be a short trip, with the oratorical textbooks serving as maps. A brisk excursion should be sufficient to suggest that there are ties which bind together the orator and the ordinary people who constitute the orator's audience. It is because of these ties that there is so much social psychological insight in the oratorical textbooks which enumerate the skills required of the proficient orator. These sorts of textbooks seek, amongst other things, to instruct aspiring orators about the nature of audiences. One of their principal recommendations is that orators should base their ways of speaking upon the mentality of the audience. In providing organized systems for the orator, the textbooks also offer systematizations of ordinariness of the audience. As a result, a knowledge of rhetoric provides more than knowledge of the specialized, professional tricks of the orator. It also can throw light upon ordinary modes of thinking.

This might seem surprising, because it is easy to suppose that, in the rhetorical situation, the orator is the extraordinary person and that the audience represents dull ordinariness. In the courtroom, it is the jury who are selected for their ordinariness, whereas the barristers are chosen for their specialist skills. Politicians will address the 'public', in order to put themselves at its head and advertisers cajole the ordinary shopper, in order to make fortunes for themselves and their clients. There is little point denying that the professional orator, ancient and modern, must possess certain out-of-the-ordinary skills. In ancient times, personal bearing, superb memory and a loud voice were all prerequisites for success. However, in certain respects orators are not figures set apart from their ordinary audiences. The confident delivery and good looks of an orator may be the envy of the audience, but the content, as opposed to the delivery, of the orator's message may not be that extraordinary.

All the classical textbooks emphasize that the successful orator should understand how an audience thinks, and, before addressing an audience, the orator should be well aware of its opinions. As Quintilian wrote, "much depends on the character and beliefs of the audience and the generally received opinion" (*Institutes of Oratory*, II, vii, 23). In the twentieth century, we find a British member of parliament and amateur theorist of rhetoric making the same point. Edgar Jones, in a book whose preface was written by the future Prime Minister and outstanding public speaker, Lloyd George, declared that the speaker "must know the people's prejudices, he must watch during the preliminary proceedings to see what manner of folk they are, and what is the general background of feeling on the subject of his address" (1912, p. 174). The crucial point was not that orators should merely know the prejudices of the audience, but also that they should appeal to those prejudices. Quintilian suggested that the orator should avoid upsetting the cherished opinions of the audience. In the same vein, Aristotle urged the speaker to be at one with the audience: "One must represent, as existing, that which is honoured by each set of people – as by Scythians, or Lacedaemonians, or philosophers" (*Rhetoric*, 1367b).

In effect, Aristotle was urging the orators to emphasize the similarity between themselves and their audiences. This point has been stressed by modern theorists of rhetoric, as E. L. Murray (1985) has shown in his discussion of the New Rhetoric of Perelman and Olbrechts-Tyteca. Kenneth Burke, in *A Rhetoric of Motives*, argues that orators must identify themselves with the opinions and values of their audiences. This is especially true if the orator wishes to change the existing opinions or prejudices of the audience. There is no point charging in to lambast the Scythians, Lacedaemonians or philosophers for their wrong-headedness. That would only anger the audience. Instead some degree of identification must be established, because, "some of their (an audience's) opinions are needed to support the fulcrum by which he would move other opinions" (Burke, 1962, p. 580). Therefore, the orator, wishing to persuade an audience, should not emphasize the gulf which separates their respective opinions. Instead, orators should try to slide their controversial views into categories which are familiar and well-valued by the audience.[1]

An example of the way in which the orator can identify with the values of the audience, even when criticizing that audience, was provided by

Gorgias. He wished to reproach the Athenians for their warlike attitude towards their fellow Greeks, but he knew that a direct criticism of his audience would be counter-productive. Instead, he praised Athenian victories over the Medes, thereby implying that only victories over foreigners truly deserved hymns of praise, whilst "victories over Greeks call for dirges" (Philostratus, *Lives of the Sophists*, p. 494). Similarly, Gordon Allport wrote that the best way to argue with bigoted racists in the United States is not to dispute the details of prejudice directly. That would emphasize the differences between the tolerant speaker and the prejudiced audience. Instead, the tolerant person should make an appeal to common values of democracy and fairness, "in essence, an appeal to the American creed" (1958, p. 331). In case the reader of these lines is a committed experimental social psychologist, then some experimental evidence on this point should be cited, lest the values of experimentalism be unnecessarily, and unpersuasively, slighted. Papastamou and Mugny (1985) have shown that a minority which expresses its point of view in a way that rigidly rejects the values of a majority is likely to be unsuccessful in altering the views of the majority. Their experimental set-up used a Marxist minority, which criticized the liberal pacifism of the majority. When the majority's viewpoint was uncompromisingly dismissed as 'bourgeois sentimentality', the minority was much less persuasive than when it expressed its view in a way which showed flexibility and some respect for the pacifist values of the majority.

If orators adapt themselves to their audiences, then the image of the powerful orator playing masterfully with the emotions of the helpless crowd is a myth. This is an image to be found in the older psychological theories of the crowd, such as those of Le Bon and even of Freud. According to this myth, the audience falls under the spell of the hypnotic orator, who shapes its views like a potter moulding clay. However, these theories consider the powers of suggestion flowing from the orator to the crowd, and they ignore the powers of the audience over the orator. It can be argued that if orators can control crowds, it is only because crowds control orators. As Cicero wrote, "the eloquence of orators has always been controlled by the good sense of the audience, since all who desire to win approval have regard to the good will of their auditors, and shape and adapt themselves completely according to this and to their opinion and approval" (*Orator*, VIII, 24). Cicero might equally have said that the orator is controlled by the bad sense, or prejudices, of the audience. This was the nub of Plato's criticism against oratory, when Socrates dismissed rhetoric as "pandering" to the common mass (*Gorgias*, 463).

Of course, orators themselves may choose to subscribe to the myth that they possess sublime powers of persuasion. Convinced of their own talents, they are liable to forget that their audiences might also share in the myth. In fact, some orators' successes are only possible because the audience colludes with the orator in sustaining the myth. Perhaps nowhere has this base and vainglorious side of oratory been more visible than in *Mein Kampf*. Continually, Hitler praised the way in which his own Superior Will regularly wrestled with, and overcame, the resistant and inferior wills of his audiences. Hitler's bragging overlooked the extent to which his audiences conspired in their own submission, by sharing the myth of the Superior Will of the leader. J. P. Stern has emphasized how important an ingredient this was in Hitler's oratorical successes: "The language of the mythology of the Will is...the characteristic language of the audience, the time and place Hitler sets out to conquer" (1975, p. 75). Under these circumstances, the shared belief in the 'extraordinary orator' united the actual orator and the ordinary audience.

Since the orator and the audience are linked together, oratory must be seen as an irreducibly social activity. At the minimum, this implies that orator and audience must share common argumentative forms. The speaker must use shapes of arguments which are recognizable to the audience. For example, Aristotle, in his discussion of different types of arguments, or enthymemes, illustrated the 'argument from parity' with the lines: "Thy father is to be pitied for having lost his children; and is not Oenus to be pitied for having lost his famous son?" (*Rhetoric*, 1397b). This declamation would be incomprehensible if the audience were unable to grasp immediately that a disputed present instance is being compared to an undisputed past occurrence. Because this much is understood, the argument from parity can be used, without its structure being explained from basic principles in a heavy-handed manner (i.e. you showed pity in the previous case, and the present case contains even more of the features deserving of pity than were present then and when this happens we feel assured in claiming...).

The link between the orator and the audience rests upon more than a sharing of argumentative forms. It also comprises a common content. If orators are identifying with their audiences, then they are emphasizing communal links, foremost amongst which are shared values or beliefs. The concept of common-sense (*sensus communis*) might be a helpful one for discussing this communal content. The orator, in identifying with the beliefs of the audience, will be treating the audience as a community bound together by shared opinions. Edgar Jones's remarks about the audience as a particular kind of "folk" illustrates this sense of community. The audience, therefore, will be presumed to possess a common-sense, agreeing that certain positions are commonly sensible whilst others are affronts. Allport's tolerant American will appeal to the common-sense belief in the rightness of democracy and to the shared principles of fairness. Gorgias played upon a common Hellenic sense of national pride. Neither would feel the need to justify these beliefs to their respective audiences, for such beliefs were ingrained into these different commonalities of what was sensible. By contrast, Papastamou and Mugny's inflexible minority showed scant respect for the sensibilities of their audience, when they dismissed its common assumptions as being so much 'bourgeois' nonsense. By applying the label 'bourgeois' to the rejected common nonsense, the orators, who would strenuously deny being 'bourgeois' themselves, were emphasizing their own non-identification with this bourgeois audience.

Common-places of rhetoric

The classical textbooks aimed to provide short-cuts for the invention of arguments. Not only were arguments, or enthymemes, categorized and listed in terms of their form, but there were also attempts to organize them in terms of content. The intention was to provide materials for the less imaginative orator or for the amateur, who needed to compose a speech. No longer would it be necessary to invent every argument from scratch. Instead, orators could turn to the appropriate section in the textbook, and there they would come across suitable arguments upon common themes. A spatial metaphor was frequently used to describe these sorts of argumentative themes: they were the 'places' (*loci* or *topoi*) of arguments. The English world 'topic' is derived from the Greek *topoi*, and the topics of arguments were the place where arguments were to be discovered.

Although the concept of an argumentative place, or topic, is an important one in rhetorical theory, there was much uncertainty about the precise nature of such places. At times, the theorists themselves seemed baffled about the origins of argumentative themes. Cicero in *De Partitione Oratoria* referred to the topics of arguments as being the mysterious places where arguments lurk (ii, 5). The translator of the Loeb edition of *De Partitione* lessens the mystery by introducing a metaphor familiar to the modern reader: *eos in quibus latent argumenta* is translated as the "pigeon-holes in which arguments are stored". Francis Bacon, in his discussion of topics, similarly gave the metaphor of places a more solid image. He commented that "the place where a thing is to be looked for may be marked, and as it were indexed; and this is that which I call *Topics*" (1858, p. 422). A Demosthenes or an Isocrates might be able to index and pigeon-hole arguments quite satisfactorily in their own minds, but the less proficient might need the written organization of the textbook. Should the relevant places in the orator's mind be sadly empty, then the textbooks would be readily stocked with appropriate rhetorical themes. In this way, the textbooks intended to offer a handy system of mental organization, based upon systems used by orators. The same metaphors of indexing and pigeon-holing appear in modern psychological theories, where the pigeon-holes and indexes are intended to represent the actual psychological properties of the memory itself. Thus, psychologists will assume that the 'topics of argument', or attitudinal beliefs, must be organized within the memory. If the orator is to summon up the topics for use in the course of debate, or if the topics are to be accessed (to use a familiar computing analogy), then the memory stores must have some system of indexing (see, for example, Schank and Abelson's computer models of beliefs and memory in *Scripts, Plans, Goals and Understanding*). As Bacon and Cicero both implied, within the mind there must be some store where the argumentative themes are to be found mysteriously, but not haphazardly, lurking.

There is, however, an ambiguity in the rhetorical concept of 'topics', which is liable to confuse the modern reader. It would be natural to assume that the 'topics' of rhetoric referred to the content of arguments, or the subject matter of an orator's discourse. Both Aristotle and Cicero wrote treatises with the title of *Topics*. The modern reader might assume that these would be the works to provide the dull orator with the handily indexed arguments, rather as the equivalent of those books of etiquette which list jokes and anecdotes to help out the unpractised after-dinner speaker. However, neither Aristotle's nor Cicero's *Topics* was a book of this sort. Both dealt principally with the forms, not contents, of arguments. In these works, the 'topics' of arguments represented the universal forms in which arguments can be expressed, rather than what would today be understood by the 'topic' of an argument. Nevertheless, the term 'topics' was not used exclusively in this way, but, rather confusingly, it was also used on occasion by ancient theorists to describe the content of arguments.

In order to avoid confusion, we will not use 'topic' in the technical sense of an argumentative form. Our concern here is with the contents of arguments, and especially with their common-sensical content. The word 'topic' was used in one way which relates directly to common-sense. In talking of the content of arguments, the rhetorical textbooks often referred to the 'common-places' (*loci communes*) of arguments. Clearly, no handbook could hope to list all the subjects on which an orator might be required to speak. Such a list would be infinite. However, the handbooks did hope to provide certain basic themes, which were common to many arguments, and these were the common topics or 'common-places' of arguments. For our purposes, the concept of common-places is an interesting one, in that it stands for the common-sense values and notions, which ideally should be shared by speaker and audience alike. In this way, the very notion of 'common-place' underlines the social nature of rhetoric, and, as will be suggested later, the very rhetorical nature of the common-places, in its turn, points to the contrary nature of common-sense.

There were two aspects to the commonality of the common-places, and both aspects were typically assumed by rhetorical theorists. On the one hand, these places of argument were common because they represented the useful platitudes, whose indexed places were frequently visited by orators. These common-places were the stock phrases of oratorical productions, to be used time and time again. On the other hand, the commonness of the common-places related to the fact that these bits of folk wisdom were commonly shared by members of the audience, and also by the speaker. Thus, the common-places were assumed to be both commonly used by orators and commonly held by their audiences. A few remarks can be made upon both aspects of the commonness of the common-places.

(a) The commonly used topic

The common-places had a certain generality, in that they were the sort of general remark which could be inserted without difficulty into different speeches. Seneca recounts that Latro had a stock of general remarks, learnt by heart, which had "no intimate connection with particular controversies, but can be quite aptly placed elsewhere too, such as those on fortune, cruelty, age and riches" (*Controversiae*, I, preface, 23). Aristotle referred to such common-places as 'maxims'. He commented that maxims can be particularly effective because of "the vulgarity of the hearers". Aristotle explained: "A maxim is...a general statement, and men are pleased when a sentiment which they already entertain on special grounds is stated in general terms." He added that the use of maxims has the advantage of giving "a moral quality to our speech". All maxims have this effect, he argued, "since the man who uses a maxim makes a general declaration of his moral predictions" (*Rhetoric*, 1395b). The moral dimension is likewise clear in Quintilian's discussion of those common-places "in which we denounce vices themselves such as adultery, gambling or profligacy without attacking particular persons" (*Institutes of Oratory*, II, iv, 22).

There was a danger that the constant use of these maxims and moral homilies would reduce them to no more than debased clichés. If the common-places were cited too commonly, they would lose their special moral force, just as constant visits by sightseers can destroy the charm of a natural beauty spot. Quintilian expressed reservations about the indiscriminate use of common-places, and he warned against the practice of relying overmuch upon ready-made maxims to the neglect of the specificities of a case: "Some speakers, for example, introduce the most long-winded common-places just for the sake of the sentiments they contain, whereas rightly the sentiments should spring from the context" (II, iv, 30). In modern times, George Orwell has denounced the decay of political language. Stale generalities, used many, many times, fill the speeches of politicians:

> When one watches some tired hack on the platform mechanically repeating the familiar phrases – *bestial atrocities, iron heel, bloodstained tyranny, free peoples of the world, stand shoulder to shoulder* – one often has a curious feeling that one is not watching a live human being but some kind of dummy: a feeling which suddenly becomes stronger at moments when the light catches the speaker's spectacles and turns them into blank discs which seem to have no eyes behind them. (Orwell, 1962, p. 152)

Orwell's complaint is that morality itself is undermined when the moral quality of language becomes merely a handy cliché. Constant repetition of hack phrases rubs away the reflective surface of these words, so that the image of ourselves and our deeds can no longer appear in the ethical looking-glass. Nevertheless, even a cliché is not completely devoid of all moral, or emotional, force. All the clichés of Orwell's hack are designed to give a certain moral quality to the discourse. *Bloodstained tyrannies* and *bestial atrocities* are hardly neutral terms. It is not entirely haphazard that one set of clichés is selected over another. Orwell's hack will be attempting to invoke in the audience a sense of moral community, in the same way that Gorgias or Allport's tolerant American were appealing to the communal senses of their audiences. In this way, the modern cliché, like the classical common-place, is a convenient means for speakers to stress their identification with their audiences. Clumsily, the tired hack, watched by the sceptical Orwell, is suggesting that orator and audience are the sort of people who should *stand together, united against all the evil forces, which beset the upholders of justice...*

(b) The commonly held topic

Because of the link between the speaker and the audience, we can expect the commonly used topic to be one that is commonly held by the audience. The common-place, or handy-maxim, will form a part of the sense of a particular community. In fact, rhetorical theorists often defined rhetoric itself in terms of common-sense, or commonly held beliefs. Most notably, Aristotle began his *Topica* with the statement that dialectical reasoning, which included rhetorical reasoning, concerned "opinions that are generally accepted" (100a). Similarly Thomas Hobbes, who introduced Aristotle's *Rhetoric* to English speakers in the seventeenth century, wrote that "the principles of rhetoric out of which enthymemes are drawn" were "common

Opinions" (Brief of the Art of Rhetorick, p. 277). Accordingly, the content of oratory was common-sense, and not technical matters which might be disputed by experts. As discussed in Chapter 5, the arts of witcraft comprise the arts of inventing arguments from commonly held materials.

A distinction must be made between two senses of the concept of 'common-sense'. There is an anthropological, or restricted, sense which confines particular versions of common-sense to particular communities or audiences. Then there is an unrestricted use, which implies that there is a common-sense to which all audiences subscribe. Some rhetoricians, particularly in the eighteenth century, did not restrict the commonality of 'common-sense' to particular communities. Instead, they supposed that common opinions would be those which were held by all thinking, or reasonable, people. For example, George Campbell in his *Philosophy of Rhetoric* (1776) suggested that the common-sense of rhetoric was composed of beliefs which were sensible "to all mankind" (1963, pp. 39–40). This extension of common-sense to the commonality of the human race goes too far. It neglects the point that the Scythians, Lacedaemonians, and philosophers all have their separate codes of honour, to be respected by the sensitive orator. There is no reason why the right-thinking Scythians or the law-abiding Lacedaemonians should accept what passes for common-sense amongst the philosophers. Similarly the democratic common-sense, to which Allport's tolerant individual appeals, is not to be found amongst the common-places of *Institutes of Oratory* – a work written to help the orator practising under the capricious autocracy of Domitian. Therefore common-sense, or the *sensus communes*, should be understood anthropologically, rather than in an unrestricted manner. Each community possesses its own common-sense, expressed in common-place, but nevertheless potent, symbols. It is these common-places which the orator is advised to invoke, even when seeking to criticize the audience. The skilful orator should be able to switch into different sets of common-sense common-places, when addressing audiences drawn from different communities.

A further distinction might be in order, for the anthropological common-sense is not to be equated with any absolute conception of common-sense. Sometimes the term 'common-sense' is equated with the good sense, or *le bon sens*, so that someone said to be using their 'common-sense' is being praised for being sensible. This absolute use of common-sense, however, conflicts with the anthropological meaning. Each audience will no doubt imagine its own common-sense to exemplify *le bon sens*, but if we say that all communities have their own common-sense, we are not implying that all are equally sensible. To make that assumption in a rhetorical context would be dangerous. Therefore, if we say that Hitler's ravings on the Superior Will appealed to the common-sense of his audience, we should, on no account, be interpreted as implying that Hitler's speeches were sensible in any absolute sense. We must always bear in mind that the *sensus communes* can be both the good common-sense envisaged by Cicero, as well as the evil prejudices feared by Plato. The present point is a much simpler one: whether the common-sense of a community appears to us as *le bon* or *le mauvais sens*, it nevertheless will exert its control over the individual orator, who seeks to make an audience of that community.

Contrary topics of common-sense

So far the suggestion that there is a similarity between the professional orator and the ordinary member of the audience has not yet been developed. In fact, far from emphasizing the similarities, the arguments of the preceding section can be interpreted as calling attention to an important difference. The professional orator is equipped to argue different cases before different sorts of audiences. Should it be a Lacedaemonian or a Scythian who requires oratorical expertise, the professional will obligingly prepare the brief. Even a philosopher can be accommodated. In other words, our expert knows all about the various common-places of the Lacedaemonians, Scythians, and philosophers. In possessing such skills, professional orators would appear to be extraordinarily mobile, in that they can move between the different places where their various audiences store their arguments. *Prima facie* this would appear so very different from the ordinary person. Whether Lacedaemonian or Scythian, ordinary persons will find themselves located in one spot, drawing upon a single set of common-places. However, there may be differences between the orator and ordinary person, but the oratorical situation also highlights similarities.

Certainly the rhetorical textbooks stressed that the orator should acquire the skills of arguing both sides of a case, and, thereby, should be able to summon up contrary common-places. Cicero states that Aristotle, in his rhetorical classes, taught young men "the fluent style of the rhetorician, so that they might be able to uphold either side of the question in copious and elegant language" (*Orator*, xiv, 46). In Roman times, young orators would engage in mock debates or *suasoriae*, taking it in turns to argue either side of a controversial matter. According to Cicero, the *suasoriae* were an important feature of oratorical training, because "we must argue every question on both sides, and bring out on every topic whatever points can be deemed plausible" (*De Oratore*, p. 109). Although the orator might be able to produce arguments for both parties to a dispute, it was not considered professionally ethical to do so in practice. Plutarch recounts how Demosthenes was much criticized because, in his youth, he wrote speeches for both sides in the same controversy. According to Plutarch, it was as if

Demosthenes had sold "to the disputants, as it were from one and the same cutlery-shop, the knives with which to wound each other" (*Lives of Demosthenes and Cicero, Parallel Lives*, p. 37).

Again, this suggests that the orator possesses an extraordinary flexibility, at least until the moment of oratorical action. Then the flexible two-sidedness of the desk-bound orator contracts into the one-sided inflexibility of the advocate on the podium. According to this line of reasoning, it would be the one-sided advocate who would resemble, and identify with, the audience. Therefore, one would expect the audience to be characterized by one-sided prejudices. The desk-bound orator, by contrast, would be a figure extra-ordinary for its store of different common-place reasonings. This sort of assumption has been made on occasions. For example, the differences between the professional advocate and the ordinary person were discussed by Samuel Johnson. According to the Doctor, lawyers should not be criticized for "affecting warmth" for their clients, nor for advancing arguments with which they might not necessarily agree. The same behaviour would be intolerable in common discourse, but there were clear differences between the arguments of a courtroom and a conversation between friends: "Sir, a man will no more carry the artifice of the bar into common intercourse of society, than a man who is paid for tumbling upon his hands will continue to tumble upon his hands when he should walk on his feet" (Boswell, 1906, Vol. I, pp. 342–343). Johnson was arguing that in ordinary discourse, people should speak as they think and their words should match their attitudes. The lawyer, on the other hand, must adopt the attitudes of the client, and must flit, during the course of an oratorical career, from one place of common-sense to another.

However, this is not the full story. Nor, in some respects, is it even the more interesting half of the tale. It omits a paradox, which arises when one considers not the arguments which might arise between communities, but those within one community. Here we have disputes in which both parties are appealing to the same audience, and therefore are identifying with the same common-sense. In a typical courtroom, both prosecution and defence must address their arguments to the same jury, and must base their arguments on this audience's common-sense. The paradox arises because both the logoi of the prosecution and the anti-logoi of the defence will be appealing to the same common-sense of the audience. Following rhetorical practice, both sides will be attempting to identify with the views of this audience. The paradox is that the two oratorical sides, although appealing to the same common-sense, will be arguing in diametrically opposed ways. In this way, the same common-sense will be the location of arguments which contradict each other.

The paradox is resolved if we assume that the common-sense of an audience is not unitary, but is composed of contrary aspects. If we make this assumption, then we can expect to find logos and anti-logos, or contrary common-places, in the minds of the audience. The opposing orators will then be playing upon these contrary tendencies. One orator will be attempting, as it were, to grab the logoi of the audience, in order to pull that audience leftwards, whilst the opposition puts its full weight upon the anti-logoi, pushing in a rightwards direction. Both logoi and anti-logoi are presumed to co-exist within the common-sense, and we can assume this state to be quite normal and not associated with the presumed *angst* of cognitive dissonance. If this assumption is made, then the gap between the professional orator and the ordinary person is narrowed. The ordinary person, whose mind is filled with the contrary tendencies of common-sense, will resemble the desk-bound orator: each possesses contrary common-places, which are lurking within the mind, awaiting the call to be used in a one-sided advocacy.

It might be objected that the contrary tendencies of common-sense represent an unstable state, which must progress towards consistent uniformity. For example, a jury must decide whether to acquit or condemn, and, therefore, one of the two sets of opposing common-places must be rejected. However, as was discussed in Chapter 5, rhetorical disagreements are often between two points of view, which are both, to a certain extent, reasonable. Choosing between the two may not imply that the one view is totally correct and the other is to be rejected as utterly erroneous. Moreover, in the case of a decision taken by a jury, there may be a rejection of the application of one set of common-places in the particular instance, but not a total evacuation of the common-places from their indexed locations in the mind. It may be decided that so reprobate is the accused that any show of mercy is inappropriate on this occasion. This would not represent a total rejection of the common-places of mercy, in favour of an acceptance of those of justice. It would merely indicate an unwillingness, after suitable deliberation, to visit the places of mercy for this particular case. Despite the decision in the particular case, the jury will continue to adhere to the common-sense that it is right to be both merciful and just. In consequence, these common-places will still be left tugging in their opposite directions. Like an advocate capable of prosecuting and defending, the jury will have retained their contrary common-places of blame and justification for future use.

The rhetorical textbooks, aiming to offer convenient sets of common-places for defence and prosecution, were embodying the spirit of Protagoras. For each issue there would be general pro and con common-places, bearing out the maxim that there were two sides to every issue. In fact, it should come as little surprise that Protagoras is credited with inventing the practice of preparing general common-places. According to Cicero, Protagoras was the first rhetorician to write out "discussions of certain large general subjects such as we now call common-places" (*Brutus*, 46).

In presenting the contrary common-places, the textbooks were, in effect, doing more than just providing aids for the orator. They were also arranging the contents of common-sense. By their arrangement of common-places, the rhetorical theorists reveal that common-sense is not a harmonious system of interlocking beliefs, but is composed of contraries. Just as the forms of argument can be arranged in opposing pairs – categorizations opposed by particularizations, arguments of quantity by arguments of quality, and so forth – so also can the common-place content of common-sense. This can be seen in relation to the three great branches of rhetoric: the forensic rhetoric of the courtroom, the deliberative rhetoric of politics and epideictic rhetoric, in which the character of individuals was discussed. Not all common-places would be equally useful in each of these three branches. Yet, when rhetorical theorists mentioned the sorts of common-places appropriate for each type, they tended to list pairs of opposing themes, or common-sense logoi and their equally common-sensical anti-logoi. In forensic oratory, arguments will be directed towards defending or prosecuting, and there are common-places of mercy and justice. Similarly there are contrary common-places for epideictic oratory, where the arguments pull towards the opposite poles of praise and blame, justification and criticism. In deliberative oratory, where political decisions might be debated, there would be common-places stressing success, morality and bravery, all contestable by those dwelling upon failure, immorality and foolhardiness. For example, *Rhetorica ad Herennium* outlined the sorts of common-places which should prove useful for a defending lawyer. These included themes about "humanity, fortune, pity and the mutability of things". The author commented that "all these common-places, reversed, will be used by the adversary, who will amplify and recount the defendant's transgressions" (II, xvii, 26). In contrast to common-places of pity, there will be those which emphasize the seriousness of justice. For example, "we show that if we indulge this man, many others will be the more emboldened to commit crimes – something which the anticipation of a judicial sentence has hitherto checked" (II, xxx, 48).

One of the clearest presentations of the contrary themes of common-sense is to be found in Francis Bacon's *The Dignity and Advancement of Learning*. He ended his discussion of rhetoric by appending a "Promptuary", or "preparatory store of common-places", which was intended to represent the "*seeds, not flowers* of arguments" (1858, p. 492, emphasis in original). The common-places were arranged in antithetical form. There were forty-seven sets of maxims or proverbs, so that each common-sensical saying was matched by an equally sensible negation. For example, the common-place that "Wisdom that comes not quick comes not in season" was opposed by "The wisdom that is ready at hand does not lie deep." Playfully, Bacon ended his list with an antithesis about argumentation itself: "He who relies on arguments decides according to the merits of the pleader, not the cause" finds itself opposed in the forty-seventh pair by "Arguments are the antidote against the poisoning of testimony."

Nor has Western common-sense tidied up its contradictory themes since the days of Bacon. Today, we could easily contrast maxims such as 'many hands make light work' and 'too many cooks spoil the broth'. The contrary nature of common-sense, and its maxims, has often been noted by the authors of social psychology textbooks. Their observations are intended to act as criticism, for in the opening chapters of textbooks we are frequently told of the hopeless confusions of common-sense. A favourite example is the contradiction between the proverbs 'absence make the heart grow fonder' and 'out of sight, out of mind'. Krech, Crutchfield and Ballachey (*The Individual in Society*), Baron, Byrne and Griffit (*Social Psychology*), Hollander (*Principles and Methods of Social Psychology*) and Severy, Brigham and Schlenker (*A Contemporary Introduction to Social Psychology*) all draw attention to the unhappy confusion produced by that particular pair of home truths. Baron, Byrne and Griffit assert that because of these contradictions, "common-sense fails us". However, help is at hand in the form of experimental social psychology, which enables the "unfounded speculation" of common-sense to be "supplanted by orderly and precise experimentation" (1974, p. 2). According to Severy, Brigham and Schlenker, the accumulation of statistically analysable data from controlled experiments will enable us to "describe the conditions under which each [opposing proverb] is true or false" (1976, p. 6). Having been confined to their appropriate situations, the maxims of common-sense will no longer be able to mock us with their contrariness.

For all the hopes of the social psychology textbooks, the confusions of common-sense are not going to be easily replaced by scientific order and precision. The experimental method is not a powerful vacuum cleaner which will suck up the confusing layer of dirt, leaving the pattern on the floor covering to shine unambiguous in its brightness. Following Quintilian's Principle of Uncertainty, we can say that there is an infinity of situations, or conditions, in which contrary proverbs may be applicable. Thus, there is an infinity of experiments to be conducted before we can have full order and precision. Because the task is infinite, and beyond the finite vacuuming capacities of all the hard-working laboratories, a degree of mess remains. Moreover, there is ample scope for argument between experimental specialists, just as there is for the upholders of common-sense. As was seen in the last chapter, psychologists can draw upon maxims about the strangeness of the human species to augment their theories of the fundamental inconsistency of many human actions, whilst other psychologists, with their different maxims and interpretations of statistical evidence, can talk of underlying consistencies.

The contrary aspects of common-sense are not confined to pairs of opposing proverbs, but, in addition, they are deeply embedded in the vocabulary of language itself. Phrases and single words carry definite implications of accusation and justification, so that a term which implies praise can be considered the contrary of one exuding blame. The very use of one phrase rather than another will, then, indicate the seed, if not the flower, of an argumentative position. What really appalled Orwell about the clichés of the political hack was that the ready, and unthinking, adoption of one set of terms precluded debate, and thereby thought, about opposing moral positions. In debate, the orator will urge the audience to consider the matter in terms of one sort of vocabulary, while the opponent will be urging the categorization of the issue under an opposing set of terms. The opponents will differ upon the appropriate categorization in which the matter should be placed. In debating this, they need not disagree about the meaning of the competing common-place categories, since both sides can appeal to common linguistic sense. As *Rhetorica ad Herennium* counselled, "no one will propose the abandonment of virtue, but let the speaker say...that the virtue consists of qualities contrary to those evinced here" (III, iii, 6). The anonymous author showed how easily adjectives can be grouped in terms of rhetorical contraries: "If it is at all possible, we shall show how that what our opponent calls justice is cowardice, and sloth, and perverse generosity; what he has called wisdom we shall term impertinent babbling, and inoffensive cleverness; what he declares to be temperance, we shall declare to be inaction and lax indifference; what he has named courage, we shall term the reckless temerity of a gladiator" (*Rhetorica ad Herennium*, III, iii, 6).

The linguistic aspect of common-places illustrates clearly how inherently contrary common-sense is. All speakers of the community will possess contrary sets of words with their respective tones of justification and criticism. The mere possession of these words means that we can take either side in the dilemmas and controversies which chance our way. Because the content of our language is two-sided, we are not always and inevitably pushed into a single position. To continue with the spatial metaphor which underlines the notion of common-places, one might note that these contrary terms will be closely located. Aristotle remarked upon this, in suggesting that "those qualities which border on a man's actual qualities must be assumed to be identical with them, for the purpose of praise or of blame;

thus the cautious man may be called cold and designing; the foolish man may be good natured, or the callous man, mild" (*Rhetoric*, 1367a). The terms could have been equally well reversed, to claim that the cold man is called cautious and the good-natured man is called foolish. The point is that terms such as 'cold' and 'cautious', or 'courage' and 'recklessness', possess opposing moral and rhetorical qualities, but find themselves in such proximity, that, in particular instances, reasonable or reasoned arguments can be made for preferring one term to its rhetorical contrary. Nor should this be considered a failure of efficient mental organization, which would be eradicated by the sort of linguistic streamlining which some modern, scientifically-minded, psychologists seem to envisage. It is because of this proximity between the undefined borders of opposites, that common-sense can provide us with dilemmas to think and argue about; and, only if there are such dilemmas and deliberation, rather than the smooth and unthinking categorization of all worldly particulars, can our discourse bear a moral quality.

Social dilemmas and common-sense

Common-sense would appear to possess two contrary aspects in its relations with argumentation. On the one hand, common-sense seems to close off arguments: certain matters will appear to be commonly sensible within a community, and consequently these matters will be accepted without argument. For this reason, the orator is advised not to attack directly the common-places of the audience. On the other hand, common-sense seems to open up arguments: the common-places, which constitute important components of common-sense, provide the seeds of rhetorical arguments. In themselves the common-places may be taken for granted, and thereby not be under argumentative attack, but they also provide the weaponry with which arguments can be conducted. In fact, such is the nature of this weaponry that common-sense openly invites argumentation and con-troversy. However, social scientists have often stressed the aspect of common-sense which closes off arguments, whereas it is the argumentative aspect which is of direct relevance to rhetoric.

The view of common-sense as non-controversial is illustrated by the sociologist Peter Berger, who suggests that common-sense defines the view of the world which members of a society will share. Common-sense repre-sents "the world *tout court* – the only real world, typically the only world that one can seriously conceive of" (1970, p. 376). According to this view, common-sense is like a giant schema, or combination of smaller schemata, through which social reality is filtered. Just as cognitive psychologists suggest that schemata tend to make ambiguous stimuli unambiguous, so

Berger suggests that common-sense removes dilemmas of interpretation and makes social life meaningful. People need not worry about interpreting every event in their lives, but instead the individual "can simply refer to common-sense for such interpretation, at least for the great bulk of his biographical experience" (p. 376). Berger implies that, through common-sense, the social customs of a community will appear natural, and thereby non-controversial, to its members. Of course, each society will have its own set of customs and there is, therefore, a multiplicity of common-senses in the world. As the anonymous follower of Protagoras wrote in the *Dissoi Logoi*: "If a group of people should collect from all the nations of the world their disgraceful customs and then should call everyone together and tell each man to select what he thinks is seemly, everything would be taken away as belonging to the seemly things" (II, 26). Each society will consider its seemly customs to be as natural as the seasons, whilst the customs of other societies are likely to be thought of as bizarrely unnatural or uncommonly nonsensical.

The rhetorical implication is that different societies will possess different stocks of common-places, locating the seemly in very different places. The author of *Dissoi Logoi* points out that the Massagetes had the habit of cutting up their parents and eating the pieces: "They think that to be buried in their children is the most beautiful grave imaginable." However, the Greeks take a dim view of such behaviour, and anyone doing such a thing in Greece "would die an ignominious death" (II, 14). If an orator were speaking on the issue of respect for parents, the sorts of common-places which would impress an audience of Massagetes would greatly differ in substance from those which might be used to catch the sympathetic attention of Greeks. To use a modern term, one might say that the cultural values of the Greeks differ from those of the Massagetes, with the value for the preservation of parental life getting short shrift amongst the latter.

The similarity between the common-places of classical rhetoric and the modern concept of values has been discussed by Perelman and Olbrechts-Tyteca. They have noted that values and common-places are both "objects of agreement", which make possible "a communion with regard to particular ways of acting" (1971, p. 74). Values, like common-places, express generalities, rather than particularities. According to Milton Rokeach, who has been the foremost social psychological investigator of values in recent years, values comprise "a small number of core ideas or cognitions present in every society about desirable end-states" (1979a, p. 49). Particular attitudes and specific actions will be justified in terms of such general values, but the values, as desirable end-states, will not themselves need to be justified. According to Rokeach, there will be common agreement, at least within a given society, that the values are generally to be valued. In this way, values, like the common-places of rhetoric, constitute elements of common-sense whose truth or desirability is taken for granted.

In his analysis, Rokeach concentrated upon positive values, such as 'freedom', 'self-respect' and 'true friendship', but the notion that values are general objects of agreement applies equally to negative values. There will be agreement that some things are utterly undesirable. Thus Bentham was referring to negative values, when he wrote of lust, cruelty and avarice as being "bad motives", and generally despised. He explained that, because of the rhetorical meaning of these terms, their badness could not be denied, nor did it need to be justified: "The fact is, that these are names which, if properly applied, are never applied but in the cases where the motives they signify happen to be bad" (*Principles of Morals and Legislation*, p. 114). So firmly are such values objects of agreement that it would provoke a scandal if someone were to show disrespect for the common-sense of decency by explicitly, and seriously, championing the values of *cruelty, avarice* and *greed*. Similarly, Orwell's hack political orator appears to be invoking unassailable values, for there will be no-one amongst the audience to declare themself in favour of *bestial atrocity* and *blood-stained tyranny*.

Although values, and common-places, are objects of agreement in themselves, they are also the means by which controversies can be conducted. They provide the seeds of argumentative logoi, and these can be opposed by anti-logoi also based upon generally agreed common-places. The controversy does not arise so much from disputing values directly, nor from an assault upon a commonly cherished common-place. Avarice, greed and lust are likely to remain as overtly unchampioned as blood-stained tyranny. The main possibility for controversy arises from two sources. There may be disputes about the interpretation of a value or there may be controversy about which value is appropriate to the case in hand. In other words, the dilemmas of categorization and particularization raise their familiar heads again: the particular essence of the general category might be disputed and so might the choice of value to categorize the particular instance.

Both sorts of dispute have been described in general terms, in the earlier discussion of argumentative forms. In Chapter 6, brief mention was made of disputes concerning the essence of political categories. Research, using Rokeach's scale for measuring values, has suggested that political opponents might express their support for the same value, with everyone, for example, agreeing that 'freedom' is a wonderful thing. However, the interpretation of this self-evidently desirable value differs markedly, and the fascist's freedom is the democrat's dictatorship (Billig, 1977; Billig and Cochrane, 1979; Cochrane, Billig and Hogg, 1979; Rokeach, 1979b). Similarly Bentham might have used the traditional moral terms of 'lust', 'avarice' and 'cruelty', but he sought to turn traditional morality upside down with his scientifically utilitarian ethics. The opponents of Orwell's political hack would also declare themselves to be appalled by *bloodstained tyrannies*, but their list of those governments with blood on their hands and murder on their consciences would be a very different list from that of the hack.

Of more direct relevance to the contrary nature of common-sense are those disputes about the appropriate value to apply to a particular case. As was argued in Chapter 6, the individual possesses more than one schema, and therefore will be faced by choices, or dilemmas, about categorizing information. Similarly, there will exist a multiplicity of values within any community, just as the members of an audience will each possess a multiplicity of common-places. Moreover, it is not merely a matter of multiplicity, but of contrariety, for the common-places of common-sense can be brought into conflict with one another. The rhetorical textbooks, in their practical exercises for young orators, demonstrated how easily this could be done. The value against avarice can conflict with that of personal achievement, lust with freedom, and cruelty with firmness, as disputants discuss whether a positive or negative value should be stuck upon the particular matter under debate. In the courtroom, the value for justice regularly collided with the countervailing value for mercy, as the prosecution stressed valued common-places which might counter those of the defence.

Vilfredo Pareto had an interesting argument to explain why societies possess multiplicities of values and why these values should conflict with each other. He suggested that principles tend to be expressed in simple, unqualified ways. However, these simple formulations are too extreme for guiding practical conduct, because, if they were followed with consistent literality, they would fail to achieve the desired result. For example, the maxim 'Thou shalt not kill' expresses a simple, unqualified principle, or value. According to Pareto, such a principle is a "statement that far oversteps the rule of conduct which one is aiming to establish and which would have to be stated in a great many more words if one were to specify in just what cases and under just what circumstances one must not kill, in what other cases one may kill, and in what other cases still one must kill" (1935, para. 1772). Therefore, there need to be exceptions and qualifications to the simple principle. These exceptions and qualifications will be justified in terms of other principles. For example, killing by the army of the state will be justified by a value for patriotism, or perhaps by the value for standing against bloodstained tyrannies. Because every absolute principle has the character of overstepping the bounds of reality, each principle needs to be held in check by the countervailing force of contrary principles. Pareto illustrated this by suggesting that the injunction to 'love thy neighbour as thyself' might be counterbalanced by a principle which "enjoins the vendetta as a duty" (para. 1772). If the latter principle sounds a bit uncommon in modern times, there is little doubt that the common-sense maxim 'charity begins at home' still retains its countervailing force.

Regardless of the specific illustrations, Pareto's general point was that, for most social actions, there will be a complexity of principles pushing and tugging in different directions. As a result, there must be contrary principles within common-sense. If Pareto is correct, then dilemmas, and potential arguments, are inherent in social life. There will always be problems and controversies arising from the claims of rival principles. For instance, there may be a dilemma whether, on this occasion, the loving of neighbours should take precedence over the demand for domestic charity. Such social dilemmas are not unfortunate accidents, but are an inevitable consequence of there being principles or values.

Because of the dilemmatic nature of common-sense, it is frequently hard to formulate clear and sensible principles to those puzzled by the dilemmas. Instead, the principles will often reflect the dilemma itself. In Chapter 4, there was a discussion of I. A. Richards's harsh criticisms of Bishop Whately's rhetorical advice. All we got from Whately, thundered Richards, was a postcard's worth of crude common-sense: do be clear, but not dry, use metaphors, but don't overdo them. Each common-sense principle is hauled back by a contrary one, lest it get unrealistically out of hand. As was discussed in Chapter 4, the advice of the experimental psychologists, with their goal of unknotting the contrarieties still unrealized, has not greatly superseded that of Whately. Perhaps we might now get an index card's worth, but we will not receive the sort of advice which turns a dilemma into clear and precise order. Advice which calls attention to contrary principles, but does not locate the precise resting place of these contrary pulls for every situation, is not worthless. Implicitly, it calls attention to the complexity of social and psychological reality, and thereby criticizes any one-sided theory, whether formal or informal, which attempts to encapsulate human activity in a single, unqualified, principle.

It is for this reason that so much sound practical advice resembles that of Whately. Opposing common-places must be balanced, just as the decision-maker must take into account contrary, but reasonable, considerations. An example can be given from the world of sport to illustrate how easily general advice can sound like the balancing of platitudes. Mike Brearley, by common consent, has been one of the most thoughtful and successful of all those who have captained the English cricket team. He is also a trained psychotherapist. In his book, *The Art of Captaincy*, there are, as is to be expected, insights into the techniques of that most technical of sports. In addition, the book is filled with the sort of profound observations about people and groups which are too rarely found in modern social psychological textbooks. Yet even Brearley, when he summarizes the captain's art, finds himself describing the contrary pulls of common-sense, in the style of Bishop Whately: "A captain must get the best out of his team by helping them to play together without suppressing flair and uniqueness" (1985, p. 13). Or, again, "a leader is to lead. But this does not mean being a martinet" (p. 277); "No one will follow a prig or a prude; but a captain cannot afford to be dissolute in his personal life" (p. 276). In each case, an eminently sensible principle is hauled back by an equally sensible counter-principle, lest the bounds of sensible captaincy be overstepped. Brearley's balancing of principles is sound common-sense, but it offers little encouragement to the reader who dreams of leading out ten others onto the pitch at Lords. Just as Quintilian realized that no rhetorical guidebook could replace the intuition of the brilliant orator, so Brearley cannot reduce the dilemmas of captaincy to precise formulae. The art resides in feeling for the required balance of contraries in the subtly different dilemmas which must be faced at every stage of every game, both inside and outside the boundary of play.

It is not only the individual decision-maker who is faced by dilemmas. Society in general, with its opposing principles of common-sense, sets puzzles for its members to argue about. In Chapter 5, the debate between the Jewish Elders and the Roman idolators was described. This was not merely a debate between two rival common-senses, but it also reflected a dilemma within the common-sense of rabbinic Judaism. Two principles of common-sense seemed to coincide, thereby occasioning philosophical and theological debate. On the one hand, common-sense stresses the omnipotence of the Deity, able to act at will. On the other hand, common-sense suggests that the world proceeds according to natural laws, which seem to restrict divine omnipotence. In their commentaries upon the debate between the Elders and the idolators, the rabbinical authorities point out that events occur which the Deity might have wished to prevent, but could only do so by interfering with the laws of nature. Therefore, the sun and the moon remain in the sky, even though they remain a constant temptation for idolatry. Similarly, the victims of rape can get pregnant, although in justice they should not. It was such dilemmas which preoccupied the Talmudic commentaries on the debate with the idolators, as sages argued about the relations and meanings of the two contrary common-sense themes of unlimited Divine power and the unstopped force of nature.

The dilemmas of contrary common-places are by no means confined to traditional societies. Modern common-places have not attained the systematic orderliness which the experimental social psychologists are hoping to prepare for us. There is much evidence pointing to the dilemmatic qualities of contemporary common-sense. In an illuminating analysis of the way poverty is talked about, Murray Edelman in *Political Language* argues that people are generally equipped with two different sets of symbols and indeed with two different vocabularies. Edelman's insights about the symbols of modern political discourse can be easily translated into insights about common-places and political arguments. As he shows, poverty is frequently blamed upon the personal characteristics of the poor. When these common-places are used, it is asserted that there are things which the poor themselves can do to improve their situation. Success stories of the self-made person, advancing by hard work and a dedicated character from poverty to wealth, will support these notions. However, on their own, the common-places which criticize the poor overstep economic reality. There is much structural inequality and economic unfairness which clearly cannot be blamed upon the poor. These matters are not repressed in contemporary common-sense, but are represented in a contrary set of common-places, which supply the seeds for a defence of the poor and a criticism of unfairness. The modern citizen, not to mention the modern concerned politician, resembles Protagoras, in that both sides of the matter can be argued. The poor can be blamed for their plight, but there is also sympathy. When we think about poverty, we oscillate between the common-places of justice and those of mercy, for both sets of arguments are commonly sensible. Politicians of one party might draw vehemently upon one of the stocks of common-places, whilst their rivals raid the other store. Their audiences will feel that there is a grain, or perhaps a seed, of reasonableness in the arguments of both sides, although at any time one side might appear far more reasonable than the other. Edelman concludes that this conjunction of sympathy and blame allows poverty to be simultaneously deplored and tolerated. In consequence, poverty continues to exist as both a fact and a social dilemma.

It might be objected that in practice, the conflict between values is more apparent than real, because, in the case of social dilemmas, there are normally agreements about which value should take precedence. Both Perelman and Rokeach have stressed that not all values are held with equal force, but there is typically a hierarchy of values. In *The New Rhetoric*, Perelman and Olbrechts-Tyteca suggest that different audiences will have different hierarchies of values and that the hierarchy is "established by the intensity with which one value is adhered to as compared to another" (1971, p. 81). Rokeach (1973, 1979a and 1979b) has provided much empirical evidence to show that individuals and ideologies can be systematically distinguished by the relative weight placed upon a small number of values. For instance, the conservatively-minded person might accord a higher position in the hierarchy of values to domestic charity than to the indiscriminate loving of neighbours; a more liberal person, by contrast, might hold fast to a hierarchy which reverses the relative positions of these values. Similarly, there is evidence that conservatives and liberals differ in their readiness to blame the poor or the inequalities of society for the existence of poverty.[2]

Even if values are arranged into a hierarchy, dilemmas are not eradicated, because two objects of agreement still collide, even if with unequal force. Although, in theory, the hierarchy may appear to offer a guideline for resolving a dilemma, it may in practice set the terms for deliberating about a particular dilemma. For example, the guideline might assert that priority should be given to one of two values. Even so, dilemmas, and potential arguments, still remain. The guideline will not prevent arguments about the precise extent of the priority which should be given to the favoured value, or whether there are special circumstances in which the priority should be laid aside. The liberal might still be more inclined to blame society for poverty, but the values of self-help still remain within the argumentative repertoire, and there will be occasions when they will insistently demand to be heard. Then, the hierarchy will not provide a convenient matrix which obviates the necessity for deliberation, argument and puzzlement about the dilemmas of common-sense.

The experimentalist may harbour the mystic vision that perfect knowledge, founded upon a statistical harmony of cosmic proportions, will resolve all such puzzles. However, in an alternative vision of perfect knowledge, the dilemmas of serious rhetorical argument may still persist. The Talmud describes the Deity as giving a clear priority to one of two values, yet nevertheless feeling the tension of contrary pulls. It is said that God, deliberating between the values of justice and mercy, prays to Himself: "May it be My will that My Mercy may prevail over My (other) attributes, so that I may deal with My children in the attribute of mercy and, on their behalf, stop short of the limit of strict justice" (*Berakhoth*, 7a). The strange, but at the same time very familiar, syntax illustrates the extent to which descriptions of internal deliberations are adapted from dialogues. This monologue, with its dialogic form, seems on one level to be a statement that the value of mercy should, in general, take priority over that of justice. Yet, since only strict justice, untempered by any mercy, is excluded, the dilemma remains about the weighting to be given to the competing claims of justice and mercy, not in general, but in practice. We could go further to suggest that, because the assertion of hierarchy takes the form of prayer, especially that of self-prayer, this itself illustrates just how serious, and even divinely perplexing, the dilemma continues to be, when the problems of particular cases are faced. Thus, even in the most uncommon place which is humanly imaginable and in which perfect knowledge is presumed to exist, common-sense continues to pose its dilemmas and to provide matters for profound deliberation.

Arguing against common-sense

A rather misleading impression of common-sense may have been created so far. The suggestion that values are generally accepted and not disputed seems to imply that the basic assumptions of common-sense are fixed and beyond controversy. That would be a gross distortion. A community's common-sense can be challenged in argument and its stock of common-places is alterable. Argumentative challenges can be mounted, in order to add to the stock, subtract from it or alter the nature of what is to be stored as the commonly sensible. As was stressed in Chapter 6, we possess the skills to unpick and challenge our schemata. Therefore, the values of common-sense, which normally constitute the means, not the objects, of argument-ation, can themselves become the very topics of controversy.

Sometimes the challenge to common-places might come from outside the community, as two versions of common-sense come into controversial collision. On the other hand, the orthodoxies of common-sense can be disputed by the invention of anti-logoi from within the society. Challenges from without and within may also be made simultaneously. Anytus, a choleric Athenian conservative, complained in the *Meno* that the foreign Sophists were undermining traditional Athenian virtues with their sceptical inquiries. Young men were being taught by these aliens to question things which should never be questioned. The philosophical temperament, which was so threatening to the common-place certainties of the traditionalists, was not confined to immigrants from outlying provinces. There were those who did not even have the excuse of foreignness, yet who were challenging old values and encouraging a new, philosophical, immorality. Protagoras, the foreigner, may have been expelled from Athens as a corrupting influence, but Socrates, the native-born citizen, suffered execution on a similar charge, with Anytus as one of his accusers.

The topic of 'race' provides an example to show that the common-places of common-sense are by no means unalterably fixed. If we consider the way 'race' was talked about in the West a hundred years ago, and compare it with polite discussion today, we might claim that Allport's tolerant person has won the argument. A hundred years ago, values for racial purity could be defended without embarrassment in ways which are no longer socially acceptable. Then, it was common-sense to talk about the value of 'pure blood' and the 'threat of inferior stocks', and these common-places were as normal in educated 'scientific' discourse as they were in ordinary talk. Ernst Haeckel, whose popular biology was admired by both Darwin and Lenin, could write about the superior Aryan race, which had "been placed at the head of all races of men, as the most highly developed and perfect" (1876, p. 321). Such has been the change of perspective, that nowadays the mere quotation of these remarks suffices as a criticism of Haeckel. Not only are racial values no longer trumpeted as being basic values, but the value of opposing the racial values needs no justification. In addition there have been changes in what are taken to be the 'facts', or natural aspects of race. Changes can occur comparatively quickly, with old 'facts', about the strangeness of other races, appearing quite suddenly as strange as any foreigner had been imagined to be. It has been said of Britain in the 1950s that "when West Indians were first employed as bus conductors there were passengers who grabbed them and then shouted to the rest of the bus that their hands were warm, and passengers who tried to see if the blackness would rub off and others who put their hands on the black man's hair for good luck" (Banton, 1972, p. 114).

One might summarize these changes by saying that the old racial values, which were once unquestioned and desirable end-states, have become taboo. In this context the word 'taboo' is appropriate. A whole collection of images, terms, and beliefs has become forbidden. Those who break the taboo are liable to find themselves ostracized, just like those who transgress sexual and lavatorial proprieties in polite company. Although a few individuals might relish being the shamans of nastiness, the majority try to keep clear publicly of this tabooed store, wishing to avoid the taint of evil, which the charges of 'racist' and 'fascist' imply. The old values of race are well beyond the bounds of respectability, and mainstream politicians, drawing upon contemporary values and identifying with the public natures of their audiences, will deny that they are 'racist'. All this might imply that some unpleasant dilemmas of common-sense have been cleared up, as the racial store of common-places has been declared locked until further notice. However, things are not quite so simple, and arguments still persist within a changed common-sense.

In the first place, the former common-places of prejudice have not disappeared entirely. They may have been removed from dialogue, or public thought, but privately they can continue to feed the obsessions of individual imaginations. If these former common-places are not fit subjects for talk, then they are not socially acceptable as thoughts, and a sense of guilt, or apology, will hang over these individual thoughts. However, the dropping of a common-place from common-sense is not simply a process of pushing the publicly unacceptable into the besieged recesses of the private mind. New taboos might have been established, as places which were commonly visited become fenced off with warning signs. Even so, the old common-places may not disappear entirely from social acceptability, and, despite taboos, the reality of racism still persists in the modern world. Detached from their old value, some racist images, beliefs, and even feelings may now travel under the protection of acceptable, and formerly contrary, values.

Evidence for the changing nature of racism has been provided by the surveys and experiments of McConahay and Sears and their colleagues (McConahay and Hough, 1976; McConahay, 1981; 1982; McConahay, Hardee and Batts, 1981; Kinder and Sears, 1981; Jacobson, 1985). These researchers have shown that 'modern racism', unlike the old uninhibited racism, is expressed in covert ways, which avoid a direct appeal to racial values. Acts of discrimination and the voicing of prejudice will be justified in terms of any value but a racial one. The modern racists, unlike those of former times, will not express opposition, in principle, to a black person marrying a white one, but they will believe that 'blacks are getting too demanding in their push for equal rights': the 'blacks' or 'immigrants' have received too many hand-outs already, so in the name of 'fairness' they should not be given...they're too pushy...undeserving...claiming special rights...and so on. Old values, except racial ones, are invoked, and the modern racist will allege that it is black people who are offending common-sense morality. According to Kinder and Sears the modern racist outlook "represents a form of resistance to change in the status quo based on moral feelings that blacks violate such traditional American values as individualism and self-reliance, the work ethic, obedience and discipline" (1981, p. 416). Even the value of equality is invoked, as the racist claims that blacks, as the victims of racism, are getting special privileges. In this way, old images and actions, which might once have been justified by racial values in a self-conscious opposition to the common-places of equality, are now justified by the old contrary value. Allport's tolerant person has won the argument only too well. The value of equality has been established as a common object of agreement, but is open to differing interpretations (e.g. Verba and Orren, 1985). Instead of eradicating the old racial feelings, the value of equality has absorbed them, thereby allowing a tortuous escape from the force of social taboo. As a result, the category of 'equality' acquires a new, and dangerously contrary, meaning. The meaning is controversial, as the bounds and the essence of this 'equality' can be challenged.

Once the fencing of a taboo has been erected, it can be torn down, and there may be those who seek to burst through the values underlying the taboo, in order to reinstate the disgraced common-places. The current taboo against anti-semitic common-places is stronger than that against racist ones, although likewise there are escape routes available. Individuals may occasionally let slip remarks, but the careless expression of prejudice differs from the determined, and deliberate, challenge to the taboo. Intentionally provocative, the challenge to a taboo can be both outrageous and frightening.

Frankfurt. About 1000 people demonstrated outside a theatre last night to stop the world premiere of a play by the late Rainer

Werner Fassbinder. The play has been branded as anti-semitic
...Set in the town's seedy red-light district, it (the play) highlights
the role of an unscrupulous Jewish property speculator called
simply 'the rich Jew'...The theatre's director, Mr Guenther
Ruele, said that the play seeks to break a taboo surrounding
anti-semitism. Fassbinder, who died this year aged 36, was one of
Germany's best known and most prolific film makers with more
than 40 films in a career that spanned 17 years.

(*Guardian*, Nov. 1, 1985)

This theatrical challenge to a taboo constitutes an instance of a minority
attempting to influence the common-sense of the majority. Any such
challenge possesses rhetorical and social psychological implications. In
recent years, a number of social psychologists have been turning their
attention to the ways in which minorities can affect the beliefs and attitudes
of majorities. Serge Moscovici and his colleagues have provided experimental
evidence to show that the judgements of the majority can be affected by the
forthright positions taken by extreme minorities (Moscovici, 1976; Mugny,
1982; Moscovici, Mugny and Van Avermaet, 1985). Some of these experiments of 'minority influence' have involved perceptual judgements of
colours (e.g., Moscovici, Lage and Naffrechoux, 1969) and the details of
such experiments about perceptual judgements may seem far removed from
the issue of common-sense. However, the basic issues involved possess a
rhetorical dimension. Minorities can challenge the previously unchallenged
assumptions of common-sense, and this challenge itself can substantively
affect the nature of the common-sense. In particular, the challenge may
force the majority to justify assumptions which were previously unjustified,
and, thereby, the status of the assumption is altered. McGuire's experiments
on 'inoculation' against persuasion, discussed in the previous chapter,
illustrate the point: a previously unchallenged common-sense asssumption
was changed, under argumentative attack, into an attitude, and, thereby,
into a controversial position.

McGuire's experiment may illustrate one of the influences which a
minority can have upon the beliefs of a majority. If people, when criticized,
search for, and successfully discover, justifications for their assumptions,
then beliefs which had been accepted uncritically may find their justifications
in an argumentative context. Once the critical challenge is answered, then
reasons for holding the original position will be found. In consequence, a
minority may exert influence, not by changing beliefs, but by forcing the
unjustified to become justified. The paradoxical implication is that a belief
may become more reasonable, to the extent to which others might find it
unreasonable. Karl Mannheim described this process on the broad level of
ideology, rather than in terms of face-to-face dispute, but the same

argumentative pattern is apparent. Mannheim suggested that conservative common-sense only justifies itself when under critical attack. The conservative mentality, he argued, tends "to regard the environment as part of a natural world-order which, consequently presents no problems". However, when the power of conservatism is threatened by the challenge of rising classes and their new conceptions of the world, then this threat "causes the conservative mentality to question the basis of its own dominance, and necessarily brings about among conservatives historical-philosophical reflections concerning themselves" (1960, pp. 206–207). In this way, conservatism, under attack, only discovers its philosophical justification when faced with the philosophical objections of its enemies.

When the conservatives try to ward off their critics in this way, they change the nature of their belief. Above all, conservatism ceases to enjoy the privileged status of being unquestioned common-sense. Instead, it becomes a philosophy to take its place in the rhetorical battles between different philosophical perspectives. By entering into argument, conservatism comes down an epistemological peg, from being 'naturally' and common-sensibly true, to being justified by philosophy, like any other rag-bag of controversial opinions. The probings of a minority, therefore, might have the effect of disrupting the epistemological status of the majority's assumptions. As Perelman and Olbrechts-Tyteca have commented, "mere questioning of a statement is...sufficient to destroy its privileged status" (1971, p. 68). In this way the unquestioned elements of common-sense can be relegated to matters of controversy, on which attitudes are expected to be held.[3]

In the same way, the challenge to a taboo can threaten the status of the taboo itself. The taboo itself is part of common-sense, in that it represents a general agreement that certain ways of speaking are not reasonable opinions, to be voiced in the acceptable controversies of common-sense. For instance, Jean-Paul Sartre in his *Portrait of the Anti-Semite*, emphasized that anti-semitism was not to be thought of as a mere 'opinion', to be placed alongside opinions about controversial issues of the day. There was, he argued, something so powerfully shocking about anti-semitism that it should be considered to lie outside matters of opinion, which could be reasonably argued about. When Sartre was writing, the taboos had not been established and anti-semitism was the polite currency of gentile conversation. Now that the taboo has been established, it too can become a matter of controversy, if attacked. Those hoping to release the common-places of anti-semitism and racism from their bonded store seek to rupture the taboo, or at least weaken its status by reducing it to a mere matter of opinion.

An example can be given of a change in epistemological status, following the challenge by a minority upon a majority's common-sense. In recent years, professional anti-semites have been making a determined bid to break through the taboo which surrounds their obsession. They reason that anti-semitism would not be so tabooed, if it had not been so discredited by Hitler's death camps. Therefore, anti-semites have been publishing material which mendaciously denies that the Holocaust took place (Seidel, 1986; Billig, in press b). Amongst Western publics, these fantasies are not taken seriously or, indeed, even noticed, except by small groups which are ideologically, and indeed psychologically, insulated from normal common-sense. Once in a while, an episode might occur to cause these notions to spread outwards from their natural, or, rather, highly unnatural, environment. When they do emerge from the circles of believers, they challenge a fact which is unchallenged in normal common-sense: namely that the Nazis systematically murdered six million Jews. The challenge can have epistemological consequences.

Such an episode occurred when Noam Chomsky, the well-known linguist and left-wing activist, supported, avowedly in the cause of free speech, the rights of a pamphleteer to deny the reality of the Holocaust. Chomsky went so far as to provide a preface for one of this writer's publications. When criticized, Chomsky defended his actions and distanced himself from the thesis whose rights of publication he was defending: "Personally I believe that the gas chambers existed", he is quoted as saying (Fresco, 1980). The phrasing is significant: the reality of the Holocaust – a reality not previously questioned – had become a matter for belief. It was as if an uncontroversial issue had suddenly become a matter of controversy, one on which attitudinal stances should legitimately be taken. No-one would say 'Personally I believe that the Americans bombed Nagasaki' or 'Personally I believe that the earth is round', unless it was thought that these were matters of controversy. On the other hand, one might say 'Personally I believe that the government is doing a grand job' or 'Personally I believe that racist ravings should not be answered', because anti-logoi to these positions are to be expected. In Chomsky's case, the contact with the challenging minority had affected his beliefs indirectly. He had not been persuaded of the rightness of the minority's thesis. Yet, unwittingly, he was expressing himself differently than before, and was talking in a way which would give comfort to the minority, in its battle against common-sense. In this way, even when the minority's specific views are rejected as being untrue, the mere existence of such contrary views can have an effect, if the perceived status of unquestioned facts is changed to controversial beliefs.

From this example, and from the ingenious experiments of Moscovici and Mugny, one might be tempted to assert a general social psychological law: the epistemological status of the majority's views will be affected by the mere fact of a minority's challenge. However, the matter is not so simple, and, as always in rhetorical matters, one should be cautious about proposing absolute psychological laws, which stipulate confidently that something must follow something else. Often so-called laws in social psychology are descriptions of rhetorical strategies. Because of the contrary forms of argumentation, each rhetorical strategy can be opposed by a counter-strategy. Therefore, we possess the possibility of reacting in contrasting ways to the same rhetorical situation. As a result, an apparently reasonable psychological law can frequently be countered by an opposing law, and these reflect different rhetorical strategies.

The simple 'law', about the effects of a minority's challenge upon the common-sense of the majority, is not an absolute psychological law, but the adoption of other rhetorical strategies might forestall the apparent inevitability of such 'effects'. For example, the challenge might be so forthrightly answered by the majority that the minority is effectively dismissed as beneath further consideration. Alternatively, the majority might treat the challenge as being unworthy of answer in the first place. In this case, the refusal to enter a debate can itself be a rhetorical strategy, based upon the recognition that the mere act of answering a question imparts legitimacy to the question. Thus, the serious historian would be well advised to refrain from discussing the reality of the Holocaust with the self-styled, anti-semitic 'experts', because to do so implies a legitimate controversy between two schools of thought.

The strategy of disdaining debate with those whose views are thought to be beyond the bounds of reasonable controversy should not be confused with a dogmatic opposition to argumentation *per se*, or with a frightened flight from rationality. The strategy assumes that limits should be placed upon argumentation, lest new common-places creep stealthily into common-sense and lest arguments which should never be opened become matters of general controversy. The strategy is, of course, a response to a funda-mental social dilemma, in which the value for free argumentation tugs in a contrary direction to that of other values. Dogmatists like Anytus may be untroubled by the dilemma, in that they put scant value upon free argumentation. Others, including perhaps Chomsky, may dismiss the dilemma, if they allow the one value of free argumentation to overstep the realities of all other values. For the rest, the dilemma can be a very real one, itself to be deliberated upon and argued about. In this case, common-sense does not merely provide arguments and dilemmas, but we can turn around upon common-sense itself. There can be dilemmas about the dilemmatic nature of common-sense, as well as arguments about argumentation. Under these circumstances, rhetoric not only includes the arguments which are voiced and the polemics which are published, but also the silences, which themselves are pointed arguments. As Longinus wrote in *On the Sublime*, there will be times when silence can be "more sublime than speech" (145).

9   The spirit of contradiction

A critic might object that there has been a basic contradiction between the themes of the previous two chapters. In Chapter 7, the possessor of attitudes was likened to an orator, arguing one-sidedly for a particular case. The person who admits to 'strongly agreeing' with a statement proffered by an opinion-sampler, will resemble Thomas De Quincey's orator who one-sidedly withdraws the mind from all other estimates. Since we all possess attitudes, this seems to suggest that we are all a bit one-sided. Our critic might say that this is all very well, but in Chapter 8 the model of the person seems to be quite the reverse of what had gone before. In Chapter 8, the contrary nature, or many-sidedness, of common-sense was stressed. People seem to possess this many-sidedness as the common-places, which fill their minds, enabling them to think and argue, tug in various contrary directions. Rather than being the closed-minded and rather obsessed orator of De Quincey's depiction, the image of the ordinary person to emerge from the last chapter would appear to be modelled upon the two-sided Protagoras, who saw no embarrassment in arguing with Socrates that virtue could and could not be taught.

The case of the critic can be developed further to suggest that there is a contradiction between the account given of attitudes and that of common-sense. The notion of 'attitude' would appear to stress the differences of belief between people within a social group, some being pro an issue and others being con. By contrast, 'common-sense' refers to what seems to be commonly shared. Now in full flow, the critic can continue with a display of deduction. If our attitudes are based upon the common-places of common-sense, then we cannot possess attitudes unless common-sense is not so commonly shared. The possessor of a strong attitude will only uphold one side of common-sense, and the two-sided upholder of common-sense cannot possess attitudes. Therefore we either possess attitudes or we possess common-sense.

In effect, our critic would be asking us to choose between a one-sided or a two-sided model of the social beliefs possessed by the ordinary person. At present, according to our critic, our account is as confusing as Protagoras's position on the pedagogic possibilities of an undergraduate course in virtue. If our critic wished to conclude the case with a jibe, it could be asserted that common-sense dictates that we should cease hiding behind our own contradictions and come out into the open to reveal our own attitudes. A one-sided or a two-sided model – we must come down on one side or the other.

A dangerous dilemma beckons, and, as Cicero advised, when faced by a dilemma posed by an opponent "you are refuted, whichever alternative you grant" (*De Inventione*, I, xlvi, 86). In such cases, one should not passively accept the question as it is phrased, but should undermine the appropriateness of the challenge. It is recounted that Menedemus, when asked whether he had stopped beating his father, refused to choose 'yes' or 'no' ('don't know' does not appear to have been offered by the questioner): "It would be absurd...to comply with your conditions, when I can stop you at the entrance" (Diogenes Laertius, *Lives of Eminent Philosophers*, 'Menedemus', xii). Like Menedemus, we should stop our critic at the entrance, by refusing to assert that either it is the one-sided orator in full oratorical flow, or it is the two-sided orator, awaiting the call to duty, who provides the sole model. Apparently Menedemus would become so angry with his critics, that his face would blacken, but we can answer our invented critic more calmly. We could claim that both the one-sided and the two-sided model on their own oversimplify the complexity of our attitudes and our common-sense. What is of interest is not a simple choice between the two, but a discussion of the relations between attitudes and common-sense, and between the one-sided and the two-sided aspects of our selves.

In consequence, the present chapter will consider some of the ambiguous aspects of attitudes, or, to be more precise, the ambiguities involved in the expression of attitudes. The ambiguities to be discussed are not those which might arise because our ways of measuring attitudes are less than perfect. They are ambiguities which arise from the rhetorical nature of attitudes as arguments in a controversy. It is important, therefore, to examine attitudes in their rhetorical context, and it will be suggested that this context affects the ways in which attitudes might be expressed. Sometimes, people may express themselves with all the one-sided inflexibility of De Quincey's orator. At other times, greater flexibility will be displayed. In order to understand such switches of expression, the rhetorical relations between speaker and audience must be taken into account, as well as the competing strategies of identification and contradiction. However, it is not only a matter of altering the force with which an attitude can be expressed, or of deciding between a two-sided formulation or a one-sided one. There are also ambivalent situations, in which people seem to turn around their own attitudes in order to express counter-opinions. On these occasions, people 'take the side of the other'. All these issues will be discussed in the present chapter and the rhetorical complexity of attitudes will be stressed.

Much of this complexity, and indeed ambivalence, arises because our attitudes are not neat bundles of responses, awaiting the opinion-sampler's clipboard, but they represent unfinished business in the continual controversies of social life.

Latitudes of attitudes

Anyone possessed of language is possessed of the capacity to formulate arguments, either of the one-sided sort, which strike directly at an opponent's position, or of a two-sided sort, which themselves contain contrary tendencies. Our one-sided and two-sided skills are contained both in the forms of our grammar and in the content of common-sense. As has been argued earlier, the syntactical skills of categorization and particularization provide fundamental forms of argumentation. A straightforward categorization that 'all Xs are Ys' can be opposed by a particularization to the effect that this particular X, for special reasons, is not really a Y. Therefore, we can make bold unqualified assertions, or categorizations, and, if we choose, we can also qualify our own assertions. The skills of qualification are very necessary, since our common-sense contains contrary elements, or values which set us dilemmas. In discussing such dilemmas, we can choose to concentrate upon a single value, or common-place, throwing all our moral weight behind a stirring, and unwavering, declamation of principle. Others might chip in with qualifications, pointing out difficulties because this principle conflicts on occasion with other moral, or practical, considerations. However, we do not have to wait for others to make these points of qualification, but we ourselves can add another side to our own categorical assertions.

Instead of assuming that our everyday orators are either the confident advocates of De Quincey's description, or are perplexed deliberators, whose words are pulled in two directions, we can say that they, like the skilled professional orator, possess different ways of talking about the world. A rhetorical topic need not be discussed in just one way. We can, if we so choose, draw upon a single common-place, on the assumption that the present matter under discussion fits neatly and unambiguously into a single, well-established rhetorical location. Or again, we can express a dilemma by drawing upon two common places, pulling the matter simultaneously to opposing locations. Our words, in this instance, will qualify themselves, and they will serve as criticisms of any unqualified or one-sided assertions about the topic.

If we turn, then, to the social psychological issue of attitudes, we should be careful not to assume that our attitudes, or the way we express them, are rhetorically simple. We should not necessarily assume that there exists a single statement which defines one's attitudinal position on a topic. As was suggested in Chapter 7, attitudes are not merely expressions of the personality or the outer rumblings of the inner psyche. Attitudes also represent positions taken in matters of controversy. We would not expect an individual, engaging in an argument, just to repeat a single statement with which that individual strongly agrees. That would constitute a rather enfeebled advocacy. Instead, we would expect the individual to argue the case in various ways, and, above all, to be able to respond to the challenges of counter-arguments, adjusting the advocacy in the light of actual or potential critical challenges. In other words, the rhetorical context of argumentation will affect the way the case is expressed or argued for, whether or not there is a deep personal, or psychic, commitment to argue for the case in the first place.

In order to examine how the rhetorical context may affect the expression of attitudes, it may be helpful to use a concept developed by Sherif and Hovland: the notion of an attitudinal 'latitude of acceptance'. In their pioneering work on the social psychology of attitudes, Sherif and Hovland found that their subjects would agree with a range of statements on a particular issue. If we possess attitudes, then we show, according to Sherif and Hovland, not so much an agreement with a single statement, but a 'latitude of acceptance', which comprises the range of statements with which we will express agreement. This range will be marked off from the 'latitude of rejection', which represents all those statements with which we are prepared to disagree. Inside the 'latitude of acceptance' will be statements expressing differing degrees of qualification. In *Social Judgement*, Sherif and Hovland report the results of a study examining the latitudes of acceptance held by Americans regarding the prohibition of alcohol. An extreme statement might express an unqualified support for prohibition: "Since alcohol is the curse of mankind, the sale and use of alcohol, including light beer, should be completely abolished." A less extreme statement might assert the same basic principle, but also introduces a qualification, based upon another valued principle, which tugs in the opposing direction: "Alcohol should not be sold or used except as a remedy for snake bites, cramps, colds, fainting and other aches and pains" (1961, p. 133). There was a small minority of people who undeviatingly adhered to the former statement and only that statement. Such people drew their beliefs narrowly around the single principle, decrying the use of demon drink even for treating snakebite sufferers. Others could allow both the unqualified principle and its principled qualification to co-exist within their latitudes of acceptance, thereby indicating their potentiality for both qualified and unqualified defences of prohibition.

It would be assuming too much to say that those who only assented to one of the statements offered them by Sherif and Hovland possess only one way of expressing their extreme views. Sherif and Hovland's list of statements did not encompass all the possible ways in which an unbending opposition to alcohol could be expressed. Nor did it deal with the different sorts of audience which might be addressed by the keen prohibitionist. Perhaps even the most rigid advocate of a blanket ban on alcohol might express themself tactfully in the face of an audience of snakebite sufferers. As was seen in the previous chapter, an extreme view can be advocated with flexibility, and the present chapter will develop this theme by examining the effects of the rhetorical context upon the expression of attitudes.

If this context is ignored, it might all too easily be thought that those committed to extreme views are trapped within a small latitude of acceptance: the same inflexible expressions inevitably come pouring out, whenever the topic in question is broached. It is not difficult to depict the extremist as someone whose inner psychic forces are so strong that they override all rhetorical factors. It matters not what audience is addressed, nor what the state of controversy is. All that counts is the inner emotions, seething and pulsating, until they gain their unchanging, and unchangeable, expression. It is possible to give examples of this sort of attitudinal fixity, which seems to have only one monotonously repeated mode of expression. Jean-Paul Sartre, in his *Portrait of the Anti-Semite*, describes his friend's Uncle Jules, who could not abide the English. Jules's family would carefully refrain from mentioning anything about England in his presence, to prevent the lava of bigotry from erupting:

> And if someone, under specific circumstances, after careful
> deliberation and as it were inadvertently, made an allusion to
> Great Britain or its Dominions, Uncle Jules pretended to go into a
> fury and felt himself come to life for a moment. Everyone was
> happy. (Sartre, 1965, p. 286)

Uncle Jules was enabled, even expected, to enjoy his bigotry in protected circumstances. His predictable explosions would occur far from any constraints of reality or from the context of serious debate. Like a rare species he could display his exotic plumage in the safety of the zoo, confident that the cage wire would deter all predators and that the keepers would provide regular food and bedding. In short, Uncle Jules's family conspired to insulate him from the serious rhetorical contexts of prejudice. Should his emotions explode, then no-one was seriously expected to argue back. Nor could Uncle Jules have expected to convince the audience. In fact, rhetorically, the audience did not count, for all that mattered to Uncle Jules was the furious delight of riding a hobby-horse at full pelt. Sartre compares Uncle Jules to the "second-hand anti-semite', whose prejudices are not held with the seriousness of the first-hand anti-semite. Unlike Uncle Jules, the first-hand anti-semite will show a greater range of expression. Prejudice will be made to sound 'reasonable', even scientific on occasions; sympathy can be expressed for the bigot's own victims; there might even be a measure of subtlety in the argument; and, sometimes, out will come the embittered hatred.

Uncle Jules, whose rhetorical contexts are explicitly restricted, should not be held up as the model of the committed possessor of attitudes. Even those who might be attached to prejudices, and who invariably answer 'strongly agree' to the questions of the opinion-samplers, might, in fact, show subtle variations in the expression of their attitudes. Sometimes they might draw from the inflexible end of their latitude of acceptance, and, at other times, in other rhetorical contexts, the tone is sweeter and more reasonable. The variety of ways in which prejudice, or for that matter any attitude, can be expressed by one and the same person is perhaps best illustrated by a biographical approach. The same person can be observed in different moods and in different circumstances, expressing themself with full variety and even incongruity. No better biographer can be cited than James Boswell. His hero, Dr Johnson, was renowned, or notorious, for his prejudices against the Scots – a common prejudice in England and a particularly serious one in the years following the unsuccessful Jacobite rebellion. At times Johnson rode his hobby-horse jocularly, particularly to joust with his young Scottish admirer: "He played off his wit against Scotland with a good humoured pleasantry, which gave me, though no bigot to national prejudices, an opportunity for a little contest with him" (1906, vol. 1, p. 360). Certainly, Johnson could phrase his prejudices with a witcraft which was much admired by Boswell:

> I once reminded him (Johnson) that when Dr Adam Smith was expatiating on the beauty of Glasgow, he had cut him short by saying, 'Pray, Sir, have you ever seen Brentford?' and I took the liberty to add, 'My dear Sir, surely that was *shocking.*' – 'Why, then, Sir, (he replied) YOU have never seen Brentford.'
> (Boswell, 1906, Vol. II, p. 445, emphasis in original)

If Johnson possessed a prejudiced attitude, or a schema of bigotry, it was not an inflexible one which demanded that all Scots be lumped dismissively together. Exceptions to sweeping generalizations were often conceded with a graceful wit, which showed off Johnson's skills of advocacy, whilst at the same time preserving the overall argument for prejudice. Boswell describes a conversation between Johnson and a Scotsman about the literary merits of Scottish authors in general, and, in particular, those of the sixteenth-century writer George Buchanan. Johnson is dismissive of Scottish literary talent, but his adversary, knowing the Doctor's admiration for Buchanan, senses an opportunity for undermining the prejudice. He asks:

> 'Ah, Dr Johnson, what would you have said of Buchanan, had he been an Englishman?' – 'Why, Sir', (said Johnson, after a little pause,) 'I should *not* have said of Buchanan, had he been an *Englishman*, what I will now say of him as a *Scotchman*, – that he was the only man of genius his country ever produced.'
>
> (Boswell, 1906, vol. II, p. 445)

At times Boswell accepted Johnson's defence that he was only treating the Scots as he found them, basing his judgements upon facts and a critical spirit, and not upon prejudices: "Johnson treated Scotland no worse than he did even his best friends, whose characters he used to give as they appeared to him, both in light and shade" (vol. I, p. 521). At other times, it could scarcely be denied that there was a darker edge to Johnson's prejudices, and then Boswell, unsmiling, would keep quiet. He found, for example, "outrageous" Johnson's suggestion that Scotsmen "loved Scotland better than the truth" and that they would "attest any thing for the honour of Scotland" (vol. I, p. 525). Nor did Boswell laugh when Johnson complained of the "disposition of your (i.e. Boswell's) countrymen to tell lies in favour of each other" (vol. I, p. 514). On these occasions, the joke had gone beyond itself and Boswell saw little humour in the "violent" and "extreme prejudice" of his mentor (vol. II, p. 125). But, on the other hand, Boswell could not forget the many personal kindnesses, which he, a Scotsman, had received from the hand of Johnson.

Johnson's attitudes towards the Scots are not easily summarized. Certainly no single attitudinal statement, of the sort to be found on a questionnaire, could do justice to their complexities and incongruities. Even Johnson was perplexed by his own prejudices (vol. II, p. 434). Uncle Jules's attitude towards the English might be more conveniently expressed, and given a precise location at the end of an opinion-sampler's scale. However, it is Jules, not Johnson, who is the exception. Existing as a protected, and happily endangered, species, Jules does not show the range of moods and the changing nuances which mark the fluctuations of normal deliberations and disputations. Within Johnson's latitudes of acceptance about the Scots would be a complicated mixture of raillery, menacing accusation, personal praise, impersonal insult, factual anecdote, protestations of reasonableness, etc. and etc. A variety of common-places would be reflected, both gloomily and cheerfully, in this general store of wit and bigotry. At different times, Johnson would draw upon different aspects of his stored opinions. Nor are these fluctuations confined to prejudiced attitudes, but, as will be discussed, they are a more general feature of the latitude we possess in the ways in which our attitudes can be expressed.

Situations for rhetoric

If most people can express their attitudes in many different ways, then the obvious question to be asked is why, on particular occasions, people might choose one form of expression over another possible form: why, for example, a moderate expression might be chosen on one occasion, but, at another time, the same person might speak about the very same issue in harshly inflexible tones. The issue of selection is one of the most basic questions associated with the concept of a latitude of acceptance. An attempt to provide some sort of answer to this question has been made by Glen Hass. His ideas, which are essentially non-rhetorical, can be used as the starting-point for an attempt to look at the rhetorical considerations which influence how people select from the various parts of their latitudes of attitudinal acceptance.

In common with Sherif and Hovland, Hass criticizes the assumption that a person's attitude can be represented as a fixed point, and he stresses that "there is a range of positions on a topic with which a person might agree" (1981b, p. 137). Dr Johnson was doing nothing extraordinary in displaying a range of expressions when talked, as he often did, about the Scots. Nor was he being hypocritical. When he spoke with a lightness of spirit, he was not disingenuously concealing his darker thoughts, but both shades of opinion had their genuine place on his attitudinal palette. Hass notes that "most people have had the experience of talking about the same topic to two different people at separate times, supporting slightly different positions in each conversation, but not misrepresenting their (unchanged) beliefs on either occasion" (p. 138). According to Hass, people choose from their latitudes of acceptance, in order to deal with the situation in which they find themselves. Thus, Hass refers to "situational demands", which "can cause an individual to shift within his or her latitude of acceptance" (p. 144).

On its own, the invocation of 'situational demands' is not particularly helpful, except to locate the issue of selection in the social situation rather than within the emotional life of the individual. However, Hass's intention is not to retreat behind vague generality – 'it all depends upon the situation' – but to take the matter further by hypothesizing what it is about situations which pushes people to alter the way they express their attitudes. To this end, he concentrates upon a basic motive, which he claims lies behind the variations of expression. The motive is to create a favourable impression of oneself, and, as such, the selection of appropriate attitudinal expressions is a form of 'impression-management'. Hass, in common with other social psychologists investigating the management of impressions, assumes the importance and the generality of this motive to impress other people: "Everyone wants to look good, especially if they are being evaluated by someone whose opinion is important to them" (Hass, p. 137). Similarly, Tedeschi describes how people wish to take advantage of "identity enhancing situations": "Actors not only want to avoid or mitigate negative reactions of others towards themselves, but they want to ensure that they reap the rewards (e.g., social approval) associated with being credited for behaving in a meritorious way" (Tedeschi and Riess, 1981, p. 8). The same sort of theme emerges in Schneider's account of the motives underlying 'impression-management': people "want to be approved for being warm or competent or some other charming characteristic" (1981, p. 29).

According to Hass's argument, the selection of attitudinal expressions is a form of 'impression-management', designed to promote a favourable image of the self. We will avoid those expressions which will cause our audience to look askance at us, and we will raid our latitudes to find those expressions which will maximize the chances of our being considered as warmly charming, or charmingly competent individuals. Hass gives some indication as to how this process might occur. He assumes that the fluctuations of expression "are very probably a frequent ingredient of social interaction" (1981b, p. 140). Participants in a conversation will select expressions which emphasize "a common ground", and as a result "they enable the interaction to run smoothly". Minor differences of opinion will be avoided and "finding an area of agreement or overlap of opinion makes an interaction much more comfortable for those involved in it" (p. 140). Naturally, other participants will look favourably upon someone who helps along the interaction in an agreeably smooth manner.

The problem with this account is not that it is inaccurate, but that it is limited, in that it omits the argumentative features of attitudes. The 'interactions' which Hass has in mind are the modern equivalents of the polite company which Dr Johnson claimed to engage in 'pretty talk'. As was discussed in Chapter 5, this prettiness is very different from the disputatious discussions which Johnson loved. In a discussion, the spirit of contradiction is unleashed, whilst, in the pretty conversation, agreement is the order of the moment. Yet, it would be to simple merely to say that the theories of impression-management ignore all rhetorical aspects of interaction, for the creation of a favourable impression has long been considered an important rhetorical skill.

However, there is a difference of emphasis between impression-management, as discussed by modern social psychologists, and its treatment in ancient rhetorical treatises. In the modern work, it appears that the presentation of the self in a favourable manner is an end in itself. Persuasiveness is a means of attaining this self-evidently desirable end as we try to influence the impressions of our fellow conversationalists and to persuade them of the goodness of our selves. In the rhetorical treatises, the emphasis is the other way round. The self is projected in order to increase persuasiveness. At the start of a speech, during the warm-up or exordium, orators are urged to create a favourable impression. The way the rhetorical theorists talked about the exordium is not so different from the way that impression-management theorists talk about the interactions which interest them. The rhetorical textbooks recommended that orators should present their characters, and those of their clients, in the best possible light during the exordium. If an orator projects a favourable image of the self, "he will have the good fortune to give the impression not so much that he is a zealous advocate as that he is an absolutely reliable witness" (Quintilian, *Institutes of Oratory*, IV, i. 7).

Quintilian did not believe that the creation of such a favourable impression was a desirable end in itself. It was a means to further the argumentative end of winning one's own case and defeating that of an opponent. Of course, the orator wishes to impress the audience, but only as a means to a further end. As Cicero wrote, "an exordium is a passage which brings the mind of the auditor into a proper condition to receive the rest of the speech" (*De Inventione*, xv, 15). Whereas in 'pretty company', one might be persuasive in order to create an impression, in the argumentative context, one projects a favourable image in order to be persuasive. What has been omitted, therefore, in the account of impression-management, has been the argumentative aspect. Nor is this a negligible aspect as far as attitudes are concerned, for, as has been argued previously, attitudes, by their nature, are positions taken on matters of controversy.

Nevertheless, in one important respect Hass's account of impression-management does coincide with the rhetoricians' descriptions of oratorical practice. In the previous chapter, it was argued that the skilled orator, who wishes to persuade the audience, should emphasize a sense of communality. The speaker should draw upon the common-places of the audience, and, as Kenneth Burke has written, the speaker should identify with the audience. If the participators in politely pretty conversation should seek a common-ground between themselves, then so should the orator in the context of argumentation. In both contexts, therefore, there is an identification of speaker with audience.

Although the 'pretty company' might be dominated by a 'spirit of accord', which enables the participants to identify warmly with each other, in the rhetorical context there is also an opposing spirit. In addition to the search for a common-ground, there is the motive to contradict, or to rebut, and this motive can tear asunder the identified common-ground. As a consequence, it is too simple to characterize the rhetorical situation as being dominated by the single principle, strategy or motive to promote favourable impressions. There is always, to use an old-fashioned phrase, a 'spirit of contradiction'. These two spirits, that of accord and that of contradiction, can pull in opposing directions. In Philip Massinger's play, *The Picture*, Ladislaus, King of Hungary, is so smitten by his Queen Honoria that he identifies his own desires with hers, and gives himself up to her command:

> 'You transcend
> In all things excellent, and it is my glory,
> Your worth weigh'd truly, to depose my self
> From absolute command, surrendering up
> My will and faculties to your disposure.' (Massinger, 1976, I, ii)

Eubulus remains sceptical in the face of the king's infatuation, and he questions Honoria's moral probity. Ladislaus replies sharply: "Be dumb, thou spirit of contradiction." Ladislaus cannot be identified simply with the spirit of accord, and Eubulus with the spirit of contradiction. In silencing the spirit of contradiction, to allow the victory of that of identification, Ladislaus was, of course, using that self-same spirit, but was turning it against his courtier Eubulus, who, in his turn, was attempting to make the king identify with his own spirit of contradiction. As this example suggests, the forces of identification and contradiction are often complexly intertwined in rhetorical situations. What remains to be discussed is the ways that these opposing spirits, and their differential weightings in various rhetorical situations, might influence the selection of attitudinal expressions.

Identification and contradiction

There will be no attempt to provide an exhaustive list of the different situations in which the spirits of identification and contradiction might affect the expression of attitudes. As has been stressed previously, a fully comprehensive list of situations is always an impossibility in social psychology and in rhetorical theory. Instead of aiming for an impossible completeness, a few general remarks will be made about three different sorts of situation: those that call directly upon the accommodating spirit of identification, those that emphasize contradiction, and those in which there is both identification with and contradiction of an audience.

(a) Situations for identification

These are the sorts of situation, envisaged by Hass, in which the participants search for the common-ground and where there is, broadly speaking, an acceptance of normative pressures. In these sorts of situation, one would not expect an individual to stick out disruptively from the average, in the way that Uncle Jules must have put an end to polite chit-chat whenever someone happened to mention the English. There is abundant experimental evidence suggesting that subjects frequently conform to the pressures of experimentally-created groups. In fact, it has been argued by Serge Moscovici, in *Social Influence and Social Change*, that social psychologists have tended to exaggerate the importance of conformity, assuming it to be the basic principle of social life. Rather than cite dozens of studies in which conformity is displayed in the social psychological laboratory, one experiment with a rhetorical theme can be mentioned. Cialdini *et al*. found that experimental subjects moderated their views when they expected to discuss issues such as euthanasia with other people whose opinions they broadly agreed with. It was the anticipation of face-to-face discussion which was crucial in producing these accommodating shifts. Cialdini *et al*. comment that the change in opinions, or more precisely in the expression of the opinions, "appears to be determined by the demands of the discussion situation" (1973, p. 105). The shifts disappeared when it was announced that the discussion had been cancelled. Interestingly, the authors interpret their results in terms of something closely analogous to the oratorical search for common-ground and identification with the audience: "Our subjects resemble the politician who revises his speech so as to best appeal to each audience's special interests" (p. 107).[1]

Social situations may 'demand', or, at least, encourage, not only the accommodation of opinions, but also the accommodation of the self. If the orator identifies with the audience, then part of the orator's self is bound up with, or is deliberately portrayed as being bound up with, the communality of the hearers. The identification might only be temporary, just as the polite tea-party might represent a temporary meeting of kindred spirits, to be ended as soon as the tea is drunk and the cakes are eaten. In this sense, the identification between the selves of the orator and audience might parallel what some anthropologists have termed 'situational identity'. Okamura (1981) has discussed this notion in relation to ethnic identity. In multi-cultural societies, such as the United States, members of ethnic groups have many other roles and identities, besides being a member of a particular ethnic group. For many social purposes, the ethnic identity is irrelevant. There will, however, be situations for which this ethnic identity will be appropriate, and, in entering such a situation, group members will switch into their ethnic identification. When in the company of fellow ethnic members, for instance at an organized cultural or religious event, then the ethnic member will display a range of ethnically-tinged actions, which would have been inappropriate in the role of all-American subway passenger, supermarket customer or hot-dog consumer. In acting ethnically, the group members will be identifying with one another, showing the appropriately ethnic parts of their selves. Not only will there be a convergence of gesture and language, but opinions will be expressed with the appropriate ethnic colouration. The result will be a solidification of ethnic identities, just as the respectably polite conversation confirms the respectable identities of those involved.

These situations of identification seem to stress accommodation at the expense of contradiction. However, contradiction is not wholly absent. As the late Henri Tajfel continually stressed, the formation of a group identity involves more than a description of the selves of those involved. Either implicitly, but just as often explicitly, identification with a group entails an intergroup distinction, as the ingroup separates itself from an outgroup (Tajfel, 1978 and 1981). An identification of common attitudes implies a drawing away from those who might hold counter-attitudes. Political scientists have discussed the effects of 'period' upon attitudes. It has been found that there is a tendency to accommodate to the general climate of opinion, as if the *Zeitgeist* represents a situation which cries out for respect. For example, in the 1970s there was a greater tolerance in the United States towards communists and atheists than there had been in the 1950s. Even those who had been adult, and presumably intolerant, in the 1950s, tended on average to be influenced by this shift of opinion and to have softened their views (e.g. Davis, 1975). On one level, these shifts can be explained in terms of an accommodation to changed norms and values. However, attitudes also have their element of criticism and controversy. Accommodation in this instance is not merely a matter of altering the content of the latitude of acceptance, but the spirit of accommodation also entails a modification to the latitude of rejection. A growing identification with the modern climate of opinion would have entailed a disengagement from younger, and less tolerant, selves. Thus, the identification of the self with the prevailing situation would be accompanied by a distancing from the earlier identifications of the self. Of course, some individuals might get left behind in the historical movement, even, like Uncle Jules, relishing a splendidly old-fashioned isolation.

(b) Situations for contradiction

Where impression-management theorists tend to fall short is in assuming that social situations are necessarily characterized by accommodation and identification. There can also be situations in which contradiction is the dominant spirit. Common-ground is not sought, but the challenges of anti-logoi are to be resisted directly. In such situations, one might see the reverse of what occurs in the situations which 'demand' accommodation. For example, the subjects of Cialdini *et al.* (1973) moderated their opinions when expecting a face-to-face discussion. However, if a confrontation, rather than a discussion, is anticipated, then there can be a hardening of attitudinal expressions. There is experimental evidence suggesting that people might select one-sided, unqualified expressions of their position, if they know that they will have to confront others who forcefully hold opposing views (e.g., Greenwald, 1969; Jellison and Mills, 1969; Cialdini *et al.*, 1976). It could be said that people are liable to prepare themselves to be one-sided orators in such situations, especially on matters which are important to them. They brace themselves one-sidedly for the clash by phrasing their position uncompromisingly, and by avoiding, at least in the first instance, those more wishy-washy expressions of their attitudes which in less hectic circumstances might have provided agreeable common-ground with fellow conversationalists.[2]

Sometimes, the selection of extreme positions from the latitudes of acceptance might be made with a view to combating oppositional arguments directly. Within a discussion, there may be a tacit agreement that disputants argue for a single position wholeheartedly. Each disputant will feel that qualifications will be provided by their fellow disputants and that, out of the clash of one-sided parties, the many sides of truth will emerge. Cicero's *De Oratore* recounts a dialogue between Roman orators, self-consciously modelling themselves on Socrates and his fellow conversationalists. The orators decide to rest under a tree, as Socrates did in *Phaedrus*, there to debate the classic dilemmas of oratory: whether orators should use tricks to obtain argumentative victory, whether nobility of style should be accorded priority over persuasiveness, and so on. Each disputant pushes a particular point of view, except for Antonius, who, amidst much self-depreciation and mockery from the rest, changes his tone on the second day. The others all talk as if the dilemmas of oratory had been resolved for them personally. This air of certainty is possible because each knows that someone else will put the other side. In this instance, the form of social interaction, far from guaranteeing a search for common-ground, is Protagorean: it is the whole group, with its members agreeing to divide up into argumentative prosecutions and defences, which expresses the spirit of the great Sophist, whilst its members can enjoy the spirit of one-sided advocacy.

De Oratore describes a situation like a courtroom battle, in which prosecution opposes defence without any thought of mutual identification, although, perhaps, each might concede that the other's case does have its element of reasonableness. Nevertheless, a distinction can be drawn between the two sorts of situations. In the courtroom, the audience and the opponents are formally distinguished. Opposing pleaders are to be met by the spirit of contradiction, whilst a rhetorical identification should be sought with judge and jury. In *De Oratore*, there is no immediate audience to whom common-place appeals could be made. Instead, the spirit of contradiction seems to have untrammelled licence. Yet, in a sense, there is an unseen audience. Just as those self-conscious imitators of *Phaedrus* had been the posthumous audience of Socrates, so they could hope that they, by courtesy of Cicero's efforts, would gain a wider attention. There can be few deliberate attempts to seek common-ground with the unknown, even unborn, audience. No special interests can be appealed to, for none are known to exist. As in the dialogue between the Jewish Elders and the Roman idolators, discussed in Chapter 5, argument seems to confront opposing argument, without the frills of packaging or knowing winks towards the audience. If the notion of an audience is relevant to this situation, in that speakers frame their words as if there is an audience, then perhaps it is the Universal Audience, of which Perelman and Olbrechts-Tyteca have written. This is the hypo-thetical audience, guided by no less than pure rationality, and only im-pressed by the quality of arguments and counter-arguments (1971, pp. 51ff).

The Ciceronian debate and the experimental situations represent examples where the reality, or the anticipation, of an extreme oppositional attitude may provoke the selection of an extreme formulation of one's own position. The examples have involved face-to-face debate between individuals. If our attitudes are aspects of a wider controversy, then whole climates of public opinion also can become extreme in the face of perceived extreme counter-opinions. In this case, a process of polarization may lead to a narrowing of the latitudes possessed by individuals. Murray Edelman has described the "bimodal value structuring", which occurs when public opinion might be "polarized into two clearly defined adversary foci" (1964, p. 175). Mass opinion will find itself grouping around a single value or common-place – whether it be that of the 'nation', 'democracy' or merely 'civilization as we know it' – opposing the threat of a counter-opinion symbolized by a despised value: "Those who hold the other value become the enemy" (p. 175). Categorized as the enemy, they are placed beyond the bounds of legitimate discourse. Under these circumstances, the common-ground disappears, as the two common-senses are drawn more tightly, and less dilemmatically, around their valued symbols.

These situations of deep social contradiction are also situations of identification. No common-ground might be sought with the enemy, but greater demands may be placed upon showing identification and loyalty with one's fellows. Individuals will feel less likely to voice qualifications, lest they be identified as agents or fellow-travellers of the enemy. In their famous experiments on American boys' camps, the Sherifs showed how the boys, once they were divided into separate, competitive groups, emphasized the differences between the groups. Group members put pressure on their fellow members to express total loyalty to their group's symbols and to renounce contact with any member of the despised enemy (Sherif and Sherif, 1953; Sherif, 1966). When this happens, the latitudes of acceptable attitudes become circumscribed within each group, with a decreasing range of positions which are taken as displaying an acceptable degree of loyal identification. Messages conveyed to the other side are not concerned with promoting impressions of warmth and competence, nor are they likely to be perceived as such. In short, these tense situations, bristling with hostilities and loyalties, tend to demand more than personal identity enhancement.

(c) Situations for identifying with and contradicting an audience

These are rhetorically interesting situations, in which a speaker identifies with an audience, but at the same time contradicts its views. As was discussed in the previous chapter, speakers are advised by both ancient and modern rhetoricians to identify with an audience, especially when the intention is to change the audience's opinions. As Kenneth Burke wrote, some of an audience's opinions should be used as a fulcrum to move others. When this occurs, the contrary forces of accommodation and contradiction must be brought into play, and the speaker will have the tricky job of navigating through waters whose currents swirl about dangerously in several directions.

The ambivalence of such situations can be illustrated by a common rhetorical ploy, which the classical rhetoricians do not seem to have directly discussed, and which has been located by sociologists as a strategy of impression-management, rather than as one of argumentation. Hewitt and Stokes attempt to develop the earlier sociological analysis of Scott and Lyman (1968), who looked at the ways people make excuses. Hewitt and Stokes concentrate upon what they call 'disclaimers'. These are remarks which are intended to deflect criticisms, particularly those criticisms which would be directed against the identity and integrity of the speaker: "A disclaimer is a verbal device employed to ward off and defeat in advance doubts and negative typifications which may result from intended conduct" (Hewitt and Stokes, 1975, p. 3). The phrase 'I'm not prejudiced' is a form of disclaimer which Hewitt and Stokes call 'credentialing' and which specifically seeks to avoid "an undesired typification" (p. 4). Such a disclaimer might precede the voicing of beliefs which might easily lead the speaker to be categorized as being prejudiced. Similarly the writer of a magazine article uses this sort of disclaimer when he begins with the statement "I am an active supporter of Universities", but then uses the rest of his column space to attack them (Jo Grimond, in *Spectator*, Feb. 5, 1983). In this case, the disclaimer is intended to prevent the author from being classed by the reader as the sort of philistine who normally attacks educational institutions.

Disclaimers are a sub-category of a general argumentative device well known to classical rhetorical theorists. Quintilian referred to the "extraordinary value" of *prolepsis*, "whereby we forestall objections" (IX, ii, 14–17). In the sixteenth century, Abraham Fraunce warmly recommended the same strategy, but called it by its alternative classical name of *praeoccupation*: it was still represented as the tactic "when we prevent and meet with that which might be objected" (*The Arcadian Rhetorike*, chapter 34). The general strategy might have been identified, but there is more to the 'disclaimer' than is contained in the classical descriptions of *prolepsis* and *praeoccupation*. The strategy, as described by Hewitt and Stokes, is not merely one of contradiction, by which prospective anti-logoi are sent on their way. It is also a device which seeks an accommodating common ground with the potentially critical audience. Hewitt and Stokes, in fact, locate the device in situations of identification. They suggest that the devices are attempts "to repair the breaks and restore meaning", when social interactions have been, or are about to be, disrupted (1975, p. 1). Certainly, disclaimers try to emphasize common ground. 'I'm not prejudiced' or 'I am an active supporter of the Universities' tell us something about the audiences which are being addressed. Respectively, the statements draw upon the values of tolerance and education, and the speakers identify themselves with their audiences, which are presumed also to value these things. However, in the disclaimer there is more than an identification, or an attempt to manage the impression which the audience might form of the speaker. There is also the element of contradiction, as the statement of a common ground serves as a brief exordium to a critical assault. It is as if the speaker clears the way for the sort of anti-logoi which might otherwise invite the hisses and boos of a hostile audience.

In addition, there is a further rhetorical dimension to the disclaimer. A strategy of this sort implies a commitment to future oratory. The disclaimer acts as a statement of faith that, on other occasions, the speaker will address the issue differently. The present remarks, so the disclaimer assures the audience, are not the only ones to be found within the speaker's latitude of acceptance. 'I'm not prejudiced, but...' seems to imply that, in other situations, the speaker would oppose a bigoted audience. Perhaps a reverse disclaimer would be offered: 'I'm no starry-eyed liberal but...' The active supporter of the Universities implies to his readers that, if faced by genuine philistines, he would turn his anti-logoi about: 'I am an active supporter of cost-cutting in education (see my article in the *Spectator*), but...' What these examples suggest is that changes in attitudinal expression are not confined to an elastic stretching of an attitudinal latitude to encompass moderate expressions, or to a contraction which excludes the moderate views. In addition to increasing the strength or flexibility of an attitudinal expression, there can be changes in its argumentative direction. The disclaimer implies that, as rhetorical situations alter, so the direction of the expressed attitudes can alter. Logoi can become anti-logoi, criticisms can be transformed into justifications, as speakers bend their attitudes towards the changing oratorical context of contradiction.

Taking the side of the other

The examples of the disclaimers show that the rhetorical contexts of attitudes are not fixed. Should the context be changed, and should the speaker be confronted by a new audience, then the expression of the attitude may be altered. The speaker might draw upon a moderate or an extreme expression from the latitude of acceptable opinions, depending upon the rhetorical situation. However, it is also possible to push this analysis further, by suggesting that the latitude itself may be altered if the context of controversy is changed. Since all attitudes are positions on a matter of controversy, they exist within a wider argumentative context. If the wider controversy changes, then the attitudinal arguments might be expected to be changed to cope with argumentative developments. Sometimes, the change may be such that the direction, rather than the force, of attitudinal expressions is turned around. Unlike Uncle Jules, protected from all but a tiny range of rhetorical situations, ordinary people may find themselves sounding like the oratorical equivalent of the poacher turned game-keeper. On some occasions they may catch themselves drawing upon arguments which they had assumed to belong to their latitude of rejection; but now they will be arguing against points of view which look suspiciously like those to be found in their very own latitude of acceptance. In short, there may be occasions when our criticisms turn to justifications and our justifications to criticisms.

This switching from defence to prosecution, or vice versa, can be referred to as 'taking the side of the other': positions which were previously assumed to represent the other side are advocated as one's own side. The description contains a deliberate echo of George Herbert Mead's notion of 'taking the role of another'. In *Mind, Self and Society*, Mead argued that an important part of the child's social development was to learn to take the roles of other people. In games, the child learns about social relations by playfully adopting other roles, and by so doing the child learns to co-operate with others (1934, pp. 253ff). Mead also suggests that this sort of play is vital to the development of thought. In Chapter 5, we touched upon these ideas, when discussing the argumentative nature of deliberation. It was mentioned that Cicero and Mill, amongst others, recommended that people sharpen their own thoughts by conducting their own internal arguments. All thinkers should mentally take the side of their critics, in order to probe the weaknesses of their own positions. By imagining an internal debate, in which we play the roles of critic and counter-critic, we can equip ourselves with the *prolepses* or *praeoccupations*, which will serve us in good stead when we encounter the actual critic.

Cicero and Mill were, in effect, talking about playing the role of the other as a practice exercise, rather than for real. However, there might also be occasions where it is not the imaginary role of the other that is played, but we publicly advocate in all seriousness the side of the other. It is not the intention to connect the occasions for taking the side of the other to any inner turmoils of emotion, which might lead to a reversal of expressed opinions. Instead, such reversals will be examined in relation to the general argumentative context of attitudes. It is because attitudes are located within a controversial context that such reversals can have a rhetorical meaning, rather than a significance which is confined to the subterranean depths of an individual's emotions. In particular two sorts of situations will be mentioned, as being occasions when people may feel a wish to advocate the side of the other.

(a) The non-identification of a non-contradictory speaker

The textbooks, both ancient and modern, emphasize that the speaker should seek a common-ground with the audience, especially if advocating a message which contradicts some of the opinions of that audience. This sound piece of advice suggests that speakers may meet with resistance if the common-ground is not established. Therefore, the advice can be turned upside down: it can be presented as a dire warning of what might happen, if the speaker fails to identify with the audience. If no common-ground is sought, then message and speaker might be summarily dismissed. An interesting situation might arise, if the speaker is ostensibly advocating a position with which the audience is *prima facie* in broad sympathy, but is doing so in such a crass way that the audience is liable to become disenchanted. Under such circumstances, one might envisage listeners being moved by the spirit of contradiction to take the side of the other against the speaker.

There have been a number of social psychological experiments which have shown something like this to occur in laboratory situations. Many of these experiments go under the heading of studies of 'reactance'. Like most components of social psychological theory, 'reactance' is not usually examined in terms of rhetoric. Usually it is defined as the angered reaction which individuals show when their freedom is restricted, and which they direct against those who have imposed the restriction. Brehm in *A Theory of Psychological Reactance* expresses it thus: "Given that a person has a free set of behaviours, he will experience reactance whenever any of those behaviours is eliminated or threatened with elimination" (1966, p. 4). Nevertheless, many of the reactance studies have not actually been concerned with the restriction of behaviour, but have been set in a rhetorical situation. The typical reactance experiment involves a speaker who does not actually restrict the freedom of the audience, but talks in an arrogantly off-putting manner. For example, Snyder and Wicklund (1976) had their speaker wrapping up his message with comments to the effect that his position was "the only rational choice", and that "you have no choice but to agree with me". It has been found, not surprisingly, that subjects will react against a speaker who talks to them in this way. This occurs even if the audience is in sympathy with the position advocated by the overbearing speaker. Under these circumstances, the audience is liable to start agreeing with opposing positions (Brehm, 1966; Snyder and Wicklund, 1976; Wright and Brehm, 1982). Also, it has been demonstrated that the audience will start formulating counter-arguments if they expect to meet the speaker (Baer *et al.*, 1980).

In such cases the speaker has signally failed to establish any sense of identification with the audience. Having been treated with scant respect, the audience, driven by the spirit of contradiction, or reactance, is liable to start arguing against the speaker's position. This might entail the audience arguing against a previously agreed stance. In order to so argue, the audience might dip into latitudes of previous rejection, and thereby it takes the side of the other. Similarly, Pritchard and Billig found that traditional women started using feminist arguments, when provoked by a male expressing traditional views in a tone which was dismissive of women generally. These women, who in the abstract might disagree with feminist positions, started taking the side of the feminists to counter the unpleasant threat coming ostensibly from their own side. As will be suggested later, such changes of expression are not to be dismissed as fits of pique or minor temper tantrums. They stem from an awareness that the meaning of an attitude changes as the context of controversy is altered.

(b) Removal of the counter-attitude

The 'reactance' effects occur when the context of controversy has been altered by changes in the way one's own side is being advocated. Instead of dealing with counter-arguments from opponents, one has to argue against those who might superficially seem to be allies, but with whom one cannot identify. The alterations in the context of controversy can also give rise to changes in the expression of the counter-attitudes. These changes also can lead the former opponent to take the side of the other, at least in certain argumentative situations.

One's own attitudes might have been developed in order to counter particular opposing attitudes. The anti-logoi of the opponent might always have prevented one's own logoi from enjoying unimpeded progress. Under these circumstances, we might have argued a case one-sidedly, secure in the knowledge that there were others to put the other side, just as the Roman orators did in Cicero's *De Oratore*. If, as Pareto suggested, a single, un-qualified principle can so easily overstep reality, then the removal of the opponents' restraining anti-logoi might have the effect of causing our own attitudinal logoi to burst forth like coiled springs which are suddenly released. The unleashing of the hitherto restrained force of our position may worry us. In order to curb our own logoi and to prevent our own attitudes running unrealistically unchecked in these changed conditions, we might then feel the need to take the side of the other. In consequence, we might start employing those arguments which previously had seemed to be the sole property of our opponents.

Boswell recounts an incident when Johnson felt the need to compress the coils of his own logoi, which had suddenly been released from the restraining pressures of anti-logoi. Boswell records of the Doctor, that "talking on the subject of toleration, one day when some friends were with him in his study, he made his usual remark, that the State has a right to regulate the religion of the people" (1906, vol. II, p. 324). Under normal circumstances, someone would care to disagree with Johnson's provocative remark, and there would ensue a discussion in which Johnson could pursue his familiar one-sided line. However, on this occasion Johnson was met by ready agreement, and it was the Doctor himself who was forced to provide the anti-logoi. Boswell recounts: "A clergyman having readily acquiesced in this, Johnson, who loved discussion, observed, 'But, Sir, you must go around to other States than your own. You do not know what a Bramin has to say for himself.'" Johnson was not going to let a pretty agreement stand in the way of an argumentative airing of a dilemma whose complexity he well appreciated. In consequence, he himself was forced to express the anti-logoi to his own attitudinal logoi, thereby opening up the matter for debate and deliberation.

Under other circumstances, the removal of the anti-logoi may lessen the need for the logoi, and, in consequence, an attitude is dropped when the counter-attitudes likewise fade into oblivion. There may not be a direct switching here, from attitudinal defender to prosecutor. What may happen is that the latitude of acceptance may change so fundamentally, that the formerly acceptable positions are no longer voiced and the rejected ones cease to be rejected, at least in the same manner. Again, the spirit of contradiction can play a crucial part in such a process. Johnson was notorious in his circle for his oft-voiced Jacobite sympathies. He would delight in shocking 'pretty company' with his outrageous, even treasonable, attitude: "One day when dining at old Mr Langton's, where Miss Roberts, his niece, was one of the company, Johnson, with his usual complacent attention to the fair sex, took her by the hand and said, 'My dear, I hope you are a Jacobite'" (*ibid.* vol. I, p. 267). His host, "a high and steady Tory" but firmly "attached to the present Royal Family", was suitably offended.

Boswell, however, suspected that Johnson's Jacobitism was motivated by the spirit of contradiction. According to Boswell, the Doctor would admit "the charge of disaffection imputed to him by the world, merely for the purpose of shewing how dexterously he could repel an attack, even though he were placed in a most disadvantageous position" (vol. I, p. 266). Attitudes are rarely expressed 'merely' for a single purpose, and Johnson's Jacobitism also represented a belief that there was another side to the matter, beyond the prevailing opinion, and that this other side should not go unexpressed in the face of general hostility. Someone was needed to take the side of the other, and Johnson, with his love of controversy, did not shrink from the burden. If the Doctor's behaviour in arguing so shocking a case seems to resemble that of Uncle Jules, then an important difference should be noted. Uncle Jules's speeches seem to be solitary outbursts of internal anger, whilst Johnson's affronts to gentility were responsive to the argumentative context. Boswell records that Johnson's "attachment to the House of Stuart" cooled as he grew older, but so, it appears, did the extreme anti-Jacobitism of his company: "Indeed, I heard him once say that after the death of a violent Whig, with whom he used to contend with great eagerness, he felt his Toryism much abated" (p. 267). In this case, as opposed to that of the clergyman, there was a feeling that the controversy, or dilemma, was being resolved, to the extent that the extreme anti-logoi were no longer being voiced. As the latitude of rejection was dying out, so there was little further use for the latitude of acceptance.

Identification and the side of the other

Taking the side of the other, when the rhetorical context changes, is not tantamount to hypocrisy or treachery. In none of the examples given does the individual deliberately dissemble, in order to present a public advocacy which differs from private thoughts. Nor, in the examples, does the individual go over to the other side, identifying with it whole-heartedly. Johnson did not become an opponent of state religion, although, for the sake of argument, he may have voiced some objections. The authors of reactance experiments might present their results as showing 'attitude-change', but there is little evidence to suggest that the changes displayed by the subjects carry over into other argumentative contexts. Nor is there unambiguous evidence that the participants in these experiments were provoked by the awfulness of the speaker into a profound re-evaluation of their general stance on the issues in question.

When someone does take the side of the other, it is necessary to understand this stance in relation to the argumentative context. In Chapter 5, it was suggested that the meaning of an argumentative statement should be understood in terms of the wider controversy. A statement's meaning does not merely depend upon the internal meanings of the words that compose it, but it also depends on the counter-statements, which are being opposed. The implication is that the same statement can have different meanings if it is opposing different counter-statements. Should the same statement be used to do very different argumentative jobs, then its meaning will alter. Thus, Johnson's Jacobitism, expressed in good-naturedly Whig gatherings, can be distinguished from similar Jacobite sentiments voiced in a gathering of conspirators, seriously seeking to overthrow the Georgian regime. As Boswell suspected, Johnson, objecting to the smug assumptions of Whiggism, would not have identified himself with the Jacobites, whose opposition was far more encompassing.

Despite the similarities between two argumentative statements, or two attitudinal expressions, they will bear different rhetorical meanings if they are directed against different targets. A different set of identifications and oppositions would then be involved. This is not just a point of theory, but also relates to the way that people interpret discourse. In a classic social psychological demonstration, Solomon Asch's students ascribed a very different meaning to a sentence expressing the desirability of revolutionary action, when they were told that the statement had been made by Lenin, than when they were told, correctly, that it had been made by Thomas

Jefferson. In one case the statement was interpreted as a message which the students could support and identify with. In the other instance the same words bore a threatening, and foreign, meaning to be opposed.

Although the differences between the meaning of a revolutionary statement ascribed to Jefferson can be distinguished from that of a similar one ascribed to Lenin, the similarities should not be ignored. It is not sufficient to say that the statements really, or essentially, are different, and then sit back with the matter closed. The fact that identically revolutionary statements can be ascribed to the founding heroes of the United States and the Soviet Union should be sufficient to provoke puzzlement. Similarly, Johnson's shifts between, and within, arguments frequently set Boswell wondering what the old boy was up to. This suggests that taking the side of the other may not be a straightforward act. Its mixture of similarities and differences may raise eye-brows and induce objections. In turn, the act may have arisen from situations in which the rhetorical climate, and its identifications and contradictions, might be ambivalent.

The switch from prosecutor to defender can arise when individuals find themselves acting in a similar way to the others, who have been regularly criticized by them in the past. Then, in order to justify the self, justifications might be taken from the others' repertoire. This can occur without the self genuinely identifying with the previously criticized others, and without the self abandoning such criticisms in the future. This is illustrated in the following example, taken from a letter to a national newspaper. The writer is a socialist, who has just published a novel with suitably left-wing themes. This long-serving critic of capitalist free-enterprise has just fallen foul of the system by which the book trade 'rates', and thereby fixes, the sales of books in advance of their publication: "Once rated, sales cannot easily be influenced by market forces", complains the well-reviewed but meagrely-purchased novelist. He concludes his letter with the declaration:

> In the long run, the only hope is to dismantle these monopolies
> and reintroduce market forces. An argument which might sound
> strange coming from a socialist.
>
> (Letter, *Sunday Times*, July 29, 1984)

The letter writer is himself struck by the strangeness of his switch from attacking the market forces to defending them, at least with respect to the limited context of publishing fiction. He has placed himself in an unusual situation by writing a socialist novel, expecting it to take its place in the bookstands alongside the usual fare about sex, warfare and cowboys. There is now a certain identity with other free-trading purveyors of fiction. His present enemies are the monopolies, which are preventing his own work from having a free share of the so-called 'free market'. Instead of throwing his critical darts at capitalism from left to right, he seems to have temporarily moved around to the other side of his target to attack it from the right. Although the rhetoric of *laissez-faire* capitalism might be used, in no sense is there a full identification with the modern heirs of Adam Smith. Once the controversy turns to socialism, the author will sharply part company with other free-traders, as the contents of his fiction make clear. The letter writer is sufficiently aware of the irony in his position.

The switching between contrary common-places may be especially marked amongst those who shift their identities between different groups. Not identifying completely with a single group, such people find themselves arguing against different positions depending upon the group context. Moving from a context in which they argue with other members of their group, people may find themselves confronted by new critics, who identify them with their erstwhile others. Then, in the face of these new critics, the spirit of contradiction may rise up, and the side of the former others is taken. Philip Ullah reports such incidents in his study of second-generation Irish adolescents living in Britain. These young people frequently switched their loyalties, not to accommodate to their social situations, but to react against them. One adolescent summed up their contrasting attitudes:

> When you're in Ireland, you find yourself sticking up for
> England – they call you English. Then when you're over here, they
> call you Irish. So you find yourself sticking up for both sides, and
> you can't feel you're either. (Ullah, 1985, p. 317)

These comments illustrate the extent to which the feelings of personal identity can be bound up with criticisms and justifications (or, to use the phrase of the young person, the business of 'sticking up for sides'). It is not simply that the desire to justify or criticize stems from an inner feeling called an 'identity', but, in a real sense, the sense of one's identity can emerge within a context of argumentation. In Ireland, the adolescents were finding that their normal feelings of identification were being denied. Perhaps they also perceived the Irish criticisms of the English to be as one-sided as the anti-Irish accusations they were accustomed to hearing in Britain. Unable to identify wholly with people in either rhetorical context, they would find themselves sticking up for the side of the other.

Similar feelings can be discerned in the comments given by the dissident Afrikaners interviewed by Joha Louw-Potgieter. These were radicals, who strongly opposed, often at great personal risk, the narrow racism and chauvinism of Afrikanerdom. However, when placed in a situation in which outsiders one-sidedly criticized Afrikaners, they would discover their hidden feelings of national identity. They even used common-places which otherwise were to be found within a latitude of firm rejection. One such dissident

Afrikaner commented that "I find that when I am abroad, I am sometimes in this crazy situation where one feels one's Boer blood boiling when one hears all the misrepresentations...but within a South African context, I don't feel this any more." Another reported similar experiences within South Africa, especially when English speakers start castigating all Afrikaners as being unenlightened hardliners: "If an Afrikaner should say that, the remark would not bother me, but if (an English) person, who can't even speak Afrikaans, says it, then it starts bothering me."

These reactions are not peculiar, but represent something which might be quite common. The argument which takes place within a group is transformed if criticisms which appear to resemble those voiced by the internal critics are to be heard from outside. Suddenly the wind of criticism may have seemed to have changed direction, bringing with it a fiercer chill. Mr Farrakhan, the American black Muslim leader, may castigate his fellow blacks for idleness and drug-taking, and he can receive standing ovations from black audiences. A white politician who spoke in the same way, especially to an all-white audience, could only be seen as being provocatively racist. On the other hand, Farrakhan's remarks about Jewish businesses will be branded as anti-semitic by Jews, even by radical Jews, who, in the safety of an all-Jewish context, might be outspoken in their criticisms. Similarly feminists will accept and voice criticisms amongst themselves, but such criticisms would be castigated as being beyond the bounds of reasonable discourse if spoken by a man. Hyam Maccoby draws attention to an incident which took place in the Barcelona Disputations of 1263, when the Jews of Spain were placed under serious argumentative threat by their Christian accusers. Nachmanides, the famous Jewish scholar, was leading the defence. At one point his Christian interlocutor started using, or mis-using, the arguments of Nachmanides's great rival Maimonides, in an attempt to undermine the Jewish interpretation of the scriptures. Nachmanides made no attempt to disassociate himself from Maimonides, but found himself defending his rival concerning those very points of argument on which in the context of rabbinic debate he would have been a fierce critic. Nor is this sort of phenomenon confined to minority, or oppressed, groups. Inside a family, insults might be swapped back and forth, but both the insulted and the insulting will band together should these same insults be heard coming from an outside source against a family member.

Such switches from critic to defender should not be confused with the hypocrisy of the impression-manager who smiles to please the company of the moment. The internal critic, who reacts defensively against criticism from outside, appreciates that the meaning of a statement does not merely reside in the words employed, but it also takes its force from the rhetorical context. So it is with criticisms which come from within and without a group. The arguments of the Christian interlocutor may have superficially resembled those of Maimonides, but they were not his. As Maccoby points out, what Nachmanides showed was "not dissimulation, but accommodation to the understanding of his audience" (1982, p. 62). The criticism coming from the outside is feared lest its uncompromising one-sidedness sweep away completely all aspects of that other side, which is, even to a small degree, the internal critic's own side. Like Johnson, the internal critic will often assume the existence, and indeed the legitimate existence, of the anti-logoi which are enjoined in debate. When that existence is threatened, and when there is no-one else to put the other side, then the internal critics may feel the need to protect their own identity and turn their criticisms outwards. They might, then, give voice to those thoughts which the external critics in their ignorance might leave unsaid, or in their hostility hope to leave unutterable.

When hearing the accusations from outside, the internal critics might feel as if the breeze of criticism has suddenly turned direction to blow sharply at their backs. They could, of course, let themselves be propelled forward with the new and fiercer wind, in order to clash head-on with those whom they habitually face in argument. Or they could show Protagorean two-sidedness, and turn around to stand, alongside their fellow foes, with their faces inclined towards the gale of contradiction. If they do this, they might use what, under other rhetorical circumstances, would be the counter-attitudes to their own controversial attitudes. They might draw upon arguments and justifications with which they are readily familiar, and do not need to invent afresh.

In a sense, people already possess such counter-attitudes, but normally keep them securely in the latitudes of rejection, under the firm and domineering eye of the latitude of acceptance. Perhaps, these counter-attitudes are stored in the memory, indexed together with handy refutations as part of an attitudinal *prolepsis*. However, when the argumentative context changes, it may be the counter-arguments which are required in the battle against new opponents. In consequence, they can be temporarily released from the shackle of their memorized refutations. The socialist writer, attacking the monopolies of the publishing houses, lets loose the free-market arguments, which are given special leave to absent themselves from their imprisonment within the latitude of rejection. Of course, it is always possible that the sudden taste of freedom may be dangerous. Once such arguments are used, the speaker may start to find them reasonable. Other people's shoes may be uncomfortable at first, but, if worn sufficiently often, the leather may stretch comfortably around the new wearer's feet. Similarly, the strange arguments may grow less strange, and, if frequently employed, they might come to belong properly to the self. In this way, there may be, by courtesy of the spirit of contradiction, a roundabout accommodation to the changed rhetorical context.

Unfinished business

The switching of a stance, whether from criticism to justification or vice versa, can represent a process of self-discovery for the individual. Having been placed in a new rhetorical context, individuals may experience an unforeseen rising of the spirit of contradiction, and in this way they may encounter a new side to their attitudes and maybe to their own selves. For example, some of the second generation Irish adolescents discovered the Englishness of their identities only when they went to Ireland. It has been reported that some British emigrants to the United States turn to the sorts of traditionalism which they would have found offensive in their land of origin. For example, one member of a cricket club in Philadelphia apparently "dresses whenever the occasion arises in the ceremonial kilted uniform of the Queen's Own Highlanders" and declares himself from across the Atlantic to be "an unrepentant imperialist and royalist" (*Observer*, July 28, 1985). These British emigrants, so full of dissatisfaction with staid Britain before they left, became aware of their feelings for their native land after they had chosen to live in an entirely different environment. Could, one may ask, their younger, impatient selves in Britain have envisaged the parades of blimpery, which afforded them so much reassurance in the United States? Similarly the dissident Afrikaners, when confronting English speaking critics, experienced feelings which did not, and could not, emerge in a purely Afrikaner context. In their case, taking the side of the other did not entail, even momentarily, a total identification with the current powers of Afrikanerdom. More typically, it was accompanied by a discovery of their pride in the history of the Afrikaner culture and an identification with a past Afrikanerdom oppressed by the British colonial power.

A change in the rhetorical situation can be seen as setting a test for an attitude which has hitherto only been expressed in a very different context. The second generation Irish adolescents tested their identification with Ireland when they moved from a familiar context to one in which the prevailing criticisms were coming from a contrary direction. Under test, the limitations to their pro-Irish advocacy became apparent. Like laws, whose essences and boundaries are revealed when tested by difficult cases, our attitudes may be put in a different, and more complex, light when an unusually testing situation arises. Already mentioned has been Boswell's oscillation between good humour and irritation when confronted with Johnson's prejudices against the Scots. Boswell was quick to spring from mild accuser to impassioned defender, when a critic, from outside their circle of friends, criticized the Doctor for being an anti-Scottish bigot. To one such critic, Boswell replied, "so illiberal a prejudice never entered his mind" (1906, vol. I, p. 389). Boswell liked to think himself free from prejudice and "sulky nationality" (vol. II, p. 434), as he urbanely discarded his provincial background to plunge into the world of metropolitan sophistication.

However, this was not the only context in which Boswell moved, and Johnson's wit was not the only form in which anti-Scottish prejudice came. In his *London Journal*, Boswell records an episode which occurred soon after he had arrived in London as a young man. He had gone to the theatre at Covent Garden, in order to see a new comic opera. When the crowd, awaiting the start of the performance, noticed the arrival of two Highland officers in full regalia, they started to shout with menace: "No Scots! No Scots!" Boswell's reaction was swift and unthinking. Rushing to the aid of his countrymen, he pushed aside all the nice dilemmas of dual nationality: "My Scotch blood boiled with indignation...I hated the English; I wished from my soul that the Union was broke and that we might give them another battle of Bannockburn" (1950, pp. 71ff). It appears that his expensively acquired English accent was also swept aside, as he shouted to his countrymen in the dialect which had always embarrassed him north of the border.[3]

The episode in the theatre can be seen as a test of Boswell's cosmopolitanism and the limits of his complaisance in the face of prejudice. Facing, not the banter of Johnson, who normally, but not invariably, knew when to stop, but the fury of a one-sided mob, Boswell responded with an equal but opposite reaction. In advance, he may have been unsure how he would have reacted had such a situation arisen, and he may have doubted whether he would show the physical courage he did. Afterwards, having passed the test of bravery, he would have known himself that much better. Not only would he know more about his reactions in moments of danger, but he would also have discovered how deeply his Scottish identification ran. Perhaps his Scottishness could be discarded in the witty conversations of London society, and perhaps he reacted against it in the worthy, provincial atmosphere of Fife, when, from afar, he had identified in his imagination with the great capital city. But placed unexpectedly in the middle of that English mob, Boswell experienced his own Bannockburn.

The alteration of a rhetorical context can provide a test of an attitude by revealing qualifications or even reversals which had not been seen in the previous contexts. Just as the essence and the boundary of a category can always be controversially tested by the difficult particular case, so our attitudes are vulnerable to the challenge of difficult circumstances. For example, the limits of our adherence to a principle may be revealed in the dilemmatic situation in which two, or even more, principles find themselves in serious conflict. The left-wing novelist discovered the limits to his opposition to the free-market economy with the publication of his book. Qualifications, which had not been made hitherto, were found necessary, after he was put in the unusual position of being a promotional salesman in the cause of socialism and increased royalties. In response to this situation, and to the pressures of the book trade, he found himself dipping into a store of common-places which previously had been forbidden by order of ideology.

It is not only the limits of attitudes which pose problems, but we may also be concerned where the essence of an attitude is to be located. Having seen an individual switch between prosecution and defence, or having heard an ambiguous disclaimer, we may wonder where the 'true' attitude is to be found. We might question the sincerity of someone who claims 'not to be prejudiced, but...', if we suspect that the disclaimer is merely a hypocritical attempt to displace criticism. On the other hand, we may still wonder where to locate the essence of the attitude, even if we do not suspect hypocrisy: does the essence fall on the side of the absence of prejudice, or on the side of prejudice, or perhaps the person is essentially a waverer? As always, the location of an essence can be accompanied by controversy.

We may believe that our doubts would be resolved if the individual were placed in a critically testing situation which forced a decision and an end to the contrary pulls of deliberation. However, the testing situation may not reveal an unambiguous essence, for it can be doubted whether the particular test was the essential one. It might be suggested that the episode at Covent Garden revealed Boswell's 'real' identification. On the other hand, it might be countered that his emotional reaction and the boiling of his Scottish blood were no more, and certainly no less, real than his laughter at Johnson's sallies. Nor is the essence of our own attitudes free from doubt, and we can be unsure about our own reactions in the critically testing situation. We can devise our own imaginary tests, and, although it might be easier to pass the tests of our fantasies than the tests of reality, doubts may not be easily removed. Boswell records Johnson's own private doubts about the nature of his Jacobitism. Johnson used to imagine himself in a critical situation in which a decision was required: "I have heard him declare, that if holding up his right hand would have secured victory at Culloden to Prince Charles's army, he was not sure he would have held it up" (1906, Vol. I, p. 266).

If the expression of our attitudes is liable to be influenced by a change of circumstances, then attitudes are essentially unfinished business. Each attitude, however forcefully expressed, must be incomplete, to the extent that future events may induce limitations and perhaps the possibility that counter-attitudes will be advocated. A social psychologist interested in measuring attitudes might possibly draw methodological implications from the unfinished nature of attitudes. Instead of asking someone whether they agree or disagree with a particular position, the researcher might probe in depth the occasions when a respondent might consider disagreeing with a chosen position. When hypothetical dilemmas are employed, they can be quite revealing. For example, Altemeyer, in his book *Right-Wing Authoritarianism*, describes the responses of liberals and authoritarians, when responding to hypothetical dilemmas in which values conflicted. Instead of asking outright whether it was important to obey the law, Altemeyer used hypothetical dilemmas to probe the limits of the authoritarians' avowed commitment to the law. In one of the situations, the respondents had to indicate whether they would approve if the government interfered illegally with the civil liberties of minority left-wing groups. In another of the dilemmas, respondents had to adjudge the appropriate sentence for a policeman convicted of brutally assaulting a left-wing protester. All these were hypothetical tests of the right-wing authoritarian's commitment to the law, in the same way that Johnson tested his Jacobitism by imagining he was playing God in the middle of the Battle of Culloden. And, just as Johnson found himself not to be an unequivocal Jacobite, so Altemeyer discovered limitations to the authoritarians' respect for legal authority.

It would be possible to probe attitudes in greater depth by following up the hypothetical dilemmas with detailed questioning. Having asked a question of the form 'what would you do, or think, if...', the researcher might follow up with supplementary questions: 'But what if someone then were to criticize you for...'. These sorts of questions, or cross-examination, are probably best used in the context of an in-depth interview, in which the interviewers need not feel constrained to establish a complete common-ground between themselves and the interviewed. In consequence, the interview would take the form of an argument, or discussion, rather than a one-sided succession of formal questions followed by brief responses. The respondents would be challenged to think about their attitudes, rather than merely express them. These deliberations might also provide the occasion for the sort of self-discovery that arguments can sometimes provoke. We can discover the reasons for expressing a point of view once we start to justify it in the face of criticism. Similarly, like those who suffered the questioning of Socrates, we might discover limitations and even reversals in our advocated attitudes, once we argue our point of view against someone who persistently raises difficult dilemmas.

Any such methodology, which used hypothetical situations to test attitudes, would not, and could not, succeed in completing the unfinished business of attitudes. Every attitude is necessarily incomplete, in that its latitudes of acceptance and rejection have not been determined for every conceivable situation. At best, the social psychologist can only get the respondents to think about a very small percentage of the infinitely possible situations which might set problems for the possessors of attitudes. Whatever light is shed upon a few hypothetical dilemmas, a vast penumbra must remain. What was earlier called Quintilian's Principle of Uncertainty can illustrate the point. This principle states that if people alter their reactions and expressions to cope with the particularities of the situation, then there cannot be fully worked out psychological laws. Because there is an infinite number of different situations, the psychological laws about the effects of situations would themselves have to be infinite to deal with these situations. If this principle is applied to the topic of attitudes, the conclusion would be that the task of completely specifying the possible latitudes of acceptance and rejection, even for a single attitude held by a single person, is potentially an infinite one.

What this implies is that we can never fully know ourselves or other people. It is not the case that we possess rigorously formulated 'belief-systems', which stamp out our thoughts and reactions in a fully determinable way. Sometimes social psychologists give the impression that, if they could only get hold of that 'belief-system' and trace its inner lineaments, all uncertainties would be resolved. However, that would be akin to supposing that a detailed knowledge of all existing statutes would enable one to predict with absolute clarity, not only the problem cases which will arise in the courtroom, but also their outcomes. Of course, the drafters of legislation can have a shrewd idea about where difficulties might arise, but these shrewd ideas are less certain than the laws of which the experimental scientist dreams. Even the shrewdest idea will have its limitations, and, in addition, changing circumstances and odd events are bound to produce dilemmas which were not foreseen. Similarly, our attitudes represent guidelines, or commitments to advocacy, but there will always be some uncertainty about the full potentialities of these guidelines. By the same token, we cannot be absolutely precise about the details of the advocacy which might actually be presented in the new rhetorical situations, which forever are posing dilemmas.

The air of uncertainty is even attached to Uncle Jules, whose attitude towards the English we seem to know so well from Sartre's description. However, let us imagine a changed rhetorical context. Instead of remaining an isolated and eccentric Anglophobe, Uncle Jules notices from his window columns of tough, young men marching past, some in uniforms, and all shouting violently anti-English slogans. Does he reveal the suddenness of Boswell, leaping from his seat, with his heart boiling with hatred against the English? Or does the spirit of contradiction, which has nourished his hatred for so long, reassert itself? Perhaps Jules sighs that the young fools do not know of what they complain, or, there again, maybe he flies into a rage that it is no longer possible to be properly anti-English with all these ignorant pseudo-Anglophobes about. All this is very hypothetical. Perhaps it is the specificities of the situation which will be uppermost. Will he look for the butcher's boy to see if he has joined the mob? If he has, what will that indicate? Or perhaps, Jules's views will be coloured by the personal characteristics of the crowd's political leader. Above all, we know little about the context which has transformed the views of an embittered eccentric into those of a mob which believes that the morrow belongs to them.

When imagining totally hypothetical situations, all manner of possibilities can be splayed out. Yet, if we were closer to Jules as a person, and closer to the events which sent the young toughs parading past his window, we might have shrewder ideas about the reactions of the old eccentric. But what would keep our shrewd ideas from being certainties, almost until the very moment Jules reacted, would be the knowledge that Jules possesses the rhetorical skills to dismiss the young Anglophobes, to turn around upon his own ideas, to herald the new saviours of the world, and much, much more. Even Uncle Jules can do all this – Uncle Jules, who in his familiar rhetorical context resembles a raucous parrot, performing a single trick for his piece of cuttle-fish. Yet, even he is possessed of the contrary syntactical forms and the contrary common-places which make one-sided argumentation, and also two-sided deliberation, possible.

The example of Jules illustrates the extent to which we live in a rhetorical world. Jules's own rhetorical skills ensure that he is not bound to a single, pre-formed response, although his anti-English prejudices may sometimes appear to have the fixity of the parrot's calls. Because Jules possesses these skills, we can formulate different views on him. Drawing attention to his incompleteness, we can debate amongst ourselves what he would do if he were placed in this or that situation. These arguments too will have an air of incompleteness. Even if one of the infinitely possible tests of his attitudes suddenly occurred, the arguments need not cease. Supposing the anti-English march does take place, and Jules stays rooted at his window sneering. But, we might wonder, would he have acted this way, had they asked him, the longest serving Anglophobe for miles around, to chair the local action group? And would he have thought the same way, if the local butcher's boy had joined the group? These matters we shall never know, but we can still debate them with animation.

If the attitudes and characters of all people are incomplete, in that unrealized possibilities remain, then not only are people users of rhetoric, but they are objects of rhetorical argument. We can debate the 'real' character or attitudes of others, wondering where, amongst the uncertainty, to locate the crucial essences. Such arguments are not to be easily resolved, either generally at the level of social psychological theory, or particularly in relation to specific individuals. Certainty may not be possible within the rhetorical world, but it is this lack of certainty which gives our choices – whether moral, personal, political or whatever – their element of risk, and, thus, their element of humanity. Our computers may rattle through their problems on their way to a certain solution with a speed which leaves us humans bemused. However, when we take time to argue, to deliberate, to oppose logoi with anti-logoi, recapturing the spirit of the arguments between Protagoras and Socrates, then we are fulfilling a truly human, if incomplete, side of our natures. We may search for the last word, but so long as human thought continues, the last word should be unattainable, for there is always more that can be said. Authors, in their vanity, might wish to believe that the last words on an issue are to be found at the end of their books. Readers, however, know that the broad barrels of criticism are too full to be bunged by a small, final, full-stop.

Notes

2 Rules, roles and arguments

1 It would be a mistake to imply that all role theorists believe that the concept of 'role' is applicable to every aspect of social life. One of the best discussions of the limitations of the concept of 'role' is to be found in Goffman's essay 'Role distance' in his book *Encounters*. Goffman here points out that individuals often distance themselves publicly from the role that they might be playing, and that they can do so in the course of actually enacting the role: "Sullenness, muttering, irony, joking and sarcasm may all allow one to show that something of oneself lies outside the constraints of the moment and outside the role within whose jurisdiction the moment falls" (1961, p. 114). When this occurs, there is clearly not a passive acceptance of the demands of the situation. Instead, the individual may be said to be arguing symbolically with the role. Latent argumentative urges may be expressed in these moments when, according to Goffman, "an individual does not march up and down like a wooden soldier, tightly rolled up in a particular role" (1961, p. 143).

2 Harré's 'ethogenic' approach to social psychology is not solely based upon using the game model. He recommends also both the dramaturgical model and the use of rituals as models of social situations (e.g., Harré and Secord, 1972; Harré, 1984; Harré, Clark and De Carlo, 1985). If the dramaturgical model is used, then we cannot assume that our scripts are necessarily complete: "As people living our own lives we are among the actors performing our parts in well or ill-defined scenes, sometimes fully scripted, sometimes improvising" (Harré, 1979, p. 192). Harré has specifically recommended using the game metaphor, together with its stress upon rules, as a model for arguments: "A quarrel can be treated on the agonistic model, where a rule-bound competitive episode is seen as the performance of a social act, such as the establishment of a social micro-hierarchy" (Harré, 1974). This implies that quarrels are to be seen as means of establishing social stability and, thereby, social rules, rather than being viewed as important entities in their own right. In this way, the quarrel is seen as subservient to something else (social order), which is essentially non-quarrelsome.

3 Le Quesne, in his *The Bodyline Controversy*, has documented the legislative consequences of the Bodyline/Leg Theory Tour. The 'leg-before-wicket' law was changed in time for the 1935 season, so that a batsman could be dismissed to balls pitching outside the off-stump. This change was designed to encourage bowlers to bowl at the off-stump and to render unprofitable the sort of

short-pitched, leg-stump bowling produced by the English fast bowlers. It should be noted that the English tactic was only employed once the advantage between batsmen and bowlers had shifted substantially towards the batsmen. Nowadays, spectators, especially in Australia, expect their team to engage in bursts of short-pitched bowling, far more intimidatory than anything produced on the unhappy tour of 1932/3.

4 There are two editions of the Talmud: the Babylonian and the Jerusalem Talmuds. All the quotations in the present work are taken from the Babylonian Talmud, which is the longer of the two. The composition of the Talmud is mentioned more fully in Chapter 5. Rabbi Eliezer ben Hyrcanus was a Palestinian scholar of the first and second centuries A.D., his precise dates not being known. Eliezer's great renown is clearly described in the Mishnah, which is the portion common to both Babylonian and Jerusalem Talmuds: "If all the sages of Israel were balanced against Eliezer, he would outweigh them all" (*Avot*, 2).

3 Protagoras and the origins of rhetoric

1 There has been a large amount of specialized material published on the history of rhetoric. Particularly useful are general historical treatments, such as Dixon (1971), Howes (1961) and especially Kennedy (1980a), which complements its scholarly text with an extremely useful bibliography. Much historical information, as well as philosophical insight, is to be found in Perelman and Olbrechts-Tyteca (1971) and Perelman (1979). The history and practice of ancient rhetoric are detailed by Clark (1957), Kennedy (1963; 1969; 1972; 1980b) and Self (1979). For Mediaeval rhetorics, see Murphy (1974 and 1978) and Caplan (1970). For historical treatments of rhetoric in the Renaissance see, *inter alia*, Ong (1958), Howell (1956), and Sandford (1965). Altmann (1983) discusses the specialized topic of Jewish rhetoric during the Renaissance. Sonnino's *Handbook to Sixteenth-Century Rhetoric* (1968) is particularly useful. Those interested in the development of English rhetoric owe a debt of gratitude to the Scolar Press, for its wonderful series of facsimile editions.

2 For detailed discussions of the Sophists, their history, philosophy and impact, see Kerferd (1981), Rankin (1983), Hussey (1972) and Guthrie (1969). All these works contain useful bibliographies. Loenen (1941) discusses Protagoras in detail, and emphasizes his conventional morality. Barnes (1982) reconstructs and analyses with great skill the philosophy of the pre-Socratics, including that of Protagoras. For English readers, Sprague's (1972) translations of the fragments of the pre-Socratics is invaluable.

3 Some of the sorts of arguments used by Protagoras have possibly been preserved in the anonymous *Dissoi Logoi*. This work presents pairs of opposing arguments on a variety of topics, and it has been claimed that it was compiled by an Ionian follower of Protagoras. Robinson (1979), in his introduction to the text, discusses the issues of authorship, and whether the author intended each of the opposing arguments in a pair to be equally convincing.

4 Plato's legend of the soul being banished by birth from the heavens, and thereby from the realms of unchanging truth, can be compared to an analogous Jewish legend. It is told in Jewish lore that, when a woman conceives, the soul is taken on a tour of heaven and endowed with perfect knowledge, which will be

forgotten at the moment of birth. One difference between the two legends is that in the Jewish legend the soul argues with the angels of heaven, putting up unsuccessful reasons why it should not be made to enter the impure sperm (Ginzberg, 1947, Vol. I, pp. 56f). The Platonic heaven, by contrast, is silently free from the sound of argument and rhetoric: there are only the noises of wings beating in the air, and of horses and chariots charging about.

5 For discussions of the different senses of 'argument', see, for instance, O'Keefe (1977) and Brockriede (1985). O'Keefe uses subscripts to distinguish the two main senses of 'argument'. He calls an individual "utterance of a sort of communicative act" an "argument$_1$," and "argument$_2$," describes "a particular kind of interaction" (p. 121). O'Keefe complains that rhetorical theorists have failed to distinguish these two senses clearly enough.

4 The science of persuasion

1 Gill (1985), in a careful discussion of ancient psychotherapy, warns against making overly simple parallels between ancient and modern practices. However, he does emphasize Antiphon's contribution as showing the emergence of "the belief that the philosopher can function as a doctor of the psyche" (p. 320).

2 Although there has been considerable research in social psychology looking at the persuasion and arrangement of messages, there has been a comparative neglect of the link between style and persuasion. Sandell (1977) has investigated this topic directly. Lind and O'Barr (1979) look at the effects of linguistic style in courtroom settings.

3 Philo viewed the Sophists, and Protagoras in particular, as being spiritual descendants of Cain. In *On the Posterity of Cain and his Exile* he writes: "Of what sort then is an impious man's opinion? That the human mind is the measure of all things, an opinion held they tell us by an ancient sophist named Protagoras, an offspring of Cain's madness" (p. 349).

4 Just as modern experiments on memory reveal that items placed in the middle of a list are the least memorable, so ancient rhetoricians recommended that one's strongest arguments should be positioned at the start or end of a speech. For example, Quintilian agreed with the traditional view that "the first place should be given to some strong argument, but that the strongest should be reserved to the end, while the weaker arguments should be placed in the middle, since the judge has to be moved at the beginning and forcibly impelled to a decision at the end" (VII, i, 10; see also *Rhetorica Ad Herennium*, 185).

5 Ancient and modern critics have frequently commented upon the rhetorical nature of Plato's dialogues. Crassus, in Cicero's *De Oratore*, remarks about *Gorgias* that "what impressed me most deeply about Plato in that book was, that it was when making fun of orators that he himself seemed to me to be the consummate orator" (I, xi, 47). Josephus commented that Plato "in oratorical power and persuasive eloquence outmatched all other philosophers" (*Against Apion*, p. 383). Similarly, Weaver, a modern critic, claims that "it is not unreasonable to call him (Plato) a master rhetorician" (1965, p. 75). For a discussion of the dramatic form of Plato's dialogues and the part which drama plays in the philosophical arguments, see Kauffman (1979).

6 The differences between central and peripheral routes of persuasion are discussed

in Cacioppo, Harkins and Petty (1981), Cialdini, Petty and Cacioppo (1981) and Petty and Cacioppo (1981). Petty and Cacioppo describe the central route as a "very rational one", in that "the message recipient attends to the message arguments, attempts to understand them, and then evaluates them". On the peripheral route, it is the peripheral aspects of the message which take the attention: "If a message is associated with a pleasant smell or an attractive source, it is accepted" (1981, p. 256). For specific laboratory studies which link the involvement of subjects in an issue with their likelihood of paying attention to the content of a message, see, for example, Petty and Cacioppo (1979 and 1984).

5   The art of witcraft

1 Ramus, in his book *The Logike*, defined logic in terms of argumentation: "Dialectic, otherwise called Logic, is an art which teacheth to dispute well" (1966, p. 17). Instead of logic then being subsumed to rhetoric, Ramus allowed the rhetoric of invention to disappear into logic. The work and influence of Ramus are analysed thoroughly in Ong's *Ramus: method and the decay of dialogue* (1958).

2 Radley (1985), in an interesting critique, has drawn attention to the similarities between the modern practice of social skills training and earlier training in etiquette. Both aim to equip individuals with socially acceptable ways of conducting themselves in polite company.

3 Aebsicher (1985) has analysed the traditional role of women in conversations. She focusses on the extent to which the concept of 'gossip' has overtones of gender, as it is represented in everyday discourse: women are expected to gossip, whilst men talk about important things.

4 Louis Jacobs in his *Studies of Talmudic Logic and Methodology* points out that the Talmud does not seem to present verbatim accounts of debates. Instead, literary devices are employed, in order to heighten the dramatic effect and emphasize the flow of debate. At times the redactors even create "an artificial form of discussion" (p. 57), by juxtaposing the words of sages from different periods. It is not difficult to discern literary editing in the debate between the idolatrous Romans and the Elders, although no other record of the exchange survives.

5 There are methodological implications from this position for cognitive psychologists. Those psychologists concerned with the tight-fisted aspects of thought often assume that thinking is a hidden and silent process. In order to observe what is inherently unobservable, psychologists sometimes ask their experimental subjects to 'think aloud' as they wrestle with logical, mathematical, or geometrical problems. The resulting 'protocols' are said by some psychologists to be a reflection of the thought processes involved (Ericsson and Simon, 1980). However, as Schoenfeld (1983) has shown, the commentary of the subjects is frequently not the sort of monologue which the cognitive psychologists had wished for. Witcraft is temporarily given sovereignty over the domain of tight-fisted thought. The laboratory subjects typically address their remarks to the audience of experimenters, often in order to rationalize a failure to solve the requisite problem. Thus, in a rhetorical context, they attempt to justify themselves in front of the critical eye of the experimenters. For cognitive psychologists, in

search of hidden thoughts, these dialogic aspects of what should be a monologic discourse are an inconvenience. However, such rationalizations, or defences designed to pre-empt implicit criticisms, are themselves thoughts. It is precisely these sort of thoughts which interest the rhetorical psychologist. Of course, such thoughts are even more readily apparent in situations where people have the confidence to 'speak their mind' in the face of criticism. In consequence, actual arguments might produce the sort of publicly available thoughts which can be studied without psychologists needing to strain their ears or their expensive laboratory equipment.

6 Categorization and particularization

1 The individualist and perceptual themes in cognitive psychology have been forcefully criticized by Moscovici (1981 and 1982). Moscovici stresses the social nature of thought by discussing ideas, beliefs and attitudes in terms of 'social representations' (Moscovici, 1984; see also Jodelet, 1984). According to Moscovici, the argumentative common-places which are discussed by rhetorical theorists (see Chapter 8) would be forms of social representations. The notion of common sense, as used in Chapter 8, is very close to Moscovici's concept of social representation. The principal difference is that 'common-places' and 'common sense', because they are linked to rhetorical theory, point towards the contrary and argumentative aspects of cognition much more directly than does 'social representation'. However, it might be profitable to explore the rhetorical dimensions of this theoretically important concept of social representations.

2 Many of the themes discussed in this section are elaborated in greater detail in Billig (1985). Although this section might give the impression that all of cognitive social psychology is dominated by the images of the prejudiced person and of the bureaucrat, this would be misleading. In particular, attribution theory is not discussed. At the root of attribution theory, which examines how people ascribe causes to events, is the image of the person as a scientist (see, for example, Fiske and Taylor, 1984; Kelley and Michela, 1980; Antaki, 1984). Although attribution theory might appear to postulate that the ordinary person is a scientist in their thinking, much of the emphasis of the research suggests that ordinary people think unscientifically, because they show many of the biases which are outlined by categorization theorists (for such critiques of attribution theory, see Semin, 1980; Billig, 1982; Gergen and Gergen, 1981). Antaki (1985) specifically argues that attribution theory, as normally conceived, is ill-equipped to deal with the rhetorical aspects of cognition.

3 A further example of the one-sided bias in cognitive theory is provided by the current interest in metaphor. In an extremely perceptive article, which emphasizes the metaphorical nature of much psychological science, Lakoff and Johnson argue that human thinking "is fundamentally metaphorical in character" (1981, p. 193). A similar point is made by I. A. Richards in *Philosophy of Rhetoric*. A metaphor points to the similarity between two things or concepts, and thus it could be called the tropic expression of the principle of categorization. Metaphor can be contrasted with metonymy, which highlights the particular features of a category of things. Thus metonymy is the tropic expression of particularization. Although it might just as reasonably be asserted that human

thinking is fundamentally metonymic, cognitive psychologists have paid nowhere near as much attention to metonymy as they have to metaphor.

4 There is experimental evidence that social categories do not possess the same structure as do Rosch's natural categories. For example, Deaux *et al.* (1985) suggest that gender categories differ importantly from the sort of natural categories investigated by Rosch.

5 Billig (1985) provides more detailed discussion on why the prejudiced person cannot think entirely in terms of categorizations as opposed to particularizations. Taylor and Crocker (1981) suggest that prejudiced people preserve their schemata by a strategy of differentiation in the face of disconfirming evidence. This strategy involves the use of particularization, in order to create sub-schemata. There is evidence that the prejudiced do not believe that *all* members of the group against which they are prejudiced possess undesirable characteristics (Jackman and Senter, 1980; McCauley and Stitt, 1978; McCauley, Stitt and Segal, 1980). Prejudiced people, it is suggested, do not use the argument of quantity, so much as the argument of quality: the undesirable characteristics are thought to represent the essence·of the group, even though it might be conceded that many group members do not display this characteristic. In this way, the prejudiced person distinguishes between 'true' blacks, Jews etc., and those deemed exceptional enough to be acceptable as best friends.

6 The Watergate scandal has become a particularly fruitful topic for semiotic and mythic analysis. King (1985) has examined the conceptual manoeuvres employed by Nixon to translate the language of scandal into that of tragedy. Eco wittily shows that Nixon's defence possessed the same mythic structure as the fairy story, Little Red Riding Hood, but the threatened president slid self-servingly heroic terms into the myth: "With the identification of hero and rescuer, the displacement of the President from the role of villain to that of hero, and the substitution of the misfortune (from the Watergate scandal to the loss of credibility), Nixon undoubtedly accomplished a masterpiece of rhetorical manipulation" (1985, p. 11).

7 The open-endedness of rules is a point stressed by the ethnomethodologists, following the insights of Garfinkel (1967). For example, Zimmerman (1971) argues that rules are only discovered when they are put into operation and tested by difficult cases (see Watson, 1978, for an ethnomethodological analysis of categorization). Coulter (1983) has shown how damaging the implications of the ethnomethodological insight are for those psychological theories which aim to produce fully determined laws.

8 The Theft Act of 1968 stipulates that a person is guilty of theft "if he dishonestly appropriates property belonging to another with the intention of permanently depriving the other of it". Amongst the many terms in this definition which are liable to become matters of legal dispute is that of property. The nature of 'property' was tested by the case of Regina versus Shickle of 1968. Wild birds, such as partridges, cannot be anybody's property because they are wild. However, the eleven partridges which Mr Shickle had removed were different. A neighbour had reared these birds from the egg by placing them beneath a hen. The question was whether partridges reared in this way constituted property or not. The court found against Mr Shickle, on the grounds that when he removed the said partridges they were not wild and therefore were

subject to larceny (see Elliott and Wood, 1974, pp. 411ff). In these tricky cases, not only are the boundaries of the law established, but the courts are forced to define the key terms with greater precision.

9 Woolgar and Pawluch, in discussing academic definitions of social problems, have introduced the evocative concept of 'ontological gerrymandering'. How the researcher defines the problem determines what is to be considered as problematical, and the boundaries of a concept can be stretched or contracted to suit theoretical convenience: 'By means of ontological gerrymandering, proponents of definitional explanations place a boundary between assumptions which are to be understood as (ostensibly) problematic and those which are not" (1985, p. 216). The concept of 'gerrymandering' implies that this is a matter of deceit or sharp practice. Although some researchers might slickly manipulate their terms in this way, the rhetorical aspects of definition (including the definition of 'ontological gerrymandering') are not merely a matter of conscious manipulation.

7 Advocacy and attitudes

1 Strictly speaking the 'foot-in-the-door' technique, as defined and investigated by social psychologists, differs from Boswell's strategy. The 'foot-in-the-door' refers to a quantitative increase between the magnitude of two requests: "Once a person has been induced to comply with a small request, he is more likely to comply with a larger demand" (Freedman and Fraser, 1966, p. 195). Boswell's strategy did not depend upon increasing the size of the demand as such, but his pressure depended upon establishing an unexceptional definition of the request. The foot-in-the-door strategy could be restated to cover this sort of technique: Once people have been induced to comply with an unexceptionally defined request, they are more likely to comply when the controversial details of the request become revealed. Of course, the strategy is by no means guaranteed. There again, neither is the 'foot-in-the-door strategy' (Cialdini *et al.*, 1975).

2 Katz, in a careful study of the phenomenology of being loved, argues that there are no agreed-upon behavioural criteria for the state of being loved. According to Katz's analysis, "the behaviour that signals love to one individual is often irrelevant to another" (1976, p. 18). The figures in Salancik's imaginary drama exploit the ambiguity inherent in the concept of 'being loved', as described in the Katz study.

8 Dilemmas of common-sense

1 Murray (1984) writes that the New Rhetoric, as expressed in the writings of Perelman and Olbrechts-Tyteca, is more interested in persuasion than in expression. Modern rhetorical theorists have shown that: "argumentative discourse is built on theses already accepted by the audience. Hence it bends every effort to find opinions and tenets upon which parties in the argument can agree and from which they can proceed" (p. 191). This stress upon the common values shared by speaker and audience can be found in one of the leading contemporary textbooks on communication. Ehninger, Gronbeck and Monroe advise that communicators need to be "highly sensitive" to the values of their

audience: "unless you can discover *common ground* – common valuative ground – between you and them, you may well be in communicative trouble" (1984, pp. 78–79; for detailed discussions of the ways in which values can be communicated, see Ehninger and Hauser, 1984, and Hart, 1984).

2 For evidence of the ways in which people of different political persuasions might attribute the causes of poverty, see Feagin, 1972; Feather, 1974; Furnham, 1982. These studies suggest that liberals are more likely to blame society for poverty, whilst conservatives are more willing to attribute the blame to the poor themselves. However, Nilson (1981) cautions against making too much of these differences. She argues that any emphasis upon differences between styles of explanation obscures a much more important similarity: liberals and conservatives both employ social and personal explanations, as Edelman predicted. Because liberals and conservatives resemble each other in more ways than they differ, Nilson argues that public opinion is not dramatically split.

3 For a discussion of "social epistemology" and the influence of minorities, see Deconchy (1985).

9 The spirit of contradiction

1 Similar experimental results, showing a moderation of views when discussion is expected, have been found by Hass (1975) and Hass and Mann (1976). The authors of these studies interpret their results in terms of 'impression-management' and the desire not to advocate an extreme position which might be difficult to defend: "It seems that the apparent changes in opinion are produced by a mixture of not wanting to appear easily persuaded and not wanting to be caught in a defenceless position" (Hass and Mann, 1976, p. 110).

2 Cialdini *et al.* stress that the shifts in expression should not be seen as 'genuine' changes of attitude. They argue that people alter the expression of their views depending upon the social situation without necessarily changing their underlying position: "Much like an elastic band, one's position on an issue may be stretched and distorted under situational pressures only to snap back to its original form as soon as the pressures are released" (1976, p. 663). They also warn that many experimental findings which are described as providing instances of 'attitude change' may, in fact, be instances of changes of expression. In other words, the rhetorical context must be taken into account if one wishes to determine whether someone has changed their basic position or has merely altered their form of expression to cope with a particular situation.

3 Boswell had availed himself of the services of Thomas Sheridan, the actor and elocutionist, who specialized in training ambitious young Scotsmen to lose their native accent. The sudden reversal to Scottish dialect under the extreme conditions of the Covent Garden mob is something which would have been predicted by Howard Giles's theory of 'speech accommodation'. According to Giles, individuals can show identification with others in discourse by moving their accents towards and away from that of their fellow interlocutors (e.g., Giles and Powesland, 1975; Giles and Smith, 1979). Thus, not only by action, but also by tone of speech, Boswell placed himself dramatically at the side of the two Highland officers and against the English mob.

References

There is a difference in the way that works by classical and non-classical authors are listed. Where several works by the same classical author are listed, these are ordered alphabetically by title, rather than by the date of the edition cited. The works of all other authors are listed in order of date of publication.

Abelson, R. P. (1979). Differences between belief and knowledge systems. *Cognitive Science*, 3, 355–366.

Abelson, R. P. and Rosenberg, M. J. (1958). Symbolic psychologic: a model of attitudinal cognition. *Behavioral Science*, 3, 1–13.

Adorno, T. W., Frenkel-Brunswik, E., Levinson, D. J. and Sanford, R. N. (1950). *The Authoritarian Personality*. New York: Harper and Row.

Aebischer, V. (1985). *Les Femmes et le Langage: Représentations Sociales d'une Différence*. Paris: Presses Universitaires de France.

Ajzen, I. (1982). On behaving in accordance with one's attitudes. In *Consistency in Social Behavior*, vol. 2, ed. M. P. Zanna *et al.* Hillsdale: Lawrence Erlbaum.

Ajzen, I. and Fishbein, M. (1980). *Understanding Attitudes and Predicting Social Behavior*. Englewood Cliffs: Prentice Hall.

Allport, G. W. (1958). *The Nature of Prejudice*. Garden City: Anchor Books.

Altemeyer, R. A. (1981). *Right-Wing Authoritarianism*. Manitoba: University of Manitoba Press.

Altmann, A. (1983). *Ars Rhetorica* as reflected in some Jewish figures of the Italian Renaissance. In *Jewish Thought in the Sixteenth Century*, ed. B. D. Cooperman. Cambridge, Mass.: Harvard University Press.

Anderson, J. R. (1985). *Cognitive Psychology and its Implications*. New York: W. H. Freeman.

Antaki, C. (1984). Core concepts in attribution theory. In *Psychology Survey*, 5, ed. J. Nicholson and H. Beloff. Leicester: British Psychological Society.

Antaki, C. (1985). Ordinary explanations in conversation: causal structures and their defence. *European Journal of Social Psychology*, 15, 213–230.

Archer, E. J. (1966). The psychological nature of concepts. In *Analyses of Concept Learning*, ed. H. J. Klausmeier and C. W. Harris. London: Academic Press.

Arendt, H. (1973). Introduction: Walter Benjamin, 1892–1940. In *Illuminations*, by W. Benjamin. London: Fontana.

Argyle, M. (1980). The analysis of social situations. In *The Structure of Social Action*, ed. M. Brenner. Oxford: Basil Blackwell.

Aristophanes (1970). The Clouds. In *Socrates: a source book*, ed. and trans. J. Ferguson. London: Macmillan.

Aristotle. (1909). *Rhetoric*. Trans. R. C. Jebb. Cambridge: Cambridge University Press.

Aristotle. (1955). *Sophistical Refutations*. Trans. E. S. Forster. London: Loeb Classical Library.

Aristotle. (1976). *Topics*. Trans. E. S. Forster. London: Loeb Classical Library.

Aronson, E. (1976). *The Social Animal*, 2nd edn. New York: Freeman.

Asch, S. E. (1952). *Social Psychology*. New Jersey: Prentice Hall.

Bacon, F. (1858). *Of the Dignity and Advancement of Learning* (1605). London: Longman.

Baer, R., Hinkle, S., Smith, K. and Fenton, M. (1980). Reactance as a function of actual versus projected autonomy. *Journal of Personality and Social Psychology*, 38, 416–422.

Banton, M. (1972). *Racial Minorities*. London: Fontana.

Barnes, J. (1982). *The Pre-Socratic Philosophers*. London: Routledge and Kegan Paul.

Baron, R. A., Byrne, D. and Griffit, W. (1974). *Social Psychology*. Boston: Allyn and Bacon.

Barthes, R. (1984). The world of wrestling. In *Barthes: selected writings*. London: Fontana.

Bartlett, F. (1932). *Remembering*. Cambridge: Cambridge University Press.

Bem, D. J. and McConnell, H. K. (1970). Testing the self-perception explanation of dissonance phenomena: on the salience of premanipulation attitudes. *Journal of Personality and Social Psychology*, 14, 23–31.

Benjamin, W. (1973). Unpacking my library: a talk about book collecting. In *Illuminations*. London: Fontana.

Bennett, W. L. (1980). The paradox of public discourse: a framework for the analysis of political accounts. *Journal of Politics*, 42, 792–817.

Bentham, J. (1982). *An Introduction to the Principles of Morals and Legislation* (1789). London: Methuen.

Berger, P. L. (1970). Identity as a problem in the sociology of knowledge. In *Sociology of Knowledge*, ed. J. E. Curtis and J. W. Petras. London: Duckworth.

Biddle, B. J. (1979). *Role Theory: Expectations, Identities and Behaviors*. New York: Academic Press.

Billig, M. (1977). The new social psychology and 'fascism'. *European Journal of Social Psychology*, 4, 393–432.

Billig, M. (1978). *Fascists: A Social Psychological View of the National Front*. London: Academic Press.

Billig, M. (1982). *Ideology and Social Psychology*. Oxford: Blackwell.

Billig, M. (1985). Prejudice, categorization and particularization: from a perceptual to a rhetorical approach. *European Journal of Social Psychology*, 15, 79–103.

Billig, M. (in press a). Very ordinary life and the Young Conservatives. In *Getting into Life*, ed. H. Beloff. London: Methuen.

Billig, M. (in press b). Anti-Semitic themes and the British far-left: some social psychological observations on indirect aspects of the conspiracy tradition. In *Changing Conceptions of Conspiracy*, ed. C. F. Graumann and S. Moscovici. New York: Springer Verlag.

Billig, M. and Cochrane, R. (1979). Values of political extremists and potential extremists: a discriminant analysis. *European Journal of Social Psychology*, 9, 205–222.

Blair, H. (1825). *Lectures on Rhetoric and Belles Lettres*. London: T. Cadell.

Bloch, M. (1975). Introduction. In *Political Language and Oratory in Traditional Society*, ed. M. Bloch. London: Academic Press.

Blount, T. (1971). *The Academy of Eloquence*, (1654). Menston: Scolar Press.

Boethius. (1973). *The Consolations of Philosophy*. Trans. H. F. Stewart and E. K. Rand. London: Loeb Classical Library.

Borges, J. L. (1971). *Labyrinths*. Harmondsworth: Penguin.

Boswell, J. (1906). *The Life of Samuel Johnson* (1791). London: Everyman Library.

Boswell, J. (1950). *London Journal, 1762–1763*. London: Heinemann.

Boudon, R. (1981). *The Logic of Social Action*. London: Routledge and Kegan Paul.

Bourne, L. E. (1966). *Human Conceptual Behavior*. Boston: Allyn and Bacon.

Brearley, M. (1985). *The Art of Captaincy*. London: Hodder and Stoughton.

Brehm, J. W. (1966). *A Theory of Psychological Reactance*. New York: Academic Press.

Brockriede, W. (1985). Constructs, experience and argument. *Quarterly Journal of Speech*, 71, 151–163.

Brown, R. (1965). *Social Psychology*. London: Macmillan.

Browne, T. (1981). *Pseudodoxia Epidemica* (1646). Oxford: Clarendon Press.

Bryant, D. C. (1965). Rhetoric: its functions and its scope. In *Philosophy, Rhetoric and Argumentation*, ed. M. Natanson and H. W. Johnstone. Pennsylvania: Pennsylvania State University Press.

Burke, K. (1962). *A Rhetoric of Motives*. Cleveland: Meriden Books.

Burnet, J. (1962). *Greek Philosophy: Thales to Plato*. London: Macmillan.

Cacioppo, J. T., Harkins, S. G. and Petty, R. E. (1981). The nature of attitudes and cognitive responses and their relationships to behavior. In *Cognitive Responses to Persuasion*, ed. Petty, R. E. *et al*. Hillsdale: Lawrence Erlbaum.

Campbell, D. T. (1964). Social attitudes and other acquired behavioral dispositions. In *Psychology: a Study of a Science*, vol. 6, ed. S. Koch. New York: McGraw Hill.

Campbell, G. (1963). *The Philosophy of Rhetoric* (1776). Carbondale: Southern University Press.

Cantor, N., Mischel, W. and Schwartz, J. (1982). Social knowledge: structure, content, use and abuse. In *Cognitive Social Psychology*, ed. A. H. Hastorf and A. M. Isen. New York: Elsevier.

Caplan, H. (1970). *Of Eloquence*. Ithaca: Cornell University Press.

Cardus, N. (1947). *Autobiography*. London: Collins.

Casson, R. W. (1983). Schemata in cognitive anthropology. *Annual Review of Anthropology*, 12, 429–462.

Caxton, W. (1899). Myrrour and dyscrypcyon of the worlde (1481). Reproduced in L. Cox, *The Arte or Crafte of Rhethoryke*, ed. F. I. Carpenter. Chicago: University of Chicago Press.

Cialdini, R. B., Herman, C. P., Levy, A., Kozlowski, L. T. and Petty, R. E. (1976). Elastic shifts of opinion: determinants of direction and durability. *Journal of Personality and Social Psychology*, 34, 663–672.

Cialdini, R. B., Levy, A., Herman, C. P. and Evenbeck, S. (1973). Attitudinal politics: the strategy of moderation. *Journal of Personality and Social Psychology*, 25, 100–108.

Cialdini, R. B., Petty, R. E. and Cacioppo, J. T. (1981). Attitude and attitude change. *Annual Review of Psychology*, 32, 357–404.

Cialdini, R. B., Vincent, J. E., Lewis, S. K., Catalan, J., Wheeler, D., Darley, B. L. (1975). Reciprocal concessions procedure for inducing compliance: the foot-in-the-door technique. *Journal of Personality and Social Psychology*, 31, 206–215.

Cicero. (1971). *Brutus*. Trans. G. L. Hendrickson. London: Loeb Classical Library.

Cicero. (1959). *De Inventione*. Trans. H. M. Hubbell. London: Loeb Classical Library.

Cicero. (1959). *De Optimo Genere Oratorum*. Trans. H. M. Hubbell. London: Loeb Classical Library.

Cicero. (1942). *De Oratore*. Trans. E. W. Sutton. London: Loeb Classical Library.

Cicero. (1942). *De Partitione Oratoria*. Trans. H. Rackham. London: Loeb Classical Library.

Cicero. (1971). *Orator*. Trans. H. M. Hubbell. London: Loeb Classical Library.

Clark, D. L. (1957). *Rhetoric in Greco-Roman Education*. New York: Columbia University Press.

Cochrane, R., Billig, M. and Hogg, M. (1979). British politics and the two-value model. In *Understanding Human Values*, ed. M. Rokeach. New York: Free Press.

Comenius. (1970). *Porta Linguarum Trilinguis Reserata* (1631). Menston: Scolar Press.

Coulter, J. (1983). *Rethinking Cognitive Theory*. London: Macmillan.

Cox, L. (1899). *The Arte or Crafte of Rhethoryke*. Reprinted: Chicago: University of Chicago Press.

Dan, T. (1964). *The Origins of Bolshevism*. London: Secker and Warburg.

Davis, J. A. (1975). Communism, conformity, cohorts and categories: American tolerance in 1954 and 1972–3. *American Journal of Sociology*, 81, 491–513.

Deaux, K., Winton, W., Crowley, M. and Lewis, L. (1985). Level of categorization and content of gender stereotypes. *Social Cognition*, 3, 145–167.

Deaux, K. and Wrightsman, L. J. (1984). *Social Psychology in the '80s*. Monterey: Brooks/Cole.

Deconchy, J.-P. (1985). The paradox of 'orthodox minorities': when orthodox infallibility fails. In *Perspectives on Minority Influence*, ed. S. Moscovici, G. Mugny and E. Van Avermaet. Cambridge: Cambridge University Press.

De Fleur, M. L. and Westie, F. R. (1963). Attitude as a scientific concept. *Social Forces*, 42, 17–31.

Dejong, W. (1979). An examination of self-presentation mediation of the foot-in-the-door effect. *Journal of Personality and Social Psychology*, 37, 2221–2239.

De Quincey, T. (n.d.). Conversation. In *Letters on Self-Education*. London: James Hogg and Sons.

De Quincey, T. (n.d.). Rhetoric. In *Letters on Self-Education*. London: James Hogg and Sons.

Descartes, R. (1962). *A Discourse on Method* (1637). Trans. J. Veitch. London: Everyman Library.

Deutscher, I. (1973). *What We Say/What We Do*. Glenview: Scott, Foresman.

Devine, P. G. and Ostrom, T. M. (1985). Cognitive mediation of inconsistency discounting. *Journal of Personality and Social Psychology*, 49, 5–21.

Diogenes Laertius. (1972). *Lives of Eminent Philosophers*. Trans. R. D. Hicks. London: Loeb Classical Library.

Dissoi Logoi. Reproduced in *The Older Sophists*, ed. R. K. Sprague. Columbia: University of South Carolina Press.

Dixon, P. (1971). *Rhetoric*. London: Methuen.

Dunning, E. (1971). The development of modern football. In *Sociology of Sport*, ed. E. Dunning. London: Frank Cass.

Dunning, E. and Sheard, K. (1977). *Barbarians, Gentlemen and Players: a Sociological Analysis of the Development of Rugby Football*. Oxford: Martin Robertson.

Eagly, A., Wood, W. and Chaiken, S. (1978). Causal inferences about communicators and their effect on opinion change. *Journal of Personality and Social Psychology*, 36, 424–435.

Eco, U. (1985). Strategies of lying. In *On Signs*, ed. M. Blonsky. Oxford: Blackwell.

Edelman, M. (1964). *The Symbolic Uses of Politics*. Urbana: University of Illinois Press.

Edelman, M. (1977). *Political Language: Words That Succeed and Policies That Fail*. New York: Academic Press.

Edwards, D. and Middleton D. (in press). Joint remembering: constructing an account of shared experience through conversation discourse. *Discourse Processes*.

Ehninger, D., Gronbeck, B. E. and Munroe, A. H. (1984). *Principles of Communication*, 9th edn. Glenview, Ill.: Scott, Foresman.

Ehninger, D. and Hauser, G. A. (1984). Communication of values. *Handbook of Rhetorical and Communication Theory*, ed. C. C. Arnold and J. W. Bowers. Boston: Allyn and Bacon.

Ehrlich, D., Guttman, I., Schönbach, P. and Mills, J. (1957). Post-decision exposure to relevant information. *Journal of Abnormal and Social Psychology*, 54, 98–104.

Eiser, J. R. (1980). *Cognitive Social Psychology*. London: McGraw Hill.

Eiser, J. R. (1985). The expression of attitude. Paper given at Social Beliefs Conference, University of Cambridge.

Elias, N. and Dunning, E. (1971a). Dynamics of sport groups with special reference to football. In *Sociology of Sport*, ed. E. Dunning. London: Frank Cass.

Elias, N. and Dunning, E. (1971b). Folk football in medieval and early modern Britain. In *Sociology of Sport*, ed. E. Dunning. London: Frank Cass.

Elliott, D. W. and Wood, J. C. (1974). *A Casebook on Criminal Law*, 3rd ed. London: Sweet and Maxwell.

Erdelyi, M. H. (1974). A new look at the New Look: perceptual defence and vigilance. *Psychological Review*, 81, 1–25.

Ericsson, K. A. and Simon, H. A. (1980). Verbal reports as data. *Psychological Review*, 87, 215–251.

Farr, R. M. (1977). Heider, Harré and Herzlich on health and illness: some observations on the nature of 'représentations collectives'. *European Journal of Social Psychology*, 7, 491–504.

Farr, R. M. (1984a). Social representations in the design and conduct of laboratory experiments. In *Social Representations*, ed. R. M. Farr and S. Moscovici. Cambridge: Cambridge University Press.

Farr, R. M. (1984b). Les représentations sociales. In *Psychologie Sociale*, ed. S. Moscovici. Paris: Presses Universitaires de France.

Fast, J. (1971). *Body Language*. New York: Souvenir Press.

Feagin, J. R. (1972). Poverty: we still believe that God helps those who help themselves. *Psychology Today*, 6, 101–109.

Feather, N. T. (1974). Explanations of poverty in Australian and American samples: the person, society or fate? *Australian Journal of Psychology*, 26, 199–216.

Festinger, L. (1957). *A Theory of Cognitive Dissonance*. New York: Row Peterson.

Fishbein, M. (1967). Attitudes and the prediction of behavior. In *Readings in Attitude Theory and Measurement*, ed. M. Fishbein. New York: Wiley.

Fishbein, M. and Ajzen, I. (1981). Acceptance, yielding and impact: cognitive processes in persuasion. In *Cognitive Responses in Persuasion*, ed. R. E. Petty *et al*. Hillsdale: Lawrence Erlbaum.

Fiske, S. T. and Taylor, S. E. (1984). *Social Cognition*. New York: Random House.

Fraunce, A. (1969). *The Arcadian Rhetorike* (1588). Menston: Scolar Press.

Freedman, J. L. and Fraser, S. C. (1966). Compliance without pressure: the foot-in-the-door technique. *Journal of Personality and Social Psychology*, 4, 195–202.

Freedman, J. L., Sears, D. O. and Carlsmith, J. M. (1978). *Social Psychology*. New Jersey: Prentice Hall.

Fresco, N. (1980). Les redresseurs des morts. *Les Temps Modernes*, 407, 2150–2211.

Freud, S. On Narcissism (1914). In *Standard Edition of the Complete Psychological Works*, vol. 14. London: Hogarth Press.

Fromm, E. (1977). *The Anatomy of Human Destructiveness*. Harmondsworth: Penguin.

Frye, N. (1982). *The Great Code: the Bible and Literature*. London: Routledge and Kegan Paul.

Furnham, A. (1982). Why are the poor always with us? Explanations for poverty in Britain. *British Journal of Social Psychology*, 21, 311–322.

Gadamer, H.-G. (1975). *Truth and Method*. London: Sheed and Ward.

Gadamer, H.-G. (1976). *Philosophical Hermeneutics*. Berkeley: University of California Press.

Gallie, W. B. (1962). Essentially contested concepts. In *The Importance of Language*, ed. M. Black. New Jersey: Prentice Hall.

Gallup, G. H. (ed.). (1976). *The Gallup International Public Opinion Polls, Great Britain 1937–1975*. New York: Random House.

Gallup, G. H. (ed.). (1980). *The Gallup Report*. London: Sphere Books.

Garfinkel, H. (1967). *Studies in Ethnomethodology*. Englewood Cliffs: Prentice Hall.

Gergen, K. J. and Gergen, M. M. (1981). Causal attribution in the context of

social explanation. In *Perspectives on Attribution Research and Theory*, ed.
D. Gorlitz. Cambridge, Mass.: Ballinger.

Giles, H. and Powesland, P. F. (1975). *Speech Style and Social Evaluation*. London: Academic Press.

Giles, H. and Smith, P. (1979). Accommodation theory: optimal levels of convergence. In *Language and Social Psychology*, ed. H. Giles and R. St.Clair. Oxford: Blackwell.

Gill, C. (1985). Ancient psychotherapy. *Journal of the History of Ideas*, 46, 307–325.

Ginzberg, L. (1947). *The Legends of the Jews*. Philadelphia: Jewish Publication Society.

Girard, Abbé G. (1970). *A New Guide to Eloquence*, (1762). Menston: Scolar Press.

Goffman, E. (1959). *The Presentation of Self in Everyday Life*. London: Allen Lane.

Goffman, E. (1961). *Encounters*. Indianapolis: Bobbs-Merrill.

Goffman, E. (1970). *Strategic Interaction*. Oxford: Blackwell.

Gorgias. (1968). Encomium on Helen. Trans. L. V. Hook. In *Isocrates*, vol. III. London: Loeb Classical Library.

Greenwald, A. G. (1969). The open-mindedness of the counterattitudinal role player. *Journal of Experimental Social Psychology*, 5, 375–388.

Greenwald, A. G. (1970). When does role playing produce attitude change? *Journal of Personality and Social Psychology*, 16, 214–219.

Greenwald, A. G. (1980). The totalitarian ego: fabrication and revision of personal history. *American Psychologist*, 35, 603–618.

Grice, H. P. (1975). Logic and conversation. In *Syntax and Semantics*, vol. 3, ed. P. Cole and J. Morgan. New York: Academic Press.

Grimaldi, W. M. A. (1972). *Studies in the Philosophy of Aristotle's 'Rhetoric'*. Wiesbaden: Franz Steiner Verlag.

Guthrie, W. K. C. (1969). *A History of Greek Philosophy*. Cambridge: Cambridge University Press.

Haeckel, E. (1876). *The History of Creation*. London: Henry S. King.

Hamilton, D. L. (1976). Cognitive biases in the perception of social groups. In *Cognitive and Social Behavior*, ed. J. S. Carroll and J. W. Payne. Hillsdale: Lawrence Erlbaum.

Hamilton, D. L. (1979). A cognitive-attributional analysis of stereotyping. In *Advances in Experimental Social Psychology*, ed. L. Berkowitz. New York: Academic Press.

Handberg, R. (1984). Creationism, conservatism and ideology: fringe issues in American politics. *Social Science Journal*, 21, 37–52.

Harré, R. (1974). Blueprint for a new science. In *Reconstructing Social Psychology*, ed. N. Armistead. Harmondsworth: Penguin.

Harré, R. (1979). *Social Being*. Oxford: Basil Blackwell.

Harré, R. (1980). Man as rhetorician. In *Models of Man*, ed. A. J. Chapman and D. M. Jones. Leicester: British Psychological Society.

Harré, R. (1981). Rituals, rhetoric and social cognition. In *Social Cognition*, ed. J. P. Forgas. London: Academic Press.

Harré, R. (1984). Social rules and social rituals. In *The Social Dimension*, ed. H. Tajfel. Cambridge: Cambridge University Press.

Harré, R., Clark, D. and De Carlo, N. (1985). *Motives and Mechanisms*. London: Methuen.

Harré, R. and Secord, P. F. (1972). *The Explanation of Social Behaviour*. Oxford: Basil Blackwell.

Hart, R. P. (1984). The function of human communication in the maintenance of public values. In *Handbook of Rhetorical and Communication Theory*, ed. C. C. Arnold and J. W. Bowers. Boston: Allyn and Bacon.

Hass, R. G. (1975). Persuasion or moderation? Two experiments on anticipatory belief changes. *Journal of Personality and Social Psychology*, 31, 1155–1162.

Hass, R. G. (1981a). Effects of source characteristics. In *Cognitive Responses in Persuasion*, ed. R. E. Petty *et al.* Hillsdale: Lawrence Erlbaum.

Hass, R. G. (1981b). Presentational strategies and the social expression of attitudes in impression management within limits. In *Impression Management: Theory and Social Psychological Research*, ed. J. T. Tedeschi. New York: Academic Press.

Hass, R. G. and Mann, R. W. (1976). Anticipatory belief change: persuasion or impression management. *Journal of Personality and Social Psychology*, 34, 105–111.

Hastie, R. (1981). Schematic principles in human memory. In *Social Cognition*, ed. E. T. Higgins, C. P. Herman and M. P. Zanna. New Jersey: Lawrence Erlbaum.

Heilman, S. C. (1983). *The People of the Book*. Chicago: University of Chicago.

Herries, J. (1968). *The Elements of Speech* (1773). Menston: Scolar Press.

Hewitt, J. P. and Stokes, R. (1975). Disclaimers. *American Sociological Review*, 40, 1–11.

Hobbes, T. (1872). Brief of the Art of Rhetorick (1681). In *Aristotle's Treatise on Rhetoric*, ed. T. Buckley. London: Bell and Daldy.

Hobbs, J. R. and Evans, D. A. (1980). Conversation as planned behavior. *Cognitive Science*, 4, 349–377.

Hollander, E. P. (1981). *Principles and Methods of Social Psychology*. Oxford: Oxford University Press.

Hovland, C. I. (1954). Effects of mass media of communication. In *Handbook of Social Psychology*, 1st edn, ed. G. Lindzey. Reading, Mass.: Addison-Wesley.

Hovland, C. I., Janis, I. L. and Kelley, H. H. (1953). *Communication and Persuasion*. New Haven: Yale University Press.

Hovland, C. I., Lumsdaine, A. A. and Sheffield, F. D. (1949). *Experiments on Mass Communication*. Princeton: Princeton University Press.

Hovland, C. I. and Weiss, W. (1951). The influence of source credibility on communication effectiveness. *Public Opinion Quarterly*, 15, 635–650.

Howell, W. S. (1956). *Logic and Rhetoric in England, 1500–1700*. Princeton: Princeton University Press.

Howes, R. F. (ed.) (1961). *Historical Studies of Rhetoric and Rhetoricians*. Ithaca: Cornell University Press.

Hunt, E. L. (1961). Plato and Aristotle on rhetoric and rhetoricians. In *Historical Studies of Rhetoric and Rhetoricians*, ed. R. F. Howes. Ithaca: Cornell University Press.

Hussey, E. (1972). *The Presocratics*. London: Duckworth.

Isen, A. M. and Hastorf, A. H. (1982). Some perspectives on cognitive social psychology. In *Cognitive Social Psychology*, ed. A. H. Hastorf and A. M. Isen. New York: Elsevier.

Isocrates. (1968). *Antidosis*. Trans. G. Norlin. London: Loeb Classical Library.

Isocrates. (1968). Helen. In *Isocrates*, vol. 3. Trans. L. V. Hook. London: Loeb Classical Library.

Jaccard, J. (1981). Toward theories of persuasion and belief change. *Journal of Personality and Social Psychology*, 40, 260–269.

Jackman, M. R. and Senter, M. S. (1980). Images of social groups: categorical or qualified. *Public Opinion Quarterly*, 44, 341–361.

Jacobs, L. (1961). *Studies in Talmudic Logic and Methodology*. London: Valentine Mitchell.

Jacobson, C. K. (1985). Resistance to affirmative action: self-interest or racism? *Journal of Conflict Resolution*, 29, 306–329.

James, C. L. R. (1963). *Beyond a Boundary*. London: Stanley Paul.

James, W. (1890). *The Principles of Psychology*. London: Macmillan.

James, W. (1920). *The Varieties of Religious Experience*. London: Longmans, Green and Co.

Janis, I. L. and Mann, L. (1977). *Decision Making*. New York: Free Press.

Jaspars, J. M. F. (1978). Determinants of attitudes and attitude change. In *Introducing Social Psychology*, ed. H. Tajfel and C. Fraser. Harmondsworth: Penguin.

Jaspars, J. M. F. and Fraser, C. (1984). Attitudes and social representations. In *Social Representations*, ed. R. M. Farr and S. Moscovici. Cambridge: Cambridge University Press.

Jellison, J. M. and Mills, J. (1969). Effects of public commitment upon opinions. *Journal of Experimental Social Psychology*, 5, 340–346.

Jodelet, D. (1984). Représentation sociale: phénomènes, concept et théorie. In *Psychologie Sociale*, ed. S. Moscovici. Paris: Presses Universitaires de France.

Johnson-Laird, P. N. (1981). Mental models in cognitive science. In *Perspectives on Cognitive Science*, ed. D. A. Norman. New Jersey: Lawrence Erlbaum.

Johnson-Laird, P. N. and Bara, B. G. (1984). Syllogistic inference. *Cognition*, 16, 1–61.

Jones, E. R. (1912). *The Art of the Orator*. London: Adam and Charles Black.

Josephus. (1966). *Against Apion*. Trans. H. St.J. Thackaray. London: Loeb Classical Library.

Josephus. (1959). *The Jewish War*. Trans. G. A. Williamson. Harmondsworth: Penguin.

Juvenal. (1967). *The Sixteen Satires*. Trans. P. Green. Harmondsworth: Penguin.

Katz, D. and Braly, K. W. (1933). Racial stereotypes and 100 college students. *Journal of Abnormal and Social Psychology*, 28, 280–290.

Katz, J. M. (1976). How do you love me? Let me count the ways: The phenomenology of being loved. *Sociological Inquiry*, 4, 17–22.

Kauffman, C. (1979). Enactments as arguments in the 'Gorgias'. *Philosophy and Rhetoric*, 12, 114–129.

Keenan, E. (1975). A sliding sense of obligatoriness: the poly-structure of Malagasy oratory. In *Political Language and Oratory in Traditional Society*, ed. M. Bloch. London: Academic Press.

Kelley, H. H. and Michela, J. L. (1980). Attribution theory and research. *Annual Review of Psychology*, 31, 457–501.

Kennedy, G. A. (1963). *The Art of Persuasion in Greece*. Princeton: Princeton University Press.

Kennedy, G. A. (1969). *Quintilian*. New York: Twayne.

Kennedy, G. A. (1972). *The Art of Rhetoric in the Roman World*. Princeton: Princeton University Press.

Kennedy, G. A. (1980a). *Classical Rhetoric and its Christian and Secular Tradition from Ancient to Modern Times*. Chapel Hill: University of North Carolina Press.

Kennedy, G. A. (1980b). Later Greek philosophy and rhetoric. *Philosophy and Rhetoric*, 13, 181–197.

Kerferd, G. B. (1981). *The Sophistic Movement*. Cambridge: Cambridge University Press.

Kinder, D. R. and Sears, D. O. (1981). Prejudice and politics: symbolic racism versus racial threats to the good life. *Journal of Personality and Social Psychology*, 40, 414–431.

King, B. T. and Janis, I. L. (1956). Comparison of the effectiveness of improvised versus non-improvised role-playing in producing opinion changes. *Human Relations*, 9. 177–186.

King, R. L. (1985). Transforming scandal into tragedy: a rhetoric of political apology. *Quarterly Journal of Speech*, 71, 289–301.

Klapper, J. T. and Loewenthal, L. (1951). The contributions of opinion research to the evaluation of psychological warfare. *Public Opinion Quarterly*, 15, 651–662.

Knapper, C. K. (1981). Presenting and public speaking. In *Social Skills and Work*, ed. M. Argyle. London: Methuen.

Köhler, W. (1947). *Gestalt Psychology*. New York: Mentor Books.

Krech, D., Crutchfield, R. S. and Ballachey, E. L. (1962). *The Individual in Society*. New York: McGraw-Hill.

Kruglanski, A. W. (1980). Lay epistemo-logic–process and contents: another look at attribution theory. *Psychological Review*, 87, 70–87.

Lakoff, G. and Johnson, M. (1981). The metaphorical structure of the human conceptual system. In *Perspectives on Cognitive Science*, ed. D. A. Norman. Hillsdale: Lawrence Erlbaum.

LaPiere, R. T. (1934). Attitudes versus actions. *Social Forces*, 13, 230–237.

Lebowitz, M. (1982). Correcting erroneous generalizations. *Cognition and Brain Theory*, 5, 367–381.

Lenin, V. I. (1972). Against boycott (1907). In *Collected Works*, vol. 13. London: Lawrence and Wishart.

Le Quesne, L. (1983). *The Bodyline Controversy*. London: Secker and Warburg.

Lever, R. (1972). *The Arte of Reason, Rightly Termed Witcraft* (1573). Menston: Scolar Press.

Lind, E. A. and O'Barr, W. M. (1979). The social significance of speech in the courtroom. In *Language and Social Psychology*, ed. H. Giles and R. St Clair. Oxford: Blackwell.

Loenen, D. (1941). *Protagoras and the Greek Community*. Amsterdam: Noord-Hollandsche Uitgevers Maatschappij.

Longinus. (1927). *On the Sublime*. Trans. W. H. Fyfe. London: Loeb Classical Library.

Louw-Potgieter, J. (1986). The social identity of dissident Afrikaners. Ph.D. Thesis, University of Bristol.

Luchins, A. S. (1942). Mechanization in problem solving. *Psychological Monographs*, 54, whole number 248.

Maccoby, H. (1982). *Judaism on Trial: Jewish-Christian Disputations in the Middle Ages*. London: Associated Universities Press.

Maimonides, M. (1963). *Guide of the Perplexed* (1190). Trans. S. Pines. Chicago: University of Chicago.

Manis, M. (1985). Attitudes. In *The Social Science Encyclopedia*, ed. A. Kuper and J. Kuper. London: Routledge and Kegan Paul.

Mannheim, K. (1960). *Ideology and Utopia*. London: Routledge and Kegan Paul.

Manwaring, E. (1968). *Institutes of Learning* (1737). Menston: Scolar Press.

Mason, J. (1968). *An Essay on Elocution or Pronunciation* (1748). Menston: Scolar Press.

Massinger, P. (1976). The picture (1630). In *The Plays and Poems of Philip Massinger*, ed. P. Edward and C. Gibson. Oxford: Oxford University Press.

Matthews, G. B. (1984). *Dialogues with Children*. Cambridge, Mass.: Harvard University Press.

Mayer, R. E. (1983). *Thinking, Problem Solving, Cognition*. New York: W. H. Freeman.

McCauley, C. and Stitt, C. L. (1978). An individual and quantitative measure of stereotypes. *Journal of Personality and Social Psychology*, 36, 929–940.

McCauley, C., Stitt, C. L. and Segal, M. (1980). Stereotyping: from prejudice to prediction. *Psychological Bulletin*, 87, 195–208.

McConahay, J. B. (1981). Reducing racial prejudice in desegregated schools. In *Effective School Desegregation*, ed. W. D. Hawley. Beverly Hills: Sage.

McConahay, J. B. (1982). Self-interest versus racial attitudes as correlates of anti-busing attitudes in Louisville: is it the buses or the blacks? *Journal of Politics*, 44, 692–720.

McConahay, J. B., Hardee, B. B. and Batts, V. (1981). Has racism declined in America? *Journal of Conflict Resolution*, 25, 563–579.

McConahay, J. B. and Hough, J. C. (1976). Symbolic racism. *Journal of Social Issues*, 32, 23–45.

McGuire, W. J. (1964). Inducing resistance to persuasion: some contemporary approaches. In *Advances in Experimental Social Psychology*, vol. 1, ed. L. Berkowitz. New York: Academic Press.

McGuire, W. J. (1969). The nature of attitudes and attitude change. In *Handbook of Social Psychology*, 2nd edn, ed. G. Lindzey and E. Aronson. Reading, Mass: Addison-Wesley.

McLellan, D. (1973). *Karl Marx: His Life and Thought*. London: Macmillan.

Mead, G. H. (1934). *Mind, Self and Society*. Chicago: University of Chicago Press.

Mead, G. H. (1982). *The Individual and the Social Self*. Chicago: Chicago University Press.

Mervis, C. B. and Rosch, E. (1981). Categorization of natural objects. *Annual Review of Psychology*, 32, 89–115.

Midrash Rabbah. (1983). Ed. H. Freedman and M. Simon. London: Soncino Press.

Mill, J. S. (1962). On liberty (1859). In *Utilitarianism*, ed. M. Warnock, London: Fontana.

Monboddo, Lord, (Burnet, J.). (1967). *Of the Origin and Progress of Language*, vol. VI (1792). Menston: Scolar Press.

Moscovici, S. (1976). *Social Influence and Social Change*. London: Academic Press.

Moscovici, S. (1981). On social representations. In *Social Cognition*, ed. J. P. Forgas. London: Academic Press.

Moscovici, S. (1982). The coming era of representations. In *Cognitive Analysis of Social Behavior*, ed. J. P. Codol and J.-P. Leyens. The Hague: Martinus Nijhoff.

Moscovici, S. (1984). The phenomenon of social representations. In *Social Representations*, ed. R. M. Farr and S. Moscovici. Cambridge: Cambridge University Press.

Moscovici, S., Lage, E., and Naffrechoux, M. (1969). Influence of a consistent minority on the responses of a majority in a colour perception task. *Sociometry*, 32, 365–380.

Moscovici, S., Mugny, G. and Van Avermaet, E. (1985). *Perspectives on Minority Influence*. Cambridge: Cambridge University Press.

Mugny, G. (1982). *The Power of Minorities*. London: Academic Press.

Murphy, J. J. (1974). *Rhetoric in the Middle Ages*. Berkeley: University of Los Angeles Press.

Murphy, J. J. (ed.). (1978). *Medieval Eloquence: Studies in the Theory and Practice of Medieval Rhetoric*. Berkeley: University of Los Angeles Press.

Murray, E. L. (1984). The significance of rhetoric in human science research. *Journal of Phenomenological Research*, 15, 169–175.

Nilson, L. B. (1981). Reconsidering ideological lines: beliefs about poverty in America. *Sociological Quarterly*, 22, 531–548.

Nuttin, J. (1975). *The Illusion of Attitude Change*. London: Academic Press.

Oakhill, J. V. and Johnson-Laird, P. N. (1985). Rationality, memory and the search for counterexamples. *Cognition*, 20, 79–94.

Okamura, J. Y. (1981). Situational identity. *Ethnic and Racial Studies*, 4, 452–465.

O'Keefe, D. J. (1977). Two concepts of argument. *Journal of the American Forensic Association*, 13, 121–128.

Ong, W. J. (1958). *Ramus: Method and the Decay of Dialogue*. Cambridge, Mass.: Harvard University Press.

Orwell, G. (1962). Politics and the English language. In *Inside the Whale and Other Essays*. Harmondsworth: Penguin.

Ossowski, S. (1963). *Class Structure in the Social Consciousness*. London: Routledge and Kegan Paul.

Palermino, M., Langer, E. and McGillis, D. (1984). Attitudes and attitude change: mindlessness-mindfulness perspective. In *Attitudinal Judgement*, ed. J. R. Eiser. New York: Springer-Verlag.

Papastamou, S. and Mugny, G. (1985). Rigidity and minority influence: the influence of the social in social influences. In *Perspectives on Minority Influence*, ed. S. Moscovici, G. Mugny and E. Van Avermaet. Cambridge: Cambridge University Press.

Pareto, V. (1935). *The Mind and Society*. London: Jonathan Cape.

Perelman, C. (1979). *The New Rhetoric and the Humanities.* Dordrecht: D. Reidel.

Perelman, C. and Olbrechts-Tyteca, L. (1971). *The New Rhetoric: a Treatise on Argumentation.* University of Notre Dame Press.

Perlman, D. and Cozby, P. C. (1983). *Social Psychology.* New York: Holt, Rinehart and Winston.

Petty, R. E. and Cacioppo, J. T. (1979). Issue involvement can increase or decrease persuasion by enhancing message-relevant cognitive responses. *Journal of Personality and Social Psychology,* 37, 1915–1926.

Petty, R. E. and Cacioppo, J. T. (1981). *Attitudes and Persuasion: Classic and Contemporary Approaches.* Iowa: Wm. C. Brown.

Petty, R. E. and Cacioppo, J. T. (1984). The effects of involvement on responses to argument quantity and quality: central and peripheral routes to persuasion. *Journal of Personality and Social Psychology,* 1984, 46, 69–81.

Petty, R. E., Ostrom, T. M. and Brock, T. C. (1981). Historical foundations of the cognitive response approach to attitudes and persuasion. In *Cognitive Responses in Persuasion,* ed. R. E. Petty *et al.* Hillsdale: Lawrence Erlbaum.

Phelps, G., ed. (1977). *Arlott and Trueman on Cricket.* London: British Broadcasting Corporation.

Philo. (1968). On the posterity of Cain and his exile. In *Works,* vol. II. Trans. F. H. Colson and G. H. Whitaker, London: Loeb Classical Library.

Philo. (1968) The worse attacks the better. In *Works,* vol. V. Trans. F. H. Colson and G. H. Whitaker. London: Loeb Classical Library.

Philostratus. (1965). *Lives of the Sophists.* Trans. W. C. Wright. London: Loeb Classical Library.

Piaget, J. (1959). *The Language and Thought of the Child.* London: Routledge and Kegan Paul.

Plato. (1969). Euthyphro. In *The Last Days of Socrates.* Trans. H. Tredennick. Harmondsworth: Penguin.

Plato. (1971). *Gorgias.* Trans. W. Hamilton. Harmondsworth: Penguin.

Plato. (1956). *Meno.* Trans. W. K. C. Guthrie. Harmondsworth: Penguin.

Plato. (1969). Phaedo. In *The Last Days of Socrates.* Trans. H. Tredennick. Harmondsworth: Penguin.

Plato. (1929). Phaedrus. In *Five Dialogues of Plato Bearing on Poetic Inspiration.* Trans. J. Wright. London: Everyman Library.

Plato. (1956). *Protagoras.* Trans. W. K. C. Guthrie. Harmondsworth: Penguin.

Plato. (1974). *The Republic.* Trans. D. Lee. Harmondsworth: Penguin.

Plato. (1942). *Sophist.* Trans. H. N. Fowler. London: Loeb Classical Library.

Plato. (1942). *Theaetetus.* Trans. H. N. Fowler. London: Loeb Classical Library.

Plutarch. (1929). *The Parallel Lives.* Trans. B. Perrin. London: Loeb Classical Library.

Popitz, H. (1972). The concept of social role as an element of sociological theory. In *Role,* ed. J. A. Jackson. Cambridge: Cambridge University Press.

Popper, K. (1966). *The Open Society and its Enemies.* London: Routledge and Kegan Paul.

Popper, K. (1976). The logic of the social sciences. In *The Positivist Dispute in German Sociology,* by T. W. Adorno *et al.* London: Heinemann.

Pritchard, S. and Billig, M. (1985). The role of argumentation in the development and expression of attitudes. Unpublished manuscript, Department of Psychology, University of Birmingham.

Quintilian. (1921). *Institutes of Oratory*. Trans. H. E. Butler. London: Loeb Classical Library.

Radley, A. R. (1985). From courtesy to strategy: some old developments in social skills. *Bulletin of the British Psychological Society*, 38, 209–211.

Rainolde, R. (1945). *The Foundacion of Rhetorike* (1563). New York: Scholars' Facsimiles.

Ramus, P. (1966). *The Logike* (1574). Leeds: Scolar Press.

Rankin, H. D. (1983). *Sophists, Socratics and Cynics*. London: Croom Helm.

Rhetorica Ad Herennium. (1963). Trans. H. Caplan. London: Loeb Classical Library.

Richards, B. (1985). Constructivism and logical reasoning. *Synthese*, 65, 33–64.

Richards, I. A. (1936). *The Philosophy of Rhetoric*. New York: Oxford University Press.

Robinson, R. (1971). Elenchus. In *The Philosophy of Socrates*, ed. G. Vlastos. Garden City: Anchor Books.

Robinson, T. M. (1979). *Contrasting Arguments: An Edition of the 'Dissoi Logoi'*. New York: Arno Press.

Rokeach, M. (1960). *The Open and Closed Mind*. New York: Basic Books.

Rokeach, M. (1973). *The Nature of Human Values*. New York: Free Press.

Rokeach, M. (1979a). From individual to institutional values: with special reference to the values of science. In *Understanding Human Values*, ed. M. Rokeach. New York: Free Press.

Rokeach, M. (1979b). The two-value model of political ideology and British politics. In *Understanding Human Values*, ed. M. Rokeach. New York: Free Press.

Rosch, E. (1978). Principles of categorization. In *Cognition and Categorization*, ed. E. Rosch and B. Lloyd. New Jersey: Lawrence Erlbaum.

Rosch, E., Mervis, C. B., Gray, W. D., Johnson, D. M. and Boyes-Braem, P. (1976). Basic objects in natural categories. *Cognitive Psychology*, 8, 382–439.

Rosenberg, M. J. and Abelson, R. P. (1960). An analysis of cognitive balancing. In *Attitude Organization and Change*, ed. M. J. Rosenberg *et al.* New Haven: Yale University Press.

Ross, M. and Sicoly, F. (1979). Egocentric biases in availability and attribution. *Journal of Personality and Social Psychology*, 37, 322–337.

Rothbart, M. (1981). Memory processes and social beliefs. In *Cognitive Processes in Stereotyping and Intergroup Behavior*, ed. D. L. Hamilton. Hillsdale: Lawrence Erlbaum.

Salancik, G. R. (1982). Attitude-behavior consistencies as social logics. In *Consistency in Social Behavior*, ed. M. P. Zanna *et al.* New Jersey: Lawrence Erlbaum.

Sandell, R. (1977). *Linguistic Style and Persuasion*. London: Academic Press.

Sandford, W. P. (1965). *English Theories of Public Address, 1530–1828*. Ohio: Hedrick.

Sarbin, T. R. (1968). Role: psychological aspects. In *International Encyclopedia of the Social Sciences*, ed. D. Sills. London: Macmillan.

Sarbin, T. R. and Allen, V. L. (1968). Role Theory. In *Handbook of Social*

Psychology, vol. 2, ed. G. Lindzey and E. Aronson. Massachusetts: Addison-Wesley.

Sartre, J.-P. (1965). Portrait of the anti-semite. In *Existentialism*, ed. W. Kaufmann. Cleveland: World Publishing Company.

Schank, R. C. (1981). Language and memory. In *Perspectives on Cognitive Theory*, ed. D. A. Norman. New Jersey: Lawrence Erlbaum.

Schank, R. C. and Abelson, R. P. (1977). *Scripts, Plans, Goals and Understanding*. New Jersey: Lawrence Erlbaum.

Scherman, N. (1979). Daniel: a bridge to eternity. In *Daniel*. Trans. and annot. by H. Goldwurm. Brooklyn: Mesorah Publications.

Schiffrin, D. (1984). Jewish argument as sociability. *Language in Society*, 13, 311–335.

Schneider, D. J. (1981). Tactical self-presentations: towards a broader conception. In *Impression Management: Theory and Social Psychological Research*, ed. J. T. Tedeschi. New York: Academic Press.

Schoenfeld, A. H. (1983). Beyond the purely cognitive: belief systems, social cognitions and metacognitions as driving forces in intellectual performance. *Cognitive Science*, 7, 329–363.

Scholem, G. (1969). *On the Kabbalah and its Symbolism*. New York: Schocken.

Schuman, H. and Johnson, M. P. (1976). Attitudes and behavior. *Annual Review of Sociology*, 2, 161–207.

Scott, M. B. and Lyman, S. M. (1968). Accounts. *American Sociological Review*, 33, 46–62.

Seidel, G. (1975). Ambiguity in political discourse. In *Political Language and Oratory in Traditional Society*, ed. M. Bloch. London: Academic Press.

Seidel, G. (1978). Ambiguité et pratique sémiotique. *Travaux de Léxicométrie et de Léxicologie Politique*, 3, 105–122.

Seidel, G. (1986). *The Holocaust Denial*. Leeds: Beyond the Pale Collective.

Self, L. S. (1979). Rhetoric and *Phronesis*: the Aristotelian ideal. *Philosophy and Rhetoric*, 12, 130–145.

Semin, G. (1980). A gloss on attribution theory. *British Journal of Social and Clinical Psychology*, 19, 291–300.

Seneca the Elder. (1974). *Controversiae*. Trans. M. Winterbottom. London: Loeb Classical Library.

Severy, L. J., Brigham, J. C. and Schlenker, B. R. (1976). *A Contemporary Introduction to Social Psychology*. New York: McGraw-Hill.

Sextus Empiricus. (1959). *Against the Professors*. Trans. R. G. Bury. London: Loeb Classical Library.

Sherif, M. (1966). *Group Conflict and Co-operation*. London: Routledge and Kegan Paul.

Sherif, M. and Hovland, C. I. (1961). *Social Judgement*. New Haven: Yale University Press.

Sherif, M. and Sherif, C. W. (1953). *Groups in Harmony and Tension*. New York: Harper.

Sherwood, R. (1980). *The Psychodynamics of Race*. Sussex: Harvester.

Shotter, J. (in press a). The rhetoric of theory in psychology. In *Proceedings of the Founding Conference of the International Society for Theoretical Psychology*, ed. J. F. H. van Rappard *et al.* Amsterdam: North Holland Publishing Co.

Shotter, J. (in press b). A sense of place: Vico and the social production of social identities. *British Journal of Social Psychology*.

Showers, C. and Cantor, N. (1985). Social cognition: a look at motivated strategies. *Annual Review of Psychology*, 36, 275–305.

Skinner, B. F. (1957). *Verbal Behavior*. New York: Appleton-Century-Crofts.

Smith, A. (1911). *An Inquiry into the Nature and Causes of the Wealth of Nations* (1776). London: Everyman Library.

Smith, A. (1963). *Lectures on Rhetoric and Belles Lettres*. London: Nelson.

Smith, J. (1969). *Mystery of Rhetoric Unveil'd* (1657). Menston: Scolar Press.

Smith, M. B. (1981). Foreword. In *Cognitive Responses in Persuasion*, ed. R. E. Petty *et al.* Hillsdale: Lawrence Erlbaum.

Snyder, M. (1981a). On the self-perpetuating nature of social stereotypes. In *Cognitive Processes in Stereotyping and Intergroup Behavior*. Hillsdale: Lawrence Erlbaum.

Snyder, M. (1981b). Seek and ye shall find: testing hypotheses about other people. In *Social Cognition* vol. 1, ed. E. T. Higgins *et al.* Hillsdale: Lawrence Erlbaum.

Snyder, M. L. and Wicklund, R. A. (1976). Prior exercise of freedom and reactance. *Journal of Experimental Social Psychology*, 12, 120–130.

Sonnino, L. A. (1968). *A Handbook to Sixteenth-Century Rhetoric*. London: Routledge and Kegan Paul.

Sprague, R. K. (ed.). (1972). *The Older Sophists*. Columbia: University of South Carolina Press.

Stern, J. P. (1975). *Hitler: the Führer and the People*. Glasgow: Fontana/Collins.

Suetonius. (1970). On Grammarians. In *Works*, vol. 2. Trans. J. C. Rolfe. London: Loeb Classical Library.

Szybillo, G. J. and Heslin, R. (1973). Resistance to persuasion; inoculation theory in a marketing context. *Journal of Marketing Research*, 10, 396–403.

Tajfel, H. (1978). *Differentiation Between Social Groups*. London: Academic Press.

Tajfel, H. (1981). *Human Groups and Social Categories*. Cambridge: Cambridge University Press.

Tajfel, H. and Wilkes, A. L. (1963). Classification and quantitative judgement. *British Journal of Psychology*, 54, 101–114.

Tajfel, H. and Wilkes, A. L. (1964). Salience of attributes and commitments to extreme judgements in the perception of people. *British Journal of Social and Clinical Psychology*, 2, 40–49.

Talmud (1935). *The Babylonian Talmud*, ed. I. Epstein. London: Soncino Press.

Tawney, R. H. (1925). Introduction. In *Discourse Upon Usury*, by T. Wilson. London: F. Cass and Co.

Taylor, S. E. (1981). A categorization approach to stereotyping. In *Cognitive Processes in Stereotyping and Intergroup Behavior*, ed. D. L. Hamilton. Hillsdale: Lawrence Erlbaum.

Taylor, S. E. and Crocker, J. (1981). Schematic bases of social information processing. In *Social Cognition*, ed. E. T. Higgins *et al.* Hillsdale: Lawrence Erlbaum.

Tedeschi, J. T. and Riess, M. (1981). Identities, the phenomenal self and laboratory research. In *Impression Management: Theory and Social Psychological Research*, ed. J. T. Tedeschi. New York: Academic Press.

Tedeschi, J. T., Schlenker, B. R. and Bonoma, T. V. (1971). Cognitive dissonance: private ratiocination or public spectacle. *American Psychologist,* 26, 685–695.

Terence. (1976). *Comedies.* Trans. B. Radice. Harmondsworth: Penguin.

Tunney, G. (1977). My fights with Jack Dempsey. In *The Sporting Spirit,* ed. R. J. Higgs and N. D. Isaacs. New York: Harcourt Brace Jovanovich.

Tversky, A. (1977). Features of similarity. *Psychological Review,* 84, 327–352.

Tversky, A. and Gati, I. (1978). Studies of similarity. In *Cognition and Categorization,* ed. E. Rosch and B. Lloyd. Hillsdale: Lawrence Erlbaum.

Ullah, P. (1985). Second generation Irish youth: identity and ethnicity. *New Community,* 12, 310–320.

Verba, S. and Orren, G. R. (1985). The meaning of equality in America. *Political Science Quarterly,* 100, 369–387.

Vinokur, A. and Burnstein, E. (1974). Effects of partially shared persuasive arguments on group induced shifts: a group problem-solving approach. *Journal of Personality and Social Psychology,* 29, 305–315.

Wason, P. C. and Johnson-Laird, P. L. (1972). *Psychology of Reasoning.* London: Batsford.

Watson, D. R. (1978). Categorization, authorization and blame-negotiation in conversation. *Sociology,* 12, 105–113.

Weaver, R. M. (1965). The 'Phaedrus' and the nature of rhetoric. In *Philosophy, Rhetoric and Argumentation,* ed. M. Natanson and H. W. Johnstone. Pennsylvania: Pennsylvania State University.

Weinreich-Haste, H. (1984). Morality, social meaning and rhetoric: the social context of moral reasoning. In *Morality, Moral Behavior and Moral Development,* ed. W. M. Kurtines and J. L. Gewirtz. New York: John Wiley.

Westie, F. R. (1965). The American dilemma: an empirical test. *American Sociological Review,* 30, 527–538.

Whately, R. (1881). *Historic Doubts Relative to Napoleon Buonoparte* (1819). London: Longmans, Green and Co.

Whately, R. (1963). *Elements of Rhetoric* (1846). Carbondale: Southern Illinois University Press.

Wicklund, R. A. and Brehm, J. W. (1976). *Perspectives on Cognitive Dissonance.* London: Wiley.

Wicklund, R. A. and Frey, D. (1981). Cognitive consistency: motivational versus non-motivational perspectives. In *Social Cognition,* ed. J. P. Forgas. London: Academic Press.

Wilder, D. A. (1981). Perceiving persons as a group: categorization and intergroup relations. In *Cognitive Processes in Stereotyping and Intergroup Relations,* ed. D. L. Hamilton. Hillsdale: Lawrence Erlbaum.

Wilder, D. A. (1984). Intergroup contact: the typical member and the exception to the rule. *Journal of Experimental Social Psychology,* 20, 177–194.

Wilson, T. (1925). *A Discourse Upon Usury* (1572). London: F. Cass and Co.

Wittgenstein, L. (1967). *Zettel.* Oxford: Blackwell.

Woolgar, S. and Pawluch, D. (1985). Ontological gerrymandering: the anatomy of social problems explanations. *Social Problems,* 32, 214–227.

Wright, R. A. and Brehm, S. S. (1982). Reactance as impression management: a critical review. *Journal of Personality and Social Psychology,* 42, 608–618.

Xenophon. (1975). On Hunting. In *Scripta Minora*. Trans. E. C. Marchant and G. W. Bowerstock. London: Loeb Classical Library.

Xenophon. (1910). Memorabilia of Socrates. In *Socratic Discourses of Plato and Xenophon*. Trans. J. S. Watson. London: Everyman Library.

Xenophon. (1910). Symposium or banquet. In *Socratic Discourses of Plato and Xenophon*. Trans. J. Welwood. London: Everyman Library.

Yates, F. A. (1984). *The Art of Memory*. London: Ark.

Zimbardo, P. G., Ebbesen, E. B. and Maclean, C. (1977). *Influencing Attitudes and Changing Behavior*. Reading, Mass.: Addison Wesley.

Zimbardo, P. G., Weisenberg, M., Firestone, I. and Levy, B. (1965). Communicator effectiveness in producing public conformity and private attitude change. *Journal of Personality*, 33, 233–255.

Zimmerman, D. H. (1971). The practicalities of rule use. In *Understanding Everyday Life*, ed. J. D. Douglas. London: Routledge and Kegan Paul.

Name index

Subject index